The Disordered Mind

"George Graham is contemporary philosophy's most gifted and humane writer. *The Disordered Mind* is a wise, deep, and thorough inquiry into the nature of the human mind and the various 'creaks, cracks, and crevices' into which it is prone sometimes to wander."
Owen Flanagan, *Duke University*, USA

"The book is a success, it is consistently insightful and humane, and conveys a clear understanding not only of relevant philosophical topics, but also of a much more difficult issue, the relevance of those topics to understanding mental illness."
Philip Gerrans, *University of Adelaide*, Australia

"*The Disordered Mind* is a must read for anyone who is a psychiatrist, psychologist, philosopher, neurologist, or mental health worker. Indeed, it is a must read for any thoughtful person who simply desires to understand more deeply and more realistically the workings of their own mind as well as the workings of the human mind in general."
Richard Garrett, *Bentley University*, USA

Mental disorder raises profound questions about the nature of the mind. *The Disordered Mind: An Introduction to Philosophy of Mind and Mental Illness* is the first book to systematically examine and explain, from a philosophical standpoint, what mental disorder is: its reality, causes, consequences, and more. It is also an outstanding introduction to philosophy of mind from the perspective of mental disorder.

Each chapter explores a central question or problem about mental disorder, including:

- What is mental disorder and can it be distinguished from neurological disorder?
- What roles should reference to psychological, cultural, and social factors play in the medical/scientific understanding of mental disorder?
- What makes mental disorders undesirable? Are they diseases?
- Mental disorder and the mind–body problem
- Is mental disorder a breakdown of rationality? What is a rational mind?
- Addiction, responsibility, and compulsion
- Ethical dilemmas posed by mental disorder, including questions of dignity and self-respect.

Each topic is clearly explained and placed in both a clinical and philosophical context. Mental disorders discussed include clinical depression, dissociative identity disorder, anxiety, religious delusions, and paranoia. Several non-mental neurological disorders that possess psychological symptoms are also examined, including Alzheimer's disease, Down's syndrome, and Tourette's syndrome. Additional features, such as chapter summaries and annotated further reading, provide helpful tools for those coming to the subject for the first time.

Throughout, George Graham draws expertly on issues that cut across philosophy, science and psychiatry. As such, *The Disordered Mind* is a superb introduction to the philosophy of mental disorder for students of philosophy, psychology, psychiatry, and related mental health professions.

George Graham is Professor of Philosophy and Neuroscience at Georgia State University and a past president of the Society for Philosophy and Psychology. He is co-author and co-editor of the *Oxford Textbook of Philosophy and Psychiatry* (2006).

The Disordered Mind

An Introduction to Philosophy of Mind and Mental Illness

George Graham

Routledge
Taylor & Francis Group

LONDON AND NEW YORK

First published 2010
by Routledge
2 Park Square, Milton Park, Abingdon, Oxon, OX14 4RN

Simultaneously published in the USA and Canada
by Routledge
270 Madison Avenue, New York, NY 10016

Routledge is an imprint of the Taylor & Francis Group, an informa business

Typeset in Franklin Gothic by
Fakenham Photosetting Limited, Fakenham, Norfolk
Printed and bound in Great Britain by CPI Antony Rowe, Chippenham, Wiltshire

British Library Cataloguing in Publication Data
A catalogue record for this book is available from the British Library

Library of Congress Cataloging in Publication Data
Graham, George, 1945-
The disordered mind: an introduction to philosophy of mind and mental illness / George Graham.
p.; cm.
Includes bibliographical references and index.
1. Mental illness. 2. Philosophy of mind. 3. Psychiatry – Philosophy. 4. Psychophysiology. I. Title.
[DNLM: 1. Mental Disorders – psychology. 2. Philosophy, Medical. 3. Psychophysiology. WM 140 G739d 2009]
RC437.5.G726 2009
616.89 – dc22
2009033537

ISBN 10: 0-415-77471-3 (hbk)
ISBN 10: 0-415-77472-1 (pbk)
ISBN 10: 0-203-85786-0 (ebk)

ISBN 13: 978-0-415-77471-0 (hbk)
ISBN 13: 978-0-415-77472-7 (pbk)
ISBN 13: 978-0-203-85786-1 (ebk)

We are ... subject to infirmities, miseries, interrupted, tossed and tumbled up and down ... uncertain [and] brittle, and so is all that we trust unto. *And he that knows not this, and is not armed to endure it, is not fit to live in this world.*

Robert Burton, *The Anatomy of Melancholy* (1621)

    And I have asked to be
    Where no storms come,
Where the green swell is in the havens dumb,
    And out of the swing of the sea.

Gerard Manley Hopkins, "Heaven-Haven," *Poems* (1918)

To try to be happy is to try to build a machine with no other specification than that it shall run noiselessly.

J. Robert Oppenheimer, *Letters and Recollections* (1980)

Contents

Acknowledgments

The conceptual puzzlements that ultimately motivated this book were planted during the Vietnam War, when I served as a psychiatric nurse's aide in a Harvard teaching hospital in Boston. So there just is no way I can thank all those who contributed to my view of mental disorder. My debts are many. I must acknowledge, however, my special and much more immediate indebtedness to Richard Garrett and G. Lynn Stephens, for their insight and encouragement; to Wake Forest University, which gave me two research leaves during which time, and during two long summers, the greater part of this book, in its present form, was written; and to Tony Bruce and Katy Hamilton at Routledge for their commitment, advice and encouragement at every stage of this project. I would also like to offer thanks to the five readers for the press, whose helpful feedback resulted in significant revisions, to James Thomas for his conscientious editorial work, and to more than fifteen philosophy graduate students at Georgia State University, where an early version of the manuscript was critically discussed in a seminar that I taught in the fall term of 2008.

I would like to remember my parents, George and Catherine Graham, for their support of my enthusiasm, as a young person, for the discipline of philosophy, and also my brother, Paul Graham, for his example of compassionate understanding of persons who suffer.

Last and most important: love and deepest thanks to Patricia, my wife, and Kathleen, our daughter, for their enthusiasm and support. This book is dedicated to Patricia, without whom it would not contain a single word.

Preface

This book tells two tales.

The first is a tale about mental illness or disorder. (I use 'mental illness' and 'mental disorder' interchangeably.) It offers a theory of mental disorder. It provides an account of mental disorder's reality, sources, causes or propensity conditions, contents and consequences, both symptomatic and therapeutic. The second is an introduction to philosophy of mind, to the essential elements of the subject. The book tells each of these two tales simultaneously. Each is tied up in the other. The two tales are one.

The second tale of elements of philosophy of mind derives its plot line from the first. It assumes that no sound and sensible philosophy of mind can be constructed without attending to the topic of mental illness and to human vulnerability to mental disorder: to such conditions as addiction, clinical or major depression, dysfunctional anxiety, and disorders of thought and comprehension.

The first tale of a theory of mental disorder inherits much of its cast of main characters from the second. It assumes that no conceptually regimented and normatively informed theory of mental disorder can be devised without taking philosophy of mind seriously and knowing something about this subject area of philosophy and of such topics as consciousness, Intentionality, personal identity, the mind/body problem and rationality.

The book is intended for multiple audiences. It is designed for undergraduate and graduate courses in various fields of study, philosophy foremost but not exclusively. It is intended as a text for courses on such topics as mind/brain, mental disorders and deficits, and puzzles and perplexities associated with human mental distress and instability. An instructor in philosophy of mind may use it to introduce the subject in an interdisciplinary manner. An instructor in clinical or abnormal psychology may use it to complement exposure to clinical literature and case studies. I hope it may also be read with profit by academic philosophers, mental health professionals, and the interested general reader.

Partly for the benefit of students I include short chapter summaries and suggestions for further reading at the end of each chapter (but one, the epilogue). The
suggestions sometimes cover topics with purposes or commitments that differ, occasionally
sharply, from my own. Or sometimes they point readers in directions not explicitly traversed
in the book. The suggestions are presented in an annotated and informal style.

The book presents my own views. It argues for my own positions. This is not to banish
other positions, but to provide purpose to the book's philosophical theorizing, which is to
seek a general philosophical and particular philosophy-of-mind-informed perspective on
mental disorder.

To help to make reading the book visually as mark free as possible, there are no footnotes
or endnotes. When a work is cited in the text this is because it is quoted or immediately
relevant to the topic at hand. The combination of in-text citations (with bibliography) and
suggested readings makes for a hefty list of readings and sources. I am sure, however, that
I have left important work and authors out of my stated sources and influences uninten-
tionally. I expect to find myself at a later date wishing that they had been cited. I apologize
in advance for omissions.

Introduction

STABILITY AND INSTABILITY

Alice trusted Howard, her husband. She had reason for doing so. He was devoted to her. Or so she thought.

When Howard died unexpectedly, Alice, in preparing for his memorial service, opened his computer file only to discover that he had recently been leading a secret and complex second life. He had married another woman, fathered a child with her, and periodically lived with both second wife and child, as he described things, while "out of town doing regular business" in Kansas City.

Alice's grief over Howard's death, which was profound, was mixed with anger and pain, which was deep. A positive interpretation of her husband's character ("Howard was a good man; he loved me and our children; and, I will miss him terribly") may have led to a better emotional adjustment to the loss than her bitter negative evaluation ("He lied to me and to the children; I did not really know him"). Alice fell into a protracted despondent mood. Two years later, still despondent, she was diagnosed with clinical depression.

Ian believes that he is the victim of a government plot. He is convinced that he is the object of a conspiracy conducted by the Federal Bureau of Investigation. "The FBI believes that I am running a terrorist cell." Ian refuses to leave his home for fear that he will be arrested. The business he owns, a men's clothing store, is faltering in his absence. When asked to describe evidence of being persecuted, Ian says that he cannot discuss the matter lest agents overhear the conversation. "The shirts in my closets are bugged with voice detectors." "The cuffs on my trousers contain electronic devices that signal my physical position to the FBI." He is diagnosed with paranoid delusional disorder.

What to do with the Alices and Ians of this world? How should they be understood? Treated? Sigmund Freud (1856–1939) famously fretted over them. He tried to fathom the mind's emotional and behavioral fault lines: its creaks, cracks and crevices. Freud also recognized that mentally disturbed human beings may and often do reclaim mental health and well-being. People recover from mental illnesses. For Freud, though, there is a prudent precondition for taking wise and measured aim at reclamation or construction of mental health. This is not to set the bar for emotional and psychological well-being too high.

The philosopher Owen Flanagan eloquently writes of the "wish to flourish, to be blessed with happiness, to achieve eudaimonia – to be a 'happy spirit'" (Flanagan 2007: 1). If Flanagan is right, that's a wish we all share. Truly to be happy, to be blessed. Freud, however, promoted a more modest aspiration. When asked by a despondent patient how he hoped to assist her in regaining mental well-being, he had this to say: "No doubt fate will find it easier than I do to relieve you of your illness." "But you will be able to convince yourself that much will be gained if we succeed in transforming your hysterical misery into common unhappiness" (Breuer and Freud 2000: 305).

Common unhappiness? Was Freud being ironic? In part, yes. Mainly, however, he was trying to be pragmatic or realistic. The conditions or circumstances of human existence, Freud thought, are such that an absolutely healthy, orderly, stable, trouble-free mental life is much too optimistic for a person to expect, whether recovering from a disorder or not. Why so? Why not absolute mental health, behavioral and emotional well-being? Why not flourishing? Because, he said, "our body is doomed to decay and dissolution," "the external world [rages] against us," and suffering comes from our relations with other people. "The suffering which comes from this … source is perhaps more painful to us than any other" (Freud 1989 [1930]: 26). We are psychologically vulnerable and unstable creatures, whom the vicissitudes and tragedies of life may inevitably wear down or pull apart. As persons we must therefore try to live dignified, productive lives all the while remaining susceptible to periods, perhaps pronounced or protracted periods, of distress, discord and instability.

To elicit an intuitive sense of our vulnerability to instability or distress, consider a brief thought experiment. The experiment is counter-factually presumptuous to be sure. Contrary-to-fact presumption, however, is no impediment to imagination.

Suppose you are none other than Mother Nature, although endowed with powers of deliberation, foresight, and decision-making of which she herself is not privy. Imagine that humankind has yet to appear on the earthen landscape. You wish to build the sort of mind that will help us as human beings to engage with life on the planet. You are not going to rely on Father Time to do this. (He takes forever.) You are going to do it yourself. If a supernatural agent is behind your efforts, you are not aware of its assistance. You are, as you conceive of the task, utterly on your own.

You wish the human mind to have different and various modes of operation and component psychological competencies, faculties or capacities. You want us to perceive, reason, desire, feel, remember, learn, intend, deliberate and decide. You want us to enter into productive social relationships. You want us to be properly situated or embedded, not just in the natural landscape, but in multiplex social ecologies and forms of social and cultural life. You want our mental activities to initiate, guide and complete goal-directed behavior and bodily movement. You want us to walk, grip, grasp, run, swim, open, close and climb. You wish us to achieve complex and ennobling purposes: to do philosophy, write memoirs, make art, organize religions, uncover scientific laws, found universities and discover cures.

Suppose that for reasons of imaginative contrast and heuristic comparison you narrow your conceptions of the possible human mind down just to two. Think of these as a *stable* and an *unstable* mind. You picture each as follows.

The Stable Mind. A human mind that is inherently stable and orderly. It possesses purity of heart and soundness of reason. It does things because it believes them to be desirable and is willing to face down the often and unanticipated aversive consequences of its actions. It assesses itself with equanimity, free of regret and self-doubt. It never loses control of itself. When entering into interpersonal relationships, it aims to ensure that these are harmonious, coordinated and cooperative. When it confronts the vicissitudes of life, chronic pain, physical illness and death, it does so with courage and fortitude. It loves with magnanimity, dreams contentedly and harbors a firm sense of personal dignity and self-respect. Its life, far from being an anarchic master, is the object of single-minded dedication and intelligent direction.

The Unstable Mind. A human mind that is inherently unstable and disorderly. It possesses conflicting motives, impulses and inhibitions as well as biases of thought and impediments to reason. It does things because it believes them to be desirable, but is unwilling to accept the negative consequences of its actions and is frequently conflicted or befuddled about just what is desirable. It is prone to regret and self-doubt. It often loses its grip on itself. When it enters into social relationships, its agency is prone to be disharmonious, discordant and uncooperative. When it confronts the vicissitudes and heartaches of life, it seeks refuge or escape. It loves with rapturous passion but also with breathtaking infelicity and self-destructive inconstancy. Its self-criticisms are harsh and unforgiving. The demands of life drive it into disarray and dissolution.

Which sort of mind would *you* make if you were Mother Nature? "An absolute no-brainer," you say. "The answer is obvious." "Stability, most certainly." True, stability lacks high drama. Its theatricality is thin. Instability, however, is riddled with dissonance and burdened with discomfort and unhappiness. It is also, of course, grossly incompatible with the desired ends of your creation. An utterly unstable mind could never do philosophy or do so sagaciously. Discover cures? Found universities? What sort of academic institutions would these be like? (If you answer, "Like those that exist today," then you must currently be a professional academic.)

What has the real Mother Nature actually done? Here's what, to the naked anthropological eye, she has designed for us. She has composed a type of mind both stable and unstable. She has mixed each form of mentality in us. She has made us orderly and disorderly, content and discontent, facing life's vicissitudes but also seeking refuge from them. True, some folks are more temperamentally secure than others. True, some people are much less able to undergo various trials and tribulations than others. But beneath our individual differences, however, is a fusion of both. Each of us is endowed with a stable/unstable mind. No person has all of the one but none of the other. Even the most unstable or discordant individual is not without some slice or sliver of stability. Even the most stable is not without a shadow of instability.

Periodically, of course, instability holds sway. When it does so, we become anxious about small things, develop imprudent patterns of thought, and slip or slide into emotional conflicts.

Small influences may unhinge a person. Then, in more serious cases, sadly, dissonance, distress and disturbance may seize truly powerful and persistent if, hopefully only, temporary dominion. A person's mind may break down or become disordered in a psychiatric or clinical sense. One or more mental capacities or psychological faculties may dissemble into harmful or hurtful incapacity, dysfunction or impairment. Thoughts may become obsessive, preferences addictive, perceptions hallucinatory, beliefs delusional, and post-traumatic amnesia may impose ignorance of one's past. Paralysed by phobic anxiety a person may avoid any and all public places. Numbed by major depression a person may listlessly disengage from people and projects once held near and dear.

Mental disorder, depending on its pulse and purport, may require professional mental health treatment or clinical address. One hopes that assistance is sound and sensible, but treatment and attention are unhelpful and even dangerous when resting on false or improper assumptions about mind and illness. The history of medical treatment for mental disorder is a checkered affair. It is benevolent and sensitive on occasion, given the state of medical knowledge at a time or in a culture. But other chapters in that history are characterized by superstition, ignorance, intolerance and inhumanity. The history of theory and treatment of mental illness is recounted in numerous texts (see suggested readings for this chapter). (It is also briefly available in a short chapter of a long book that helps to carry my name [see Fulford et al. 2006: 143–59].) I do not wish to repeat it here. I do, however, want briefly to sketch more recent phases. This short historical sketch should help to show why it's important to have a sound and sensible understanding of mental disorder. Such an understanding is one, I claim, in which the subject of philosophy of mind, in particular, ought to play a prominent role, to be outlined in a moment and presented in detail throughout the book.

ONE BRIEF HISTORY

In late nineteenth and early twentieth century in Western Europe the category of mental illness or disorder was applied only to the most serious problems and pathologies of mentality, namely those identified, in effect, with psychoses, severe manias or depressions. Emil Kraepelin (1856–1926), arguably the leading psychiatric taxonomist of the period, attended primarily to three main types of disorder. Kraepelin spoke of dementia praecox (roughly, schizophrenia), depressive illness (manic primarily but not exclusively), and paranoia, a term he used broadly to refer to delusional disorders (one form of which is persecutory). For him mental illnesses fell into a small set of discoverable types, identified by symptom and family history. Hospitals and asylums purported to treat (even if all that they sometimes succeeded in doing was house) persons with such illnesses. Most people who wished help for less severe or disabling disturbances, which went by names such as "nerves," "neurasthenia" or "hysteria," did so with general medical practitioners. These were doctors who did not identify themselves as specialists in mental health. Rest and diet were popularly recommended cures for less severe cases. For the wealthy but worried 'well', occasional respites at health spas aimed to regenerate one's spirits. For all battered souls, the clergy were available.

Then, later into the early twentieth century, mental illness diagnosis and treatment underwent a dramatic transformation. Freud was the major force for change. He and his disciples helped to turn clinical insight and therapeutic resource into a distinct medical specialty. This field is known now, of course, as psychiatry.

Freud published his first major work, *The Interpretation of Dreams*, in 1900 (1958 [1900]). He died in 1939. By the time of his death, in the words of Rutgers University's Allan Horwitz, "the most basic ways of thinking about mental disorder had changed" (2002: 40). Psychiatry had become a distinct specialty within medicine. Its range of application had expanded to consider less severe disturbances than psychosis or incapacitating depression. The mental malaises or psychological infirmities that formed the focus of Freud's psychological theory, such as anxiety, obsession and sexual frigidity, were described as manifestations of unconscious conflicts festering within the lives of all human beings: the ill, the worried well, and even the well. The primary function of therapy or treatment was to uncover those hidden conflicts and the manners in which people effectively adjust, or fail to adjust, to social and cultural demands. Some attention was given to diagnosis and to identifying categories of disorder, but one and the same set of symptoms or patient complaints was thought, in theory, to stem from just about any form of disorder. So, taxonomic labels failed to carry uniform and reliable conditions of application. Chronic fatigue, headaches, and weight loss may signify obsession in one individual, phobia in a second person or sexual frigidity in a third. Horwitz aptly sums up Freudian diagnostic practice: "only deep, extensive, and intensive exploration of the individual personality could indicate the true meaning of any symptomatic presentation" (2002: 45).

Freudian thought was widely endorsed and medically institutionalized. It dominated thinking about mental disorder until the 1960s, when it fell into quite rapid decline. The organizational, economic and social situation of psychiatric medicine, once again, underwent a transformation. Weaknesses in the Freudian framework became apparent. To be sure, Freudian psychology was not well suited for understanding the nature of or best treatment for truly severe psychoses (Hobson and Leonard 2001; Beam 2001). A desire for detailed and reliable clinical diagnosis became widespread (Bentall 2004; Horwitz 2002). Psychiatry grew biomedical. The field became convinced that patient distress and complaint were symptoms of specific and tractable illness types or disease categories. A proliferating range of ailments of consciousness and behavior were thought to merit classification as distinct and distinguishable disorders.

Drugs emerged as critical for the understanding and treatment of mental disorder. Chlorpromazine was introduced in the 1950s for the treatment of severe psychoses like schizophrenia. Monoamine oxidase inhibitors and tricyclics were widely deployed for the treatment of major depression. Presuppositions of drug therapy – foremost, the assumption that specific illnesses require specific drugs – imply that it makes a difference for care and treatment whether a set of symptoms is diagnosed as, say, clinical depression or schizophrenia. Depression should be targeted with one drug. Schizophrenia addressed with another. No longer was one Freudian style of therapy sufficient for all disorders. References to Freudian phenomena such as "repression," "sublimation, "Oedipal dilemma" as well as to the Freudian unconscious were charged with being unscientific and clinically unsound

(Grunbaum 1984; Horwitz 2002). Freudians, as they do today, continued to function in the profession, although Freudian-style psychiatry and its conceptual brethren moved to the perimeter of psychiatric medicine. Freud was often cast as a scapegoat for problems or false starts in the profession. Psychiatry as a profession did not blame Freud for contributing to its social and cultural prominence. Few professions lament prominence. Freud, however, was criticized for burdening the specialty with opaque concepts and elusive forms of clinical treatment. No doubt, certain effective counter-criticisms of the anti-Freudian momentum in psychiatry were willfully ignored (Lear 1998: 23). But non-Freudian biomedical trends became secure. Fine-grained diagnostics and illness-specific medication became the prescribed aspiration of the medical specialty.

The twentieth century now has ended, of course, and the twenty-first begun. Understanding and treatment of mental illness is in post-Freudian biomedical full bore. Psychiatry has moved from the language of mind and mentality to that of brain science or to mixes of mind/brain languages, such as cognitive neuroscience and cognitive neuropsychiatry, but in which brain science more or less is the desired canonical tongue. Preference for reference to the neural holds the day. The methods and manner of neuroscience, it is widely presumed, offer the best understanding of and treatment for mental disorder. It is only a matter of time, some say, before psychiatry will become a sub-discipline of neurology (Ramachandran 2003). Indeed such neurological sub-disciplinary status just is what one prominent observer says already has taken place in psychiatry. "Psychiatry and neurology [is] one specialty" (M. Taylor 1999: viii).

True, interest in the brain is not new to psychiatry. When Wilhelm Griesinger (1817–68), a professor of psychiatry at the University of Berlin, authored the first editorial of the *Archives for Psychiatry and Nervous Disease*, a journal he founded in 1867, he wrote: "Patients with so-called 'mental illnesses' are really individuals with illnesses of the nerves and brain" (see Bentall 2004: 150). (Freud himself attempted to take brain science seriously. After, however, an early effort to reconcile his developing psychological insights with the limited knowledge base of neuroscience available during his lifetime, he abandoned the attempt [Kitcher 1992].) But the immense popularity of neuroscience within psychiatry is a distinctively post-Freudian phenomenon and represents the "culmination of [the biomedical] trend within the profession" (Bentall 2004: 151).

Brain science, of course, is deeply relevant to explanatory understanding and clinical treatment of mental disorder. No one should deny that. But does a danger of post-Freudian neuro-mechanical hubris lurk within preference for brain science and associated reliance on drugs and disease-modeled modes of treatment? Consider drug treatment. So-called 'atypical' antipsychotic medications (namely drugs that produce fewer side effects than 'typical' antipsychotic medications) that were so vigorously endorsed, as recently as a decade ago, for being more efficacious than psychotherapy and even more so than their immediate pharmaceutical predecessors (like the tricyclics), are now, in the words of psychiatrist Paul Applebaum, "recognized as having substantial therapeutic limitations and often problematic effects of their own" (2004: vii).

Some critics complain that while Freud 'pathologized' normal variations in psychological diversity by portraying behavior as the expression of unconscious and unresolved conflicts, the pharmaceutical industry today exerts its own independent 'pathologizing' effect on our understanding of a mental disorder. Drug companies encourage the creation of often what in fact, if perhaps not always in intent, are suspect categories of mental disorder (Horwitz 2002). Neuroscience may have exorcized the elusive Freudian Unconscious from the mind/ brain. But commercial forces, critics say, are selling a bill of mixed neurochemical goods to a specialty of psychiatry that is over-enthused about an image of mental disorder as brain based and robustly biomedical (Luhrmann 2000; Elliott 2003 and 2004).

WHAT IS THIS BOOK ABOUT?

This book? Neither Freud nor contemporary medical culture is what this book is about, although reference to each figures in the narrative. What is it about?

In the rest of this introductory chapter, I propose to describe what this book is about and then outline its nine chapters and epilogue.

This book articulates and defends a theory of mental disorder. If offers a conception of what a mental disorder is and how best to explain it as well as to appreciate what human vulnerability to mental disorder reveals about the nature of mind and mentality.

The theory that the book proposes is distinguished by its attention to issues in philosophy of mind as well as to questions about norms or standards for a mental disorder. A rival brain-science-centered theory of mental disorder is examined and rejected, which I call the *neurological disorder* theory of a mental disorder.

I don't hope to make brain scientists quiver (not that I could, even if I wished – which I don't). But I argue that the best theory one can currently aim for of a mental disorder should focus as follows: Seek for explanations of a mental disorder that combine references to brute, a-rational neural mechanisms and to the rationality of persons. Examination of the immediate forces behind a mental disorder reveals that they carry two distinct inscriptions. "Made by unreason" and "Made by reason."

Made by reason? The theory of mental disorder that I offer and defend is characterized, in part, by promotion of a concept of mental disorder, closely tied to a description of the nature or character of the *rational* mind, broadly understood. Persons are rational agents. We think and do things for reasons. We respond to reasons that we have for thinking and doing things. The theory of mental disorder offered in this book defends the claim that elements of reason and rationality help to constitute and define distinctively mental activities such as believing, hoping, desiring, deciding, thinking and the like. It holds (i) that the reason-responsiveness of a psychological faculty or capacity is impaired or truncated in a mental disorder, but (ii) that it is not obliterated or destroyed. Reason is partly but not fully incapacitated in a mental disorder. Certain behaviors cannot be considered as symptoms of a *mental* disorder, as opposed to those of a pure and severe neurological disorder (such as advanced Alzheimer's disease), unless they satisfy (no matter how deficient or 'gummed up' in manner) at least some minimal standards of rationality, coherence or 'logic'. I describe various ways in which the rationality associated with different forms of mental disorder is truncated or impaired by neural mechanisms not themselves expressions of brain damage.

Reason's deficiencies should be no surprise in a disorder, of course. Approach Ian and it is hard not to notice that he is devoid of good evidence for his fear that the FBI is conspiring against him. Spend time with Alice and it is difficult not to miss that her depression is taking a heavy toll on her ability to care for herself and her children, whom she loves. While in the gloomy throes of depression her volitional capacities are stymied. She often does not get out of bed in the morning, complaining that she cannot rise. She lacks the will or motive to face the day. But our absence of surprise, of course, doesn't make it easy to understand how a disorder 'gums up' the mind's works.

It may help readers if I had a name for the theory of mental disorder that I offer in this book. Since I claim that our explanatory understanding of a mental disorder requires the twin frameworks of both psychological and neuroscientific explanation, I am tempted to call it the *twin theory*. But since I give pride of place in the theory to the truncated presence of rationality in a disorder, I am also tempted to call it the *truncated rationality theory*. In the end, though, I have no name for it. The theory is not without precedent. Various other discussions of mental disorder take it for granted that mental disorders result from the interplay of rational and a-rational or brute causal sources. Certainly Freud made such an assumption. He proposed that psychiatric patients be treated as rational agents, but those whose reasons for behavior were distorted by the irruption of various forms of 'a-rational noise' (instincts, cultural and other forces) into their space of reasons (a phrase of Sellars 1997). Freud tried to finesse his ignorance of the neurobiological/neurochemical details. He relied imaginatively on the fact that remarkably good first approximations of explanations of disturbed behavior may be achieved by proposing that self-destructive instincts and other forces operate beneath the horizons of a patient's consciousness. But whatever the name or label, this book offers a theory of mental disorder, a theory that is connected in robust measure with concerns in philosophy of mind.

Philosophy of mind. What is that?

Philosophy of mind is the subject or sub-discipline within the discipline or field of philosophy that systematically addresses several deep and puzzling problems of mind and mentality. The problems are deep and puzzling, in part, because they resist straightforward scientific dissolution or empirical or clinical resolution. Psychiatry is not philosophy, of course, but it does presuppose philosophic commitments and in philosophy of mind uppermost. If certain deep and puzzling philosophical problems are resolved in one manner rather than another, then much of psychiatric theory and clinical practice may or should thrive or flounder on such results (depending on the resolution).

Once we excise the presumption that mental disorders are brain disorders from our understanding of a mental disorder, a primary task for philosophy of mind in the theory of mental disorder is to show how notions of consciousness, rationality, Intentionality and psychological explanation (among others) can and should be deployed within a theory of mental disorder. They may do so without facing threat from neuroscience of being rendered explanatorily irrelevant or conceptually enervated.

To take a quick example of the germaneness of philosophy of mind to the topic of mental disorder, clinicians and researchers schooled in a categorically biomedical approach to psychiatric diagnosis sometimes presuppose that disorders and ordinary mental disturbances are utterly different and belong to two exclusive and discontinuous categories or domains. Think of delusions, for instance. 'Either delusional or not delusional' is a presupposition of this school of thought. But an 'either/or' pattern of botanizing the delusional/non-delusional distinction is indulged at the expense of truth. No matter how false or bizarre the attitudes of a mental health patient, it is usually possible to find people who hold equally false or bizarre attitudes, but who are quite normal and healthy. Avidly searching for a definitive or precise mark of a delusion is hunting for a hard-and-fast criterion where none exists. A suitably philosophy-of-mind-informed theory of delusion, based on exploration of notions such as rationality and self-comprehension, should serve to caution clinicians about just when and how to proceed with a delusional diagnosis.

References to neither the unwelcome causes nor bizarre contents of a delusional attitude suffice to explain what makes it delusional. Or so I argue. Rather, on my view, the consequences of an attitude – by which I mean, in a case of delusion, the harmful or imprudent and reason-unresponsive manner in which a person manages the attitude and acts in terms of it – all help to make an attitude delusional. As between cause, content or consequence, it is on the cusp of consequence that the nature of delusion courses. Ian is in the grips of paranoia. Understanding his delusional state requires a proper description of its consequences. Locked doors. A bankrupt business. Fear of others as unwelcome intruders.

That, in a nutshell, is what the book is about. It offers a theory of mental disorder that does not relinquish the theory to, but deploys, brain science. It demonstrates how elements of philosophy of mind should operate in an account of mental disorder. In pursuit of such ends and others, it argues that it is absolutely essential to understand the truncated or impaired presence of reason and rationality in a mental disorder.

It promotes one other big general thesis as well. This is *realism* about mental disorder. A *realist* about mental disorder is someone who claims that mental disorders truly exist. They are real. Those who assert that no condition of a person should be thought of as a mental disorder are mental disorder anti-realists. Mental disorders are not real. They don't exist.

I am a mental disorder realist.

How so? What does mental disorder realism mean to me?

The planet Mars illustrates one way in which something may be thought of as real. Mars depends on no mind whatsoever for its existence. It is mind-independent. Objective. Real. If no mind existed, Mars could.

Not so a mental disorder. A mental disorder is a condition of mind. It is mind-dependent. If no mind existed, no mental disorder could exist. But the existence of mental disorder is not mind-dependent in the same manner in which Mahler's Fifth Symphony or the babysitter's favorite TV shows are mind-dependent. The existence of such things depends on people's thoughts about and classifications of them. The symphony, for example, depends on Mahler's composing the score. The existence of the sitter's favorite TV shows depends on her selecting certain shows to watch rather than others and her preferences and tastes. But no one composes a mental illness. No one selects from which disorder to suffer.

Another way of thinking of something as real is to think of the fact that it exists as perceptually obvious or readily recognizable by the naked eye. For example, the fact that a table or mountain exists is perceptually obvious or readily recognizable by the naked eye.

Not so mental illness or disorder. A wide and complex range of behavioral goings on is relevant to recognizing a mental disorder. When a disorder as such is observed, it is observed only in the context of a broad range of human practices and with a proper store-house of empirical and normative concepts and categories at the observer's disposal. No naked eye can spot the fact that a person has a mental disorder. Only one properly clothed can recognize that fact.

Still another way of thinking of something as real is to think of it as something whose existence is so widely thought to be true that no reasonable person doubts it. Again, though, that is not the case with mental illness or disorder. A goodly number of reasonable people deny the existence of mental disorder. Some theorists say that to speak of certain mental disturbances or distresses as mental disorders is simply an arbitrary medical convention. Other ways of talking about human mental distress can and should be deployed. Just as we no longer think of Pluto as a planet, we should no longer think of major depression as a mental disorder or illness.

When I speak of mental disorders as real, I don't mean that they are mind-independent. I don't mean that they are obvious observationally. I don't mean that their existence is immune to the doubts of reasonable persons. I mean four things, each of which is defended in one place or another over the course of the book.

First: Mental disorders exist independent of whether we have a theory about them, think about them, or classify people as subjects of mental illness. Just as someone may have a somatic illness or bodily injury independent of whether we realize it, so a person may suffer from a mental disorder without our recognition of this fact. Mental disorders are not mind-independent. But they are act-of-classification-independent. Mars would exist whether we classified it or not. But this is because Mars could exist if no mind existed. Mental disorders could not exist in a mindless world. But they could exist in a world in which no one classified mental disorders.

Second: Mental disorders are discoverable. By this I do not mean that mental disorders are precisely distinguishable from non-disorders or that they do not possess ragged edges or imprecise borders. Instead, I mean that they are suitable foci of investigation and analysis, inductive generalizations can be made about mental disorders, and whether someone is the subject of a disorder cannot be settled just by recognizing that they are disturbed or upset. To qualify as a disorder a condition or disturbance must meet certain standards or norms. Success or failure in meeting such standards or norms also is discoverable.

Third: The evaluative standards or norms for being a mental disorder are such that, when a person has a mental disorder, there is something wrong with them, wrong with their mental and behavioral activity. They are in condition that they ought not to be in. Their behavior is not just harmful to them (and perhaps to others), but expresses or exhibits a truncation or impairment in the reason-responsive operation of one or more basic psychological faculties or capacities of persons. It is no mere performance error.

Finally fourth: In speaking of realism about mental disorder, I also mean that fears about the displacement or dispensability of reference to mentality in our description and explanatory understanding of a disorder on grounds of its neurological basis are unfounded. For understanding some human afflictions, such as blinding brain lesions, hemiplegic cerebral palsy, quadriplegia, conduction deafness and so on, brain science and the associated language of somatic disease or illness is canonical and exclusionary. But this is not the case for understanding a mental disorder. A-rational and mind-centered-rational factors each interact to produce a mental disorder. Though not the only signatory, the mind *qua* mind puts its inscription on the sources of a disorder. We cannot recognize a mental disorder without uncovering that mark.

Here are more advance details.

TOPICS AND THEMES

Numerous mental disorders are discussed in the book, some more than once. These include among others: clinical or major depression, dissociative identity disorder (DID), acute anxiety (in some forms), addiction, religious delusions, and paranoia. Several non-mental neuro-logical disorders that possess psychological symptoms also are examined. These include among others: Alzheimer's disease, Down's syndrome, and Gilles de la Tourette syndrome.

In this book I outline a way in which to understand the distinction between mental disorders and non-mental neurological disorders with psychological symptoms. I do this in terms of exemplars, prototypes or (more or less) uncontested examples of each. (I use 'exemplar' and 'prototype' interchangeably.) I claim that the partition or boundary between mental and non-mental physical or neurological disorders is not a chasm, although it is real in spite of that. It is, if not a hard fact, a soft fact.

Many mental disorders have features in common with non-mental physical or somatic illnesses including forms of apposite or appropriate treatment. Drugs may help with anxiety disorder as well as with Tourette's. Psychotherapy may assist with some symptoms of Parkinsonism as well as of major depression. Some of these issues of distinction and difference are discussed in Chapter 2, where I consider two defining features of the mental – consciousness and Intentionality (a technically named phenomenon to be defined in due course, namely in the third section of Chapter 2 in particular).

Chapter 3 examines what makes a mental disorder undesirable or disorderly. It inspects, ultimately to dismiss, albeit gingerly, the proposition that mental disorders are disease-like entities or processes. Or more exactly: it urges us not to confuse the issue of whether mental disorders are diseases with the question of whether people *really* do have mental disorders. There may not be a straightforward answer to the question of whether disorders are diseases or to the related question of whether they are (using a term from philosophy of science) natural kinds. But this is not a compelling reason to abandon the proposition that a disorder is a real or objective sort of condition. A mental disorder does not need to be a disease entity or a natural kind to be real or to exist. The third chapter also addresses the following question: What role does the *Diagnostic and Statistical Manual of Mental Disorders* (APA 2000) play in helping, or failing to help, mental health professionals? The manual classifies mental disorders based on courses and symptoms, but not on their causal origins or propensity conditions. Is that good or bad? I think it bad. So do many other theorists.

Chapter 4 outlines two types of skepticism about the nature and existence of mental disorder. It sketches a framework for dealing with the mind/body problem in a manner that permits (but does not require) avoiding dualism and which preserves the very idea of the mental in the category *mental disorder*. The fourth chapter also outlines an approach to the often hidden potential for contestability over the norms and values presupposed by somatic- or bodily-illness attribution. The idea of a mental disorder is not values neutral. But neither is the notion of a somatic illness.

Because worries about standards or norms for disorder are thought to have drastic implications for the existence (or non-existence) of a mental disorder, we ought to be on the lookout against construing those standards in a wrong-headed way. Consider the statement that Ian is paranoid. Is there a way of telling the story of what it means for him to be paranoid that replaces talk of his paranoia with talk of social and cultural conventions governing the attribution of 'paranoia'? What would that mean? Well, maybe it means that in Boston Ian is thought paranoid, but in Singapore he is thought not. Ian's behavior may be classified as paranoia in one culture or under one set of social conventions, but not in another. This may be so even if his behavior (of locking doors, neglecting his business, and so on) is exactly the same in each setting. According to the picture just sketched, there is no explanation of whether a person has a mental disorder independent of references to cultural conventions governing disorder attribution.

Chapter 5 takes up the problem of norms or standards for a mental disorder. It argues that rationality is essential to mindedness. Our mentality carries with it a presupposition of rational connectivity between our mental states and behavior. Not a rationality that is immune to deficiency or that is *a priori* perfect (whatever that might mean). But a rationality that makes some forms of human behavior more reasonable or responsive to reason than others. Chapter 5 argues that even though the very idea of rationality is not amenable to precise analysis or description, rationality is a basic or constitutive feature of mentality and Intentionality. The most agreed-on forms of mental disorder exhibit capacity deficits or decrements in the rationality of their associated behavior.

Two other norms or standards for what counts as mental disorder are examined in the fifth chapter. One is that of cultural convention (mentioned with reference to Ian and paranoia just above) and the other is that of an evolutionary/current environment mismatch. Each is found wanting.

Chapter 6 outlines a decision procedure for specifying the psychological capacities or mental faculties impaired in prototypical or exemplary mental disorders. The relevant capacities when impaired or disabled preclude leading a decent or satisfying life. A crucial analogy is pursued between the idea of a desirable social order and the concept of a desirable mental order or set of mental faculties or psychological competencies. Key work in the analogy is performed by deploying an analogue of a famous thought experiment of the Harvard philosopher John Rawls (1921–2002). It is this thought experiment that gives the chapter its ironic title of 'an original position'. The sixth chapter concludes by describing the multidimensional concept of a mental disorder that, by then, has been constructed over the course of the preceding chapters.

The next three chapters examine a series of mental disorders in light of the concept of mental disorder proposed in the sixth chapter. Addiction is examined in Chapter 7 along with an illustration of the complementary roles of psychological or mentalistic and neurological frameworks in our explanatory understanding of a mental disorder.

Misgivings are offered about the scope or import of non-human-animal models of addiction. The central lacuna in non-human-animal models of human addiction is that such models are unable to identify or help to describe (given the cognitive limitations of non-human animals) the failure of self-responsibility that is essential to human addiction. The plausibility of one of the central claims in the book also is illustrated in this chapter. This is that even though mental disorders are not brain disorders, neuroscience helps to illuminate their nature. A variant of the dopamine theory of reward is offered in an attempt to account for one of the main steps in addictive behavior patterns (namely relapse). In so doing the theory assumes that the brain of an addict is not malfunctioning, but is performing just as Mother Nature may have designed or intended or neurological standards should allow. Over time the brain of an addict may become damaged, of course, but if that happens, then the condition that once was a mental disorder has become a neurological disorder.

Delusional disorder is examined in Chapter 8. Delusions are a disorder or reason truncation in our capacity for comprehension of self and world. Two sorts of delusions are the focus of the eighth chapter, one of religious grandiosity, the other of paranoia. In discussing paranoia, I apply insights from the epistemology of conspiracy theories to help to describe the particular form of mistrust of people that characterizes paranoid delusions. The discussion of religious grandiosity focuses on the case of Jesus Christ. Was Christ deluded in believing himself divine? I am interested in the case of Christ not because of its religious significance, but because it helps to vividly illustrate a feature of delusion that has not been consistently appreciated in the literature. This is that subjects of delusion are in the grips of a special sort of complex higher-order stance toward certain of their lower-order beliefs, thoughts or feelings. This stance, which G. Lynn Stephens and I dub the *delusional stance*, distinguishes the case of Christ, who apparently was not in the grips of the delusional stance (for reasons to be discussed) toward conviction in his own divinity, from the case of a truly deluded person whose mismanagement of various beliefs, thoughts or feelings exhibits a pragmatic "disability that ... characterizes and [may require] clinical involvement" (Bell et al. 2006: 224; see Stephens and Graham 2004 and 2007).

Chapter 8 also explores what it means to be in proper or comprehending contact with the world – a world that is often unobvious and ambiguous in its facts or states of affairs. It briefly examines certain faulty or problematic presuppositions of two controversial theses in the contemporary mental health literature. One is known as depressive realism; the other promotes the purported 'healthy' exercise of so-called positive illusions. Neither thesis encourages proper cognitive contact with the world.

Chapter 9 sketches an approach to the nature of personhood that permits understanding some puzzling failures of self-comprehension associated with schizophrenia and certain delusions. One failure is expressed in the Cotard syndrome in which a person may claim that they are dead or fail to exist. Another is expressed in delusions of thought insertion in which a person has trouble identifying their own conscious mental activity as their own. Chapter 9 also briefly examines DID (or multiple personality disorder, MPD) to learn whether it contains lessons about one of the basic psychological capacities desired and required by all of us as persons. This is the ability to locate ourselves temporally/historically – to know where we are in time as well as in our own personal history.

The Epilogue offers a defense against an objection to the manner in which I encourage mental disorders to be identified. I take it that mental disorders do not have precise or discrete boundaries. They lack sharp edges. So, because of this assumption, together with other aspects of my analysis, some critics may charge that I allow too much clinical elbow room for persons to seek medical help for distresses or disturbances that are not true or genuine disorders.

In the Epilogue I argue that we should permit disturbances that fall outside the range of exemplars or prototypes of a disorder to count as suitable or potentially suitable for clinical assistance, not just because of the needs of individual patients, but because of our general human susceptibility to mental instability, as well as the inherent difficulty of precisely distinguishing between disorders and non-disorders. I defend the clinical implications of this position.

While no single chapter is devoted to ethics, over the course of the book I briefly consider a few moral problems surrounding mental health research, clinical practice, and social policy. These considerations are influenced by stands I take on philosophy-of-mind issues in the theory of mental disorder. One is the question of whether benevolent or compassionate treatment of a victim of delusional paranoia morally requires empathetic understanding of their paranoid world view. We persons, of course, differ in our capacities for empathy or projection, just as we differ in our moral motivations. Some of us possess rather limited capacities to imaginatively simulate the inner lives or attitudes of others. But, morally, should possessing *some* empathy for deluded persons count as part and parcel of clinical care? That is one of the moral questions I examine in the book.

Generally speaking, one key for me in the proper treatment of mental disorders is to help people to maintain or recover their dignity and self-respect. The problem of dignity and self-respect preservation is viewed by me as a special instance of a challenge that we all face as human beings. The challenge is to achieve a responsible and productive response to life's heartaches and misfortunes by giving them a "meaningful place in one's progress through life" (Velleman 1991: 55).

To mend or heal from a disorder in a self-respecting and dignified manner requires discovering a positive or purposeful place for past or present episodes of disorder in the future course of a person's life. The fact that a person has or has had a disorder is no personal discredit or sign of poor judgment or faulty character. It is an expression of vulnerability to instability that all of us harbor in our psychological make-up.

Achieving a purposeful place for episodes of disorder often consists of dealing with conflicting alternative interpretations of one's past. Caution is required though. Exaggerated emphasis or endless rumination on past episodes of disorder runs the risk of missing lessons present in other phases or chapters in one's history.

Influential among efforts to emphasize thinking about the past in a process of recovery is the Freudian presumption that acquiring truths about one's childhood is critical for mental health. Revive the distant past, remember forgotten experiences, and return to recollected trauma. As two observers put it, "to Freud ... falling like a shadow over every ... life is the significance of early injuries to the self." "A kind of ... scar that then must burden ... later development" (Gross and Rubin 2002: 94).

I am leery about the therapeutic efficacy of persistent rumination on past scars. Especially scars inflicted in the distant past. Two reasons constitute warrant for caution. One is sociological and comes from research on different ways in which people respond to bad experiences. Ruminative responding seems, for many people, to be immensely unhelpful. It leads to the recall of more negative memories, more negative interpretations of past events, and more pessimism about finding effective solutions to present and future personal problems (see Bentall 2004: 264). The other basis for caution is epistemological or evidential and stems from appreciating that a person's past often just is too vast, inaccessible and riddled with heterogeneous and ambiguous events to serve as the primary focus of reconstruction or recovery. The past (especially the personally distant past) may be a highly indeterminate place when viewed from the vantage point of one's current evidential or epistemic perspective. Not just in the ambiguities it presents to our feelings and recollections, but, perhaps more profoundly, in the indeterminacies it poses to our efforts at discovering interpretative significance. More helpful and optimistic, for me, is the forward-looking attitude of the philosopher and psychologist William James (1842–1910). James urges us to aim at constructing interpretations of the past that help to secure good results for future behavior. Past accuracy is less important than future utility, assuming that, normally, there often are numerous ambiguous past events about which factual surety cannot be achieved. "Few of us," writes James, "are not in some way infirm [but] our very infirmities can help us unexpectedly" (James 2002: 29). To be helped, however, he notes, a person must realize that "there are dead feelings, dead ideas, and cold beliefs, and there are ... live ones and ... everything has to re-crystallize around [them]" (2002: 218).

James's admonition to focus or crystallize on live ideas or attitudes that assist in future reclamation is not aimed at denying the past suffering and misfortune that is part of a disorder, but at trying to reverse its polarity. Negative past experiences of depression, acute anxiety, or delusion may become positive in delayed consequence when they contribute to reconstruction, reconstitution or reformation – to determining how to behave or to think purposively in the future – and are viewed in that progressive light. Getting the past in accurate pictorial detail is less important than sculpting the future properly.

"My residents and I," writes one senior psychiatrist, "end up teaching [patients] how to situate their symptoms, problems, and miseries within a larger life trajectory" (Sadler 2004a: 359). Constructing a future trajectory rather than achieving a past accuracy – if one has to choose where to devote one's energies between them, the first is to be preferred.

Ask Alice. To overcome her anger and despondency, Alice should not deny that her husband lived a lie. He did. That fact is painfully obvious. But there may well be other aspects of her relationship with Howard that fail to admit of so obvious and negative an interpretation. One such aspect may be whether he loved his second wife more than he did Alice. Perhaps he did not. Perhaps Howard's trips to Kansas City stemmed from a desire to hide a shameful and embarrassing relationship with the second woman rather than from a deep and preferential love for his second spouse. The attempt to hide is not a welcome trait on his part, to be sure, but it does not necessarily reflect a preference for the second woman.

Alice needs emotionally to breathe again. She needs to feel that she mattered to Howard. If it is not obvious whom he preferred, then, other things being equal, she may have good reason to believe or hope that she herself was his deepest and most important love. Persistent brooding over the fact that he deceived her and fathered another child offers no such relief.

If there really are mental disorders, and if these are conditions whose behavior (or aspects of it anyway) is controlled or explained by forces of mind described in mind-language terms, a theory of mental disorder should illuminate just what it means for mentality to exert or exercise control. The problem of finding a genuine causal-explanatory role for mind in mental disorder is especially challenging for a theory like the one offered in this book that locates or describes some of the controls in the language of brain science, but says that subjects of mental disorders do not suffer from damaged brains or neurological disorders. If it is possible for neurological disorders and mental disorders to pull apart in some way, though the boundaries between them may not be sharp or precise, space is left open for mental disorders to be real and distinct disorders. In psychiatry surely not every problem is also philosophy of mind's problem, but the characterization of mental disorder partly is.

CHAPTER SUMMARY AND SUGGESTED READINGS

This chapter introduced the main topics of the book and outlined the manner in which I plan to address them.

It offered a general, orientating and heuristic description for why we persons are vulnerable to mental disorder. The human mind is a mix of the orderly and disorderly, the stable and unstable. I noted the importance of Freud to the history of psychiatry. I urged that a theory of mental disorder needs to acknowledge its dependence on philosophy of mind. I noted that, in order to recognize that sort of disciplinary dependence, this book introduces and describes elements in philosophy of mind of particular relevance to the theory of mental disorder.

All of us are prone at least at times to spiral out of rational or reason-responsive control. Such spirals or episodes when they constitute a mental disorder cannot be fully understood just in terms of the language of mind. Brain science, too, must enter into the explanatory picture. But I've claimed that mental disorders are not brain disorders even if or though they are based in the brain. This claim awaits defense in the book. It is one of its main themes and central to what I mean by being a realist about mental disorder.

The chapter also outlined the remaining ones of the book. A general description of the category of mental disorder is promised together with a discussion of norms or standards for disorder. A host of topics both in philosophy of mind and the theory of mental illness will be discussed.

On Freud, Raymond Fancher's *Psychoanalytic Psychology: The Development of Freud's Thought* (Norton, 1973) is a helpful general introduction to the development of Freud's ideas. The philosopher Edward Erwin has edited a useful and topically extensive one-volume encyclopedia on Freud and Freudianism entitled *The Freud Encyclopedia: Theory, Therapy, and*

Culture (Routledge, 2002). The cast of contributors includes Marcia Cavell, Morris Eagle, Clark Glymour, Adolf Grunbaum, Karl Pibram, Louis Sass, Donald Spence and numerous other prominent philosophers, scientists and medical professionals.

There is no lack of books on the history of the identification and care of mental illness. A representative selection includes: H. F. Ellenberger's *The Discovery of the Unconscious* (Basic Books, 1970); G. E. Berrios and R. Porter (eds), *A History of Clinical Psychiatry: The Origin and History of Psychiatric Disorders* (Athlone Press, 1995); E. Shorter's *A Brief History of Psychiatry* (Wiley, 1997).

A comprehensive single-volume treatment of the philosophy and psychiatry intersection, which is designed primarily for pedagogical and research purposes, is K. Fulford, T. Thornton, and G. Graham's *Oxford Textbook of Philosophy and Psychiatry* (Oxford University Press, 2006). This text contains extensive bibliographic entries on a wide range of inter-field topics. Large portions stem primarily from materials used in the master's program in the philosophy and ethics of mental health, developed in the philosophy department of the University of Warwick (UK) by Fulford, Thornton and others.

Two collections of readings that deal with topics at the intersection of philosophy and psychiatry are G. Graham and G. Lynn Stephens (eds), *Philosophical Psychopathology* (MIT Press, 1994) and Jennifer Radden (ed.), *Philosophy of Psychiatry: A Companion* (Oxford University Press, 2004). On the centrality of philosophy (not of mind but) of science to a proper understanding of both psychiatry and mental illness, Dominic Murphy's *Psychiatry in the Scientific Image* (MIT Press, 2006) is an important contribution to the literature.

A broad elementary introduction to philosophy of mind is my *Philosophy of Mind: An Introduction* (Blackwell, 1998). There are a number of general collections of prominent and influential papers in philosophy of mind including T. O'Connor and D. Robb (eds), *Philosophy of Mind: Contemporary Readings* (Routledge, 2003) and B. Gertler and L. Shapiro (eds), *Arguing About the Mind* (Routledge, 2007). Gertler and Shapiro's collection includes several papers on what mental disorders may reveal about mind and mentality.

Three websites are useful reference tools for readers of this book.

One is Christopher Perring's site entitled *Metapsychology Online Reviews*. This site contains reviews of books of many different types, from memoirs and self-help books to texts and philosophical monographs, on a wide range of mental health issues, including philosophic topics. Its address is: http://metapsychology.mentalhelp.net.

Another is the *Stanford Encyclopedia of Philosophy*, an award-winning resource on a wide range of philosophic topics. Its address is http://plato.stanford.edu.

Still another is the philosopher David Chalmers's popular and sophisticatedly organized site for online papers on philosophy and matters mental. It includes papers on philosophy of mental illness. Its address is: http://consc.net/mindpapers. Also see *PhilPapers* via: http://philpapers.org.

An entire journal is devoted to publishing papers at the philosophy/psychiatry interface and includes articles by philosophers and mental health professionals. The journal is *Philosophy, Psychiatry, and Psychology*, published by Johns Hopkins University Press.

Numerous professional organizations offer colloquia and special meetings or symposia on philosophy and psychiatry. These include the Association for the Advancement of Philosophy and Psychiatry and the Society for Philosophy and Psychology. Oxford University Press publishes a book series at the philosophy-and-psychiatry interface entitled *International Perspectives in Philosophy and Psychiatry*. A website is maintained in connection with the series and related activities. It is entitled *International Network for Philosophy and Psychiatry*.

2 Conceiving mental disorder

I state an obvious fact. The task of describing the conceptual make-up of the category of mental disorder is truly daunting.

Mental disorder is such a big and varied category of states and conditions. How can one meaningfully decide what mood disorders, anxiety disorders, personality disorders, delusional disorders, impulse control disorders, etc., have in common? But this chapter aims to give the task a try. Or more exactly: it aims to begin the task. The chapter is about how to construct a sound and sensible concept of mental disorder. Not just of disorder or of the reference of the term 'mental' in 'mental disorder', but of the category *mental disorder* itself. This chapter helps to set the stage for the theory of mental disorder to be constructed and applied in the rest of the book.

MENTAL DISORDER HAS CONSEQUENCES

The very idea of a *mental disorder* has numerous consequences of diverse types. Classification deploying the concept affects millions of people in a variety of different ways and settings.

Scientists and mental health professionals specialize in the study and treatment of mental disorder. Patrons, benefactors and governments support mental disorder research. Psychiatric drugs and therapies are dedicated to the amelioration of mental disorder. Lawyers and legal advocates argue that if their clients suffer from certain disorders this reduces liability for crimes. Consumers select insurance companies on the basis of whether they reimburse for treatment of mental disorder. Scientific journals, professional associations, patient support groups, book publishers, and websites devote themselves to the topic of mental disorder. Reference to mental disorder is prominent in the autobiographies,

biographies and memoirs of scientists, political figures, soldiers, scoundrels and saints. People's self-conceptions, family aspirations, and social goals often are affected by whether they or those whom they love are classified by mental health professionals as subjects of a mental disorder. Talk of disorder – albeit in this case, loose and informal – appears in descriptions of ordinary moods, problems and emotional disturbances. We speak of ourselves as 'seriously depressed', being prone to 'panic attacks', or 'addicted to work', and so on.

It is difficult to escape from the idea of mental disorder. Indeed it seems difficult to escape from disorder oneself.

A recent survey by R. C. Kessler and associates, published in the prestigious *Archives of General Psychiatry*, claims that nearly half of the citizens of the United States suffer from a mental disorder at some point in their lives (Kessler et al. 1994). Is that true? Does a label or concept with *that* many personal and social consequences apply to so many individuals in just one country alone? The accuracy of statistics like those offered in the survey depends, of course, on the validity or legitimacy of the concept of a disorder that it deploys or presupposes. Skeptics charge that such surveys typically fail to deploy sound and sensible concepts of a mental disorder (see Elliott 2003; Horwitz 2002; Horwitz and Wakefield 2007; Wakefield 1999). Unsound and insensible instruments, they charge, classify numerous cases of non-disorder as disorders and therein overestimate the prevalence and epidemio-logical range of instances of mental disorder. Some skeptics assert, too, that legitimate boundaries have yet to be drawn around a concept of mental disorder (see Bentall 2004; Poland et al. 1994). One well-situated observer even claims that "psychiatrists do not know what they mean explicitly by mental illness/mental disorder" (Colombo 2008: 70).

Robert Schumann, no doubt, had a mental disorder. To all informed ears Schumann (1809–56) is one of the greatest composers of classical music who has ever lived. But, tragi-cally, Schumann suffered from a profound and periodically recurring depression. So profound, in fact, that he starved himself to death in an asylum, where he had insisted that he be placed after a failed suicide attempt. He had jumped into the Rhine River (Ostwald 1985).

Just as we don't wish people who lack mental disorders to be classified as if they harbor them, we don't wish people, like Schumann, who are subjects of a disorder being treated so poorly or incorrectly that they become suicide statistics. So: We need a *good* concept of mental disorder. We need a concept that identifies real cases of disorder and helps us to treat people with disorders well. We need to enact conceptual rectitude in the very idea of a mental disorder. Or we need to do this as best we can.

WHAT SHOULD A THEORY OF MENTAL DISORDER DO?

No concept of a mental disorder other than that proposed by or presupposing a good theory of mental disorder suffices as a good concept. A concept with rectitude. So, what should a theory – a sound and sensible theory – of mental disorder do?

A theory of mental disorder should consist of several components. First and foremost, it should describe what a mental disorder *is*. It should offer a *concept* of mental disorder.

This means it should describe the nature or constitution of a mental disorder and help to distinguish (as best a theory can) mental disorders from disorders that are not mental, such as purely somatic illnesses such as Parkinsonism or diabetes, as well as from non-disorders or 'mere' problems of or disturbances in living, such as grief over the death of a loved one or anxiety over exams or possible loss of one's job.

The need to offer a concept does not mean that the concept must be constituted by a clinically tractable list of necessary and sufficient conditions for the category *mental disorder*. If such a list existed, disturbances or distresses would count as in the extension of *mental disorder* just in case they satisfy each and every member of the listed conditions.

Consider an imaginary list of the necessary-and-sufficient-condition type.

C_1 –.
C_2 –.
C_3 –.
C_4 –.

Now imagine filling in the blanks with descriptions of purported conditions or characteristics of a mental disorder, whatever they may be. Once filled in, if correct, and if we wish to know whether a particular distress or disturbance is a mental disorder, then we should consult the list. When a disturbance possesses each and every element in the list, then and then only does it count as a mental disorder.

Hardly anyone believes that necessary and sufficient conditions for being a mental disorder truly exist, however. No such list has attracted consensus among informed professionals. Indeed, whenever such a set is proposed, which occurs rarely, theorists tend to be immensely skeptical. Rightly so. To mention just one example, consider the proposal, due to Jerome Wakefield, that a mental disorder should be analyzed as the harmful failure of a mental faculty to function as Nature designed (Wakefield 1992). Something is a mental disorder if and only if it is a harmful mental dysfunction. By such a standard being blind as a result of brain damage is a mental disorder. Mother Nature made eyes to see, presumably. Blindness is harmful. Sight is a form of conscious experience and so, of course, it is mental. So, blindness is a harmful mental dysfunction. But a concept of mental disorder surely should not classify blindness when caused by brain damage as a mental disorder. Psychiatrists don't treat it; ophthalmologists and neurologists may try.

Worry about necessary and sufficient conditions does not infect the application of all concepts. Compare and contrast the case of mental disorders with that of numbers. Consider the very idea of the number zero. Historically, the idea of zero developed after that of the positive integers. One reason for this is that the sheer possibility of *zero* struck many people as mysterious and paradoxical. How can something be that particular number if truly it is nothing (a zero)? Note, however, that by the standard of possessing necessary and sufficient conditions, zero is easy to define. It's a number in our number system with the following special property: 0 is an additive identity such that just when it is added to any number, say, *a*, the result is always *a*. Talk of 'just when' is talk of necessity and sufficiency for being zero.

Numbers are abstract, neat and formal, however. So, they are definable in terms of necessary and sufficient conditions. Mental disorders are concrete, messy and empirical. So, they aren't so definable. And borderline cases of a disorder are debatable as to whether they are disorders or not.

In saying that the concept of mental disorder lacks necessary and sufficient conditions, I am agreeing with psychiatrist Nancy Andreasen, when she says that it possesses "debatable boundaries" (Andreasen 1984: 35). I am, however, disagreeing with those who charge that its debatable boundaries mean that the concept of a mental disorder just is a catch-all concept, utterly resistant to regimentation or conceptual rectitude (Gorenstein 1992: 14). Plenty of good and useful empirical concepts have debatable boundaries. Take the notion of a 'book', for example.

You, I assume, are holding an instance of the proper application of this concept in your hands right now. You know how to talk about books, to refer to and classify them. But, I suspect, you recognize, too, that there is plenty of conceptual elbow room for debate over what exactly counts as a book. There are fuzzy borderline (non-exemplary, non-prototypical) cases. Must a book have pages? Must it be printed? Can it be stored in a computer file? Can an author carry a book around in their head? Is a comic book truly a book? To debate how best to answer questions like those is neither to deny that, objectively speaking, books really do exist nor to doubt whether you are reading a book. It is not to assert that 'book' is a catch-all term or that we don't have the foggiest idea whether books are housed in libraries.

How may the very idea of a book be characterized if not by listing necessary and sufficient conditions of application? What enables the term 'book' or our use of it to successfully identify objects even though it is contestable in various ascriptions? Here's how.

The term 'book' is not messy or contestable in all of its uses. Some applications are prototypical or exemplary. Consensus applications, if you will. *War and Peace*, for example, is a consensus application of the term. No truly informed person would deny that Tolstoy's masterpiece is a book. Others are foil applications, by which I mean clear cases of non-books (e.g. a single blank piece of paper on a desk). No truly informed user of the word 'book' would be tempted to classify a single blank piece of paper as a book.

A characterization of the very idea of a book can be extracted from exemplary applications. Then, when instances of use of the term drift toward foils (clear non-cases), however, the wisdom of the applicability of the concept becomes increasingly contestable or debatable and eventually dissolves.

Here's a description of what the word 'book' means (extrapolating from consensus applications): "A set of written, printed, or blank pages fastened along one side and encased between protective covers." That's how my desk dictionary defines the term. The description applies both to the object you are reading at present and to *War and Peace*. But it fails to apply to, say, a single blank piece of paper. True, some candidate books (e.g. a manuscript in your computer file) are not covered by such a characterization. But uncontroversial or exemplary cases are covered. Borders between exemplary books and non-books (foils) are, as noted, contestable or debatable. We can debate rights of semantic immigration (should comics be counted in as books?) and emigration (should the manuscript in your computer be counted out as a book?). But clear-cut cases are clear-cut and to condemn a whole or entire concept to catch-all status just because various instances of application provoke controversy and doubt is to misunderstand how sound and sensible empirical notions often work.

Eleanor Rosch understands how sound and sensible empirical notions often work (Rosch 1978; see also Margolis and Laurence 2003). Rosch, a psychologist at the University of California at Berkeley, says it goes something like this. People begin by using a word to describe cases to which the word is intended to apply. Over time the word's application may then be extended to novel cases by a successive series of similarities, resemblances and analogies with the initial cases. So, for instance, someone first calls an object a 'book' if it is a set of written printed and bound pages, and so on. Then someone calls a second object a book because it resembles the original object in certain ways, if not in every way; then, the process continues. Up to a point. What point? That depends. Sometimes the resemblances in the mind of the speech community are too thin, metaphorical, or confusing to merit the term 'book'. Or perhaps other terms will do better. The book on my desk is a book. The 'neural code' in my head, unwritten and unbound, is not. It's just a neural code. But extensions sometimes stick. Comic books cost much more today than they did when I was a child. They're books despite not possessing truly protective covers.

Failure to possess necessary and sufficient conditions is devastating for a number concept. But it is no liability for an empirical notion like that of a book. Nor, I assume, is it a liability for the notion of a mental disorder. Besides which, for a concept like that of a mental disorder to possess such conditions (or more exactly conditions that are thought to be such) arguably is not a blessed event. A list of purported necessary and sufficient conditions would overly or unwisely constrain whatever findings medical science may discover about a disorder. Suppose, for example, the American Psychiatric Association decides (wrongly, I would say) that something is a mental disorder only if it is a brain disorder or a neurological impairment, deficit or disability, namely the expression of a broken brain. Mental disorders are neurological disorders, so dictates the higher councils of the Association. Call this purported necessary condition 'C_3'.

Faced with this piece of judgment or legislation, psychiatrists, neuroscientists, neuropsychologists and others would be urged to try to discover, identify and describe impaired or disabled mechanisms within the brain that are just what C_3 says are properly referred to as mental disorders. If C_3 is true, it must be possible, in theory at least, to tell a brain impairment story about any and all properly classified mental disorders. That is, it ought to be possible to state all the facts about what makes a mental disorder a *disorder* in neurological or brain science terms. Indeed, a lot of mental health professionals already are attracted to a broken brain/neural disorder conception of a mental disorder. A psychiatrist, for example, may tell her depressed patients that depression is "a brain disorder, just like epilepsy." "Just as you would take drugs for epilepsy, you should take them for your mental disorder."

Some of the reasoning behind the broken brain conception of a mental disorder is represented by the following line of argument.

(1) The mental somehow is nothing other than the physical, the neural.
(2) *X* is a mental disorder.
(3) So, *X* is a physical disorder, a disorder of the brain.

Consider, though, an analogous inference about your computer. A software state of your computer is nothing other than a hardware state. So, a software malfunction is a hardware malfunction. Or:

(1*) A computer software state is nothing other than a hardware state.
(2*) *Y* is a malfunction in the software.
(3*) So, *Y* is a hardware malfunction, a disorder of the hardware.

But, of course, it does not follow that if a computer's software fails to function properly that this means its hardware is broken. If my computer finds the wrong price for a desired airline ticket, this could be a hardware problem or it could merely be a software problem (or an instance of misinformation at the airline's website). Peculiarities in software may be responsible for errors in processing even if there is no corresponding malfunction in the computer's physical machinery (see Arpaly 2005: 283; Wakefield 2006: 129).

An alternative and more attractive theoretical possibility, when it comes to describing a mental disorder (and one for which I possess much sympathy, as will be evident throughout this book), is ruled out by C_3's broken-brain necessary condition for a mental disorder. This is that the brain of a person with a mental disorder may be healthy or in good working order, given proper neurological standards, even though the person's mental condition or state is a mental disorder. Or as I wish to put it: Mental disorders may be disorders *in* the brain (realized in the brain or 'hardware') without being disorders *of* the brain (or neural malfunctions or impairments).

I am not alone in holding the view that mental disorders may be based in an unbroken brain (see Arpaly 2005 and Wakefield 2006; see also Graham and Stephens 2007 and Stephens and Graham 2009a). But I may be willing to extend, develop or hold fast to this view in ways others are not, such as by making it central to the very idea of a mental disorder in which conceptual rectitude is enacted, as well as to (what I call) *realism* about mental disorder. If we understand a mental disorder as a brain disorder and recount its story just in terms of a damaged brain, while this does not imply that we are mistaken in thinking of the condition as a disorder (after all, it is a neurological disorder), it does rule out thinking of a disorder as a *mental* disorder (or so I argue). Realism about mental disorder says that mental disorders are honest-to-goodness mental conditions or states of persons. While this need not entail that they are non-physical in nature, realism about mental disorder (on my view) does preclude, as will be argued later in the book, understanding a mental disorder in exclusively and exhaustively neuroscientific terms.

What is of interest to me in disconnecting the notion of a mental disorder from the thesis that mental disorders are neurological disorders is preserving a special theoretical perspective to understand just what makes a disorder *mental*. To say, for instance, that Alice and Ian are subjects of a mental disorder is to say that how they think, feel and deliberately or intentionally act are among the sources or propensity conditions of their disorders and that how they think, feel and act is *not* attributable to a neural impairment or disorder even if, or though, neural activity is involved.

Of course, it may be objected that any pattern of neural activity that serves as the physical basis of a mental disorder qualifies, by this fact alone, as a neural disorder. Such a piece of conceptual legislation, however, is not what neurologically enamored investigators mean when they propose that a mental disorder is nothing other than a neural disorder. An enormous scientific investment is being made in finding the neural mechanisms that underlie mental disorders. Often this investment is based on the premise that mental disorders are nothing other than disorders or impairments of brain mechanisms. Nancy Andreasen writes in a chapter of *Brave New Brain* entitled (and note the title) "Broken Brains and Troubled Minds" that "Psychiatrists ... have steadily recognized that mental illnesses are ... cells in our brains [gone] bad [and] this is expressed at the level of systems such as attention and memory [in disorders] such as schizophrenia and depression" (Andreasen 2001: 7) (words in brackets inserted by me).

What is being proposed by referring to mental disorders as disorders of the brain or cells gone bad is that various neurologically specifiable breakdowns occur in the brain (due to a developmental trauma, injury or pathogen, just to name three sorts of causes) and that such breakdowns constitute or compose the conditions referred to as mental disorders. So, a mental disorder is a type of brain disorder. It is not merely realized or embodied in the brain (in its cells, as it were) but is itself a form of bad cells or neural damage or impairment.

Given the purpose or intent behind the broken-brain view, it is contrary to its scientific aspiration to propose that 'brain disorder' should be defined first in terms of the conceptually prior notion of a mental disorder and then and then only recommend that the notion of a mental disorder should be re-described as that of a brain malfunction or disorder, all the while continuing to use the criterion of a mental disorder as the criterion for a brain disorder. The whole effort of identifying mental with neural impairment would be viciously circular. It would make the notion of a brain disorder depend on the notion of a mental disorder rather than the other way around. The identity of a mental with a neural disorder (urged by Andreasen, Griesinger and others) is supposed to mean that the very idea of a neural disorder (properly regimented) should be used to describe what makes something a mental disorder. It is not supposed to mean that the *mere* fact that the brain is the physical basis of a mental disorder means that the brain itself is disordered in cases of mental disorder, namely possesses 'cells gone bad' to restate Andreasen's catchy phrase.

The general distinction that I am making here between that of a disorder being *in Z* (say, the brain) versus *of Z* (say, a neural or brain disorder) is quite orthodox in medicine. Consider somatic illness. The presence of pain, fever, cough, nausea, vomiting, diarrhea or fatigue does not necessarily mean that something is wrong with a person's body or soma even though, of course, such events are unpleasant. Fevers and diarrhea, for instance, may, on occasion, be a body's evolutionarily selected defenses against disease, danger or bodily damage (see Nesse and Williams 1996). Fever or diarrhea may mean that the body is functioning well. Perhaps it is ridding itself of dangerous toxins. Some somatic distresses, including discomforts whose aversive qualities warrant medical treatment and amelioration, may not be physical illnesses. In such cases we do not speak of a disorder (an impairment, dysfunction, breakage or incapacity) of the body in order to identify the sources of discomfort. A fever or case of diarrhea may be a disturbance in the body without being an illness of the body. Analogously, a mental disorder may be a disorder 'in' the brain without being a disorder 'of' the brain.

Of course, it may be difficult empirically to tell apart the character of a healthy brain that underwrites a mental disorder from that of a broken brain that underwrites a neurological illness with psychiatric symptoms. Consider, for example, Tourette's syndrome, which (I assume) is a neurological disorder. It is marked by facial tics, forced vocalizations and involuntary profanities. There are a number of hypotheses for the possible forms of brain damage responsible for the disorder, early brain damage or childhood infection among them. But it is not obvious, just from what the Tourettic person says, whether they are suffering from a neural impairment (brain damage or infection) with psychiatric symptoms or, instead, angrily, as part of a mental disorder (paranoia perhaps), intending to indulge in hateful speech acts under conditions, say, of stress or emotional arousal. We may be inclined to say things about them like "As part of her mental illness she really hates me and wants to insult me." But suppose the proper scientific picture is: "No, no, no, she does not hate you or intend to insult you." "Her speech reflects no deliberate intention." "She is undergoing a burst of impaired electrical activity in her brain." "The sounds appear as speech, real profanities, but they aren't." "Her cells have gone bad."

There is a difference between saying that the subject of Tourette's hates or distrusts the people at whom they curse and saying that their profanities are not speech acts (or real curses) at all but the expressions of impaired electrical activity. The first may be apposite in describing Tourette's symptoms as a mental disorder, but the second is the sort of remark appropriate to thinking of Tourette's as a neurological disorder (which it is, I assume).

If conceptual rectitude cannot be achieved by reference to necessary and sufficient conditions or through identifying disorders using neurological criteria, then how is it best achieved? Fortunately, there is another way in which to characterize *mental disorder*. It's been outlined above in the example of a book. This is to recognize that the concept of a mental disorder has uncontroversial or prototypical instances of application or exemplars. An uncontroversial instance or exemplar is a case that competent and informed observers or qualified judges agree (or at least currently or widely agree) is a mental disorder. Then, reference to prototypical or exemplary features of such cases provides information about how best to characterize the idea of a mental disorder. Reference to a disorder's prototypical features also *fallibly* characterizes a disorder. If a certain disorder now is classified as mental but somehow is later discovered to be a neurological disorder, then the condition should fall out of the category of a mental disorder and be reclassified as a deficit or disorder of a broken brain.

Anyone who thinks that just because we now believe that a disturbance counts as a mental disorder (exemplary or otherwise), it must forever be thought of as such, misunderstands the investigatory mission of medical science and its complementary disciplines. Ian's paranoia may be thought of as a mental disorder until perhaps it is discovered that a specific site in his limbic system is damaged and is responsible for his reason-unresponsive distrust of other people. It would be time then for brain science to take over the explanatory understanding of his disorder.

A theory of mental disorder should have other elements as well. It's not all about the concept of a mental disorder, of course. Second, there should be a list that specifies which disturbances are mental disorders. Such a list is known as a taxonomy or nosology of mental disorder. The taxonomy should identify categories of mental disorder, such as 'clinical depression' and 'paranoid delusional disorder'. Third, connected with the second component, there should be a description of the constitutive elements of particular disorders. What makes a clinical depression a case of depression? Delusion a delusion? Fourth, the theory should explain why disorders are undesirable conditions of persons and normally require medical/psychiatric address or clinical amelioration. Or as I like to put it: The theory should answer the following question: What impairments of basic psychological capacities or mental faculties make them disturbances of clinical importance or psychiatric significance? Finally, fifth, a theory of mental disorder should tell us how to treat or care for people with a mental disorder and how persons may recover or reconstitute their mental health. I will have things to say about each of these topics over the course of the book, although not much about the fifth. But first things first.

The question being asked is: What is *mental disorder*? How should the category or concept of a mental disorder be characterized?

Consider a real example of a mental disorder (if somewhat hidden in history). Consider the case of Virginia Woolf (1882–1941), English novelist and essayist. Woolf committed suicide by drowning herself. Why did she do such a dreadful thing? Here's a plausible hypothesis: Woolf feared a complete depressive breakdown (having had major depressive episodes in 1895 and 1915) from which she believed that she could not recover. In a suicide note to her husband, Leonard Woolf, she wrote that "I shan't recover this time." "I begin to hear voices." "I can't fight it any longer" (quoted in Slavney and McHugh 1987: 31). Quentin Bell wrote of Woolf's episodes as follows: "Her sleepless nights were spent in wondering about whether her art, the whole meaning and purpose of her life, was fatuous, whether it might be torn to shreds by a discharge of cruel laughter" (quoted in Slavney and McHugh 1987: 31). Woolf's disorder, in the words of Philip Slavney and Paul McHugh, two psychiatrists at Johns Hopkins who have studied her case in retrospect, "shaped her development as a person and as a writer, affected her closest relationships, and eventually claimed her life" (Slavney and McHugh 1987: 116).

The symptoms of Woolf's particular disorder consisted, in part, of a complex set of conscious experiences of self and world: anxious sleepless nights, doubts about her art, fear of public humiliation, grief over the loss of her London homes during the Blitz, and so on.

A large body of research examines the general sort of subjective situation and social circumstance in which someone like Woolf may have been embedded (see Klinger 1977; Emmons 1999; see also Abramson et al. 1989). When a person is committed to a life-defining goal (in her case, that of being an accomplished writer), persists in intense and challenging efforts to achieve it, but simultaneously fears or believes that the likelihood of success is negligible or slim-to-none, they may feel trapped or intractably stymied, helpless or impotent. They may believe that they can neither approximate that goal nor effectively disengage from it. Perhaps such a person's conception of their own merits as a person depends on the goal's pursuit but is, as the person fears, most likely to be frustrated. When this happens, when a person is driven to succeed but feels bound to fail, their commitment to themselves and to their own well-being may collapse or tumble. They may become incapable of prudently taking care of themselves or of protecting their own good or personal well-being. Whether this describes Woolf's situation and the main forces behind her depression (namely a sense of entrapment or helplessness) may be debated, of course. (I am assuming, for purposes of illustration, that it does.) But certainly Woolf lacked a prudent capacity for responsible self-management. Despite her successes and attentions of those who loved her and admired her work, she ended up committing suicide.

So, what, then, is a sound and sensible concept of mental disorder? Rather than travel through this and a number of chapters to reveal my final answer, I shall state it now. Then, after working through the next several chapters, I plan revisit the statement in the sixth chapter, having in the meantime detailed both its meaning and rationale and adding additional features to it.

There are four different parts to the concept of a mental disorder that I propose. It goes like this (remember, subject to later refinement and addition).

The notion of a mental disorder, prototypically understood, is the notion of a (i) disability, incapacity or impairment in one or more basic or fundamental mental faculties or psychological capacities of a person, that (ii) has harmful (or highly likely harmful) consequences for its subject. The disability or impairment possesses a special sort of proximate or immediate origin or source. It is (iii) brought about by a balance or mix of mental activity, on the one hand, and (what may be called) brute a-rational neural mechanisms (though not of the sort exemplified in a brain disorder), on the other, and (iv) is one in which the interaction or intersection of such forces endows the disorder with a truncated 'logic' or impaired or compromised rationale distinctively its own. A depressed Alice may not get out of bed. A paranoid Ian may remain locked inside his home. Woolf may commit suicide. Just why such people do such things rather than others is explained, in part, by the rationales behind their depressions and paranoia. The depressed Alice does not wish to face the day. So she stays in bed. The paranoid Ian does not wish to face other people and possible agents of the FBI. So he locks his door. Woolf fears another breakdown.

If I am right and this notion of a mental disorder is sound and sensible, then Woolf's depression, Alice's depression, and Ian's paranoia are instances of a mental disorder if each reflects a harmful disability of one or more of their basic psychological capacities, and springs from two sorts of factors, one characterized in neural terms, the other in mental terms, that put them at serious risk for harm (e.g. for committing suicide). For instance (to oversimplify for illustrative purposes): One possible neural mechanism behind certain aspects or features of depression is high levels of stress hormones (among other factors). Certain levels may help to distribute a despondent mood throughout a person's psychological economy. One set of mental forces (among others) behind depression may be a belief in one's helplessness or impotence. This belief may lead to a severe decline in self-care. ("I can't help myself, so why bother to try?") The mood effects of high levels of stress hormones combined with belief in personal impotence and a decline in self-care may help to 'rationalize' some of a depressive's behavior. Committing suicide may possess a sad, sorry and truncated rationale.

Andreasen appears to recognize the power and relevance of the two sorts of forces that I mention as responsible for a disorder (in [iii] above). She writes: "As we think about mental illnesses, we will be mindless if we address only the brain and brainless if we address only the mind" (Andreasen 2001: 29). Properly interpreted, that's part of my position. But I hasten to add that by identifying mental disorders with disorders of the brain (or with cells gone bad), Andreasen accepts a form of explanatory reduction of mental disorder to that of a neural disorder. And that most certainly is not my view: neither the identification nor the reduction.

How do I come up with the above characterization of a mental disorder? Is it warranted? What does it mean? Which concepts in philosophy of mind are presupposed by it? What do those concepts mean? The four sub-theses (of [i] through [iv]) of the concept that I propose require substantial analysis and motivation, which they will receive over the course of the next several chapters. And one key concept will be added to the mix of notions in the concept of mental disorder. This is appeal to the notion not just of mentality but of the rationality and reason-responsiveness of a person.

I now plan to do the following. I will divide up the question of 'What is mental disorder?' into two sub-questions. One is: What is *mental* about a mental disorder? The other is: What constitutes the *disorder* of a mental disorder? In one way or another, these two questions will occupy me all the way up to the end of Chapter 6, when I will return to the above concept of a mental disorder. Hopefully, by then, I will have successfully explained what the concept means and why it is worth endorsing. Numerous disorders of different types will need to be discussed as well as various concepts that are part of philosophy of mind. Rectitude will rectify. Or at least it's worth a try.

THE MIND OF MENTAL DISORDER

A huge book sits on my shelf. It's a reference book that I sometimes consult when conducting research on mental disorder. It's nearly a thousand pages long and entitled *Neurobiology of Mental Illness* (Charney et al. 1999).

It's a book with a big hole in it. Not a physical hole. A semantic hole. For despite its title, the word 'mental' is not mentioned in the index, let alone described or defined in the book. So, then, how on earth was it decided by the editors which illnesses to examine in the book? Anxiety and mood disorders are examined. But so, too, are tic disorders. Schizophrenia is examined, but so, too, are Alzheimer's and autism. Depression surely is a mental disorder. But tics? Alzheimer's? Such classifications are dubious and need argument. It needs to be shown why, say, Alzheimer's possesses not just mental symptoms (which, of course, it does) but the sort of causal origin or source that makes it a mental disorder. The big book offers no such argument. In the title the word 'illness' wears the conceptual pants. 'Mental' is left conceptually naked or without explication.

In the literature on mental disorder, applications of the term 'mental' are often deployed without conceptual attire or semantic explication. Bengt Brülde and Filip Radovic note with a tone of lament that in "almost everything that has been written about the concept of mental disorder ... focus has not been on what makes a disorder *mental*, but on what makes a mental disorder a *disorder*" (Brülde and Radovic 2006: 99). The philosopher Dominic Murphy likewise bemoans such neglect: "psychiatry contains no principled understanding of the mental" (Murphy 2006: 61).

Brülde, Radovic and Murphy are right. The very idea of the mental deployed in psychiatry as well as in the theory of mental disorder typically is unexamined or at least under-examined by psychiatrists and others writing on mental disorder. That is unfortunate. Witness the book on my shelf.

Murphy does try to offer a start, however. He writes: "'the mental' covers states and processes that play a very direct role in intelligent action, including processes such as perceiving, remembering, inferring, and a wide variety of motivational states" (Murphy 2006: 63).

Not bad – for a start. But the question arises as to just what constitutes the mentality of the states and processes that he mentions. What is the principal or foremost difference between mentality and non-mentality? Why, for instance, is my perceiving the hair on my head mental, but growing the very same hair not? Murphy seems skeptical about being able to answer such general questions about mentality without, as he says, waiting to learn what the "sciences recommend" (Murphy 2006: 64). But we don't need to hold our semantic breaths. There is no need for that. We may offer *some* analysis of mentality, and then science, broadly understood, may of course try to refine or revise our effort. In the meantime we are not in the pre-scientific dark.

We may pick out the domain of mental by identifying various prototypical examples of mentality (e.g. thinking, sensing, perceiving and so on) and then extrapolating a general description. As Eric Olson remarks:

> We agree on a wide range of typical and characteristic ... mental phenomena. ... No one doubts that beliefs, memories, intentions, sensations, emotions and dreams ... are mental phenomena, and that earthquakes and temperatures are not.
>
> (Olson 2007a: 264)

If we do so, if we extrapolate a general description, and this is the technique used in the discipline of philosophy of mind, then what do we find? What we find, I believe, is that mentality is constituted by two elements, aspects or features. These two features are consciousness or conscious phenomenology, on the one hand, and Intentionality (a technical feature to be explained just below), on the other.

"The mental begins and ends with consciousness and intentionality." "Consciousness and intentionality help to define the mental *qua* mental." So write Terence Horgan, John Tienson and I in summarizing what the philosophy of mind tells us about the very idea of mind (Graham et al. 2007: 468). That's what philosophy of mind says is the mental: states or conditions of persons (and of other creatures) that are conscious and states or conditions possessed of Intentionality. I need to explain.

Presumably, among all the things that there are, some are mindless, some minded. A brick is mindless; so, too, is an earthquake. But we persons possess minds of our own. What is the basis for this distinction? Between being minded and mindless? In what does it consist? It consists, in the broadest sense, in the fact that neither bricks nor earthquakes harbor perspectives or possess the power or ability to consciously represent their selves or the world. Self or world fails to appear to bricks or earthquakes in any way at all. A brick is unaware of itself. A quake, although it may bring horrors to the world, bears no thought of the world that it effaces. By contrast all sorts of things (including ourselves) appear to us persons in all sorts of different and distinct ways. A box of chocolates may appear to us as a thank-you for a job well done. An architect's papers may appear as a blueprint, prescribing the construction, measuring the spaces and places of our intended home.

To say that we have perspectives or powers of representation is to say two things. One is that representations of self or world are subjective, in the sense that they exist only as had by us as minded subjects. The other is that our experiences and conscious representational states are about things, or directed at things, other than themselves.

The first or subjective aspect of mindedness or perspective possession is referred to (by philosophers) as consciousness, phenomenal experience or conscious phenomenology. The smell of mothballs, the bitter-sweet taste of dark chocolate, the vividness of thoughts of our native country, the wistful memory of last week's wedding, the dread of tomorrow's snow storm. What characterizes each and every one of these experiences is that there is something it is like to a person to undergo them (see Nagel 1974). There is something it is like to possess a conscious perspective on the world and ourselves: to smell mothballs or to dread a storm. This something it is like is sometimes referred to as the qualitative or phenomenal character of an experience. Some philosophers use the word 'quale' (singular) or 'qualia' (plural) to refer to this character. On occasion I have joined in this use. But here, in this book, I plan to refrain from deploying terms like 'quale' and 'qualia'. This is because certain technical philosophical controversies would be encouraged that I wish to avoid and are unnecessary for the tasks of the book (but for some detailed discussion of qualia talk see Graham and Horgan 2002 and 2008).

The second or directedness aspect of possessing a perspective means that our mental states are about something – the world or ourselves. Franz Brentano (1838–1917) called this aspect of mindedness 'Intentionality'. (The adjectival form of the word is 'Intentional', but use of this term should not be confused with calling something intentional in the sense of its being purposeful or deliberate. See just below.) The word 'Intentionality' refers to the aspect of a mental state or attitude in virtue of which it is directed at, is of or about, or represents something other than itself (Brentano 1995 [1874]; see also Searle 1983). Intentionality is exemplified when a desire is for dark chocolate, a fear is of flying, or a mathematics professor wonders how best to describe a Cauchy sequence for her students.

Intentionality, it should be noted, has no special connection with intending or being intentional in the common English sense, in which, for example, I intend to eat dinner tonight or to begin a new aerobic exercise regime. Intending is but one form of Intentionality, among numerous others. (So as not syntactically to confuse 'intending' or 'intentionally' with 'Intentionality', I deploy a convention, common among philosophers, of capitalizing the first letter in 'Intentionality' when used to refer to Intentional phenomena, i.e. mental phenomena possessed of aboutness or directedness.) Thus, for examples, beliefs, perceptions, desires, intentions, and memories are Intentional (note the "I" in a capital) states (i.e. states with Intentionality or directedness), as are emotions such as fear and joy, pride and shame, love and hate. Any mental state that is directed at or about something other than itself is an Intentional state. Your visual perceptual experience of this page, for instance, is possessed of Intentionality. Note, too, that although this page certainly exists, some things or events that a mental state or attitude may be about do not exist. A song says, "I saw Mommy kissing Santa Claus underneath the mistletoe last night." Mother was there. Mistletoe was in place. But Santa, of course, was nowhere to be found. Mother cannot kiss Santa for he does not exist, although children may sing of him or misperceive of Daddy as Santa (see Harman 1998).

While the basic idea behind that of Intentionality or Intentional states or attitudes is that of directedness to a thing or object, 'thing' or 'object' is interpreted in a very broad way: material entities (cars) or abstract objects (numbers), properties (standing under the mistletoe), states of affairs (kissing mommy), or facts (that Dad is dressed up like Santa). Indeed, anything whatsoever that a person may think about, or direct their attitude toward, may count as an object of thought. Even, as just noted, non-existent objects may count as the Intentional objects of Intentional states.

Back to consciousness. Conscious or phenomenal experiences come in many varieties. Talk about consciousness permeates all discourse, prose and poetry, ordinary and special. Consciousness is the most vivid feature of our mental lives – of our being minded or possessing a perspective. As William James (1997 [1910]: 71) put it, "The first and foremost concrete fact which every one will affirm to belong to inner experience is the fact that consciousness of some sort goes on."

One of the most striking features of conscious experience is that the content or character of experience is directly apparent or immediately evident to its subject. You know directly of what you are thinking. You know, for instance, whether you are thinking of, say, chocolate ice cream or mother kissing Santa. You needn't observe the expression on your face in a mirror to decipher such facts. Mirror observation does not tell you. You know immediately. If, however, another person is sitting next to you, they must rely on your behavior and verbal report to identify what you are thinking of or even if you are thinking about anything at all. As the head of a coma research group recently put it, "conscious awareness is a subjective experience that is inherently difficult to measure in another human being" (Laureys 2007: 87). Indeed.

Jones shot Phaedeux (pronounced 'Fido'), his dog. Jones gave thought to shooting Phaedeux. Jones did so on purpose or intentionally. But we may wonder, what was Jones thinking about in shooting the poor little creature? That the dog barks too much? That Phaedeux is getting too old and arthritic and needs to be put out of his misery? That the dog had bitten his little son, Jones junior? (Jones would not tolerate that.) What was on his mind?

Jones had a perspective, a mind of his own, in shooting his dog. But what was it? We need to ask him. He, by contrast, knows first-hand. "Phaedeux bit junior," he thinks to himself.

A second prominent feature of consciousness is that even if some conscious states are not possessed of Intentionality, an important and pervasive number of conscious states are Intentional or possess aboutness. Your present visual experience, for example, would not be the visual experience that it is if it did not seem to you to be directed at a book on the subject of mental disorder. My present thought would not be the thought that it is unless it appeared to me that I am thinking of Jones and Phaedeux.

Intentionality, if perhaps not as vivid as consciousness, is just as central to mindedness or to our being minded and having a perspective. Unlike the computer keyboard on which I am typing right now, which is attitude-less, I have various attitudes (beliefs, desires and so on) directed toward my self and environment. The computer keyboard thinks of neither self nor world. It literally is thoughtless.

One of the most significant aspects of Intentionality, evident on reflection, is that Intentional states have a structure analogous to acts of speech. Just as I may ask whether such-and-such is the case or promise that so-and-so will be the case, so I may hope that something is the case, fear that it is the case, or desire that it be the case. In each instance, the content of an Intentional state (what it's about) is describable by a sentential clause or propositional phrase: a *that*-clause. I fear *that* Woolf suffered from a severe form of depression. I know *that* Santa was not under the mistletoe last night.

Many items in the world other than minds possess Intentionality or aboutness and serve as vehicles of Intentional content. The blueprints of a house, maps, representational paintings, words of a language, speech acts, novels, and road signs. The Intentionality of mentality, however, is unique. Mentality has Intentional content built right into it, as it were, as opposed to the map of a city which derives its Intentionality from the manner in which it is designed or interpreted by readers or users. A map expresses a perspective (that of the cartographer). But it does not have a perspective. The perspective is not in the map. It must be read into the map. The mind's Intentionality or aboutness is un-derived. It inheres in it or is intrinsic to it. Something was literally on Jones's mind when he shot his dog.

Underived or intrinsic Intentionality is sometimes referred to as original Intentionality. The words or verbal inscriptions in this book mean and refer, and thus have a form of Intentionality, but it is extrinsic to them and originated or derived from me when I wrote them down. For instance, suppose I write the string of letters or word 'bello'. If I were a speaker of Latin, I might mean *war* by this word; if Italian, I might mean *beautiful*. The point is not that such a string is devoid of Intentionality. The point is simply that its Intentionality (what the string symbolizes, represents or is about) is a function of what I and other speakers use the word to mean or refer to.

The notions of consciousness and especially Intentionality are critical (as we will learn in detail later) for understanding the role of the mental in mental disorder. The philosopher Jennifer Church, in discussing the conscious Intentional states distinctive of depressed people, for instance, quotes a remark of a forlorn character in a movie by the distinguished late Swedish film director, Ingmar Bergman (1918–2007). Everything in the world, the character says, is getting "meaner and grayer" (Church 2003: 175). An explanation of what it is like to be depressed, Church observes, "must take account of [a] correspondence between *what* is ... felt and *what* is ... perceived" (175). "The felt qualities of [a] depressed state ... are the perceived qualities of the objects around" the depressed person (Church 2003: 176). Depression is the state; grayness and meanness appear in the world outside the depressed person. To feel depressed is (in part) to perceive the world as mean and gray.

Church's observation generalizes to other sorts of mental disorders. In disorders mental states typically cited as conscious and Intentional (such as being depressed or anxious about something) possess Intentional contents that are inseparable from their subjective or what-it's-likeness or phenomenal character. "The ... qualities of a depressed state are the perceived qualities of the objects around." Woolf's conscious Intentional states of depression, for example, were part of her experience of self and world – a self and world that had particular depressing qualities or objects for her and that, to use Church's apt term, corresponded to her depressed mood or feelings. The same may also be said of, say, an anxious state. The qualities of an anxious state are the perceived qualities of various objects around the anxious person. My present state of agoraphobia, for instance, would not be the state that it is if it did not seem to me as if the crowd in the mall where I shop is dangerous and threatening.

While philosophers of mind agree that the marks of mentality are consciousness and Intentionality, they disagree about how best to understand these features as well as about the relationships between them. Brentano, for his part, claimed that Intentionality is irreducible to and not constituted by anything physical. It's something non-physical. But other philosophers try to show that Intentionality can and should be understood in physical terms.

Some philosophers claim that Intentionality and consciousness are inseparably connected and that neither Intentionality nor consciousness, in an ultimate sense, may occur or be possible without the other (see Graham et al. 2007 and 2009). But other philosophers argue that Intentionality can and commonly does occur without consciousness and/or that consciousness can and commonly does occur without Intentionality. Some Intentional states or attitudes (say, unconscious beliefs or desires) are not conscious; some conscious states (say, moods) are not about anything. The relevance of such claims and debates to our effort to enact rectitude in the concept of a mental disorder is difficult and complex to appraise, first because such claims are rarely raised in the context of discussions of mental disorder (remember the big book on my desk), and second because debate about the nature of consciousness and Intentionality is one area in which Murphy's hesitancy to speculate about the mental before science has contributed may be prudent.

Or perhaps on occasion not. Sometimes scientists try to lend a helping hand, but, alas, not always in a genuinely useful manner. Relevant example? Some diagnostic manuals presuppose that the word 'mental' refers to, in addition to states of consciousness or Intentionality, sub-personal, non-conscious information-processing states that neither occur in consciousness nor, strictly speaking, possess directedness or aboutness. How so?

Consider ideomotor apraxia (Rogers 1999: 101). Are the origins of this condition (which will also be visited later in the book) mental/psychological or not? Ideomotor apraxia is a disorder in the execution of simple gestures (say, walking around a table or combing one's hair), even though the ability to carry out more complex acts (e.g. walking through Central Park in New York City) may be preserved.

Whatever science may say about the complexities of using a term like 'mental' in extended or non-prototypical applications, it lies in the nature of mentality itself to place constraints on just what counts as mental. The natural purpose of locomotion or movement is to move the body across the ground. Walking requires repeated patterns of using, abandoning and regaining "a balanced stance on the ground with the alternate legs" (Brooks 1986: 181). At the end of a posture or stance, for example, the supporting leg must be behind the trunk of the body, with the toes of the walker poised for take-off. At least three principal joints are involved in walking: the ankle, knee and hip. By and large, such locomotive activity is managed by subcortical and spinal centers and requires the activation of all sorts of neural control signals to govern individual muscle movements (e.g. knee flexors or ankle extensors). We may think of these signals as a form of information, as bits of synergistic charge or discharge. But the information (the charge and discharge) is devoid of Intentional content. It consists simply of bursts of electrical energy. Though the walker's thoughts are about something (e.g. finding a seat at the table), his motor neurons are not about anything at all.

Sub-conscious, sub-personal information-processing activities of various sorts, no doubt, play utterly critical causal-explanatory roles in ideomotor apraxia, but they do not occupy *mental* (psychological) roles in the sense of being conscious or Intentional. Certainly they are not part of the perspective of the subject of the disorder. Indeed, any intimate connection between mindedness and perspective is severed if we think of sub-personal information-processing as constitutive of the mind of a disorder. An ankle joint just does not have a point of view. Nothing appears to it. The person whose ankle it is has a perspective. Things appear to them.

No one should classify ideomotor apraxia as a mental disorder. Yet some psychiatric diagnostic manuals appear (note: I say 'appear') to do just that (APA 1987: 48).

So, how does mentality figure in *mental* disorders? What role or roles do consciousness and Intentionality play in a mental disorder? I will make a few brief remarks about this topic here, but plan to return to it in more detail periodically throughout the rest of the book.

M. S. Moore claims that whether a disorder is mental is "related in some way to the symptoms exhibited by the person, not to the species of causation involved" (Moore 1980: 57). I agree with the first half of Moore's claim, but disagree with the second.

Appearing as symptoms constitutes a truly important role for the mental (and thus for consciousness and Intentionality) in a mental disorder, as testified by the list of exemplars that I plan to offer in the next section of the chapter. Each and every disorder on that list is constituted, in part, by vivid and often harmful symptoms of conscious and Intentionality sorts and, indeed, of conscious Intentionality (of Intentional states or attitudes that are parts of conscious experience). As Richard Bentall puts it: "[C]ommonly recognized forms of psychopathology involve some kind of abnormality of conscious awareness" (Bentall 2007: 130). Bentall offers two brief examples of the relevance of conscious symptoms with Intentionality to the concept of a mental disorder:

> [D]epressed patients are usually excessively aware of negative aspects of themselves, and are often tormented by memories of enterprises that have ended in failure. Anxious patients ... are typically extremely vigilant for potential threats in their environment.
>
> (Bentall 2007: 130)

Vigilance directed to the outside world and its threats are distinctive of anxiety. Tormented negativity about self haunts the severe depressive. Each of these sorts of states is both conscious and Intentional (or possessed of directedness). There is something it is like to be tormented about oneself as well as to be anxious about perceived threats. Contrary to Moore, however, mental causation (or causal-explanatory reference to a disorder's mental origins or propensity conditions) is also an important role for mentality in a mental disorder as opposed to a non-mental illness or disorder. None of the exemplars (again, to be offered momentarily) can be understood in their conditions of onset or emergence without reference to conscious and Intentional states in which the contents of these states are efficacious. Mere mental symptoms are completely and utterly insufficient for calling a condition a 'mental disorder'. Did Woolf kill herself and do so intentionally because she felt hopelessly trapped or did she do so accidentally because of a defective alteration of neurotransmitter function due to Parkinson's disease? It's important to know what causes or helps to cause a set of symptoms if we are to grasp what sort of disorder a disorder is and what sorts of behavior its symptoms are. Depression-related deliberate suicide is one thing; accidentally killing oneself because of a prefrontal lobe dysfunction in an episode of lost motor control is another.

Moore's view is unacceptable for the same reason that it is unacceptable to classify visual blindness as a mental disorder when it is caused by a brain lesion. It confuses the type of disorder (whether mental or non-mental) with the type of symptom. (And it presupposes that symptoms themselves can properly be individuated and understood independent of discovering their origins.) Here is an analogy. Suppose that each of us has a sore throat, which type of sore throat do we have? If mine is caused by streptococci and yours is not, mine is a strep throat and yours is not. Causes make a difference. Symptoms reveal a disorder. Causes help to determine its type.

So, we have to be careful in using disorder words or terms for disorders. Given that each of us is 'depressed', does this mean that we each are subjects of a mental disorder? If my depression is part of the fact that I have Huntington's disease, which is a chronically progressive neurodegenerative disorder characterized by a movement disorder, dementia and psychiatric disturbances (including paranoia and depression), my depression is an aspect of a neurological disorder (or so I assume) – Huntington's disease. But if your depression is caused, in part, by experience of job loss or perception of marital decay, or if, more generally, it somehow requires reference in psychological or Intentionalistic terms (terms that presuppose Intentionality) for its explanation, then, on my view, it is a mental disorder. It is (what I would call) clinical or major depression.

I will have much more to say about the causes or sources of disorder as well as of symptoms in the course of the book. And that includes a bit more in the last section of this chapter. Right now, though, I want to turn to the problematic question of how to identify exemplary disorders.

EXEMPLARS OF MENTAL DISORDER

Two general means suggest themselves for identifying exemplars or prototypes of mental disorders. One is to deploy a universally endorsed taxonomic manual and simply to adopt the disorders mentioned in that manual as prototypical mental disorders. As we will learn in the fourth section of Chapter 3, there is no such manual. Or more precisely, the most favored manual is not without plenty of informed and qualified critics. It is widely criticized. The second general way is to pick out the most conspicuous and frequently identified disorders as exemplary, using distinct but overlapping standards of conspicuousness and frequency. This in itself is a complicated procedure, but a brief effort along these lines will, I believe, serve to pick out a set of disorders that attract sufficiently wide consensus and consent.

Arthur Kleinman, a professor of psychiatry and anthropology at Harvard, remarks that "many medical anthropologists are suspicious about the idea of culture-bound disorders" (Kleinman 2000: 302). The suspicion is not unfounded. A mental disorder if prototypical is not a disorder just of the Chinese or French Mind but of the Human Mind. Symptoms may be culturally or environmentally variable, of course, but a disorder, prototypically speaking, lays more firm or exemplary claim to qualifying as a disorder of mind if it afflicts people across distinct cultural or contextual niches. (Compare: Diabetes is not Canadian diabetes. It is, as it were, diabetes-diabetes. True, an outbreak of diabetes may appear in one place. But being place-bound is not essential to the condition.) So, one way in which to identify an exemplary disorder is to insist that a disorder is exemplary or prototypical just when it is cross-cultural and then seek to identify cross-cultural disorders. Non-exemplary disorders may be culturally unique, and certainly certain symptoms may be niche specific, but not a disorder of a broadly consensual sort.

A possible example of a culture bound (hence not exemplary) disorder that Kleinman mentions is known as Chinese railroad psychosis, which is also known as *shenjing shuairuo*, although this perhaps is more likely to be a culturally specific manifestation of neurasthenia (chronic fatigue) or a symptom of (the more general disorder of) depression. But what are some cross-cultural disorders?

Kleinman claims that five general types of disorder are cross-cultural. These are: major or clinical depression, bipolar depression, schizophrenia, brief reactive psychoses and a range of anxiety disorders "from panic states through phobias through to obsessive compulsive disorder" (Kleinman 2000: 302).

Insisting that exemplars must be cross-cultural is not free of empirical difficulty. It may be tough to distinguish between, on the one hand, cultures functioning as varying and shifting contextual scaffolds for a cross-cultural disorder's expressed symptoms and, on the other, cultures as harbors of specific sorts of disorders. Might not the defining features of a disorder include *niche-specific* features, wherein a disorder is "comprehensible only in relation to some [cultural] norm or other cultural factor" (Murphy 2006: 253)? Take eating disorders, for instance, such as bulimia. Young white American females feel pressure to be thin more so than their Navajo Indian counterparts. Quite generally, the epidemiology of bulimia tends to follow Euro-American ideas of beauty as they spread through other cultures. The conscious perception by young women of Euro-American ideas of thinness and beauty and the attendant social pressures on them to be physically attractive reinforce ideas of thinness as something desirable. This may help to explain the incidence rates and epidemiology of bulimia in certain cultural settings.

Is bulimia more like Chinese railroad psychosis (culture specific) or more like major depression (cross-cultural)? If Kleinman's list is sound and exhaustive, bulimia (not mentioned on his list) is not an exemplary disorder. It's more like Chinese railroad psychosis (assuming this is a culture specific disorder). Or perhaps it is a culturally tethered or socially structured set of symptoms of one of the general disorders which Kleinman lists. Perhaps it is a form of depression, anxiety or obsessive compulsive disorder with a distinctive grip on young women. One female victim of anorexia nervosa, a condition similar to bulimia, reports: "I knew that I had a certain strength … that would really show up somewhere." "I skipped breakfast." "I just couldn't fit the calories into my regimen." "I always 'watched it'" (Costin 1998: 243–4). She obsessively compulsively watched it.

Allan Horwitz remarks that "in the broadest sense symptom profiles … fit the illness norms of particular cultures" (Horwitz 2002: 116). Symptom profiles may be culturally tethered, but exemplary disorders themselves? With Kleinman I assume not. To be an exemplar or prototype (remember: I am using these two notions interchangeably) is to be cross-cultural. In this way suitably informed observers, whether in Dakota or Singapore, should be able to reach agreement on certain cases of a disorder, namely an exemplary disorder.

It would reinforce the wisdom of adopting a list of exemplars like or similar to that of Kleinman if its members could also be identified on grounds other than merely cross-cultural presence. Are there other grounds? Yes, at least two of them.

So, here is a second and connected way in which to devise a list of exemplary disorders. It consists of examining surveys or reports of the prevalence or incidence rates of mental disorders worldwide and then picking as exemplars only those that are most prevalent or possess the highest rates of global incidence. Skeptics do question, as earlier noted, and perhaps sometimes should question, the methods employed for gathering prevalence rates in statistical surveys. Methods? Sometimes just self-reports of symptoms when elicited in standardized interviews conducted over the telephone. "Diagnoses based on [personal] recollection," Randolf Nesse complains, "are biased by strong tendencies to forget" (Nesse 2001: 180). For that and other reasons, self-reports may be unreliable. But the following two facts are striking and useful for us to note about the main surveys that, to my knowledge, have been conducted to date.

One is that reports come from several different sources and survey instruments including the World Health Organization, the United States Epidemiological Catchment Area survey, and the National Comorbidity Survey (Kessler 2005; Kessler, Bergland et al. 2005; Kessler, Chiu et al. 2005; WMHSC 2004). The other is that whether occurring in the United States or elsewhere depressive disorders and anxiety disorders are thought to be the most prevalent, often followed in some countries, such as the United States, by substance or alcohol abuse or impulse control disorders (also known as addictions) (see also ESEMeD/MHEDEA 2000 Investigators 2004). This fact about prevalence rates for depression and anxiety disorders dovetails more or less with part of Kleinman's list. Depression and anxiety disorders are prominent on his list. Substance abuse or addiction is also present on his list, if understood as instances of (what Kleinman calls) compulsive disorder. (Later in the book, in Chapter 7, I explore whether addiction is a form of compulsion.)

A third method for identifying exemplars is owed to a theoretician and clinician who is one of the most prominent critics of the standard manners and modes of disorder identification. I have already mentioned him in this chapter. This is Richard Bentall (2004). Bentall's rather iconoclastic (albeit not totally idiosyncratic) idea about categorizing types of mental disorder goes something like this.

Popular taxonomies of mental disorder are either, at best, grossly unhelpful and misleading or, at worst, rest on a serious category mistake. The category mistake is that they encourage or presuppose a biomedical disease model of mental disorder. Disease models should be rejected, says Bentall. (I myself plan to examine disease models of mental disorder in the next chapter.) Mental disorders, says Bentall, are not diseases. Diseases typically have discrete edges, which distinguish themselves from each other and are discontinuous from normal variations in health. The sorts of mental health problems faced by the patients of psychiatrists just are not like that, says Bentall. Psychiatric troubles or maladies do not have discrete edges. They are hard to distinguish from normal, albeit otherwise immensely distressful, conditions. There is, for example, no obvious cut-off point in the diagnosis of depression that suggests a uniform basis for distinguishing between being grief-stricken or profoundly sad, on the one hand, and being clinically depressed, on the other. So, it is best not to think of people's psychiatric troubles or complaints as disorders if this means thinking of them as diseases. It's best to think of them, says Bentall, as just that, namely troubles or complaints with which people need help. As Bentall puts it, once troubles or complaints have been identified and explanatorily understood, there is no "ghostly" illness, disorder or disease "remaining that also requires explanation." "Complaints are all there is" (Bentall 2004: 141). Complaints are classes of disturbances that are "troublesome" and "worthy of [professional] attention" (Bentall 2004: 142).

Bentall is not making Moore's claim that causation is irrelevant to the classification of a mental disorder. He is saying that a 'disorder' consists in symptoms or complaints plus origins of a non-disease type.

Complaint- or trouble-orientated lists of 'disorders' like the one I am about to mention of Bentall are not without critics. Bentall is not without replies (Bentall 2004: 144). I don't wish to endorse his approach or complaint terminology in this context. I simply wish to cite his list.

Bentall mentions the following complaints as the ones most commonly seen by clinicians (Bentall 2004: 488). Complaints about or disturbances of depression, mania, paranoia, incoherence, hallucinations and negative symptoms (flat affect, affective blunting, anhedonia, apathy, impoverished speech, among others).

What is striking about Bentall's list, at least to me, is that it overlaps with Kleinman's in certain respects as well as with global prevalence rates and incidence data, although it is devised from an utterly different taxonomic perspective. This is the perspective of someone who is skeptical about current diagnostic practices and labels. Depression (major or clinical depression) is mentioned on each list. 'Mania' is part of what it means for a depression to be bipolar. But mania also may count, depending upon how it is described or understood, as a feature of a range of anxiety and impulse control disorders. Blunting, apathy and anhedonia are features of depression as well, of course. Incoherence and hallucinations are constituents of schizophrenia mentioned by Kleinman. Paranoia may be part of depression as well as mania and anxiety.

We certainly don't get a perfect match between the three lists. Perhaps such imperfection spells doom for thinking of mental disorder prototypes or exemplars. I think not. The proposed list of exemplars (which follows below), which is for something as complex as a mental disorder – unlike something as simple or relatively straightforward as a book – just is (in my book here) a sort of heuristic or organizational device. It helps to give us reference points for regimenting or constructing a notion of mental disorder. Besides which a proposed list is not an unquestioned entity. Some parts may need to be deleted as we learn more about various conditions. Other conditions may also be added. In any case, the three lists overlap in various ways. Some items are mentioned or appear on each. So, with such similarities or overlaps in mind, I assume that we are warranted in considering the following as disorder exemplars or prototypes.

- Depression (including major depression and depression with mania).
- Anxiety disorders (including phobias and some types of paranoia).
- Disorders of incoherence (including delusional disorders).
- Disorders of reactivity or impulse (including addiction or substance abuse and some forms of both mania and obsession).

So, now back to the question: Just what chores or functions does mentality (consciousness and Intentionality) play in disorders or conditions of the above-mentioned sorts? For a disorder to be a prototypical or exemplary disorder, it must include what roles for the mental?

ROLES OF THE MENTAL IN MENTAL DISORDER

The mental plays two primary roles in mental disorders. The first (already noted) consists in its role as main or central symptoms. The second, a role mentioned but not yet really discussed, consists in being part of a disorder's propensity or onset conditions, origins or causes.

Figuring in both symptoms and onset conditions or sources is not the only role of mentality in mental disorder. Psychotherapy for mental disorders, with reliance on reasoning and conversational address, focuses directly on a subject's conscious Intentional states. So, consciousness and Intentionality may also play roles as focal points for a disorder's therapeutic address. Still another role? Some subjects of certain disorders know that they have a disorder or that something is wrong with them. This first-person knowledge is sometimes referred to as diagnostic insight and is, as a form of knowledge, constituted by conscious Intentional states. I say 'certain disorders', since for other types of disorder diagnostic insight on the part of a subject is utterly absent. In delusional disorders, for example, diagnostic insight is missing and often disturbingly so, making it difficult to offer therapy voluntarily to a person (Fulford 1989 and 1994; Currie 2000). Deluded people don't think of themselves as deluded. After all, how could they? If I believe that I am God incarnate, but also believe that I am deluded in believing this, the thought that I am God incarnate will impress me as unwarranted or unfounded. So, in my own eyes, I should abandon it. Insight, however, is present in certain other sorts of disorder. Victims of obsessive thinking, for example, often complain of the obsessive and interruptive character of their anxieties and thoughts, and this fact helps to distinguish, clinically, between a deluded subject (who may think that nothing is wrong with them) and a victim of obsessive thinking (Goodwin and Guze 1996: 4).

Aside, however, from certain forms of therapy and cases of illness insight, consciousness and Intentionality have two *main* roles, as noted, in a mental disorder. In symptoms. In sources or causes. What, then, about sources?

Something is seriously incomplete and over-broad in a concept of mental disorder if it is applied only on the basis of a disturbance's being mental in symptoms alone. Only if our explanatory understanding refers to feelings, beliefs, memories and other mental states or attitudes as causes or sources is a disorder mental. Why so? The answer, as noted above in discussing Moore, is that to understand what type of disorder a disorder is (whether mental or somatic), it is necessary to go beyond or inside symptoms to learn how the symptoms arose, otherwise even the symptoms themselves may not be properly described or understood. This is a point I made earlier in the chapter but it bears repeating.

Parkinson's disease is a degenerative disorder of the brain characterized by progressive tremor, slowness of movement, and rigidity (Litvan 1999: 559–64). Mental symptoms may be part of the symptom profile of this disorder in the form of failing memory, problems with concentration, and difficulties in initiating goal-directed activity. But do such symptoms make Parkinson's a mental disorder? No, they do not. Consciousness and Intentionality play no role whatsoever in the onset or course of the condition. Degeneration of part of the midbrain (known as the substantia nigra) with subsequent decrease of a chemical messenger known as (striatal) dopamine is a probable cause of Parkinsonism. It is a purely somatic disorder or disease, namely a disorder *of* the brain, albeit a disorder with some harmful symptoms of a mental sort. Neurological problems or deficits irrupt into the space of reasons in Parkinsonism and in severe cases essentially swamp a person's ability to control various forms of bodily activity.

How do the rigid motions of a victim of advanced Parkinsonism compare with Alice's remaining in bed in the morning? How much like the slow movement of the Parkinson's patient are the lethargic and unwelcome steps taken by Alice when she spots a window that needs to be closed from a bitter winter wind and rises from underneath her covers? Compare the explanation for Parkinson's disease with that for Alice's loss of motivation (which, I am saying, stems from her protracted grief and perception of personal helplessness [(Abramson et al. 1989; Abramson et al. 1978]). To explain the slowness of Alice's steps we must refer to her own self-conception or to how she thinks of herself and her situation. If we are to intervene in her depression, we may try to influence how she understands her husband's love for her and her parental responsibilities toward her children. In a case of Parkinson's, we must aim directly to manipulate its neurobiology/neurochemistry (no small chore as diminishing returns from dopaminergic therapy may sometimes contribute to further motor performance deterioration [Litvan 1999: 563]). No association between motor performance and a person's self-comprehension is at all evident.

A key feature of Alice's sort of depression is that conscious representations of self and world, namely states of consciousness and Intentionality, play critical roles not just in the symptom profile of the depression but in its origins or conditions of onset. It is, in particular, in attitudes of a self-referential nature that people experience themselves as helpless or aggrieved and therein may become depressed.

That a depression (or type of clinical depression) springs from such mental sources such as learned helplessness does not mean that the sources function to the exclusion of brute a-rational somatic/neural conditions. It is my view (mentioned earlier and to be explained later) that mental disorders are produced by a mixture of mental and brute somatic factors. In mental disorders there is both mentality and neurobiology/neurochemistry (the second 'gumming up' the works of reason, as I like to put it). Perhaps the brain of a subject of helplessness depression suffers decrements of neurotransmitter function derived in part from perceptions of the person's own helplessness or frustrated efforts to avoid negative outcomes. The subjective experience of a depression may exemplify the interplay between such perceptions and its underlying neurochemistry.

It's easy to see, by contrast, that nothing like a key causal role for Intentionality occurs in exemplary cases of somatic or bodily illness. Breast cancer neither arises from nor disappears under pressure from a person's Intentional states (states with Intentionality). Cancer growth has somatic sources and may remit only under chemical forces. It would be ridiculous to try to cure breast cancer by, say, doses of Freudian psychotherapy.

Assuming that mentality plays a key causal role in exemplary mental disorders, it is worth wondering how we should answer questions about the *legitimacy* of the diagnosis of a mental disorder. Symptoms often present a nasty practical problem to the diagnostically conscientious clinician, who often must spend time and energy in deciding whether a particular cluster of symptoms expresses a *mental* (rather than a brute somatic) disorder. Borrowing a term introduced by the philosopher Nelson Goodman to distinguish, in the visual arts, between original paintings and inauthentic copies, exemplary mental disorders in their origins bear the *autograph* (stamp or mark) of mentality (Goodman 1968: 113). They carry the mark of the mental in their sources or propensity conditions. A mental autograph on some of the sources of a disorder helps to distinguish a disorder that is authentically or legitimately mental from one that is not.

Compare and contrast a case of mental disorder with Alzheimer's disease. Alzheimer's is characterized by progressively worsening memory, language and visual spatial skills, as well as changes in personality. Victims may also become depressed, apathetic, aggressive, and lose insight into their condition. As the disease progresses, delusions and paranoia may occur. But is Alzheimer's a mental disorder? Although its precise proximate physical origins are not known, it is known, I believe, that Alzheimer's has exclusively brute somatic or neuronal causes, namely likely degeneration of various sorts of processes in cortical and possibly subcortical neurons. So, it is not a disorder in which consciousness and Intentionality figures in its onset. No 'autograph of mentality' is present in its sources, although mental decrements are present in symptoms and some such symptoms do, in fact, help to produce or sustain their own elements of dramatic personality change. (The disorientation or sense of helplessness produced by severe memory loss may be responsible, for example, for the depression and paranoia often observed in victims of Alzheimer's.) Moore may wish to classify it as a mental disorder. I do not.

There is much more that can, should and will be said as the book continues about exemplary mental disorders being mental in their causes as well as symptoms. For the nonce, however, I am done with the topic of the mind of mental disorder. I plan to turn in the next chapter to our second question about mental disorder. This is: What makes a mental disorder disorderly – a disorder? I approach this question by asking what makes a mental disorder undesirable.

CHAPTER SUMMARY AND SUGGESTED READINGS

Mental disorder. What's that? Counting anything as a mental disorder requires having a theory of mental disorder. This chapter offered a brief sketch of the aims of a theory of mental disorder. Coming up with a good concept of a mental disorder is one of them. I argued that exemplars of mental disorder may serve as a constructive basis for a concept of mental disorder. I described how we may identify exemplars and I offered a list of them. Taken too seriously a list of exemplars (at this early stage of investigation) may lead us astray. So we must be careful. It is not written in stone and each member of the list must ultimately be understood in terms of its origins or sources and symptoms.

What is the mind of a mental disorder? I noted that the concept of mind or mentality that operates in the description of exemplary mental disorders possesses two referents. One is to the consciousness of a state or attitude. The other is to the Intentionality of a state or attitude. Every conscious state or attitude has a qualitative or subjective character to it. It is like something to its subject. Intentionality is the aspect of mentality in virtue of which mental states or attitudes are about or directed at objects or states or affairs, both real and imagined. If I have a belief, it must be a belief about something. If I have desire, it must be a desire for something. Each state refers beyond itself.

In mental disorders of exemplary sorts the properties of consciousness and Intentionality play at least two roles. One is in symptoms of disorder and the other is in its origins or sources.

The social setting of psychiatric medicine is explored in Allen Horwitz's *Creating Mental Illness* (University of Chicago Press, 2002), T. M. Luhrmann's *Of Two Minds: The Growing Disorder of American Psychiatry* (Knopf, 2000), and Carl Elliott's *Better Than Well: American Medicine Meets the American Dream* (Norton, 2004). Each book also offers timely and provocative critiques of cultural or non-medical influences on psychiatric (and in Elliott's case, general medical) practice.

On concepts and the human conceptual system, prototypes and the like, Eric Margolis and Stephen Laurence's "Concepts," in S. Stich and W. Warfield (eds), *The Blackwell Guide to the Philosophy of Mind* (Blackwell, 2003), is a short, accessible and informative survey of the cognitive science of concepts and conceptualization.

On the question of just what a theory of mental disorder should accomplish, Richard Bentall's *Madness Explained: Psychosis and Human Nature* (Penguin, 2004), and Nancy Andreasen's *Brave New Brain: Conquering Mental Illness in the Era of the Genome* (Oxford University Press, 2001), offer a pair of contrasting perspectives. Bentall's book is also a helpful short introduction to clinical experimental practice. Andreasen's contains useful information about the neuroscience of mental illness and the history of psychiatric medication. Sharing Andreasen's admiration for neuroscience is J. Allen Hobson and Jonathan Leonard's *Out of Its Mind: Psychiatry in Crisis: A Call for Reform* (Perseus, 2001).

Much has been written on consciousness and Intentionality. Good short introductions to these phenomena are available in John Searle's *Mind: A Brief Introduction* (Oxford University Press, 2004). Advanced readers may find B. McLaughlin, A. Beckermann and S. Walter's edited, *The Oxford Handbook of Philosophy of Mind* (Oxford University Press, 2009), a valuable reference tool, especially parts II (on consciousness) and III (on Intentionality).

The disorder of mental disorder

Just what type of a disturbance or distress is the disorder of a mental disorder? It is undesirable, no doubt. But what makes it undesirable? In this chapter I describe some of the features of a mental disorder that help to make mental disorders undesirable. Not all of them. Some of them.

WHAT MAKES MENTAL DISORDER UNDESIRABLE?

Writers on mental health and illness sometimes complain that the psychiatric use of the term 'disorder' is a conceptual embarrassment. "I am wary of the word 'disorder'," writes Ian Hacking (Hacking 1995: 17).

Wary or not, however, the term serves as an alternative to a number of other terms. It is common to speak now not just of a mental illness, for example, but of a mental disorder. This is not because the expression 'mental illness' is no longer used. It is widely used. (I use it in the subtitle of this book. I use it interchangeably with talk of disorder.) Sometimes, though, the expression 'mental illness' is used to refer not to a disorder or behavioral condition as such, but to the subjective or personal experience of having a disorder. It is used to refer to the what-it's-likeness or conscious phenomenology of a disorder, say, of a depression or paranoid delusional disorder. The what-it's-likeness of being depressed certainly is different, subjectively, from that of being paranoid. The what-it's-likeness of schizophrenia is distinct from that of addiction. And so on. Disorder talk, by contrast, is never used for something exclusively phenomenological. There is more to a mental disorder, so-called, than just its what-it's-likeness either in state or attitude. There is the behavior: locking one's doors, not getting out of bed, and so on.

The general intention behind the concept of a disorder when applied to a mental disturbance or distress is to try to capture at least three facts central to a disturbance. These
three facts help to explain why a mental disorder is undesirable or a *disorder* and something
bad or disorderly as such. A condition that people *ought not* to be in. (I say 'help' because
other facts are also proper to disorders as such, as we will learn in later chapters.)

It is important to recognize, in preparation for describing the three facts, that the classification of a mental condition or state as undesirable or bad for a person is different from
saying that it is undesired or thought bad by the person. A disorder may be undesired,
depending on the condition, but it may not be. An addictive behavior pattern may be
undesired, for instance, but perhaps not when its subject is high on a drug or winning wagers
at a casino or horse track. Such a pattern, however, still is *undesirable*, whether or not the
person appreciates this fact.

So, what are the three facts that help to explain why disturbances that are classified as
mental disorders are undesirable and 'disorders'? The first fact is that a disorder is harmful
or dangerous. A person is much worse off or markedly more poorly off when subject of a
disorder than if mentally sound and healthy. So, for example, a person in the midst of, say,
a major depressive episode, or someone in the grips of an obsessive compulsive disorder,
is poorly off. Not only may these particular conditions feel bad (again, not all disorders or
episodes of a disorder may feel bad), but they are associated with harmful or deleterious
behavior. The harm of a disorder may take the form of pain and suffering. It may take the
form of death or a significant risk of death. Or it may take the form of being unintelligible or
incomprehensible to oneself.

Being incomprehensible to self is no mere insignificant occurrence, like the transient
ignorance associated with occasional absent-mindedness or garden varieties of forgetfulness or muddled thinking. Self-incomprehensibility is a severe burden, a self-stultifying
impairment. Victims of certain disorders just do not understand why they think, feel or act
as they do. They vigorously distrust their own husband, although he has done no harm to
them. They are deeply despondent, although they have just won a Pulitzer Prize. They are in
the dark about themselves.

Being in the dark about one's own person means that an individual is incapable of rational
self-scrutiny or taking proper responsibility for self. Consider clinical depression. One of
the most intriguing hypotheses in Freud's psychopathology is his notion that in a case of
depression a person may develop free-floating or content-diffuse anxieties or concerns as
well as loosened affective or emotional connections with previous sources of pleasure and
satisfaction. Some depressed people care or are emotionally concerned, to employ Jennifer
Church's apt terminology, "for everything and nothing" (Church 2003: 181). Which is to say:
Everything matters just as much to them, but also alas, just as little, as everything else.
So, in effect, nothing matters or stands out, neither the activities of daily living nor normal
bonds of home or heart. A person loses emotional connectivity with previously cherished
goods. Engagement with the world may go flat or become sullen. Yet such an individual
has perhaps just won, say, a Pulitzer Prize or married a much desired soulmate. So, why
can't someone in such a situation get their world to be emotionally resonant again – to be
affectively cared for again? A depressed person just may not know why. They may be in the

dark about themselves. "How could this happen to me?" "Why aren't I happy?" "I should be happy." "Shouldn't I?"

Depression is commonly classified as a mood disorder. But, of course, depression is much more than that. A remark made by Annette Karmiloff-Smith about neurodevelopmental disorders applies to depression as well as to other sorts of mental disorder. This is that "a totally specific disorder [is], ex hypothesis, ... extremely unlikely" (Karmiloff-Smith 1998: 390). Depression, for instance, is not just a mood disorder or specific to feeling or affect. It also is a disorder of care and emotional commitment as well as, oftentimes, of self-comprehension (notions to be discussed later in the book).

The second fact about disorder that helps to make a disorder undesirable concerns its non-voluntary and ultimately personally uncontrollable nature. Experiencing a mental disorder is not something a person willfully does. The onset of a disorder is not deliberate. It is not a self-"disordering" – not a self-authored or deliberate effort to become disordered. One becomes disordered without intending and despite wanting not to be disordered. So, too, getting oneself out of a disorder is not under direct or voluntary control. One can no more 'snap out of it', say, out of an obsessive compulsive or paranoid delusional disorder, than a person can snap out of scurvy or malaria.

Take depression again. A clinically depressed person cannot be persuaded to stop being depressed just by being told of the costs, risks or liabilities associated with being depressed. Being depressed is not a choice to be frowned on and rejected after a concerted risk assessment or analysis of its costs and benefits. A person can't help it. Often depressed people are acutely aware of its costs. All of which may mean that an individual in the grips of a disorder like depression may require help or assistance from others or from mental health professionals to be free of its incapacitation or to reduce its range or prominence. A person with a disorder may be unable to live decently, if at all, without the aid or assistance of others, especially during crises or periods of high and imprudent risk.

We are used to people needing aid and assistance with somatic disease or injury. A victim of breast cancer may be unable to survive without assistance (drugs, surgery and so on) and the generosity and competence of others. So, too, a person who suffers, say, from a mental disorder like agoraphobia or delusional disorder may be unable to function well or appropriately without the aid of others.

The third fact presupposed by the concept of disorder is that a disorder is not excised or extirpated from a person's psychological make-up or economy just by mere addition of other psychological resources. A disorder "gums up the works" and upsets the "proper working order" of mentality (Feinberg 1970: 287–8). The mind of a mental disorder is not made orderly or healthy just by endowing it with other psychological assets. So, someone who suffers from, say, paranoid delusional disorder and who is incorrigibly and imprudently distrustful of others is not released from the grip of paranoia just by being endowed with added doses of creative imagination. Added imagination may make their paranoia worse. A vivid imagination may more deeply entrench unwarranted convictions about why other people should be distrusted. A depressed patient who suffers from low self-esteem is not automatically cleansed, psychologically, of their excessively self-critical habits just by being given special opportunities for social affiliation (a larger family, extra friends, and so on).

Social contact may worsen a depressive condition when, in a darkly mood-ridden contrast and comparison with others, a person feels less successful, lovable or worthy of the better-ments of social life than other people.

Compare the situation of a mental disorder with a somatic injury in this respect of not being excised by compensatory additions. A person with a broken leg is not freed of this misfortune, the misfortune of the break does not disappear, just if they are endowed with more muscular arms or enhanced ocular acuity. As long as the leg remains broken, they are injured or in bodily ill-health. Likewise, as long as a depressed patient remains pessimisti-cally self-critical, or a paranoid person persists in unwarranted social distrust, they are worse off. They are in mental ill-health. Such is the undesirability of a mental disorder. It gums up the mind's works.

So, a mental disorder is not just a mere "alien condition involuntarily suffered" (like a transient headache, for example), to use an apt expression of the philosopher Joel Feinberg (1926–2004), quoted also just above, but is something for which the simple grafting on of other psychological capacities, so to speak, neither heals nor covers up its wound (Feinberg 1970: 287–8). Unless the disorder itself is addressed, and its 'gum' removed by means that are proper to a condition's content and character, a disorder gets in the way of a person with the condition. It makes their life worse.

Just how much worse depends on circumstances, cases and contexts of course. Being worse off does not mean that disorders are always and utterly devoid of some measure of compensation or secondary gain. It has been claimed, for example, that susceptibility to paranoia may encourage a healthy distrust of others in aberrant and truly threatening social environments (Jarvik and Chadwick 1972). It has been widely claimed that several prominent scientists and creative artists have flourished in their craft if not person despite (because of?) the travails of a bipolar disorder (Simonton 1994). Different contexts or cases may offer different forms of compensation. But who would voluntarily and knowingly pay such steep prices for those 'gains'? The alleged gains, no matter how arresting, do not eliminate the disorder. A disorder leaves an individual in harm's way and in need of reconstitution or address.

So: It's no wonder that conditions classified as disorders are undesirable or thought of as 'disorders'. They are harmful, non-voluntary and not directly addressed or treated with mere added ingredients or without regard to an addition's fit, suitability or contextual appropriateness.

MORALLY THERAPEUTIC INTERLUDE AND LURE OF THE DISEASE MODEL

One presupposition behind referring to the incapacities, disabilities or impairments operative in the 'gummed up works' of a disorder is that the symptoms or behaviors expressive of disorder are not transparently explainable or understandable. A performance lapse may have nothing whatsoever to do with a disorder (with an incapacity, disability or impairment). Put me on a bar stool with a bunch of college chums, where I am challenged to down three pints of ale, and I may drink with reckless abandon. But this does not mean that I am an alcoholic, nor does it imply that I will subsequently develop the feelings, attitude and preferences that make me a substance abuser. Competencies or abilities don't always reveal themselves when or as they should or could. To the extent that I possess or over time develop alcohol consumption constraints, I will be able to refrain on other occasions.

The presence of symptoms of a disorder is explained by reference to an *underlying* disability, incapacity or incompetence in a person's psychological make-up. As long as the disorder endures, its symptoms, depending on environmental circumstances, may persist. (I am saving for the sixth chapter, discussion of just which incapacities are proper to mental disorders of the exemplary varieties.)

Given that mental disorders incapacitate or gum up, as noted, persons with disorders often require special care, intervention or treatment. Questions of care, intervention or treatment may be immensely complicated. Care of a person with a disorder usually is not some one thing, like dispensing a medication, and (as noted above) it should not be depicted as a mere add-on or graft to a disorder. The character or type of care should stem from the character of the disorder as well as from the uniqueness of the individual person affected or hurt by the condition and their interests and needs.

In referring to the person with a disorder, it must also be emphasized that there is more to a disorder, of course, than the disorder. There is *this* particular person with the disorder. Let me briefly explain what I have in mind here by referring to the uniqueness of the individual and by speaking of complexities of treatment.

Whatever care or aid is given to an individual with a disorder should, of course, be subject to moral constraints. It should be consistent, as best we can tell, with a person's self-respect and sense of personal dignity (see Nussbaum 2006). We certainly shouldn't try to 'heal' or restore 'order' to a person in a manner that demeans or disrespects them.

One form of disrespectful or undignified treatment is to encourage unquestioned and imprudent reliance on psychotropic drugs. Prescriptions for antidepressant and antipsychotic medications have skyrocketed in the last decade, due, in part, to the resistance of health insurers to pay for cognitive psychotherapies and the hours and labor often required in psychotherapeutic treatment. Psychotropic medications are among the best-selling drugs and best-selling new drugs. Among the most popular patented drugs in 2005, for example, was one named *Cympalta* (duloxetine), an antidepressant medication, which had secured Federal Drug Administration approval only in 2004 and earned US$667 million for its manufacturer, Eli Lilly (Klume 2007). Drugs, however, often have deleterious side or long-term negative effects, both known and unknown.

Richard Bentall (2004) offers the following striking example of the unwelcome effect of a drug on none other than himself.

> I was a [volunteer] participant in [an] experiment ... in which I received 5 mg of droperidol, and became restless and dysphoric to the point of being distressed. I burst into tears. ... I had a hangover for days. ... The doses in these experiments were far lower than those typically given to patients.
>
> (500)

Overenthusiastic use of or reliance on medication, Bentall adds, has "led to a worldwide epidemic of avoidable iatrogenic [treatment-induced] illness, causing unnecessary distress to countless vulnerable people" (Bentall 2004: 501). It is not Bentall's position that "the use of psychiatric drugs is always wrong" (504). But drugs, he cautions, harbor risks that must be factored into their use and application. Even the most popular medications may be harmful.

A timely example may help to illustrate what I mean. One of the most widely prescribed medications for depression is a family of drugs called specific serotonin reuptake inhibitors (SSRIs). Here, roughly, is how they work in the brain. Signals are sent between brain cells (neurons) by chemicals known as transmitters. One of the most common of these chemical messengers in the brain is 5-hydroxytryptamine, known more commonly as serotonin. This chemical is also found in the intestine (as well as in bananas). When a transmitter like serotonin is released and activates a receptor on the adjacent brain cell, its excess is delivered back into the releasing nerve ending in a process known as reuptake. There it is stored for later recirculation. In serotonin's case a specific reuptake process operates through a transporter molecule. SSRIs block that process of reuptake. So, serotonin 'washes over', as it were, the adjacent cell. This increase of serotonin is thought to combat or help to combat depression, on the hypothesis that depression is due in some measure to a decline of serotonin in the brain. One may question that particular hypothesis, of course, although that is not the point I wish to make here. I am aiming for another caution.

One difficulty with SSRIs is that they are not designer drugs. That is, they do not target just depression, for although they do block the reuptake of serotonin, they also work wherever the same chemical process occurs elsewhere in the body. This includes the intestine. So, some patients experience intestinal side-effects, such as diarrhea and nausea.

Alas, for all we know, the side or long-term effects of certain drugs may stymie some perfectly healthy reactions. Some evidence from non-human animal models suggests that social animals undergo fluctuations of serotonin levels in response to natural or normal stresses in their species' life, such as a rise or fall in social status (see Edwards and Kravitz 1997). So, an animal that enjoys high social status, but experiences a decline of place in its social hierarchy, may undergo a drop in serotonin levels and exhibit depression-like symptoms such as withdrawal and body self-absorption. To speculate: This may be an evolved defense mechanism, like some cases of fever or diarrhea in instances in which a toxin has been ingested. As Neil Levy notes, perhaps social withdrawal "allows one time to recuperate from the ... decline in status" and to ensure that "the decline ... is reversed or at least halted" (Levy 2007: 82; see also Watson and Andrews 2002). A person who merely shrugs off dramatic loss of social prominence may fail to appreciate what it takes to deserve or merit the fruits of hard-won social labors. So, an episode of depression (not something truly harmful or clinically deleterious) may help an individual to get their act together or to secure other benefits of a personal nature (see Graham 1990). A serotonin decrement is not necessarily a bad thing.

The power of drugs to restore mental health derives from the ways in which they are used and, often, from how they are understood or interpreted by the persons who consume them. One cautionary fear is that drugs may create unnecessary psychological dependencies or autonomy losses that are imprudent and debilitating. If your house is broken into or your job is lost, and you become depressed, this may not indicate, of course, that you should be prescribed antidepressant medication. Carl Elliott, a philosopher trained also as a physician, complains that people may rely on "beta-blockers or Paxil to take the edge off business presentations, Ritalin to improve our attention and concentration, Prozac to give ... the confidence to apply for a promotion" (Elliott 2003: 153). Elliott notes: "some situations call for depression or ... anxiety." But "some things call for fear and trembling" (Elliott 2003: 157).

Drugs and chemical manipulations are not alone in posing dilemmas in the diagnosis and treatment of disorder. Diagnostic taxonomies and psychiatric labeling also raise difficulties. Ethical or moral difficulties. Erving Goffman's classic studies of the potential stigma of mental illness show that diagnostic categorization sometimes constitutes an affront to a patient's dignity and self-respect (Goffman 1961 and 1963). Dignity and self-respect are undermined by labeling when a person suffering from a disorder is perceived not as the individual whom they are, but as one of a general type "without significant individuality and diversity, defined entirely by their [diagnostic] characteristics" (Nussbaum 2006: 191). To classify someone who is not well and in need of help into a de-individuating pigeonhole is a recipe for prescriptive tyranny.

Prescriptive tyranny may take different forms. I mention two.

One consists of causing a person to lose hope in their condition or circumstances. One patient describes the effect on him of being labeled as follows.

> By approaching my situation in terms of [my] illness, the system has consistently underestimated my capacity to change and has ignored the potential it may contain to assist that change. ... The major impression I have received is that I am a victim of something nasty, not quite understandable, that will never really go away and which should not be talked about too openly in the company of strangers.
>
> (P. Campbell, as quoted in Radden 2009: 173)

Another form of prescriptive tyranny is noted by Nomy Arpaly (Arpaly 2005). The fact that a person possesses a mental disorder does not automatically mean that they are not blameworthy, praiseworthy or personally responsible for their behavior. Suppose a woman's husband is clinically depressed and diagnosed as such but, as a result, she treats him like an impotent child – utterly helpless. Suppose also that in "treating his suffering [in this demeaning way] she misunderstands [the condition] and aggravates it" (Arpaly 2005: 297). Treating him like a child humiliates him. She should be forgiving and supportive, true, but she may also harbor legitimate resentment or negative reactive attitudes for certain forms of misbehavior on his part. On occasion, label or no label, he does misbehave and he needs to know this. Anything less fails to respect him as a person. The label 'depression' should not cover all of his sins or enervate her person-respecting reactive attitudes toward them. "We are not limited," the philosopher Ferdinand Schoeman aptly remarks in a paper on alcoholism, "to one response" (Schoeman 1994: 201). Schoeman observes: "Our thinking about what is fair to expect of people must respect the ambiguities implicit in our understanding of what individuals can do" even when they are subjects of a disorder (Schoeman 1994: 195). Anything less is treating them less than they deserve.

Colin King is a stigma survivor. At 17 years old, King was misdiagnosed with schizophrenia. He has since completed a PhD in institutional racism at the University of London and worked as a mental health practitioner. He is a black man.

King remembers, during one period of hospitalization, "looking at the open ward, my acne making me look like I had a second face, mortified, life became morbid, with no purpose, no pride, no joy, and no ambitions, cut off; you begin to think that life is like that all the time" (King 2007: 21). Diagnostic labeling and treatment, he says, may make a person feel as if their personhood had been "objectified ... under rigid labels" (26).

When various mental health professionals observed King, they saw a man in need of treatment. They reacted to him as a person who would function better on medication; an underachieving, social misfit. The mental health profession would have done much better service for King, of course, and treated him with dignity and compassion, if they viewed him not primarily as a patient with a medical problem, but as a person in a behavioral predicament, facing a personal challenge. King's primary challenge was not the medical problem of, say, controlling his angry outbursts, but the personal problem of becoming a more able and stable person, whatever the impediments of his disorder or situation.

Is there any way in which to guard against over-reliance on drugs and the overblown power of labeling? No doubt, we need a conception of mental disorder that helps to reveal when as well as how drugs should be used and diagnostic labels applied. That's a tall and complicated order. It may not be possible to cleanly and clearly deliver on it. But one model for the disorderliness of a mental disorder that has been proposed in response, in part, to that tall order and which attracts numerous clinicians and mental health professionals is that of a somatic disease or bodily illness. This is sometimes called the biomedical disease model of mental disorder. In broadest terms it goes something like this: Somatic diseases and bodily illnesses constitute a class of negative health conditions recognized by medical and lay people alike. We know or surely seem to know when a condition should be classified as a somatic disease, treated with drugs, and labeled as, say, malaria not measles, syphilis not scurvy, carbon-monoxide poisoning not cancer. For such and other reasons it is both sound and sensible to conceive of a mental disorder on the model of a somatic disease. A person may be classified as someone with leukemia with no over-reliance on drugs or as victim of ovarian cancer with no social stigma. This is not to say that somatic diseases are never treated with unnecessary drugs or that social or cultural stigmata never affix to somatic maladies. (Just think of the early years of AIDS diagnosis and its contribution to homophobia.) However, still, some say, it's promising and helpful to picture depression as like epilepsy or paranoia as similar to breast cancer. The semantic admonition behind such a biomedical program (sometimes said to be part of the discipline of biological psychiatry) is to classify each condition, whether somatic or mental, as a disease entity.

Is it fit, proper or wise to think of disorders as diseases? It would help in answering this question if there was true uniformity or consensus over just what a disease model of a disorder is or precisely means. Truth be told, there is not (compare Andreasen 2001 with Guze 1992). But still the question is worth exploring, if we may make some assumptions, two to be exact, about what a disorder as disease means so as to help to frame discussion. What exactly is to be said for a biomedical disease model of disorder? Are mental disorders disease entities? I now wish to explore this question.

ARE MENTAL DISORDERS DISEASES?

First assumption: Any picture of the semantics of the notion of a somatic disease as a set of finitely specifiable and empirically tractable necessary and sufficient conditions of application is mistaken. The notion of a disease, however, does possess prototypical, exemplary or paradigmatic conditions of application. (Again, I use such terms, adding 'paradigmatic' to the mix, interchangeably.) What I mean by this remark is that the concept of a disease picks out conditions or states of persons that *tend to have* certain properties or features. Some such conditions or states tend to have the features of a disease in spades or with truth conditional robustness. States that tend to have them in spades are paradigms, prototypes or exemplars of somatic disease.

Reference to paradigms, prototypes or exemplars doesn't help to classify each and every disease or exclude non-exemplary diseases from the class. Prototype semantics is like that. Each of a Rembrandt self-portrait and the self-portrait of a weekend hack is properly described as a painting, although only the first is an exemplar. Each of the Boston Marathon and Monty Python's Marathon for People with Directional Disorder (when the gun goes off folks run in dozens of different directions) is a marathon (though etc.). But acknowledging the existence of prototypes or exemplars is incompatible with a semantic spirit of *hands-off conceptual rectitude* that permits people to define 'diseases' pretty much as they please.

Second assumption. What somatic conditions or bodily states do I believe should be put on the list of prototypical somatic illnesses or diseases? Here, for me, are some exemplars:

- Infectious diseases (for example, malaria and encephalitis)
- Diseases of the bronchopulmonary system (for example, emphysema)
- Diseases of the kidney (for example, medullary cystic disease)
- Diseases of the liver (for example, hepatitis)
- Diseases of the blood (for example, leukemia).

The list may go on, alas, almost indefinitely: diseases of nutrition (like scurvy), metabolism (like lipomas), endocrine system (like Cushing's syndrome), bone and joints, and so on. We are somatically fragile creatures.

Assumptions made. Are mental disorders diseases or sufficiently akin to diseases to be classified as a form of disease? Are delusional disorder, agoraphobia and depression sufficiently similar to malaria, scurvy, hepatitis or leukemia?

I am not asking if mental disorders are *physical*. It may be that some sort of physical-identity thesis is true or that mental events are nothing but brain events (a topic to be explored in Chapter 4). But, if so, the sheer physicality or neurophysical basis of a disorder does not necessarily mean that mental disorders are diseases (for a reason that I will mention in a moment). I am asking here if mental disorders are disease-like on *other* grounds, grounds which are not directly connected with the issue of physicality, but which are sufficient to qualify disorders as diseases.

Similarly, I am not asking if mental disorders are disorders *of* the brain or central nervous system and therein diseases by virtue of being neurological disorders. Often (as noted earlier in this book) mental disorders just by virtue of being thought to be neurophysical are also said to be disorders of the brain (neurological disorders) and therein diseases, assuming that brain or neurological disorders are diseases (e.g. Andreasen 2001). I assume that we should distinguish between disorders that are based in the brain from those that, in addition, are disorders of the brain (such as a blinding brain lesion, Parkinsonism or Pick's disease). My main reason for promoting this distinction (as noted throughout the book) is that the norms or standards for healthy and proper brain function are not the same as those for satisfying or prudent personal activity or rational or reason-responsive behavior, just as, say, the norms for good computer hardware are not the same as those for good software.

Nomy Arpaly (2005: 283) remarks:

> If computers are completely physical, and yet one can meaningfully distinguish hardware and software problems, then it is possible that though human beings are completely biochemical, one can still tell mental states and problems [apart] from non-mental biomedical states and problems.

So, mental activity may constitute a disorder even if the brain does not malfunction, but is in good working order, and even if the mental ultimately is neurophysical. If the disorder in/of brain distinction is apt, and I assume it is, then the case for claiming that mental disorders are diseases cannot rest on assuming that mental disorders are brain or neurological disorders and that brain disorders are diseases.

So, I plan to explore whether mental disorders are diseases independently of considering whether they are physical or whether, if physical, they are brain disorders. So: Are they diseases?

In my judgment the best answer to this question depends on at least two factors. The first concerns symptoms. The second causes. I say 'at least' because there is a third factor that is operative in at least some, if perhaps not all, cases of mental disorder but that rarely is operative in cases of somatic disease. Ian Hacking refers to it as the *looping effect* of human kinds. I will have something to say about Hacking's idea applied to mental disorders later.

First symptoms. Prototypical or exemplary symptoms of a mental disorder are multiple and there are or certainly seem to be no symptomatic hard edges or discrete boundaries between normal variations in human mental health and disorder. Take clinical depression, for instance, of the sort exhibited in what is called a major depressive disorder. Unlike malaria, scurvy and typical bodily diseases like leukemia, there are no blood tests, *X*-rays, biopsy results, or skin sores available to make a diagnosis of depression. Symptoms of a major depressive disorder include what are called a "syndrome" or "syndromal cluster" of symptoms, such as: feeling sad, blue, tearful; loss of pleasure; change in appetite (either increased or decreased); sleep disturbance (either trouble falling asleep or sleeping too much); being agitated, restless or slowing down; feeling worthless or extremely guilty; thinking of killing oneself; and other symptoms. The sheer multiplicity and contextual variability of symptoms is a source of major problems in diagnosing the condition as well as in distinguishing depression not just from periods of sadness, unhappiness or demoralization but also from personality traits such as melancholia and negative global attitudes like nihilism or pessimism. "Everywhere we look," writes Richard Bentall, "it seems that [mental disorders] exist on continua with normal behaviors and experiences" (2004: 115).

By contrast the symptoms of a prototypical somatic disease (like malaria or scurvy) tend both to be few and to be discontinuous with normal variations in human physical health. Neither malaria nor scurvy is continuous with normal variations in human somatic health. Malaria, for example, is an infectious disease in which people suffer from fever and anemia. It is not a normal variation in body temperature or in the oxygen-carrying component of the blood. (I will have more to say about symptoms momentarily.)

Second, consider the factor of causes. The causes or proximate sources of a mental disorder are prototypically multiple, and there are no successful explanations of mental disorders that cite a single main cause or even a few main causes. The prototypical causes of a bodily disease, by contrast, are not multiple, and there are plenty of successful explanations of bodily disease that cite a single main cause. Victims of malaria, for example, all suffer from a rupturing of red blood cells caused by a species of parasitic protazoa carried by mosquitoes that inject the malarial parasite into the bloodstream. Victims of depression, by comparison, do not suffer or appear to suffer from any such single cause. Losses of major and diverse sorts are among the most frequently proposed candidates for sources for depression. Loss of an intimate relationship or of a loved one with whom one has had a deep attachment. Loss of self-respect after a sudden and unexpected decline in social or economic status. Loss of health after a person has become the victim of a somatic disease (cancer, chronic nutritional ailment, and so on). Loss of effective, purposive agency in a situation of learned helplessness. Stress (often associated with the threat or perceived prospect of loss) has also been proposed as an influence or vulnerability factor. Financial hardship, marital decay, or a move to a new city among strangers, these are among the stresses associated with some instances of depression. So, too, guilt has been cited as a possible influencing condition. Religious guilt, for example, may make one vulnerable to depression, and may take the form of an intense and unforgiving sense of sin.

The above motley assortment of candidate sources of depression is a far cry from pinpointing defective ascorbic acid synthesis as the triggering precipitant of scurvy or of the malarial parasite as the proximal cause of malaria. Nor is the motley assortment of losses and stresses associated with some specific and identifiable (at least by our current scientific lights) underlying pathophysiology or proximate and specific neuromolecular causal mechanism or trigger responsible for the symptoms. Some scientists hope for an as yet unfound underlying molecular neuropathology ('cells gone bad', as it were). And, indeed, more than one medical scientist has associated such a hoped for discovery of "one biological abnormality" or "biologic marker" as something that would help to warrant depicting a mental disorder as a disease entity (Heninger 1999: 89). Given, however, the variety of depression's diagnostic syndrome and the diverse and contextually various and culturally scaffolded ways in which a depression's symptoms are expressed, such a neurochemical discovery seems quite unimaginable.

The variety that characterizes both the causes and symptoms of a typical mental disorder not only makes for an ultimately imperceptible grading from the prototypically or frankly disordered to the non-disordered, but it tempts some observers to extend the category of mental disorder into shady and conceptually contestable and unregimented areas. Harvard psychiatrist John Ratey, for example, has written of something he calls "shadow syndromes," which are, he claims, milder forms of mental disorders and which, he notes, if accepted as disorders (and he urges that they should be) would mean classifying far more people as disordered than do current and already super-generous schemes of diagnostic classification like the *Diagnostic and Statistical Manual of Mental Disorders* (DSM) (Ratey and Johnson 1998).

But back to the issue of the causes of a mental disorder. Explanatory references to various sources or contributing causes of a disorder like depression help to form what I like to call *propensity explanations* of a disorder. Propensity explanations identify factors or processes that contribute to a strong tendency or disposition for events to occur. Propensity explanations are at work in the disciplines of history and political science, for example. Consider a political revolution. Why, for example, did a certain violent political revolution occur? Suppose the following is part of the best explanation: In the summer of 2010 there was a growing and seething discontent among a large portion of the population, and when the economy collapsed late that October, the discontent turned to violence. The combination of discontent and economic collapse brought about the revolution. It did not do so simply double-handedly. Some inflammatory remarks of a popular right-wing political entertainer and radio commentator played a role. So, too, did other factors, such as the absence of strong political leadership in the minority political party. But revolutionary tendencies hit a feverish pitch when the stock market imploded.

Such is a propensity explanation. It is eminently compatible with a successful propensity explanation that the explained or partially explained event, contrary to fact, may not have occurred or eventuated. Propensities as such are not necessitating forces. They don't make events inevitable. Propensities (as I am using this notion) are strongly affecting, robustly influencing, or profoundly encouraging. The onset of revolution was profoundly encouraged by background discontent and foreground economic collapse.

In speaking of a propensity explanation I do not mean to refer specifically to what is sometimes called a statistical explanation or an explanation that refers to measurable statistical probabilities. Some propensities may be modeled or quantified as mathematical probabilities, of course, but not, I believe, those streaming toward mental disorders of exemplary sorts. Rather, I mean to refer to a species of what may be called a *how-likely explanation*. Take, for example, the fact that a certain person had a major depressive episode. This episode, if explained by a propensity explanation, is not necessitated by loss of a job or spouse or predisposing features of a sour or dour personal temperament. Statements about a job loss, even when supplemented by reference to aspects of temperament or to other biographical or situational contingencies, account only for why the episode might have been expected or anticipated by a knowledgeable observer. A questioner might ask, "How likely was it that the person would become clinically depressed?" And this question may be answerable by pointing to facts about the person or the situation that more or less strongly contributed to the onset of the depressive episode.

Why only such a partial or non-necessitating explanation? This is because an episode of disorder has so many different and complex aspects. It is immensely difficult to get a causal-explanatory grip on the phenomenon. Stephen Haynes briefly describes the sort of complexity confronting explanation of a mental disorder as follows:

> The task facing the [explainer] is overwhelmingly complex. Each client typically presents several concomitantly occurring behavior problems and is imbedded in a complex social setting. [T]here are multiple potential causal factors for these behavior problems.
>
> (Haynes 1992: 3)

In accounting for a mental disorder, our explanatory understanding comes up against a plurality of partially contributing sources, not just background or distal forces and situational variables but proximate or immediate influences, into an overall configuration of conditions that help to bring a disorder into existence. There is no apparent immediate causal trigger in the total configuration nor is the set of sources as a whole necessitating. This is not to deny that there may be necessitating causal triggers for certain aspects or features of a disorder. (A despondent mood, for instance, may possess its own precipitant neurochemistry.) But it is to deny it for the complex whole.

Consider, again, depression. A propensity explanation for a major depressive episode may put into focus the role that, say, death of an intimate or loss of a job may play in the tendency to feel helpless and pessimistic. Then, it may trace a path from the occurrence of such events through to deteriorating aspects of a person's self-confidence or to intense or frequent stressors. The stressors themselves may generate an excess of adrenal stress hormones, which, once initiated, may precipitate or exacerbate a negative mood. In some cases, there may be a point, a threshold perhaps, at which the gradual accumulation of small and otherwise unremarkable changes in a person's outlook or mood yields a large and overt transformation. An episode of clinical or major depression may then emerge in exemplary form. A great deal of background activity may be needed to build the person up (or down) to such a threshold point, or a person may, perhaps by virtue of temperament or learning history, be pre-possessed with a primed vulnerability for a major depressive episode. A simple loss, a mere disappointment, a routine stress, may somehow swell in some individuals into a profoundly negative and despondent condition. For other people only a dramatic calamity may help to serve as a source for depression, and then (in a case of calamity) aspects of the causal landscape even when informed by the languages of neurobiology and neurochemistry elude reference to precise powers of necessitation.

In speaking of the loosely probabilistic or momentum-like nature of a path to a disorder, I do not mean to *a priori* preclude the operation within a disorder of an unknown main, single underling neurobiological/neurochemical spring or unified causal mechanism, but the glaring absence of evidence to date for the operation of such springs or mechanisms in prototypical mental disorders offers, I believe, good inductive reason not to expect them. Of course, it is always open to someone to insist that, for instance, a major depressive episode has some, as yet undiscovered, narrow final pathway of causes that can be triggered in various ways. But absent a rather doctrinal or *a priori* pre-theoretical commitment to the presence of a narrow causal set behind a disorder like depression, the current evidence for such a set (given also depression's many and variable symptoms) seems, as noted, utterly non-existent.

Propensity explanations of a disorder like depression, it should be noted, are compatible with referring to the natural law-likeness or lawfulness of processes that may be part of or contribute to propensity to depression (or, more generally, to a disorder). Perhaps certain sorts of neural processes, such as a sudden and dramatic decline in serotonin levels, if they could somehow be isolated from other neurochemical forces, do in a lawful manner produce, say, a protracted bleak or despondent mood.

Similarly, nothing in a propensity explanation precludes thinking of various forces behind or processes within a disorder as constituted by types of events, processes or entities classified (in the language of philosophy of science) as *natural kinds*. Natural kinds are special sorts of substances or processes in the world. Natural kinds are types of events, processes or entities studied by natural sciences (like the quarks of physics or the neurons of neurobiology), referred to in scientific laws or represented in mechanical models, and assumed to be parts of the act-of-human-classification-independent causal structure of the world. Chemical substances like lead, gold and water are standard examples of natural kinds in the literature. Types of neurochemical processes, say among neurotransmitters like serotonin or dopamine, may be natural kinds and, if so, then insofar as reference to such processes is part of the successful propensity explanation of a disorder, natural kinds may help to govern certain specific aspects of a disorder's emergence.

I am reluctant, however, to classify mental disorders themselves as natural kinds. My reluctance to classify mental disorders as natural kinds is not that disorders are unnatural. Disorders are naturally occurring events. Human beings naturally are vulnerable to them. Nor is it based on the assumption that only processes or entities that are discretely bounded and fail to admit of borderline instances qualify as natural kinds. Types of mental disorders lack such boundaries and contain borderline instances, to be sure, but this is not why they fail to count as natural kinds. Some writers on natural kinds claim that taxonomic classifications of animal species refer to natural kinds. If that is so (and I don't wish to appraise the claim here), and if, for example, terms like 'monkey' or 'dog' refer to organisms that qualify as natural kinds, certainly those categories admit of borderline instances. Spineless, armless monkeys. One-legged, hairless three-eyed dogs. Nor, finally, is it premised on the assumption that disorders are not objective states of affairs or that they are conditions that are perniciously culturally relative and unfit objects of medical scientific discovery and analysis. Mental disorder anti-realism is not my line. I am a mental disorder realist.

My reluctance about conferring natural-kind status on a mental disorder stems from the fact that mental disorders fail or certainly appear to fail to emerge in a law-like fashion or to arise whole cloth from physical causal mechanisms (or through the operation of unified causal essences, to use an expression of Richard Samuels [2009]). It also stems from the fact that violations of norms or standards of prudential reasonableness or reason-responsiveness are presupposed in the attribution or notion of disorder. Disorders gum up the works of mind and mentality, broadly understood. Disorders have (what may be called) a normative mode of being (they are bad for a person) and not just or only an empirical mode of being (they affect a person). (Much more will be said about such topics in Chapter 5.)

Descriptions of norms are not proper parts of natural science. It is one thing for a lump of sugar to fail to dissolve in a hot cup of Earl Grey tea. There is nothing untoward on the lump's part in such 'dissolute' behavior. It would be absurd to suggest that the lump is acting imprudently or unwisely. A category mistake if ever there was one. It is quite another matter, however, to be clinically depressed and to disengage from emotional and personal attachments once held near and dear. It is part of the very idea of clinical depression that such disruptive disengagement is how people ought *not* to behave. The reason responsive operation of certain key features of human mentality (such as, in depression, the capacity for enduring emotional commitment) are impaired or truncated in depression as in other disorders. Not obliterated, as happens in some neurological disorders, but truncated.

Finally: Just because mental disorders are not natural kinds does not mean that they are relegated to the metaphysically feeble status of socially constructed categories of activities like touch football games or TV shows that your sister Bernice loves. If you are the subject of a disorder this is an objective fact about you. It is not dependent on anyone's classification of you or your situation. Your parents don't decide whether you are clinically depressed. The properly regimented canons of psychiatry determine the standards for that.

I am tempted to coin the awkward expression 'classificatory decision-independent', or CDI for short, for such objective facts (and I will have more to say about this topic later in the book). Mental disorders are conditions that cannot occur without beings with minds or emotions and attitudes. Nobody can be clinically depressed or schizophrenic without possessing thoughts, perceptions, feelings and so on. But if we are realists about mental disorder, as I am, then although without minds we would have no mental disorders, with respect to the category *mental disorder* there are facts of the matter as to whether someone is depressed, agoraphobic or deluded. Such disorder-facts are not fits of decisional or classificatory fiat or evaluative judgments of mental illness and ill-being that just about anyone is entitled to make. Some judgments or determinations of the presence of a mental disorder deserve to be dismissed and brushed aside. Others deserve assent.

So, then, again, why not classify mental disorders as diseases? If depression, to remain with this example, is to qualify as a disease, and diseases are properly represented by the likes of malaria and scurvy, then a disease conception of depression puts pressure on our explanatory understanding of a depression to find its main single cause or limited range of causes. For better or worse, however, we currently have no good reason to believe that depression's main causes are single or few. In fact, attempts to identify its cause as if main and single, which often stem from a desire to conceptualize depression as a disease, typically focus not on life events (like the loss of a spouse, a gradual erosion of self-esteem, and so on) but on hypotheses about the biochemistry that underlies depression. The main cause of depression? Not phenomena such as loss, grief, stress or a sense of sin but, say, a significant depletion of cells in the prefrontal cortex, a region of the brain that helps to detect reward and punishment and may serve to shift mood from one state to another. However, in cases of depression, again, to stick to this example, candidate distinctive forms of neurochemistry have not been shown to be consistently predictive of depression. And, as noted above, descriptions of alleged neurochemical powers sufficient to produce depression also fail to distinguish between moods or attitudes indicative of depression and those of a non-depressed but 'merely' sad or demoralized individual. No doubt, partly because a disorder such as depression is a complex condition, with no sharp symptomatic edges, and contains a rich mix of conscious and Intentional or perceptual states, the language of neuro-biology/neurochemistry proves to be an incomplete (not blunt but incomplete) explanatory instrument when it comes to describing depression's onset or origins.

We are not done yet with the question of whether mental disorders are diseases. Two distinguishing features have been mentioned: symptoms and causes. I am claiming that neither the typical causes nor typical symptoms of a disorder tend to be like those of a typical disease. Is there also perhaps a third distinguishing feature? There is, I believe, a third distinguishing aspect or dissimilarity. It is this.

Merely knowing that one is a victim or subject of, say, scurvy and knowing of its symptoms does not by itself affect the course or character of the condition. Knowing that it is associated with bleeding gums and multiple purple spots on one's skin plays no direct role whatsoever in the occurrence or appearance of those symptoms. Scurvy is what it is regardless of how it is conceived or classified by its victim. It is caused by a prolonged deficiency of ascorbic acid (vitamin C), which the body cannot synthesize. It commonly occurs in the spring, perhaps in part because of the relative lack of fresh fruit and vegetables during winter months. Of course, receiving a diagnosis of scurvy may and should motivate a person to embark on vitamin therapy. Just knowing, however, that one harbors scurvy and knowing of its symptomatic expression does not by itself affect the course or character of the illness. By contrast, just such a knowledge-and-illness interplay or epistemic/pragmatic symbiosis can and sometimes does occur in prototypical cases of mental disorder. To be told that one is clinically depressed, say, typically includes sharing predictions about how one is expected to react or to feel about negative or unwelcome events. A person's knowledge of expecta-tions may push and pull them to feel or behave in ways that conform to the predictions. Ian Hacking calls this feature of a state of affairs in which knowledge of one's classification helps to entrench or reinforce the evidence base for the classification (and disorders are not alone in possessing it) an interactive or *looping effect* (Hacking 1995: 105, 121).

Looping is not confined to disorders. Numerous non-medical and social-role-occupying conditions of persons are prone to interactive or looping effects. To dub someone before their ears as a 'musical genius', for instance, may affect their attitude toward their future capacity for achievement. It may elevate their personal standards or expectations.

The hypothesis of looping in a case of a mental disorder, such as depression, is that knowledge of one's diagnosis may affect the character of one's condition. (Note: 'Disorderly' effects may result from looping even when the offered or shared diagnosis is mistaken. When or if that happens looping may contribute to a phenomenon known as iatrogenesis in which a condition is created in a clinical setting. I do not discuss iatrogenesis here.) The depression or condition, in such a case, is not simply *there* as it is in a chemical kind, such as water or salt, with its character fixed independent of human observation, classi-fication and interpretation. A person is not simply *there* with their feelings and behavior evolving independently of the depressed (or so-classified) person's self-understanding of the category. A person who is aware of the fact that he or she is so classified may modify their behavior, in part, to fit the classification. Nothing like this happens with scurvy, malaria, or cancer. In scurvy the gums become swollen and anemia with resultant pallor sets in. One is not disposed to these symptoms by virtue of knowing that one has scurvy.

Imagine that you have failed an entrance exam to medical school, and that your life's dream is to become a doctor. Off-hand you explain your performance in a number of non-self-critical ways. "The examiner gave incomplete instructions" or "Bad luck but I'll try again." Self-confidence is secure. Circumstances, you think, were out of kilter. But now assume the following: You have been diagnosed as suffering from a depressive disorder and have been told nothing of its potentiality to remit. Learning of its symptoms, you recognize that it is expected of you that you will slink away and blame your own stupidity or lack of conscientious preparation, not instructions or sheer bad luck, for an exam failure. You are also expected to be unstable in self-esteem or self-confidence. Partly because of these pronouncements, you may go into an emotional free fall. You may think of yourself as low in self-esteem and easily humiliated. "It's pointless for me to take the test again." "I've not got what it takes." Such occurrences and attitudes would be instances of looping. It is not that you are prone to free fall just by virtue of the depression (though, of course, you may be). But the fact is that your response to failure is affected by your beliefs about how, as a depressive, you ought to behave. Classifying yourself a certain way may contribute to being that way. The dynamics of the condition may be affected by diagnosis of the disorder. As Hacking remarks, the conditions susceptible to looping "change the ways in which individuals experience themselves – and may even lead people to evolve their feelings and behavior in part because they are so classified" (Hacking 1999: 104).

The nature and precise forms of looping, or what Hacking means by the concept, are neither completely transparent nor uniform. But at least in rough terms the phenomenon is widely recognized within psychiatry. As the psychiatrist John Sadler puts it: Many patients think of themselves in "DSM jargon" and live out their "self-identity in a diagnostic concept" at least partly because of their knowledge of it (2004a: 359, 358).

But if one wonders how mere knowledge of a diagnosis may mold one's behavior in a case of mental disorder, an explanation in the context of a mental disorder of looping should start, I believe, by recognizing that we are dealing with an individual whose rationality is in various relevant respects still perhaps very much intact, albeit in other respects (connected with the specific disorder, if the diagnosis is veridical) impaired or truncated. Learning that one is diagnosed as clinically depressed, for example, may produce beliefs about what is *appropriate* behavior for a depressed person, namely how one ought to behave and feel if one really is depressed. In this way what helps to sculpt a person's behavior is sensitivity to believing that they ought to behave in certain ways if they truly are 'depressed'.

I personally like to think of a shared diagnostic classification, in a case of mental disorder, as a kind of what might be called, in effect though not intent, quasi-command or quasi-imperative. The mental health professional says to the patient, in effect: "You are depressed." "Behave *this* way." The behavioral influence on a person of this quasi-imperative may be reinforced by such facts, among others, as the patient's need for help, proclivity to defer to authority or desire for self-definition and understanding.

Not so with somatic diseases. The course of hepatitis or scurvy is not affected by knowing or being told just that one possesses the disease, no matter how rational or irrational one's apprehension of its symptoms. ("You have scurvy." "Make your gums bleed." To speak of a quasi-command harbored in the case of a shared somatic disease classification would be an absurd depiction of the pragmatic force of the categorization.)

Or more exactly. Not so with somatic diseases in their normal course or character. Anomalous causal connections or a-rational causal chains between knowledge of a diagnosis and the character of an illness may occur. Knowing that I suffer from a cardiovascular disease may make me so nervous and upset that it induces episodes of a dangerously irregular heart beat and an attendant disease may achieve heightened resonance. Wayward cases aside, however, the typical contour of a somatic disease is not directly affected by such knowledge.

So, are mental disorders diseases? My take-home point or conclusion about disorder and disease actually is two long alternative take-home points. One bold. One humble.

The bold one goes like this. What does the biomedical disease model of mental disorder tend to encourage? It tends to encourage, I believe, a conception of a mental disorder that is committed to, or pushes us to search for, a narrow range of causes for a disorder, symptoms that are discontinuous with normal variations in human health and well-being, and a disorder-identity immune to looping effects – effects that appeal to a subject's sense of appropriate behavior for someone with the disorder. Such theoretical encouragements are inappropriate or ill-suited for the category of a mental disorder. Mental disorders don't satisfy or tend to comply with those demands. So, they are best understood as not diseases.

But the second point (the humble one) goes like this. I am not without misgivings about denying that mental disorders are diseases. I assume that diseases like malaria and scurvy are exemplary. But someone might ask: 'Why not count, say, hypertension as a disease exemplar?' No firm boundary between abnormal and normal variations in arterial health or function helps to distinguish hypertension from healthy states. And if causes of a disease that are distal (say, deleterious eating habits or stressful cultural circumstances) are counted as among its sources or propensity conditions, some diseases (again, such as hypertension) may look much like mental disorders in their multitudinous and risky propensity conditions. One person's penchant for cheesy omelets may resemble (in its distal causal powers) another's loss of a job or death of a loved one.

So I confess that I see no utterly indefensible taxonomic ill in classifying a disorder as a type of disease but only *provided* that we are not misled into thinking that the mental disorder marathon runners, so to speak, are headed in the same direction as many diseases. Namely: A track with a narrow range of causes, symptoms more or less clearly delineated from normal patterns of human mental diversity, and immunity to looping. That is not the path through the woods of a mental disorder. Many diseases run in that direction; mental disorders do not.

In general, systematization and regimentation of the concepts and categories of mental disorder should be judged basically by how well important purposes are served: by the theoretical utility of its distinctions; by how well it analyzes, orders, sorts and organizes various types of ailments or afflictions; by how helpfully it obliterates obstructive boundaries to medical-scientific investigation and therapeutic treatment as well as by how successfully it discourages premature celebration of what are likely to turn out to be scientific dead-ends. A harsh dichotomy between mental disorder and somatic disease does not serve those ends. But nor does warm and indiscriminate embrace of a disease model of disorder.

Carl Hempel (1905–97) was one among a group of distinguished philosophers from Central Europe who came to the United States in the 1930s. He is the author of one of the great introductions to any field of philosophy (in his case, the philosophy of science) and was a major figure in twentieth-century philosophy of science (Hempel 1966). In 1959 Hempel was invited by the British psychiatrist, Edwin Stengel, to present a paper on psychiatric classification at a conference in New York City under the auspices of the American Psychopathological Association. In that paper Hempel (1965a: 151–2) claimed that the following should be expected of a classificatory system such as a system that categorizes mental disorders.

> In scientific research [entities] are often found to resist a tidy pigeonholing of any kind. ... [S]ome of the objects under study will present the investigator with borderline cases, which do not fit unequivocally into one or another of several neatly bounded compartments, but which exhibit to some degree the characteristics of *different* classes.

Scurvy and malaria possess tidy pigeonholes – one cause, symptoms discontinuous with normality, no looping. Depression does not. Depression is the upshot of propensity factors, harbors symptoms continuous with normality, and typically is vulnerable to looping. Such is the fate of a mental disorder. Not nested in a pigeonhole but perched on a wide, bumpy and permeable plateau.

A PROBLEMATIC DISORDER AND THE PLACE OF DSM

My chosen method in this book for constructing a theory of mental disorder includes breaking the very idea of a mental disorder up into two parts. One is that of 'the mental' and the other is that of 'the disorder'. (Not that these two parts can be kept totally distinct even when only one is the focus of attention.) The main topic of this chapter is the disorder of a mental disorder. We've learned a few things about this. A mental disorder gums up the psychological or mental works. It does not have discrete edges. (Gum is like that, is it not?) It may not be best understood as disease process or entity. But we have not completed the process of examination. There is more to learn.

Much more. To illustrate some of what remains, let's examine a case that represents a difficulty in understanding what a disorder is. The case is a troublesome sort of disturbance of unknown origin and is, as yet, professionally undecided in categorization. First, we need some imaginative stage-setting.

Suppose you enter a store to purchase a bar of candy. You pick up the brand you like. You hand the clerk some money and he gives you the proper change. You leave the store, walk out onto the sidewalk, remove the wrapper, and start eating. The bar is made of rich dark chocolate and crisp, chewy nuts. You say to yourself, "That's delicious."

This is a piece of ordinary human behavior. Nothing special. Nothing distressful. Nothing abnormal. The clerk barely notices the transaction.

Contrast. Suppose that the next day you visit a doctor's office with whom you have made an appointment. She is an orthopedic surgeon. You tell her that you wish to have your left leg amputated. You tell her that it feels as if it is not yours. It feels strange and unfamiliar. "It is not overtly crippled," you say. "Or at least I can and do walk with it." "But it feels like something alien." "Even when I look at myself in the mirror, I don't perceive it really as mine." "I am not me with this leg." You ask her to remove it surgically and to arrange to have it replaced with a prosthetic limb.

The surgeon is astounded. She examines your leg and finds it to be perfectly healthy. No tumors, no apparent neuromuscular disease. "I cannot amputate a healthy limb," she says. "But I am in profound discomfort," you reply. "I have spoken to four different surgeons in the past year and none of you seems to understand my feelings." "Don't you have an obligation to relieve my suffering?"

Most certainly, this is no ordinary human behavior. No bar of candy. There is something incredible about it. You strike the doctor as in acute distress. She certainly appreciates the dramatic anomaly of your complaint. For better or worse, you impress her as possibly being ill, psychiatrically, or as suffering from a mental disorder. Being a surgeon, she is not sure just what this disorder may be, however. So, she asks you to wait in her outer office, while she makes a private professional phone call. While you are absent, she calls a former medical-school classmate, who now is a senior professor in the psychiatric department of a distinguished university medical center. She describes your case to him. He tells her that you may be a sort of patient sometimes colloquially described as a 'wannabee'. A wannabee is someone who wants to have a healthy limb amputated and claims to be emotionally dissociated from the limb. He says that you may be suffering from a disorder that has come to be known, in some circles, more technically, as body integrity identity disorder (BIID). It's a disorder, he says, in which a person undergoes a chronically distressful mismatch between a part of their body and the part as they experience, feel or emotionally engage with it. "Whereas," he remarks, "some people who actually are missing a limb feel as if it is present, in, say, phantom limb pain, other individuals feel as if a body part that actually is present and functioning is, in some sense, also absent – not a proper part of them." "That's the essence of BIID."

Then, he warns her: "In the absence of access to surgery, some sufferers have deliberately injured the affected limb or body part." "Tourniquets, dry ice, and even chainsaws have been used." "The intent has been either to remove the limb or to injure it so badly that a surgeon has had to remove it."

Her former classmate has no particularly decisive advice to give. Unfortunately, too, he practices psychiatry in a distant city, for otherwise your surgeon would perhaps send you to him for a consult. But he does recommend a psychiatrist in your immediate area for that purpose. "You might consider sending your patient to him," he says. "Psychiatry may have a critical part to play here."

Where should your doctor turn? Resting in her bookshelf, but rarely consulted, since she is an orthopedic surgeon, is the most recent version of the American Psychiatric Association's *Diagnostic and Statistical Manual of Mental Disorders*, first published in 1952, and now in its fourth edition (APA 1994 [DSM-IV] and 2000, with text revised [DSM-IV-TR]). (Hereafter I shall refer to the various editions of this book as DSM-I, DSM-II and so on. I use 'DSM' to refer to recent editions of DSM in general.) In popularity and influence, DSM is the international Bible of psychiatric diagnosis. Other diagnostic manuals exist, written by psychiatrists, psychopathologists, clinical psychologists, and others. However, these guides or tool-kits are either similarly organized, like the World Health Organization's *International Classification of Diseases* (now in its tenth edition and often referred to as ICD-10; see WHO 1992), or fail to have an equally significant impact on clinical practice as does DSM. (That's an overgeneralization perhaps. Goodwin and Guze [1996] enjoys readership as well as do other texts. But DSM is the text of dominating influence.)

The first two editions of DSM, published in 1952 (APA 1952) and 1968 (APA 1968), more or less reflected the popularity, at the time, of Freudian psychology. Many of Freud's patients suffered from disorders now described as forms of anxiety disorder (such as obsessive-compulsive disorder, panic disorder and so on). Freud offered explanations of these disorders that made appeal to what he regarded as the misdistribution and repression of unconscious psychic energy or forces in people. So, Freud's psychological theory came to be known as "dynamic" or "psychodynamic" psychology. As noted in the first chapter, dynamic psychology pictures mental disorders as symptom-unspecific operations of unconscious mechanisms, not as discrete symptom-specific disorders. Repression of normal sexual instincts, for instance, may lead one individual to a case of sexual perversion, but another to compose a novel. "The hysterical symptom," Freud wrote of one sort of symptom, "does not carry [any particular] meaning with it, but the meaning is lent to it, soldered to it, as it were; in every instance the meaning can be a different one, according to the nature of the suppressed thoughts which are struggling for expression" (Freud 1963 [1905]: 57). The third edition of DSM, published in 1980 (APA 1980), departed quite drastically from its two predecessors. Here, briefly, is what led to that departure and to DSM-III's creation.

Multiple research studies had indicated that psychiatric diagnosis, even using DSM-I and DSM-II, tended to be unreliable and inconsistent, not just between different countries (the United States and the United Kingdom), but with respect to the same patients in the same hospital or institution when examined by different clinicians. Improving consensus between clinicians was taken to be the primary goal or desideratum of DSM-III. One of the intended fruits of consensus, *reliability* so-called, is to be able to classify large samples of patients in the same diagnostic category, so that they might be pooled in research studies, serve as pedagogical reference points in the education of mental health professionals, and meet the financial strictures of insurance companies and managed care organizations, which do not reimburse without uniform diagnostic categories across distinct cases.

So, DSM-III was constructed. It defined disorders through the description of syndromes or symptom sets, quite regardless of possible underlying causes and in a manner that is isolated or that stripped away from the social or biographical contexts in which a disorder may arise. For better or worse, this meant that DSM-III freed clinicians from the need to secure detailed knowledge of a person's history or social context in order to diagnose. As Nancy Andreasen puts it, "DSM criteria encourage physicians to jump ... into inquiring about specific signs and symptoms without [getting] to know the patient as a unique individual" (Andreasen 2001: 184). Sadler adds: "The DSM has little to say about the biographical life histories of patients." "It offers no dramaturgy, no climax, no denouement" (Sadler 2004a: 358).

Though quasi-imperious in purport and impact within the mental health field, the reliability-orientated framework of DSM has evoked a substantive share of skeptical apostates or critics. Criticism takes two main forms. One is moral or sociological. It charges collusion between economic and commercial interest groups (drug and insurance companies, for example) in promoting the DSM-like system of diagnostic categories and the medical profession. As one critic observes:

> Symptom-based logics generate inflated prevalence estimates. They also show how these estimates are created and perpetuated because a number of particular groups have distinct interests in demonstrating the presumed pervasiveness of mental illnesses in the community.
>
> (Horwitz 2002: 91)

A second and related but philosophically deeper form of criticism concerns the scientific or empirical credentials of DSM. Many critics charge that DSM fails to satisfy the goals of a good psychiatric taxonomic system, which include not just reliable diagnosis, but providing a framework for prognosis, treatment, and ongoing scientific research. Mere consensus is not enough. In essence, designers of recent editions of DSM (as well as of ICD) more or less determined their criteria for what counts as a psychiatric diagnostic category by seeking consensus or agreement among their fellow clinicians rather than by focusing on additional and in some ways more important goals such as determining the legitimacy of the various diagnoses (a desideratum known as validity), giving descriptions of the typical social settings of onset, characterizing courses of and variations within different disorders, and learning whether the diagnostic categories themselves, in the words of Richard Bentall, "are useful in predicting either long-term outcome or response to particular treatment" (Bentall 2007: 131).

Jeffrey Poland, a philosopher and one of the most outspoken and articulate critics of DSM, summarizes his critical attitude toward DSM's construction this way:

> Empirical evidence is not used in many [taxonomic] decisions; rather, loosely constrained speculations regarding concepts, coherence with other systems [like ICD], face validity, and consensus of the field are taken to suffice for making a decision [as for what to count as a disorder]. Even when empirical evidence is employed, it is often not clearly relevant, or, even when relevant, the decisions are only loosely connected to the evidence cited. Many of the [deliberations about accuracy of diagnosis] are quite meaningless.
>
> (Poland 2001)

The social/biographical setting of the onset or appearance of a disorder, for example, is not to be treated lightly. DSM does treat it lightly.

Certain environments seem to help to produce or scaffold certain symptoms. As noted earlier, symptoms of an eating disorder or anxiety disorder like anorexia nervosa, for instance, are rare outside of Western post-industrial societies, where the majority of cases are young white females from middle- to upper-middle-class families (see Brumberg 1988). A Navajo Indian with the disorder is an anomaly, which fact should reasonably discourage the diagnosis of that sort of case (among the Navajos) as an instance of anorexia.

The taxonomic categories deployed in DSM-III have proliferated with each successive edition or textual revision. The first edition of DSM was a small pamphlet-like book with a gray cover and roughly 100 labels for disorders and symptoms. DSM-IV-TR, the most recent edition, is as thick and about as heavy as a brick with more than 800 pages of definitions, criteria, glossaries and related materials (APA 2000). It purports to identify about 400 distinct conditions as disorders or symptom types. The hundreds of diagnostic categories that appear in DSM-IV-TR are a motley collection that includes social phobias, generalized anxieties, gender confusion, and attention deficit hyperactivity, among many other classifications, as types of disorders. So, in effect, non-traditional disorder categories are described within the covers of DSM alongside more traditional ones like major or clinical depression and schizophrenia. In the words of Rutger's sociologist Allan Horwitz, the newest edition of DSM "categorizes an enormous diversity of human emotions, conduct, and relationships as distinct pathological entities" (Horwitz 2002: 2). Another and ironic observer has estimated that the fifth edition of DSM (now scheduled for 2012) will likely have 1,256 pages and contain 1,800 diagnostic criteria (Blasfield 1996). From handbook, through brick, to imposing monument.

The general scientific weaknesses of DSM are not pursued as a specific topic in this current book. Much has been said and continues to be written about them in other sources and by other observers (see Poland et al. 1994; Horwitz 2002; Bentall 2004; Murphy 2006; see also Caplan 1995). Let's return to your hypothetical case.

Your doctor's psychiatrist friend neglected to mention that BIID does not yet appear in DSM. Reading a description in the manual, she hopes, would help her to figure out what to do and whether it is wise to turn to the services of a consultant psychiatrist. She believes that the concept of a mental disorder is a considerable conceptual distance from normal forms of bodily injury or typical disease. So, she wonders what health norms are relevant in the situation that you are in. Is it that a person must *feel* their body as their own? She does not know how surgery could restore or reconstruct that feeling. Perhaps the bizarre feeling is transient and ephemeral. Perhaps it represents a mere passing fall in certain types of neurotransmitters. So, perhaps there is no need to do anything other than to see you again in a few months. "Is this really something that ought to be surgically corrected by removing a limb?" she asks herself.

The surgeon opens her copy of DSM-IV-TR. BIID, as just noted, is not mentioned in DSM-IV-TR. Dr Michael First, a psychiatrist at Columbia University in New York, who coined the expression 'bodily integrity identity disorder', and has become something of a specialist in the condition (and is also one of the central players in the project to create DSM-V), is among medical professionals urging its inclusion in DSM-V (First 2005). If First succeeds (and given his prominence he may), and DSM-V appears in 2012, you in your hypothetical condition may be classified in 2012 as a case of BIID. But formal recognition must wait. In the meantime what should be done? What now? (We are supposing, of course, that your visit is taking place before the appearance of DSM-V.)

Diagnostic indifference is not an option. The surgeon suspects she should categorize you. She just does not know how. She describes an alternative possible course of action. It's the one suggested by her former classmate. She phrases it as follows: "I need to be assured, before I even begin to consider removing your limb, that you are emotionally and rationally of sound mind." "So, would you be willing to see a psychiatrist and to have their evaluation directed back to me?" "You and I can then meet again after you meet with them."

"I know what you are thinking," you reply. "In a world where people are born without limbs or lose arms and legs in war or to accidents or disease, only a disturbed person would wish a healthy limb removed." "But my limb *really* is not healthy." "If it was, why would it make me suffer so?" "Besides which, I don't want to see a psychiatrist." "I just don't trust what they will say."

Not trust a psychiatrist? Given its checkered history and the moral dilemmas posed by labeling, overextended drug use and so on, psychiatric diagnosis is not an uncontroversial specialty. Toward the end of his life and career, Karl Menninger (1893–1990), a distinguished psychiatrist and member of the family that founded the Menninger Clinic, wrote a letter to Thomas Szasz (1920–). Szasz, although a psychiatrist, is a famous (infamous?) arch-skeptic about the validity of the concept of mental disorder. One observer of Szasz's career as a psychiatry critic has described him as like a "musician who does not like music." On past occasions Szasz had been critical of Menninger. Menninger, however, graciously wrote a letter to Szasz with the following remark: "I am sorry that you and I have gotten apparently so far apart all these years." "You tried; you wanted me to come there, I remember. I demurred. Mea culpa" (letter to Karl Menninger, 6 October 1988; see http://www.szasz.com/menninger.html).

Mea cupla? Why did Menninger ask, rhetorically perhaps, for forgiveness from an infamous disorder and anti-psychiatry skeptic?

I cannot speak of Menninger's reasons. They are not evident in the letter. But certainly neither he nor Szasz is alone in worrying about the legitimacy of the concept of a mental disorder or in harboring distrust of diagnostic psychiatry (though Szasz is an extreme case). The particular and specific vicissitudes, above mentioned, of DSM aside, the very idea of a mental disorder (no matter the taxonomic manual) has been the subject of controversy and criticism. Is the World Health Organization to be trusted when it claims that "450 million people suffer from mental disorders in both developed and developing countries" or that "one in every four people ... develops one or more mental disorders at some stage in life" (WHO 2002)? Not only, as noted earlier, has the presumed categorical domain of mental disorder historically been much smaller than it is now, but a whole new family of mental health professions (therapists, counselors, etc.) has propagated itself since the 1960s, each claiming to diagnose psychological distresses and prescribe remedies for mental disorder.

Is there perhaps something deeply wrong or categorically mistaken with the very idea of mental disorder or with the notion that mentality is gummed up by something that deserves to be called a disorder or illness? Should psychiatric diagnosis and psychiatric medicine be distrusted? Rather than worry about what a mental disorder is (disease? complaint? neural impairment?), or which manual to use in diagnosis (DSM?), shouldn't we wonder *if* it is? Are mental disorders real, honest-to-goodness conditions?

I want to get back, of course, to the topic of the proper meaning of the term 'disorder' in "mental disorder" later in the book (in Chapter 5 in particular), but before doing so I plan in the next chapter to examine skepticism concerning the very idea of a mental disorder and, with it, some of the metaphysical and values assumptions of medicine.

CHAPTER SUMMARY AND SUGGESTED READINGS

What makes a condition or mental disturbance worthy of diagnosis as a disorder? The answer that I offer in this chapter, and which is developed later in the book, consists of referring to mental disorders as gumming up the mental works of a person, of their mind, as it were, and in a manner that is harmful, involuntary, and typically requires treatment or assistance from others. The need for treatment or assistance raises questions about the moral status and not just the therapeutic effects of clinical care as well as about the self-respect and dignity of the person with a disorder. The dual dimensions of treatment as a therapeutic act and as a moral relationship with a patient may suggest that somatic diseases constitute a good model for mental disorder. If so, clinical diagnosis necessitates looking beneath or beyond the symptoms of a disorder to a disease process or entity that is responsible for the symptoms. Such a model is known as the biomedical model of mental illness. Although advocacy of the model usually is combined with an attempt to understand mental disorders as instances of a broken brain, it does not have to be associated with such an attempt. A mental disorder may be pictured as a disease process or entity without also being classified as a neurological disorder.

The biomedical model has been developed in different ways, depending on the conditions to be taken as exemplars of bodily disease and as prototypes of mental disorder, respectively. By picking certain illnesses as exemplars, this chapter has argued that mental disorders probably are not best understood as disease-like entities. They don't have the same numerically limited range of causes that diseases normally or often do and they lack the relatively precise margins often available for somatic illness between health and illness. They are also susceptible to a looping effect typically absent in somatic disease. Looping effects, so-called, connect the diagnosis as known to its subject with a disorder's course or progression.

The chapter also paints a picture of some of the conceptual difficulties associated with DSM, a major diagnostic manual for mental disorders. At the heart of those difficulties are doubts about the scientific and clinical utility of the manual.

A detailed and systematic attempt to characterize the disorder of a mental disorder has been made by Jerome Wakefield. A prolific writer his "Disorder as Harmful Dysfunction: A Conceptual Critique of DSM-III-R's Definition of Mental Disorder," *Psychological Review*, 1992, 99, pp. 232–47, is a good introduction to his approach. Allan Horwitz and Wakefield apply the latter's characterization to the question of how to distinguish between sadness and clinical depression in their *The Loss of Sadness: How Psychiatry Transformed Normal Sorrow into Depressive Disorder* (Oxford University Press, 2007). Wakefield's analysis is subjected to negative critical scrutiny in D. Murphy and R. Woolfolk, "The Harmful Dysfunction Analysis of Mental Disorder," *Psychiatry, Philosophy, and Psychology*, 2000, 7, pp. 271–93. See also B. Gert and C. Culver, "Defining Mental Disorder," in Jennifer Radden (ed.), *The Philosophy of Psychiatry: A Companion* (Oxford University Press, 2004), and R. Woolfolk, "Malfunction and Mental Illness," *Monist*, 1999, 82, pp. 658–70. DSM's definition or characterization of a mental disorder is the subject of criticism in S. Wilkinson's "Is 'Normal Grief' a Mental Disorder?," *Philosophical Quarterly*, 2000, 50, pp. 290–304.

A useful set of papers on moral and ethical issues associated with psychiatric diagnosis and treatment is S. Green and S. Bloch's edited collection, *An Anthology of Psychiatric Ethics* (Oxford University Press, 2006).

Three accounts of the nature of disease are L. Reznek's *The Nature of Disease* (Routledge, 1987), Kenneth Schaffner's *Discovery and Explanation in Biology and Medicine* (University of Chicago Press, 1993), and Paul Thagard's *How Scientists Explain Disease* (Princeton University Press, 1999). A short but informative explication of disease models of mental disorder is offered by Dominic Murphy in his "Psychiatry and the Concept of Disease as Pathology," in M. Broome and L. Bortolotti (eds), *Psychiatry as Cognitive Neuroscience: Philosophical Perspectives* (Oxford University Press, 2009). In this same collection Richard Samuels's "Delusions as a Natural Kind" provides a nuanced defense of the proposition that delusions constitute a natural kind. Samuels's paper is a helpful guide to the literature in philosophy of science on natural kinds.

On dangers of overenthusiastic use of psychiatric medication, see D. Healey, "The Three Faces of Antidepressants," *Journal of Nervous and Mental Disease*, 1999, 187, no. 3, pp. 174–80, and his *The Anti-Depressant Era* (Harvard University Press, 1997).

The complex and multifunctional character of psychiatric diagnosis and the social power of labeling are briefly explored in John Sadler's "Diagnosis/Antidiagnosis" in Jennifer Radden's book (above cited). See S. Kirk and H. Kutchins, *The Selling of DSM: The Rhetoric and Science in Psychiatry* (Aldine, 1992) for a detailed history (with authors' critical judgment) of the progression through some of the editions of DSM. A short but telling critique of DSM is J. Poland, B. Von Eckardt and W. Spauling, "Problems with the DSM Approach to Classifying Psychopathology," in G. Graham and G. L. Stephens (eds), *Philosophical Psychopathology* (MIT Press, 1994).

For a discussion of diagnostic and moral dilemmas confronting requests to amputate healthy limbs, see Tim Bayne and Neil Levy, "Amputees by Choice: Body Integrity Identity Disorder and the Ethics of Amputation," *Journal of Applied Philosophy*, 2005, 22, pp. 75–86. Many 'wannabes' are eager to deploy psychiatric diagnostic labels for their condition, in order, they hope, to medically legitimate their requests for surgery. New forms of requests for amputation and for labeling are taking place in the virtual communities and private chat rooms of the Internet. See Louis Charland, "A Madness for Identity: Psychiatric Labels, Consumer Autonomy, and the Perils of the Internet," *Philosophy, Psychiatry, and Psychology*, 2004, 11, no. 4, pp. 335–49.

4 On being skeptical about mental disorder

One of the most provocative questions to ask about mental illnesses or disorders is: Are there any? Radical skeptics or categorical reality deniers of the existence of mental disorder I call *anti-realists* about mental disorder. Mental disorders don't happen. Affirmers, like me, I call *realists* about mental disorder. Mental disorders happen. They are not just possible but actual.

Isn't it wholly absurd to deny the existence of mental disorders? After all, we have diagnostic manuals to identify them, don't we? Psychiatrists seek to treat them. Doctors are not trying to trick people into thinking that they have them. The anti-realist agrees, of course, that there are thick manuals and well-intended psychiatrists. Anti-realists don't reject the existence of people who believe that mental disorders are real or of books that purport to identify disorders. They reject the existence of mental disorders. They say: There is no such condition as clinical depression. There are only people who believe in the existence of clinical depression. There are no such conditions as delusional disorders. There are only conventions for classifying people as subjects of such disorders.

Is anti-realism warranted? Some intelligent people find various arguments compelling for the position. In this chapter I plan to look at two varieties of anti-realist argument: *metaphysical skepticism* and *moral skepticism*. I plan to outline each form of skepticism and then to critically inspect it. First I offer a brief description of each form.

Metaphysical skepticism: Very briefly, and leaving out details, some medical scientists and others believe, on broadly empirical and philosophical or metaphysical grounds, that reference to the mentality of a mental disorder should be and hopefully will be (if this has not already occurred in certain cases) superseded or displaced by a brain-centered or physicalistic and non-mentalistic understanding of mental disorder. Given such displacement, no condition deserves, they think, to be classified as a mental disorder. The number of mental disorders, just like the number of unicorns and goblins, is zero.

Moral skepticism: Very briefly, and leaving out details, some critics of the very notion of a mental disorder charge that the attribution of mental disorders to people is a morally unacceptable or ethically misbegotten practice. It is morally unacceptable because it is a human-dignity-violating or respect-for-persons-undermining process. If we truly, it is said, wish to help people who suffer from mental disturbances, we must jettison the concept of a mental disorder or illness and replace it with alternative ways of thinking. These alternative ways should help us to understand and treat people who are mentally disturbed or troubled as compromised, although still responsible and not-ill agents. No condition deserves, they think, to be labeled as a mental disorder. Describe it as an unwelcome condition no doubt, but not a mental disorder.

I am not enamored of either form of radical skepticism or anti-realism about mental disorder, although I am convinced that each harbors important and useful lessons for the theory of a mental disorder. The merits of these lessons are independent of their anti-mental-disorder case. The main lesson of metaphysical skepticism is that the category of mental disorder has implications for our understanding of the causal-explanatory power of the mind in the physical world. These implications must be properly understood and addressed if a concept of mental disorder is to apply sensibly to persons. The main lesson of moral skepticism is that a diagnosis of mental disorder is morally contestable territory. Protection or preservation of a person's dignity and self-respect should be a constraint on diagnosis and treatment. Ethically demanding standards for diagnostic labeling and care should be observed. When the social power of psychiatric diagnosis is overlooked, "we risk overlooking the moral impact diagnosis has on people's lives" (Sadler 2004b: 175).

In this chapter both lessons will emerge over the course of examining each form of skepticism. First I plan to examine metaphysical skepticism about mental disorder.

MENTAL DISORDER AND THE MIND/BODY PROBLEM

Consider the famous mind/body problem. This is the problem of the place of consciousness and Intentionality or of mind in the physical world. The general form of the problem, which has occupied the attention of philosophers and others since ancient times, is represented by two facts about human beings that seem to be categorically distinct: physical facts, such as that I am six feet tall, with my feet planted on the ground, my head held high; and mental facts, such as that I *believe* I am six feet tall, *want* to keep my feet planted on the ground, and *decide* to hold my head high. These seem like two categorically different sorts of facts, expressive of two very different sorts of features of persons. For one thing, the mode of existence of the first sort of fact (the physical one) has nothing to do with the conscious feelings or Intentionality-infused attitudes of people. The truth of the proposition that "Graham is six feet tall" has nothing to do with my or anyone else's state of mind. It is true no matter what I or anyone else thinks, feels, or believes. It possesses what philosophers call mind-independent truth conditions. But the truth of the proposition that "Graham believes that he is six feet tall" is utterly dependent on what I think or believe. Its mode of existence (as a mental fact) depends on my state of mind. It *is* a state of mind. It possesses mind-dependent truth conditions. So: Just what is the relation between these two sorts of facts and features? The one mind-independent. The other mind-dependent.

It hardly needs saying that this is a difficult question. There is no general consensus about its correct answer. This is not an uncommon occurrence in philosophy, of course. In debates about prominent philosophical topics, especially of a metaphysical sort of which the mind–body problem is one example, there are no "knock-down, iron-clad, settled once-and-for-all arguments for, or against" a proposed resolution of a topic (Swoyer 2008: 18). "No recipe that forces a uniquely correct answer" (ibid.). There are famous attempts to answer the question of what is the relation, say, between mental and physical facts, mind and body, and, just as in philosophical debates about other topics, one must weigh the costs and benefits of each proposed answer. I plan to restrict myself to outlining and examining two of the most famous attempts to solve the mind/body problem. I will do so without considering all of the pros/benefits and cons/costs that attach to each position. One is *dualism*. The other is *physicalism*.

Each of these metaphysical positions comes in different forms. Dualism, for example, may be substance (or thing or individual object) dualism or property dualism. Here I will understand dualism as substance dualism, though much that I say about it can be rephrased as a commentary on property dualism.

Physicalism, as the name suggests, says that a person, me or you, or what we refer to when we use the first-person-singular pronoun ('I', 'me', 'moi', etc.), is a physical thing made up entirely of physical things (organs, cells, particles and the like). Just as a clay statue is composed entirely of clumps of clay, and has such properties as mass and weight and a position in space, we persons are composed entirely of clumps of biochemical physical matter, and have such properties as mass and weight and a position in space.

Physicalists, of course, also believe that persons think and feel, but physicalists think that mental facts that are true of a person are a species of physical fact. The most popular physicalist view is that thoughts and feelings are identical with states of a person's brain. The brain is the organ of thought and feeling. It is the thing that thinks and feels. This version of physicalism is called the psychophysical *identity theory*. Of course, no individual brain cell thinks, even if it is indirectly involved in thinking. It cannot produce or harbor a thought on its own. Many cells and special networks or systems of cells and brain areas must be involved in a direct and literally thought-full way in mental activity.

Dualism is a denial of physicalism. It is the thesis that human persons have a "dual"-nature. Not a single (physical) nature. But people have a composite, bifurcated or compound nature. Mind and body. The mind is intimately connected with a certain physical thing, a human organism or body (including brain), but the mind is, strictly speaking, a non-physical thing. This is a thing not composed of physical particles. It is a thing without weight and mass, and having no position in physical space.

Dualists maintain that the mind is the basis or vehicle of mental facts (facts about beliefs, hopes, desires and so on). The body including brain is the basis or vehicle of physical facts (facts about height, posture and so on). That I am six feet tall is a physical (or body) fact and is true of my body. That I believe I am six feet tall is a mental (or non-physical) fact and is true of my mind.

Dualists of all stripes worry about how best to describe the relation between mind and body, given that the mind is non-spatial. What is it for a person's mind to be part of them or in them (or indeed *them*) if it is not spatial? The worry goes like this: if I have a thought, and the thought occurs to me, but it does not occur in my body/brain (because it is not spatial or e.g. part of the cellular activity of my brain), it seems that there would have to be two manners or ways of being *in a person*. In you but not spatially in you (the way in which a thought is in a person). In you and spatially in you (the way in which a particle or organ is in a person). No dualist can avoid thinking about such a worry. (I will consider an aspect of the worry later in a discussion of the problem of mental causation and something that Jaegwon Kim calls the *pairing problem* [Kim 2003].) The worry attaches to every form of dualism even those forms that equate the mind of a person with the person themselves or which claim that the person is, strictly speaking, a mental substance. (When Descartes famously says that he can conceive of himself existing without a body, he is not saying that his mind can exist without a body. He is saying that he is a mind and that it/he can exist without a body.) It seems one sort of fact for something to be in the body. It seems another sort of fact for something to be 'in' the person or mind.

Metaphysical skepticism about mental disorder, of the sort that I am about to discuss, takes physicalism about the mind–body seriously. It sides with physicalism against dualism and supposes that dualism should be rejected. It also assumes that the proper rejection of dualism is equivalent to claiming that mental disorders do not, strictly speaking, exist. They are unreal. The reasoning behind metaphysical skepticism about mental disorder goes like this.

It is said: The very idea of a *mental* disorder is an historical and unscientific anachronism. It presupposes that unlike non-mental physical or somatic disorders or bodily diseases (such as scurvy, cancer and so on), mental disorders are disorders of a non-physical thing, substance or entity, namely the mind. Associated with this allegedly non-physical thing are certain purported defining properties (such as non-extension in space) that are unshared by anything physical. But, so this form of skepticism continues, there are no non-physical things. The assumption that immaterial minds exist just doesn't mesh with a sound and sensible medico-scientific picture of the world or cohere with a properly informed understanding of the motion of matter and movements of the body. So, any so-called 'mental' disorder, if it is a disorder of some sort, must somehow really be physical in nature. Not mental. Calling a disorder 'mental' is a metaphysically misleading misnomer. (Some anti-dualist critics add to this anti-dualist thesis an extra claim about mental disorder. This is that mental disorders are not just physical and non-mental or in the brain but disorders *of the brain* i.e. neural disorders. This is a thesis that I already have discussed in the book and will continue to critically examine independently of examining the mind/body problem. I believe that the thesis is false. To suppose that mental disorders are brain-based or physical is not to concede that mental disorders are disorders of the brain. But I am not discussing the neurological disorder or brain-damage view of mental disorder here in this chapter.)

The following argument is a more formal statement of the anti-dualist criticism:

(1) Somatic illnesses or physical diseases are one kind of disorder. Mental illnesses or disorders are another kind of disorder. Each is a distinct kind or type of disorder.

(2) Somatic illnesses are illnesses in the body. In order for a mental disorder to be a distinct type of disorder from that of a somatic illness or physical disease, it must be a disorder in a thing or entity that is not physical. The mind.

(3) But no thing or entity is a non-physical entity. There are no non-physical things.

(4) So, there are no (distinctively) *mental* disorders. This is not an accidental fact, as would be the case if no person currently just happens to be the subject of a mental disorder. It is a metaphysical fact, namely a fact about the nature of reality. No person can have a mental disorder. Insofar as there are no non-physical entities or things, there can be no mental disorders. No person can be *mentally* ill.

The main idea behind the skeptical argument is that the very idea of a mental disorder has no application to any thing that is real. Minds as such are not real, strictly speaking. Brains are real, of course, but minds are not. Insofar as minds are not real, strictly speaking, there are no mental disorders or illnesses of mind.

Perhaps unexpectedly self-critically, given the authors and its audience of mental health professionals, DSM-IV expresses sympathy for this anti-dualist position. It says the following: "Although this book is titled the *Diagnostic and Statistical Manual of Mental Disorders*, the term *mental disorder* unfortunately implies a distinction between 'mental' and 'physical' disorders that is [an] ... anachronism of mind/body dualism" (APA 1994: xxi).

Anti-dualist/pro-physicalist sentiment also appears in a wide variety of other guises in the literature on mental disorder. Michael Allen Taylor (1999: viii), for instance, affirms it in a popular textbook on clinical neurology. Taylor writes:

> Psychiatry and neurology [is] one field. [M]ental illness is not "mental" at all, but the behavioral disturbance associated with brain dysfunction and disease.

Not mental at all? This is because, so Taylor assumes (note also Taylor's talk of brain dysfunction and disease), no mental things exist. Brains do; minds don't.

Many thinkers (this author included, of course) continue to believe that mental disorders are real, honest-to-goodness conditions of people and that the category *mental disorder* does apply to certain disturbances or distresses of persons. The expression 'mental disorder' is not a misnomer. It is not an anachronism. It is not unscientific. So, the conclusion that there are no mental disorders is not acceptable.

In reply to the metaphysical skepticism, two general lines of defense may be offered. One consists in defending dualism. It rejects the third premise, which means, in effect, that it rejects physicalism (the proposition that the mind is nothing other than something physical or the brain), and it may be outlined as follows.

Pro-dualism: the first line of defense

Dualism depicts mental disorders as separable from physical states or conditions, although causally interacting with them. It claims that mental disorders can be, and sometimes are, causes and effects of physical activities in the brain, body and physical environment. However, dualism claims that there can be no *physical* theory or description of a mental disorder. Any theory of a mental disorder must include reference to non-physical facts as essential pieces of information about a mental disorder. This means not just that a theory of mental disorder must use mental terminology and refer to conscious experiences and Intentional states or attitudes (i.e. states or attitudes with directedness or Intentionality), but, also, that this mental terminology or language must be interpreted as referring to properties or features of a non-physical, weightless and intangible entity – the mind.

So, one line of defense against the metaphysically skeptical criticism is to defend dualism and a dualist depiction of a mental disorder. It consists in attacking the third premise mentioned above, namely that nothing is non-physical. It would argue that the mind is both real and non-physical. It is separable from the brain. The brain is implicated in both the origin and treatment of mental disorder. For mind and brain interact, no doubt. But the mental is not something neural. The mental of a mental disorder inheres in a special non-physical entity.

There is, dualists maintain, a very special and intimate way in which the mind both affects and is affected by the body/brain. I alluded to it just above. The mind of a person immediately or directly causes changes in their body/brain without directly causing changes in any other organism or individual. Conversely, the body/brain directly causes changes in a person's mind without directly causing changes in any other mind. Call this mind/body mode of bidirectional causation *direct interaction*. Consider an episode of a mental disorder. Suppose a person is suffering from a panic attack. Anxiety, say, immediately causes changes in various neurochemicals in a person's brain (say, in noradrenaline). These changes in turn bring about further changes in the anxious mood of the person, perhaps adding generalized and excessive fear to the anxiety. Each sort of change is directly caused in the person. The anxiety immediately affects no one's brain but that of the person with the disorder. The neurochemical changes immediately affect no one's mood but that of the person.

All this raises the following question, of course. Does dualism offer a truly promising or perspicuous approach to matters mental including the topic of mental disorder? It may be thought that there is a sound sociological reason for dismissing dualism. This is that it is unpopular among scientists. "Today, most scientists do not accept dualism" (Frith and Rees 2007: 9). But dismissal on grounds just of scientific or medical unpopularity really isn't sensible, for, as Christopher Frith and Geraint Rees (each scientists), just quoted, aptly note, dualism does recognize that "the brain [has] a key role in linking matter and mind" (Frith and Rees 2007: 9). Dismissals of dualism sometimes rest on simplistic caricatures of the position, as if, for example, it is anti-brain. But by insisting that there are direct causal interactions between neural and mental activity, dualism does give some pride of place to the brain, albeit, not the referential (reverential?) throne offered to it by physicalism. Dualism respects the physical domain in certain ways; but, dualism denies its explanatorily unbridled range or reach in questions about the behavior of persons.

From the perspective of developing a concept or theory of mental disorder, a dualist conception of it has at least two potentially appealing features. For one, dualism readily (if perhaps not very plausibly) explains why neuroscience is an incomplete explanatory instrument when it comes to addressing many of the questions that we wish to answer about a mental disorder. On a dualist conception of a mental disorder, neuroscientists may inform us about neurotransmitters, the activity of cells, and so on. This information may be useful in helping to understand the sources and treatment of a mental disorder. In addition, however, to considering disorders in neural terms, there are disturbances of consciousness and Intentionality in a mental disorder, which, I am arguing in this book, are distinctive of a mental disorder. So, on a dualist conception, if a disorder is a mental as opposed to a brute somatic or body/brain disorder, reference should be made to consciousness and Intentionality as features or aspects, not just of the disorder, but also (says the dualist) of something non-physical. The mind. That is why (again, says the dualist) neuroscience is an incomplete explanatory instrument. It fails to make the necessary reference to the non-physicality of consciousness and Intentionality.

Dualism's second potentially appealing feature is that it offers a ready (again, if perhaps not terribly plausible) answer to the question of why medical science ought to contain a specialization in psychiatry. Why not just clinical neurology, as Michael Alan Taylor recommends? If mental disorders are not physical and therein not neurological, they are not neurological disorders. Medicine needs a specialty that is uniquely devoted to the health and illness of a non-physical mind, namely the personal subject of experience, albeit in a manner that also attends, as neurology does (for a dualist), to neural causes and effects of mental activity. A dualistically informed psychiatry should fit the bill.

Dualism also possesses arguments purportedly in its favor that are totally independent of understanding a mental disorder. These arguments are based on a number of claims about consciousness and Intentionality. I mention two related arguments but do not discuss them here.

(1) The *limits of physical science argument* claims that we cannot account for certain aspects of human behavior in physical scientific terms. One version of the argument goes like this. If we try to conceive of thoughts or feelings arising in the brain out of the interactions of physical particles, or networks or systems of physical cells, we rightly draw a blank and incredulous stare. We are incredulous not just because we don't fully understand the activities of the brain. We are incredulous because the activities are physical. The mere fact that they are activities of physical particles (neurons, and so on) seems to pose insuperable challenges to explaining thoughts and feelings in physical scientific terms. No matter how deeply we examine the physical structure of neurons and the biochemical transactions that occur when they fire, no matter how many physical facts we discover, we still appear to leave something out that demands a further explanation. That is why and how *this* collection of neural and chemical activities produces *that* thought or *this* feeling, or any thought or feeling at all. Between the two, namely neural activity and thinking/feeling, there is an "explanatory gap" (Levine 2009: 284). This is a gap we seem unable to bridge by the acquisition of additional physical information.

(2) The *physically descriptive elusiveness of subjectivity argument* claims that the conscious, phenomenal or subjective *like-thisness* aspect of a conscious experience cannot

be described in physical terms. Nothing in brain science or in any other manner of impersonal physical description can describe what it is like to you to taste a bitter-sweet piece of dark chocolate, to vividly relive your grandmother's funeral or to struggle to learn how to speak and understand a language that is not your native tongue. The quality or character of conscious experience is fundamentally private or perspectival. Comprehending it requires adopting a certain perspectival or experiential point of view. But comprehending physical activities is not perspectival or experiential. Grasping the atomic weight of gold is possible for a person who is deaf and blind, whereas grasping what hearing or seeing is like requires having acoustic and visual experiences. Conscious character does not lend itself to impersonal physical- or brain-science description.

I don't wish to endorse either of these two arguments or to spend time here trying to decide how best to develop or interpret them. (I and legions of other philosophers have written or helped to write about the issues involved in them. See, for example, Graham and Horgan 2002; Graham et al. 2009. See also the Suggested Readings for this chapter for additional recommendations.) If there is anything to them, and I believe there is, it does not ultimately lie in support for dualism, however. It lies in the fact that mental phenomena pose problems for the metaphysics of mind/body, period – whether for dualism or physicalism (see Graham and Horgan 2002). As for dualism it is no less difficult to explain how an immaterial thing or non-physical entity can produce or harbor thoughts and feelings than for a brain to produce or harbor them – either metaphysical possibility seems puzzling. As Eric Olson puts it, "It is no easier to explain a thing's ability to think on the assumption that it is immaterial than it is on the assumption that it is material" (Olson 2007b: 153). Also, if the subjectivity or perspectival privacy of conscious experience poses problems for the position that consciousness is a brain process (and I believe that it does), then why should it be assumed that subjectivity is less of a problem for something that is not in space but interacts with the brain? The bitter-sweet taste produced by your nibbling on a piece of dark chocolate may not be explicable or describable in physical-science terms, but is it any less inexplicable if we assume that there is something non-physical or immaterial 'inside' you?

Suppose, though, that, for whatever reasons, dualism somehow enjoys warrant, perhaps not decisive (whatever that would mean), but warrant enough to be taken seriously. If so, one way of proceeding would be to learn if a dualistic theory of mental disorder can be developed that combines the best interpretations and defenses of each of the just-mentioned arguments (and others) while, at the same time, helping to make sound and sensible sense of a mental disorder. Of course, this would be an immensely ambitious project: to develop a dualist theory of mental disorder. It would occupy a huge book all by itself. The nature of dualism is complex and various. Work would also have to be done to defend a dualistic theory of mental disorder in light of contemporary attitudes and practices in science and mental health medicine, where so much attention is being given to the role of the brain and central nervous system and wherein many medical scientists tend to favor a neuroscientific theory of mentality. Adding an account of just how dualism may accommodate neuroscience in a theory of mental disorder would add still another layer to a dualistic theory.

Taking on a complex and ambitious project like that of a dualistic theory of mental disorder makes sense only if we concede that certain characteristic features of mental disorder should be interpreted as properties of a non-physical thing (or in some other pro-dualist way). However, perhaps we don't need to make any such concession. Perhaps we don't need to assume that dualism is true in order to be *realists* about mental disorder i.e. in order to maintain that mental disorders are genuine and a distinct category of ill-health from somatic or bodily illness.

Fortunately, there is a second and alternative means of deflecting metaphysical skepticism about the very idea of mental disorder. It is one that ultimately sidesteps debate over the truth of dualism.

The first line of defense against metaphysical skepticism, as noted above, focuses on the third premise that there are no non-physical entities. It defends dualism. But a second and alternative line focuses on the second premise. This is the assumption that if a mental disorder is a real honest-to-goodness disorder, then it must be a disorder in a non-physical entity or thing.

The second line consists in arguing that mental disorders can be distinct from somatic or physical illnesses or disorders even if mental disorders are not themselves disorders in a non-physical thing. It presupposes that the category of mental disorder, while perhaps compatible with dualism, does not require it. The category is also compatible with depicting mental disorders as physical or based in the brain.

Metaphysical cohabitation: the second line of defense

Contrary to what some observers (Taylor, for example) seem to think, one may assume that the mind ultimately is something physical and that mental processes are brain processes and yet go right on thinking that some forms of human behavior (such as those associated with a mental disorder) are best understood (if only in part) in terms of reference to conscious states and Intentionality. It's this sort of possibility that I wish to explore here, not so much an explicit matter of mind/body metaphysics, as a matter of how best to understand a mental disorder.

Some preliminary stage-setting is required. We should remind ourselves that, despite anti-realists and radical skeptics, the distinction between mental and non-mental somatic or physical disorders is well recognized within medicine. There is a medical specialty that deals with mental disorders (psychiatry). There is an institute of the US federal government that supports research into mental disorder (National Institute of Mental Health). There is a branch of the British National Health Service (Mental Health Services) that deals with mental illness. There are specially trained personnel (mental health professionals) who deal with people who are subjects with mental disorders, and there are special treatments (e.g. psychotherapy) and medications (e.g. antidepressants) that are regarded as appropriate and effective for those disorders. Fully accredited medical schools, doctoral programs, and other institutions provide training for mental health professionals and support research designed to understand and ameliorate mental disorder. Each year many thousands of people are diagnosed as suffering from some type of mental illness or disorder. The validity or legitimacy of these diagnoses is accepted by both the public and medical professionals alike and, frequently, by those who have been diagnosed.

Does all that presuppose dualism? Does it imply that the mental is something non-physical? No, it does not. Here's why.

It must be recognized that not every distinction is a dichotomy, i.e. is a separation between two contrary categorical types of features or entities. Some distinctions are dichotomies. Some are not. The distinction between being, say, dead and alive is a dichotomy. One and the same person cannot be both dead and alive. However, a distinction like that between standing, say, 6 feet tall and weighing 175 pounds is not a dichotomy. One and the same person can both be 6 feet tall and weigh 175 pounds. So, likewise, one and the same condition of a person may be (absent argument to the contrary) both a physical condition and a mental disorder. The contrast pair 'physical/mental' when applied to a physical condition versus a mental disorder may be a distinction that is not a dichotomy. This would be the case if, say, the mental is a distinguishable form or variety of the physical, just as height is a distinguishable physical feature from that of weight. The mental is (so this line of reasoning goes) that particular variety of physicality that is best described in mental terms, i.e. in terms of the language of consciousness and Intentionality. The somatic or bodily, by contrast, is a type of physicality that is best described in physical scientific terms, i.e. in terms, say, of natural or physical science (and without reference to consciousness or Intentionality). If one wants to refer to, say, the Intentional content of a state or condition or to the what-it's-likeness of a conscious experience, the language of mind is the appropriate – indeed inescapable – language. If one wishes to talk of ion channels, one should use the language of neuroscience.

Does such an approach to the mental disorder/somatic illness distinction make sense? Is there empirical applicability or traction to it? First off, there is reason to believe that conscious and Intentional states are physical states and part of the physical world. Physicalism has its supports (as we will see momentarily). But then, as paradoxical as this may seem, there is also reason to describe such physical states in mental- and not brain-science terms. This is not because describing conscious or Intentional states in the language of brain science is dreary or unaesthetic. It is because mental descriptions are the best terms in which to understand certain forms or features of human behavior. Just as, in some cases, I must refer to a person's weight rather than to their height, so in some cases I must refer, for example, to a person's autobiographical memory rather than to cellular and molecular networks in their hippocampus.

But what reason is there for believing that mental states are part of the physical world? To bring this reason into sharp focus, I need to describe a serious difficulty for dualism. The assumption that states of consciousness and Intentionality are states of a non-physical entity (or of a non-physical sort) creates a problem that dualism appears unable to solve. It is known as the *problem of mental causation*.

Imagine that you are severely depressed. One morning you are faced with the choice of staying in or getting out of bed, and then washing, dressing and going to work. You decide to get out of bed, make the effort to get out of bed, and lo and behold, succeed. You get dressed and head off to work. It took, we may suppose, considerable effort on your part to rise up out of bed and to prepare for the workday. You had to combat a strong impulse to remain in bed – an impulse grounded in your despondent mood.

The decision and movement (getting out of bed) must have been causally linked together in an appropriate manner for the decision to produce the effect, namely getting out of bed. Note, however, that if minds are non-physical (if dualism is true) then mental causation of the physical (e.g. causation by decision) fails to appear up to the motor task. Non-physical minds and the decisions they allegedly bring about seem too weightless, ethereal or 'soulful' ever to move limbs or to be linked together with getting out of bed. A diagnosis of depression explains why it is difficult to get out of bed, but dualism appears to metamorphose an effortful difficulty into a causal mystery. How can something non-physical, like a decision, move, actually move, something that is physical?

Princess Elizabeth of Bohemia (1618–80) worried that dualism could not account for the actions of mind on body or in the physical world. She wrote to the philosopher René Descartes (1596–1650), the father of modern dualism, about it. "How [can] a man's soul," she asked, "being only a thinking substance ... determine animal spirits so as to cause voluntary action" (see Kim 2003: 66). The philosopher Jaegwon Kim has recently offered a 'bohemian' variation, one of numerous in the literature, on Elizabeth's critical query.

Kim writes: "The radical non-spatiality of mental substances rules out the possibility of invoking any spatial relationship for cause-effect pairing" (Kim 2003: 71). Then Kim adds: "Temporal order alone will not be sufficient to provide us with such a basis." For causes and effects to be paired or linked, Kim says, "we need a full space–time framework" (2003: 74). The trouble, says Kim, with mere temporal order (say, the fact that an alleged mental cause occurs just before its effect but not in physical space) serving to pair a cause with an effect is that temporal order alone cannot pair or link a cause with its effect. Causal relations must be "selective and discriminating, in the sense that there can be two [events] with identical [temporal] properties" and one, but not the other, causally produces the effect (2003: 73). Which event is the producer? This is the one, says Kim, with the right linkage in space to the effect, namely an event with the right spatial properties. So, it is spatial relations, such features as distance, orientation, etc., and not just temporal relations (such as being before or after), that are required to pair or link causes with their effects.

The following example may help to illustrate the point that Kim has in mind. Consider how, with some imaginative reconstruction on my part, an important historical document was accidentally discovered near Nag Hammadi in Egypt in 1947. (Imaginative reconstruction? I am not striving here for historical accuracy. I am trying to make a philosophical point with an example.) A Bedouin goat-herder searching for a lost goat in the barren wilderness (or for treasure, depending on how the historical evidence is read) near the north-west shore of the Dead Sea tossed a stone into a cave and heard it strike something. He did not know just what had been struck. But he was curious. So, he went into the cave to learn what he had hit. He discovered an ancient earthenware jar that contained several old scrolls. He sold them to a cobbler and part-time antiques dealer, and after news of the startling discovery reached others and biblical archeological scholars heard reports of the find, more scrolls were discovered in surrounding caves. Hundreds of items, some in mere fragments, were found. The set of them all is called the Dead Sea Scrolls.

Now imagine that at the exact same time at which the herder threw a stone into the cave, another herder, a companion of the first, standing near to him had the following thought. "I wish to hear a sound from the cave." Suppose that at the very same moment in which the friend had completed this thought, the sound was heard. What caused the sound? Was it the friend's wish? Or was it the stone striking the jar?

Suppose each of the stone throw and the wish bore the same temporal relation to the sound coming from the jar. The movements of both stone and thought occurred just before the sound. But note how temporal order alone does not tell us what made or caused the sound. Being struck by a stone? Being the Intentional object of a herder's thought? We also need, as Kim puts it, some way of discriminating and picking out the right event to link with the effect of the sound. We need a 'full space–time framework'. This network offers, conceptually, a diverse range of physical concepts (of mass, shape, size, velocity, direction and orientation) with which to identify causes of physical effects. Within such a physical framework we are able to identify the stone as the cause of the sound. It is only because the stone impacted the jar, literally, mechanically hit or struck it, and did so at such-and-such a velocity and so on that a sound was produced and heard by the herders. The second herder's wish or thought had nothing whatsoever to do with the noise.

Commonsensical as this idea of Elizabeth and Kim may sound (no pun intended, well, not quite), a dualist must insist that it is utterly wrong-headed. Mind moves matter even if it does not do so through its spatial or mechanical properties. It has none. But this is, to say the least, a mysterious or immensely puzzling idea. How can something independent of its spatial or physical features make matter move (a jar to sound, a person to rise from bed)? Dualists have tried to take the mystery or puzzle out of the idea. But think about it.

Evidently, minds, if non-physical, do not stand in spatial relations to anything. Temporal relations, yes. Spatial relations, no. They lack velocity, mass and so on. So, one thought cannot be any more near to a jar, strictly speaking, if it is non-spatial, than any other thought. This means that the second herder's thought is not a fit candidate for the cause of the sound. There is no way to pair or link it causally with the noise.

Descartes himself puzzled over how non-physical minds could possibly interact causally with physical objects in space. "At one point," notes William Lycan, "he suggested gravity as a model for the action of something immaterial on a physical body; but gravity is spatial even though it is not tangible in the way that bodies are" (Lycan 2003: 48).

What goes for jars goes for bodies. No thought can move a body. Only something spatial can. Or so the anti-dualist mental causation criticism goes.

Back now to the example of the bed. Suppose you are trying to decide whether to get out of bed and there is a 'moving stone' (a neural or neuromuscular process) in you that is active just before you start to rise and (at the exact same time) also a decision of the form 'I shall now get out of bed'. Suppose that this decision takes place 'in' a non-physical substance or thing. We, if Kim is right, cannot use the temporal proximities of these two events (the neural process and the decision) to the action of rising out of bed to identify the cause of rising. Each bears the same temporal relation to the rising. We need, Kim would urge, a full space–time framework to individuate or specify the actual cause. We need to refer to the spatial connectivity of the neural process with the activity of rising. Only by referring to neural events or processes are we able to explain the rising from the bed i.e. to link or pair a cause with its effect. A non-physical decision lacks the proper connection and clout.

This isn't the place to enter into a detailed analysis or assessment of Kim's argument. But I would like to make two brief comments about it.

The first is that one way in which to hold that mental events can produce physical effects is to abandon dualism and to maintain that mental events themselves are nothing but brain events. Again, as noted earlier, this is the doctrine of *physicalism* or one species of it (the so-called *identity* theory). Our bodies have no non-material entities 'attached'. Instead of sheering off decision-making from the brain, think of deciding as a brain process. Suppose, for example, that a decision to get out of bed is one and the same as a process in the sensorimotor and limbic systems. If the decision to get out of bed is a neural state or neuromuscular process, this state or process may then produce or help to produce (given the spatial constraint) getting out of bed.

The second comment is that Kim's account of why causality requires a space–time framework in which to operate is one way, as noted above, of developing Elizabeth's worry about dualism and mental/physical causation. Closely related ways have also been deployed in the literature. Another way of expressing the same worry is in terms of the concept of transfer of conserved quantities of energy or momentum between objects or events involved in causal relations and goes, very roughly, like this (see Levin 1979: 85).

For any caused physical event (say, getting out of bed), there has to be a chain of events leading to that event, and this chain must occur in a medium wherein links in the chain can transfer their energy or momentum from one link to another in temporal succession. Call this transfer the transmission of 'causal oomph'. A non-physical medium is a medium of energy or momentum in name only. It is utterly oomph-less. Only a physical medium possesses the requisite causal relations. Non-physical entities do not. So, on this view, in the case of the jar and the sound, mechanical energy or momentum is transferred from the stone to the jar, then via the surrounding air to the ear, where it is perceived as a sound. But on a dualist theory, in the case of the jar and the sound, there is no medium in which the non-physical 'energy' or 'momentum' (to assume for the sake of argument that it may make sense to speak of such things) of a thought can travel. The thought never reaches the jar. If you are a dualist, vague and mysterious talk of direct interaction between mind and body is no substitute for developing a model of causation that can explain the power of mind in the physical world and that also is consistent with dualism.

I now wish to put commentary on Kim aside. I want to extract a moral or lesson about the metaphysics of the mind–body problem from the problem of mental causation. One lesson of taking the problem of mental causation (or, for that matter, the symmetric problem of physical causation of the mental) seriously and of worrying about what it means for dualism is that dualism is beset with the difficulty of explaining how states of consciousness and Intentionality can both be non-physical and produce effects in the physical world. The seriousness of the problem of mental causation combined with the importance of reference to causal powers of mind for understanding a mental disorder (e.g. for explaining why a depressed person struggles to get out of bed) and for understanding much of human behavior in general means, I believe, that dualism should surely not be regarded as the option of *sole metaphysical* choice for the explanatory understanding of a mental disorder. We also need a non-dualistic alternative for understanding disorder. This should be an option that preserves explanatory reference to mentality in our understanding of a mental disorder (thus preserving the *mind* of a disorder) but does not require that we cavort with dualism.

Should it be physicalism? Should it be the identity theory – the theory that identifies the mental with certain activities in the brain? Suppose we adopt the identity theory. If so, there is a tough question to be addressed if we assume physicalism and make appeal to a presumed identity of mental events with brain events to help to explain how mental events can produce changes in the physical world. Under such an assumption, mental events are causes of events in the physical world, in the body, in behavior, and so on, in virtue of their *physical* characteristics. So, it seems, we should be able to *describe* states of consciousness and Intentionality in physical terms or as physical characteristics. If, say, the intention or decision to get out of bed is nothing other than a neural event or set of neural events, then we should be able to describe it in brain science or neural terms, should we not? Such terms presumably pick out the sources of the causal powers of brain events. (Remember this is the hope or aspiration of metaphysical skepticism about mental disorder. Not to deny that people have problems thinking and feeling, but to describe such problems in neurological terms – with *mental* illness talk left out.) But it is hard to see how we can exchange talk of conscious and Intentional states (decisions and the like) for physical-language talk. Not only do arguments like the limits of physical science argument and the physically descriptive elusiveness of subjectivity argument pose problems for physical descriptions of the mental. But does any neuroscientist really purport to offer such descriptions?

A popular neuroscience text asserts that "mental illness is ... the consequence of patho-logical processes in the brain" (Bear et al. 2007: 684). It says on the very same page that mental disorders are "diseases of the body, just like cancer or diabetes." But when I inspect this book for a description of the origins of a motor activity, like that of, say, getting out of bed, I find remarks like the following:

> The somatosensory and posterior parietal areas, parts of the prefrontal cortex ... are thought to play a role in generating the intention to move and converting that intention into ... action.
>
> (Bear et al. 2007: 461–2)

As I read the passage here is what is being said. Brain activity generates an intention to move, which, in turn, is somehow converted into movement, again, by brain activity. So, we are given back talk of Intentionality, talk of the very same processes of decision-making and intention formation that as a physicalist one would, it seems, wish brain science to couch in neuroscientific terms. But the text does not offer what's wanted. It mentions intention. It does not attempt to describe the process of intending in neural terms. We are offered surmises as to which brain systems or areas underwrite movement. Underwriting an intention is one thing. *Being* an intention is another.

But suppose brain science is ultimately unable to tell us of the physical constitution of mental states or attitudes, such as intentions, decisions and the like, we may still be warranted in being physicalists about the mental. How so? Well, for one thing, one might be a physicalist just because one believes that the only *type* of real causation is physical causation and that mental causation must somehow be physical causation if mental causation is to qualify as causation. If minds are causes, minds must be brains. Never mind if we never describe mental causation in physical terms or succeed in exchanging the language of mentality for that of brain science.

Bertrand Russell (1872–1970) once complained that the more abstract the "ism's" that we postulate, the more we may hope to understand, but the harder it is to believe that all that postulated metaphysical machinery is true. Russell makes this sort of complaint in a famous theft-over-honest-toil passage. He says: "The method of 'postulating' what we want has many advantages; they are the same as the advantages of theft over honest toil. Let us leave them to others and proceed with our honest toil" (Russell 1993 [1919]: 71).

It is important that neither dualism nor physicalism (nor any other metaphysical "ism") should get crowned as the victor on matters mental without our laboring hard over how to explain particular cases of human behavior and mental disorder. The unavailability (assuming it is unavailable) of a physical language for conscious and Intentional states is a mark against physicalism (albeit not decisive). But the difficulty of solving the cause/effect-pairing problem is equally a mark against dualism (albeit perhaps not decisive). And it seems unlikely to me that we will settle on which mind/body metaphysics is best without continued toil over how best to explain and understand mental disorder. So, I am not going to embrace a particular metaphysics of mind/body in this book. Instead I plan to help myself to a metaphysically agnostic or ecumenical strategy. This is a strategy, which, as promised above, is compatible with physicalism (of a sort) but also with dualism. Here is how its dialectical wheels work.

First a short background anecdote, which is adapted from an example of the philosopher Fred Dretske (1988). Suppose a talented soprano in an opera by Puccini sings an aria, and this is followed by a glass on stage shattering. What her song is about or its Intentional content, namely unrequited love, plays no role in causing the glass to break. If the aria had not been about love but about something else (say, waffles or sea salt), or even if it consisted of nothing but nonsense syllables, as long as she hit the high notes, the glass would have shattered. An idea owed to the philosopher James Woodward helps us to understand the causal relation at work here (Woodward 2003). Hitting the high notes (HH) caused the glass to shatter (GS). On Woodward's account, a causal relation is a relation between two variables (e.g. HH, GS) that can take on different values (e.g. either hitting or not hitting the high notes), and HH causes GS just in case the value of GS would change under some intervention or manipulation on HH. For example, if a crazed opera fan was to have jumped onto the stage and vigorously hugged the singer, thus preventing her from hitting the high notes, no shattering would have been produced by her voice. Or, if the singer had only hit notes lower in pitch, a vibration or two might have been produced in the glass, but it would not have broken.

Now compare. Here is a case of mental causation. Suppose in singing about unrequited love, her singing, in addition to shattering the glass by virtue of its high notes, is accompanied by the audience sobbing and breaking into tears. Is the Intentional content of the song (what it is about, unrequited love, UL) causally efficacious in producing the sobbing and tearing (T)? Again, on Woodward's account, UL is the cause of T if and only if the value of T would change under some intervention on UL. If the audience would not have sobbed and become teary had the soprano sung about waffles or sea salt, this gives us reason to believe that the fact that her aria was about unrequited love caused the audience to sob. Content is not efficacious in causing the glass to shatter, because the aria could have been about waffles or sea salt and the glass would still have shattered had the singer hit the high notes. But in singing about unrequited love the audience sobbed.

This may sound like a neat approach to uncovering causation, and it is, I believe. Simply intervene in a process and see what happens. In, say, the case of Agoraphobic Arthur, considered in the next chapter, causally explaining the onset of an episode of a major panic attack by reference to his fear of heart failure amounts to answering the question of what would happen to Arthur if he no longer felt his heart pounding when he was in a crowd of people. He might not panic. But we are not always in a position to intervene (so, we may have to manipulate variables hypothetically in the imagination), associations between events are not always invariant (oftentimes they are probabilistic or propensity-like), and background conditions are causally relevant and sometimes difficult to specify with precision (the beauty of Puccini's music and the text of the opera may also have contributed to the audience's tearful reaction). And, while it is helpful to conceive of interventions or manipulations as well-designed experimental interventions (hypothetical or otherwise), we must not picture them as exclusively the products of human agency. If a brick falls on the glass on stage, this, too, counts as an intervention in the glass's integrity.

All that granted, what is the anecdote's lesson for how to avoid taking sides in the physicalism/dualism debate if we are to understand a mental disorder? A particular kind of causal efficacy is definitive of mental causation. This is Intentional-content efficacy i.e. the power or potency of states or attitudes with Intentionality (see e.g. Arpaly 2005). Provided it is possible for the physical states or brain processes of a person (if physicalism is true) or for their non-physical mental states (if dualism is true) to possess Intentional content, and for the content of such states (what they are about) to play a causal role in the sources or origins of a mental disorder, no choice between the two metaphysical positions (physicalism or dualism) with respect to a disorder needs to be made. We may be physicalists and still admit to a role for mental causation in mental disorder. Or we may be dualists and, by way of the dualistic bifurcation, distinguish between somatic and mental disorders. Such a metaphysical choice between dualism and physicalism may need to be made on other grounds (parsimony, compatibility with physics or ethics, or whatever), but we ourselves can explanatorily understand a mental disorder without making such a metaphysical choice. All we need, metaphysically or mind/body speaking, is commitment to the causal efficacy of states or attitudes with Intentional content and to the real existence of such states or attitudes.

Or more exactly, all we need is such a commitment together with commitment to whatever else is required in association with the causal efficacy of attitudes if we are to understand the origins of a mental disorder. This is an important 'whatever else' proviso. One other commitment also is needed (as I explain in the next chapter). This is the recognition that, in the words of John Searle, "Intentional phenomena are subject to constraints of rationality" (Searle 2001: 108). It is constitutive or partially definitive of Intentional content and of the causal efficacy of Intentional content that it is subject to rationality norms or standards. So, for example, it is part of the explanation for why the audience sobbed and became teary on listening to the aria about unrequited love that this was a reasonable or sensible reaction for them to have (especially given the background text or story of the opera). If they had had an irrational obsession to remain stoical, the aria would not have been effective in eliciting tears or sobbing. If things had been different, then there would have been no tears and nary a sob.

So, here is what I will assume about the metaphysics of the mind/body problem in what follows in this book. I assume what I call *the way of metaphysical cohabitation.*

The physicalist says: mind is a clump of matter. The dualist says: mind is not matter though it matters in the physical world. I shall refuse to choose. A presumption of dualism may cohabit with an understanding of mental disorder. A commitment to physicalism may cohabit with an understanding of mental disorder. Dualism may be more vulnerable to worry than physicalism (which is my view, namely, dualism is less attractive than physicalism). But the cohabitation assumption is that our ability to explain and to understand a mental disorder has nothing directly or explicitly to do with the truth or falsity of dualism and it is not threatened by the truth of physicalism, provided that brain states are or can be bearers or vehicles of causally effective Intentional content. This last point, by the way, is consistent with what Dretske himself thinks. Mentality is causally effective in the physical world insofar as Intentional content is effective and also if Intentional content is an aspect of physical states.

Let me turn to a brief analogy to help to illustrate some of what has just been said about not directly adopting a particular mind/body metaphysic if we are to understand mental disorder. Consider the following thought experiment to illustrate our reliance on reference to Intentional content in the explanation of behavior.

Suppose a Martian visits Boston. Suppose it disguises itself as a male human being so as not to arouse suspicion. It/he then observes a Boston Red Sox baseball game in Fenway Park, but knows nothing about baseball. He sees players in motion and deploys what he knows of the physics of moving bodies to comprehend the game. A person sitting right next to the Martian is an avid baseball fan. This person knows the 'score' or rules of the game. The Martian mentions to the fan that since the game consists of bodies in motion he knows what is happening in the game. He knows this, he says, because he knows physics. The fan is astounded. The fan knows physics, too. He teaches quantum mechanics at the Massachusetts Institute of Technology. But, he claims, there are essential features of baseball that the language of physics is utterly ill-equipped to describe. The fan says that all the activities in the game are physical, true, but when it comes to baseball the science of physics is an incomplete explanatory instrument. One such feature of the game is that players run from base to base. What accounts for this fact? Not just physics. Sometimes a player is trying to steal a base. Base stealing is not described in any physics text. Another such feature of the game is that some batters, when at home plate, refrain from swinging at certain pitches although they are poised to swing. This is because, in some cases, there are two strikes against them and they fear striking out. These facts, too, cannot be understood without understanding the rules of the game. To know the game and how to explain its activity is to know the rules. It is also to assume that players know and observe them as well. Physics cannot tell that sort of story. So says the fan.

The Martian puts the following provocative claim to the fan: "The expression 'rules of baseball' implies a distinction between norms or rules of the game and laws of bodies in motion that is an anachronism of baseball/body dualism." "We can translate behavior that conforms to the rules of the game into the language of the Book of Physical Motion." But the fan chuckles at the Martian's physicalistic hubris. He replies that regardless of whether baseball is a physical game, holding that baseball-by-the-rules should be kept distinct from natural-laws-for-bodies neither commits one to nor presupposes any sort of baseball/physics dualism. The fact is that for theoretical reasons (such as being able to describe and explain activities on the field) as well as for practical purposes (such as being able to enjoy the game), the movements of baseball players in motion must often be classified as importantly different from, say, the behavior of a ball itself when hit into the bleachers or hurled across the field. "We don't have," the fan says, "a physics of the game of baseball." "There is physics *in* baseball, of course, as witness the trajectory of a ball or the speed of a base runner." "The game of baseball is a physical game." "But there is no physics *for* baseball." "To grasp what is happening in a game one has to approach it from the players' perspective – from the perspective of those who are playing the game and know how it is played." "One has to approach it in terms of the *content* of the conscious or Intentional states of players in the game – their fears, beliefs, aspirations and knowledge of the game."

There is no doubt that the fan is right, is there? Some activities that take place in a game, such as the parabolic curve of a baseball in flight, can and should be described purely in physical terms. Projectiles in motion under the control of gravitational forces. But to treat the whole game in this explanatorily threadbare manner misses the contested purpose of the contest. It's a game in which physics is relevant, but not a game of mere bodies in motion. It's a game of baseball. Regardless of what scientists at MIT or on Mars may be able to tell us about why baseballs move in the way that they do, players and fans remain experts on certain other key aspects of the game.

The moral of the game story is this: Matter sometimes isn't all that matters when it is in motion. Sometimes we have to talk about mind, Intentional content, and the efficacy of content. We have to refer to mentality. The dualist will resist the conclusion that mental states are ultimately physical. The physicalist will insist that mental states ultimately are physical. But we have to approach the mental in a mental disorder (or in a baseball game) in a manner that suits the sort of labor or toil required for our purpose (e.g. the explanatory understanding of a mental disorder). The language of mind and mental content is needed to understand mental disorders independently of the ultimate truth or falsity of dualism or physicalism. Or such is my assumption. Such a metaphysically bypassing attitude toward the mind/body problem, namely, that for purposes of understanding a mental disorder (and much of human behavior in general) it makes no real difference how the metaphysical problem is solved, will hardly satisfy an advocate for immediate doctrinaire metaphysics any more than a carafe of wine will quench the thirst of a dehydrated third baseman after a double-header in the hot July Boston sun. But this conciliatory or cohabitation attitude does not deny metaphysical truths (if, for instance, physicalism is true, it's true), it merely deprives them of current explanatory relevance for tackling certain questions about a mental disorder.

Now let's turn to the second criticism of the idea of mental disorder. It's a criticism with a moral purpose, albeit with hefty metaphysical underpinnings (not discussed in detail here).

MENTAL DISORDER AND RESPECT FOR PERSONS

In this section of the chapter I plan to combine a number of different critical claims that have been leveled against the category of mental disorder, all of which share the following assumption. Characterizing a person as the subject of a mental disorder is a form of disrespect or an indignity to them as a person. I call this the *respect for persons* argument for anti-realism about mental disorder. It needs some stage-setting. I am going to begin with something hypothetical and imaginary.

Suppose we discover that a number of college and university students are dramatically and unhappily concerned with grades. Suppose this concern leads to imprudent and reckless behavior (e.g. pulling 'all-nighters' which cause sleep-deprived students to do poorly on tests and to risk somatic ill-health) and needlessly redundant activity (e.g. repeating class-note reviews on too numerous occasions); that these students are temperamentally predisposed to be more concerned about status-orientated intellectual performance than their classmates; and that their states of grade anxiety are accompanied by statistically abnormal activity in the verbally dominant left hemisphere of the brain.

Suppose a psychiatrist, who has helped to make these discoveries, joins the team composing DSM-V and argues that disturbances and behaviors distinctive of grade hyperconcern deserve their own classificatory status in DSM-V. Systematically preparing notes, updating class files and reviewing assignments before exams are good work habits, the psychiatrist argues. However, repeating these activities, when they already have been conscientiously performed, and doing so in redundant and oftentimes ritualistic ways; and, then, failing to gain rest or sleep, so that concern with grades occupies the waking day and causes sleepless nights, is, the psychiatrist claims, a special sort of disorder. The psychiatrist has a name for it. Grade obsessive disorder. GOD, for short. In a respected professional publication the case for GOD as a special disorder is summarized as follows:

> Grade obsessive disorder meets all the reasonable criteria for being a mental disorder. It consists of a syndrome of behaviors. There is evidence that it reflects the bothersome activation of the central nervous system. It is associated with sleep disturbance and with various cognitive dysfunctions – in particular, the inability to do well in academic performance despite being intelligent and well prepared. It should be regarded as a special and distinctive type of disorder.

What sort of argument would be mounted *against* classifying GOD as a disorder? One general answer is what I am calling the respect-for-persons criticism. It goes like this (and will take the next three paragraphs to state).

What does it mean to respect persons? To respect persons is, in part, to treat them as responsible for their own conduct and behavior. When we scold a dog for chewing on a rug, for instance, we are trying to train him. We do not hold the dog responsible for his conduct. We try to correct him. (We may hold the dog's owner accountable for correcting or failing to correct the dog. But we don't charge the dog with correcting itself.) People, however, unlike dogs, should be treated as capable of being reasoned with about their conduct, and as deciding to behave as they do, selecting their goals, and directing their own behavior. We should respect their rationality and reason-responsiveness and treat them as responsible agents. If a person were, say, to obsessively chew on a rug, we should not aim to train them. We should help them to modify their own behavior and to become better at reasoning about how to behave.

Some people have unusual preferences, unshared by others, or imprudent desires, harmful to themselves (wishing to chew on rugs, for example). But an unusual or imprudent desire just is another desire or preference. There is no good reason for believing that it needs to be 'cured' by classifying a person as mentally ill. Some people like to gamble, whereas others have a taste for saving money. Some people become listless and despondent in response to life's misfortunes, whereas others respond to setbacks as challenges that they are eager to overcome. Some folks chew on candy, others chew on rugs. To refer to people as mentally ill, as the philosopher Eric Matthews puts it in a recent paraphrase of a notorious advocate of respect-for-persons criticism, the psychiatrist Thomas Szasz, "is to deny the human dignity of the 'mentally ill' by denying them their ... power to choose how they will behave" (Matthews 2007: 311–12). Some people like to risk their lives in extreme sports, whereas others like to sit on a couch with an electronic remote control for their television and watch soap operas. If some people have the bad luck to be born with temperaments that lead them to 'stress out' with poor academic performances, we should expect them to recognize that this reaction is not conducive to their own welfare. We should expect them to take whatever steps are necessary to combat this source of unhappiness. If they fail in that expectation, the responsibility to change is ultimately their own. Their mental welfare is their business, not that of the medical profession.

To continue with the criticism: Focusing on the anxious or obsessive behavior of students and classifying it as a disorder, dehumanizes a young person and pictures them as non-autonomous, non-responsible objects of medical manipulation in need of therapeutic assistance. To categorize someone as a victim, in particular, of GOD is to discourage them from taking responsibility for their emotional and behavioral academic problems. Each and every student needs to learn to manage their own desires and to cope when academic achievement falls below a desired baseline. Worrisome socially, a classification such as GOD may also serve as a legal basis for exclusion of certain people from normal or desirable patterns of student social life – an exclusion that is a violation of their civil liberties. Individuals diagnosed as victims of GOD may be stigmatized or discriminated against when seeking to join a fraternity, sorority or social club. Labeling them as disordered also allows psychiatrists and other mental health professionals to assume a position of unwarranted judgmental authority over otherwise socially intimidated and medically poorly informed non-psychiatric educational professionals of a college or university. A medically uneducated dean of students, for example, having read of the alleged disorder in Time or Psychology Today may require either that (a) students diagnosed with GOD take plenty of extra time with exams, which would be unfair to un-GOD-like students, or (b) refrain from enrolling in certain courses (which would be unfair to the anxious students themselves) on grounds that it would exacerbate GOD's symptoms. Meanwhile, parents conscientiously shepherding their children's applications to colleges and universities may turn to psychiatrists for advice on whether their son or daughter is a potential victim of GOD, thus enhancing the power and expanding the scope of mental health professionals into what otherwise should be the private lives of individuals. "The judges of normality are present everywhere," wrote the French philosopher–historian, Michel Foucault (1926–84). "We are in a society of the teacher-judge, the doctor-judge, the educator-judge, the social-worker judge" (Foucault 1977: 304). Do we also want physicians to be the student-judge? Indeed we do not.

The above critical claims are offered here, for illustrative purposes, against counting GOD as a mental disorder. GOD as a classification is a construction of my imagination, of course. But I mention a full set of critical claims and wage it against GOD, because it includes the moral charges that various critics level against the very idea of a mental disorder, no matter the alleged type of condition. Addiction. Depression. Obsession. Even schizophrenia. It is said: People's minds or reasoning capacities are not to be treated, trained or 'fixed'. People ought to be regarded as responsible individuals who, in the final analysis, have control over their own behavior and can be reasoned with. Granted, some people may need or welcome help from others to cope with emotional and behavioral problems. But non-medical assistance is one thing (especially when requested); medical labeling and involuntary treatment or intervention is another. In brief: labeling and involuntary treatment is morally inconsistent with human dignity, with respect for persons.

Each claim within the set above represents its own cluster of potentially distinct issues. Also, although the set is not intended as an explicitly metaphysical criticism, it does, of course, harbor contentious metaphysical assumptions about human agency and the powers of reason and self-control especially for people who are distressed and disturbed.

Disorder and respect

When the various claims in the respect for persons argument are put together and used as an objection to the very idea of a mental disorder (and not just to the proposition that GOD, alcoholism, etc., is a disorder), what should happen? Is the category of mental disorder somehow in and of itself disrespectful? Undignifying? Surely, classifying someone as a victim of cancer, diabetes or scurvy does not disrespect them as persons. So, then, why believe that there is something inherently disrespectful or morally unacceptable about describing a person as a subject of a mental disorder?

For disorder skeptics of the respect-for-persons type, the difference in moral attitudes toward persons reflected in the ascription of a somatic as opposed to a mental disorder is that, in the second case, it's the mental powers and faculties of a person that are the object of categorization, whereas in the first it's 'merely' the body. That difference, say critics, makes a big moral difference. How so? Well, consider, for the most famous description of the nature and importance of this difference, Thomas Szasz's attack on the idea of mental illness (Szasz 1960, 1972, 1974, 1982 and 2001).

Szasz charges that ascribing a mental disorder to a person, unlike the ascription of a somatic or physical illness, reflects essentially contestable value judgments that are often moral and socio-political in character, rather than (what he assumes to be) well-defined and more or less value-free somatic- or biological-illness categories. Being depressed, anxious and so on are problematic disturbances, certainly, but they are not illnesses, not disorder classes. Or so Szasz claims. To call them illnesses or disorders, says Szasz, confuses what is sickness with what is difficulty, medicine with morals. When persons are treated as patients with a mental illness, Szasz claims, the door is wide open to disrespect and indignity: for giving people less credit (or discredit) for their behavior than they deserve: for manipulating them: for failing to respect their powers of reasoning and personal preference. In the case of a somatic ailment, by contrast, that particular door to disrespect is closed. The very idea of a physical illness is comparatively value-free. Or at least it is free of reference to or an assumption of essentially contestable values. Saying that a person has cancer poses no affront to them as a person. But saying that a person is addicted to alcohol or beleaguered by GOD does.

Is Szasz correct? Whether he is correct that the very idea of a mental illness presupposes essentially contestable values is not the issue I plan to address here. (The value presuppositions or norms for mental disorder will be examined later in the book, primarily in the next chapter.) But is Szasz correct about the notion of bodily or somatic illness? Is the very idea of a somatic illness truly value-free? Or at least contestability free? If it is not, then it is irrelevant whether the concept of mental illness presupposes contestable or unsettled values. Evaluative asymmetry between somatic and mental disorder vanishes. Moreover: if the very idea of a somatic illness, although not value-free, surely is sound, then so, too, may be the very idea of a mental disorder. It's not as if the latter presupposes value or valuation, whereas the former does not.

Attempts have been made to define bodily disease or somatic illness in value-free terms and a fortiori in terms that do not reflect contestable values (see Boorse 1975). But values are presupposed by the notion of somatic or bodily disease. The very idea of a bodily disease is not value-free and its presupposed values are not without at least some measure of contestability (as will be argued in a moment). The fact that the notion of bodily illness is susceptible to values contestation is under-appreciated by some of the more prominent critics of Szasz.

R. E. Kendall is the former President of the Royal College of Psychiatrists in the UK and is the author of a number of influential pieces on whether mental illness is a genuine illness (Kendall 1975, 1985 and 2001). Kendall, although critical of Szasz's dismissal of the category of mental illness, accepts (or appears to accept) the assumption shared with Szasz that if a condition is to qualify as a genuine illness, then it must be described in value-free scientific or biological terms. Contrary, however, to both Szasz and Kendall the very idea of bodily illness or disease cannot achieve a normatively disinterested or value-neutral standard.

The attribution of bodily illness and disease presupposes norms and values, standards of efficient and proper functioning of the body's organs and of its other systems (cellular and so on), and notions of normative defects in those systems. This is not just because the purpose of medicine is premised on the disvalue of pain and reduced life expectancy (as Szasz himself admits). But it is due to the fact that the notions of bodily health and physical well-being are evaluative or normative through and through. As the book jacket to a recent book on human vulnerability to illness warns, "The next time you get sick, consider this before you pick up aspirin: your body may be doing exactly what it's supposed to do" (Nesse and Williams 1996). But who is to say what the body is supposed to do? Supposed to do by what standards, which norms? For whom exactly? For you, our species, your genes? Drug manufacturers, who believe you should never get headaches or run fevers but should take their medication?

Suppose you are an obstetrician–gynecologist. Suppose one of your pregnant patients complains of severe morning sickness. Is this a hormonal dysfunction? A mark of poor somatic health? It's called a sickness isn't it? If pregnancy was a disease, we might think of morning sickness as a symptom and be committed to its diminution. However, naturally, we don't think of pregnancy as a disease. But why is that? Appreciation for its utility during, say, the Stone Age, as an instrument of needed population growth, is irrelevant today. Humankind may well profit from a dramatic decline in growth of population. More of the world's limited resources would be available to distribute to the poor and needy. So, what about a drug for eliminating morning sickness? Is that a good thing? A bad thing? Such a drug, if pregnancy is a good thing and not an illness, might actually be bad, depending on how it is used. Nausea and associated food aversions during pregnancy may help a woman to avoid spicy plant toxins or foods produced by bacterial and fungal decomposition, thus contributing to lower miscarriage rates and healthier, heavier neonates.

My neighbor is allergic to cats. Is this a dysfunction? Something bad? Could it be an allergy that protects them from a dangerous toxin? Should they take drugs to suppress the allergic reaction and restore them to 'proper bodily well-being'? But suppose it is shown that eighteen out of twenty people with untreated cat allergies are less likely to develop blindness than those who take medication for them. How is this to be understood? Are those with the allergies in a healthy somatic condition? Or suppose that some adolescents possess abnormally heightened vulnerability to physical injury when playing high-school or intramural sports, and that this decreases their reproductive fitness. Suppose, also, however, on a personal plus side, the condition makes for greater academic success, superior performance on IQ tests, temperance in the consumption of alcohol, and dramatically reduced visual impairment rates. Who's to say whether these pre-adults are physically ill rather than that their body is behaving precisely as it should?

Much of what passes for the value-freeness and incontestability of the category of physical illness or somatic disease rests on two facts about values or norms presupposed by physical illness diagnosis. One is that the values often are not obvious, but they are hidden behind social practices and conventions. The other is that when obvious, such values typically are not questioned or debated because they are widely shared. Physical illness classification often rests on near universal human aversions to injury, pain and death. Even so, considerable elbow room for contestation and critical scrutiny is present in somatic-illness attribution, even if few people have the stomach for it. Especially if or when social and environmental conditions change or the cost of health care rises sharply, then contestation about norms of bodily health previously unquestioned may abruptly bubble up to the social and discordant surface.

Lawrie Reznek writes as follows: "Diseases are so classified because they ... make us worse off" (Reznek 1987: 159). But if the world were suddenly to change so that it is "filled with useless noise," something that once was a disease, such as otosclerosis leading to deafness, might not be classified as a disease. This is because "it would not make us worse off" (Reznek 1987: 160).

Let me try to clarify and defend the proposition that the very idea of physical illness is vulnerable to value contestation, with a distinction between two types of goods or values. I have in mind the distinction between instrumental values, that is, things valued as means to other things that are valued, and categorical values, that is, things valued for their own sake.

Some health/illness values are instrumental. Others, at least in a broad or general human context, are categorical. By way of illustration, consider, again, the value of pregnancy. Suppose that medical scientific research establishes that the experience of morning sickness protects fetuses from deadly food toxins. Morning sickness helps to ensure that more healthy fetuses survive until birth. Would not medicine, then, have shown objectively or scientifically that morning sickness is a value-free proper function of, say, the hormonal system of pregnant women and not a genuine sickness or illness? Not quite. All that would have been shown is that a type of *instrumental* value is possessed by morning sickness; namely, if pregnancy is categorically good and morning sickness is the only, the best or the most reliable means by which to avoid ingesting certain harmful toxins, then it is better to undergo morning sickness than to eliminate its occurrence by, say, taking symptom-dissolving medication. Morning sickness allows more fetuses to crossover healthily through the threshold of neonatal life.

The instrumental value of morning sickness does not settle whether morning sickness is incontestably valuable or good. For that proposition to be true, it needs to be decided whether pregnancy is good, categorically. And warranting a decision like that requires debating the merits and demerits of pregnancy and the reliability of morning sickness as a gatekeeper against toxicity.

Generally, if a decision is to be reached as to whether this, that or another condition of the body, its organs or systems is healthy and well rather than unhealthy and unwell, we have to accept some categorically evaluative or normative standards for what counts as good or bad states of affairs for persons and their bodies (pregnant or not pregnant, with or without cat allergies, with or without deafness or blindness, and so on). Categorical standards may be anything but incontestable and immune to critical scrutiny especially when contexts change or situations shift. The question of which conditions of the body to treat categorically (pregnancy good, pregnancy bad) calls for, as Carl Hempel has put it, "standards which are not objectively determined by empirical facts" (Hempel 1965b: 89). Even the most pedestrian sureties about the value of certain somatic conditions may be disrupted if our environment shifts, and with it the value or disvalue of certain bodily states. Reznek offers a clever if chilling example:

> Albinism – the failure to produce the pigment melanin – is a pathological condition because it fails to protect the skin from the sun's rays. But suppose that the amount

of light in our world was greatly reduced (in a nuclear freeze), so albinism would be valuable because it would enable the skin to synthesize vitamin D from the small amount of light available.

(Reznek 1987: 86)

The moral of Reznek's little thought experiment? The value-laden character of the very idea of somatic illness is often more than skin deep. Evaluative assumptions often rest buried within the taxonomic conventions of the ascription of somatic illness.

It is worth noting that once we accept the proposition that the concept of a somatic disease is normative through and through, and that such norms or values may be or become contestable, we may reflectively appraise standards for bodily disease on normative grounds, debate their wisdom and then proceed to conduct medical science accordingly (see Levy 2007: 94–103). (I will make an analogous point for the concept of mental disorder later in the book.) Acting as if standards for physical health are objectively neutral and value-free ultimately hurts the cause of physical medicine just as much, if perhaps not more, than it does the case for mental disorder. It is impossible to define standards of physical health and somatic well-being without appealing to potentially contestable norms.

Now back to the category of a mental disorder. Part of what worries Szasz and others about the values underpinning the notion of a mental disorder is legitimate anxiety about some of the norms or evaluations that, over history or in different cultures, have supported the attribution of mental disorder. During the Renaissance and through to the conclusion of the eighteenth century, for example, there was a marked tension and disjunction between treating individuals with mental illnesses as suffering from natural ailments or as possessed by malign spiritual forces. Demonology, witch-hunts and the torture and execution of the mentally troubled were not uncommon. Contestable or worse, utterly despicable cultural, political and moral values at particular times and in particular places have characterized our explanatory understanding and treatment of mental illness. (The category of somatic illness has also had its share of witch-hunts, of course.) Wise and compassionate apprehension about abhorrent social possibilities repeating themselves helps to motivate some critics to polarize the distinction between mental and non-mental, physical illness and to dismiss the first as controversially value-laden and misjudge the second as value or contestability free. But history, in this case, should make only for a cautionary tale. Not a dismissive one.

So, what about *mental disorder*? May this still be a personally disrespectful category even if the category of physical illness possesses its own zones of value contestability? True, the attribution of a mental disorder does not always serve the interests of those who are diagnosed. (Certainly attributing a pseudo-disorder like that of GOD would not!) Attribution of a mental disorder, depending on how this is understood, conducted or implemented, may inhibit recovery and an effective return of personal well-being. As one 18-year-old with a diagnosis of schizophrenia puts it, "The belief held by hospital staff was that I would be powerless to influence the return of psychotic symptoms that could at any moment strike again" (May 2004: 246). Another person, diagnosed with a mental illness, writes of his being labeled as follows: "[I was] placed in the category of persons whose experience is devalued ... simply because at a certain time or times I lost contact with the ... view of reality agreed upon by my peers" (P. Campbell 1996: 57).

Fortunately, safeguards against the misuse and misapplication of the category of mental disorder have been imposed on psychiatric practice. Fortunately, too, a number of counter-judgmental and anti-discriminatory responsibility themes have been absorbed into current mental-health-care practice, in movements like those of patient power and of user services and user-led research, in the popularity and selling power of anti-psychiatric medication literature, and in the organization of mental health services along multidisciplinary and patient-as-person-centered lines (see Bracken and Thomas 2005).

Alas, it is true, too, that with the ever-swelling nomenclature of DSM, more and more forms of human behavior are classified as disorders and 'medicalized', and the sad day may come when a bizarre category like that of GOD may push its way into the pages of our diagnostic manuals. Fortunately, however, both the idea and the extended range of the concept of mental disorder are under constant critique, vigilance and modification (see Horwitz and Wakefield 2007). Likewise, just as there are situations in which people are disrespected when classified or treated as mentally ill, so there are cases in which people's lives are transformed or reconstructed much for the better by receiving a mental disorder diagnosis, along with the care and medical attention that they need. (Styron [1990] and Jamison [1995] offer vivid personal testimonials of the help which is often received by mental illness patients.)

Anyone who has lived through what Bentall calls − referring to their commonness, not blandness, for certainly they are not bland − "the ordinary tragedies of life" will appreciate that many challenges and disappointments in life provoke profound psychological distur-bance and scars − the death of a beloved spouse, a humiliating embarrassment in the eyes of one's colleagues, friends or family, the inability to care for one's children, and so on (Bentall 2004: 239). Some people adjust to such events. Some persons manage to manage, so to speak. It's tough but they survive more or less intact. However, other persons come apart and become destabilized, if only for a time. Some seek or need assistance. Some need medical assistance. In fact, sometimes, the very same sort of grief, humiliation or sadness that moves, in the words of Karl Jaspers (1883–1969), "one individual to the psychiatrist as a sick person ... will take another to the confessional as one suffering from sin and guilt" (Jaspers 1963: 780).

What should the profession of medicine do? Should the profession insist that no such difficulty deserves to be classified as a disorder and treated in medical terms? When people behave in a manner that surely seems to require medical help, when they profoundly or profusely complain or are troubled, then the clinical responsibilities of psychiatry appear clear, urgent and demanding. A physician must ascertain the content of a patient's complaint, symptoms or behavioral signs and try to do something about them − based on the common-sense assumption that for most people what is wanted is absence of pain and suffering, some measure of pleasure in existence, a range of opportunities to engage productively with other people, to work, to complete normal human tasks, to live a decent life.

I am a philosopher and not a clinician, although as a young man in my twenties I spent an informative lessons-filled year as an aide in the psychiatric unit of a Harvard teaching hospital in Boston. As I see matters, the clinically compassionate 'coalface' of mental disorder has always been the problem of relieving suffering and helping to build or restore psychological well-being. So, even though the respect-for-persons critique of the category of mental disorder has important lessons that need to be assimilated into mental-health-professional practice, ultimately it presses for an unhelpful and overly dismissive agenda. It is one thing to build respect for persons into psychiatric practice (no small or uncomplicated order). It is another to dismiss the whole enterprise of disorder attribution and treatment as morally misbegotten. The first task, namely incorporating respectful safeguards, is necessary. The second, namely dismissal of the very idea of mental disorder on respect-for-person grounds, is overbearing and uncompassionate. Besides which, as we will see in the chapters to follow, there are honest-to-goodness disorders of mind. Persons do, mentally, breakdown or destabilize.

CHAPTER SUMMARY AND SUGGESTED READINGS

In this chapter we examined two grounds for skepticism about the existence of mental disorder and about attribution of the concept of mental disorder. Each has a lesson to teach. But neither warrants dismissal of the category.

One form of skepticism assumes that talk of mental illness is regrettably dualistic. This is metaphysical skepticism. The other form of skepticism assumes that the category of mental illness is morally misbegotten and indefensible. This is moral skepticism. Neither warrants anti-realism about mental disorder. The cautionary lesson of metaphysical skepticism is that problems of mind/body and mental causation confront the category of mental disorder. The cautionary lesson of moral or respect-for-persons skepticism is that psychiatric labeling and treatment can do more harm than good.

I argued that mind–body dualism certainly is not required of our understanding of a mental disorder. I argued that whether classifying a person as mentally ill morally disrespects them is not a function of the category of mental illness. It is a function of not observing proper ethical constraints in the treatment of persons.

In this chapter we also explored whether the very idea of a somatic illness or disease is value-free. Our verdict is negative. The proposition that the idea of bodily illness or disease is value neutral and categorically normatively unproblematic is, I claimed, unfounded. Why this concern with values? It is because we do not want to rule out thinking of mental disorders as real honest-to-goodness conditions of persons on the grounds that, *unlike* the notion of a bodily disorder, the very idea of a mental disorder is value-laden and rests on tendentious value judgments. There is no such 'unlike'.

No topic in the philosophy of mind has felled more trees and required more paper than that of the mind–body problem and the closely associated problem of mental causation. An edited collection in the philosophy of mind that contains many important papers on each problem (including the paper by Kim discussed in this chapter) is Timothy O'Connor and David Robb's *Philosophy of Mind: Contemporary Readings* (Routledge, 2003). E. J. Lowe's "The Problem of Psychophysical Causation," in that volume, may help to diminish the surety of a reader's anti-dualist skepticism. Among single-authored books to consult on the mind–body problem are D. M. Armstrong, *The Mind–Body Problem: An Opinionated Introduction*

(Westview, 1999); J. Heil, *Philosophy of Mind* (Routledge, 2004, 2nd edn); J. Kim, *The Philosophy of Mind* (Westview, 2005, 2nd edn); and J. Searle, *Mind: A Brief Introduction* (Oxford University Press, 2004). The topic of mental causation is the subject of John Heil and Alfred Mele's edited collection on *Mental Causation* (Oxford University Press, 1993). On the first-person experience of mental causation and of being a conscious and deliberate agent, Terence Horgan, John Tienson and I have written "The Phenomenology of First Person Agency," in S. Walter and H.-D. Heckmann, eds, *Physicalism and Mental Causation: The Metaphysics of Mind and Action* (Imprint Academic, 2003). See also J. Hohwy, "The Experience of Mental Causation," *Behavior and Philosophy*, 2004, 32, pp. 377–400. See also Tim Bayne and Neil Levy, "The Feeling of Doing: Deconstructing the Phenomenology of Agency," in N. Sebanz and W. Prinz, eds, *Disorders of Volition* (MIT Press, 2006).

A novel and science-inspired defense of the identity thesis may be found in Robert McCauley's "Reduction: Models of Cross-Scientific Relations and their Implications for the Psychology–Neuroscience Interface," in P. Thagard (ed.), *Philosophy of Psychology and Cognitive Science* (Elsevier, 2007). On the inability to understand the mental in physical terms, Colin McGinn's *Problems of Philosophy: The Limits of Enquiry* (Blackwell, 1993) contains an inventive, engaging and non-technical discussion of the topic.

A representative set of Thomas Szasz's papers is available in his collection entitled *The Medicalization of Everyday Life* (Syracuse University Press, 2007). A short introduction to Thomas Szasz's attack on psychiatric diagnosis and the very idea of mental disorder/illness (an introduction that is conceptually orthogonal to the approach to Szasz that I offer in this book) may be found in chapter 2 of B. Fulford, T. Thornton and G. Graham's *Oxford Textbook of Philosophy and Psychiatry* (Oxford University Press, 2006), along with a detailed bibliography. In a paper entitled "Suspicions of Schizophrenia," which appears in M. Cheung, K. Fulford and G. Graham (eds), *Reconceiving Schizophrenia* (Oxford University Press, 2007), the philosopher Eric Matthews says the following of Szasz. He is "mistaken to be against . . . psychiatry" but "ultimately right" to insist that patients should be treated as "human subjects with problems rather than simply machines to be repaired" (p. 326). A short but helpful survey of anti-psychiatry criticisms (with special attention to the phenomenon of stigmatization) is John Sadler's "Diagnosis/Antidiagnosis," in J. Radden (ed.), *The Philosophy of Psychiatry: A Companion* (Oxford University Press, 2004).

5 Seeking norms for mental disorder

Mental disorders are not brain disorders. Or so I have argued. This is true, I have claimed, even though or if mental disorders are brain based. The disorderliness of a mental disorder is connected with its being undesirable and its undesirability is constituted, in part, by the fact that a disorder makes a person worse off and does so involuntarily. Diseases do that too, of course. They make persons unwillingly worse off. But mental disorders are perhaps not best understood as forms of disease. I have argued for those claims as well.

I am not finished examining what makes a mental disorder disorderly or undesirable. In this and the next chapter I hope to complete the task.

In this chapter I turn to the question of norms or standards relevant to negative judgments or appraisals of a person's mental condition that help to warrant the attribution of a disorder to a person.

It is a tough question. Norms for disorder. What are they? A little saintly assistance may help.

DESPAIR, DEPRESSION AND DISORDER

St Augustine (354–430) was born in Tagaste in the North African province of Numidia in AD 354. Augustine's *Confessions* is one of the literary and autobiographical masterworks of Western literature. In it he describes his quest to find a meaning or purpose to life and his dramatic conversion to Christianity. To him, for him and in him, purpose was Christian purpose. Without it, he says, he suffered from intellectual confusion and emotional turmoil.

Augustine mentions that his mother once "found me in a dangerous state of depression" (Augustine 1992: 90). Was he subject to episodes of a mental illness? Clinical or major depression? Nancy Andreasen says yes. She writes:

> No medical texts are extant from the early medical period, but literary and historical evidence indicates that the absence of texts does not bespeak the absence of illness. St. Augustine has confessed to his struggles with the hopelessness and despair of depression.
>
> (Andreasen 1984: 144)

Confession to depression? Is Augustine's autobiography a tale, in part, of his personal struggle with a mental disorder? If given a chance and been fast forwarded to current times, would the venerable, but unhappy, saint consult a cognitive-behavioral therapist or embrace a drug regimen of a selective serotonin reuptake inhibitor (Prozac)? True, Augustine does speak of periods, one just noted, of despondency. Here, for a second instance, is how he describes his grief on the loss of a friend in death:

> Everything on which I set my gaze was death. My home town became a torture to me; my father's house a strange world of unhappiness; all that I had shared with him was without him transformed into a cruel torture. My eyes looked for him everywhere, and he was not there. I hated everything because they did not have him, nor could they now tell me 'look, he is on the way', as used to be the case when he was alive and absent from me. I had become to myself a vast problem.
>
> (Augustine 1992: 57)

But was he suffering from clinical depression? The mental disorder? Augustine? Imagine that a psychiatrist enamored of medication says to him, "No, despair over finding a purpose to life is completely unwarranted." "Yours is a chemical problem." "Likely it is located in your endocrine or stress response system." "Your auto-regulatory mechanism for cortisol production probably is impaired."

Nomy Arpaly remarks that "being told that one's cherished beliefs or emotions are symptoms of a ... disorder ... can be insulting, however ... compassionate" may be the underlying intention (Arpaly 2005: 285). Augustine, no doubt, would be insulted. "My problem is not with life's purpose?" So he may exclaim. "It's with my hormones?"

Augustine, I believe, does not confess to clinical depression, but rather, aside from normal periods of unhappiness (such as his grief over the death of a friend), he confesses to what the philosopher Richard Garrett aptly refers to as philosophical despair. Garrett writes: "When an individual comes to the ... conclusion that not simply their own life but everyone's life is, as a whole futile, then we have ... philosophical despair" (1994: 74). For Augustine the struggle to overcome a fear of life's futility took a religious or spiritual turn. He describes himself as on a search for a transcendent purpose to human existence. Augustine discovered this purpose, he reports, only in belief in the God of Christianity. When his mother discovered him in a depressed state, "I had lost all hope of discovering the truth" (1992:

90). But later he prays to God: "Late have I loved you, beauty so old and so new, late have I loved you" (1992: 201). "I feel but hunger and thirst for you … to attain the peace which is yours" (1992: 201).

Of course, Augustine's unhappiness may be based in part in hormonal activity. But while saying that his unhappiness may be based, in part, on hormone levels may be saying something that is true, it is not saying much, for we still may meaningfully ask both what his unhappy condition is about or directed at (what is its Intentional content?) and whether it is somehow made reasonable or sensible by what it is about. It may make sound sense, depending on background conditions, for someone to be unhappy if he believes that human life is utterly meaningless or purposeless.

Compare: Consider becoming sad because of a disease such as Addison's disease in which one's adrenals no longer produce cortisol, and wherein the sadness occurs no matter of what one thinks. A person may believe life to be immensely purposeful and yet may still feel quite despondent. To use the language of the last chapter, one cannot change whether such a person is unhappy by intervening in their conception of life's purpose. Unlike Augustine's unhappiness, which is associated with fear that life is not worth living and which is woven into a protracted and frustrated search for meaning and direction, the unhappiness of a person caused by Addison's disease is neurochemically fastened onto the disease and not responsive to reason or argumentation. Commitment to Christianity is no antidote for Addison's.

Carl Elliott complains of the tendency of contemporary psychiatric culture to categorize too wide and motley a variety of human distresses as "scientific problems defined by the language and techniques of psychiatry" (Elliott 2003: 157). A recent book laments that the extreme popularity of antidepressant medication is making Americans "comfortably numb" (Barber 2008). Be numb, not disturbed, not writing confessions in North Africa.

Complaints about over-medicalizing human distress are apt even if their purport is imprecise or unclear. Over-medicalization "violates," in the words of Jennifer Radden, "our intuitive sense that [various] forms of suffering are importantly different" (Radden 2009: 102). Not every 'disorderly' or distressful mental condition qualifies as a mental disorder. Some conditions do, of course. But others do not. Moreover, the distinction between forms of suffering that are and those that are not mental disorders is of critical importance. It not only influences the lives that people live but helps to identify and legitimate psychiatric medical practice.

Andreasen, I believe, over-medicalizes Augustine. Augustine, the saint, sought God. A student at Princeton or Cambridge may try to escape from the clutches of GOD (grade obsessive disorder). Neither behavior is indicative of a mental disorder. Each individual is in a distressed or unwanted condition, to be sure. But that is not enough, certainly, to qualify for the diagnosis of a mental disorder.

What is? Enough? What norms or standards are involved?

ANXIETY AND DSM

Let's look at a case of real disorder. An exemplary one. A case with specifics.

The case to be examined is adapted from a real case, discussed by Kraepelin, who, as noted in the first chapter, helped to provide the conceptual foundations for the modern style of classification of mental disorders of which DSM is the most prominent example. The real case was discussed in 1904 in Kraepelin's *Lectures in Clinical Psychiatry* (1968: 262). Assume that the context for offering the case is Grand Rounds of a Department of Psychiatry of a distinguished university hospital and medical center.

> Arthur A., a school teacher, has been in the hospital two weeks. He is thirty-six years old and entered the hospital of his own accord in order to be treated here. He is reluctant to be part of today's Grand Rounds. When told that he would be presented at Rounds, he became agitated and said that being paraded in front of so many strangers all at once might cost him his life. He did not explain what he meant by that remark, but he begged to sit in the corridor before the presentation so that he could see the audience enter gradually before him. "I just cannot face so many people all at once," he said.
>
> Arthur says that one of his sisters suffers as does he from fear of public places. He also says that his fearful condition began when he had to study for entry exams to graduate school. He became intensely afraid that he would fail. He became short of breath and dizzy. He felt his heart pounding rapidly. Sweat poured down his face. Because of these physical reactions he feared that he had a serious heart disease. His internist tried to assure him that he was in good cardiac health, but assurances fell on deaf ears. For this reason, Arthur sought out cardiac specialists and visited several heart clinics, his fears about his heart increasing steadily. Again, despite receiving optimistic assessments, he persisted in believing that he had a bad heart. He found that he could not cross public plazas or walk into busy stores. He stopped taking buses because of apprehension about accidents and crashes. He had an opportunity for an ocean cruise and vacation, which he declined, fearing that the boat might capsize. The fears, he says, aggravated his heart condition, which he says makes public concourse an emotional bridge that he cannot cross.
>
> His wife describes him as "chicken-hearted," afraid of all sorts of diseases and of crowds. Arthur himself admits that his fears and anxieties feel morbid, and that they keep him from leading a normal life, yet he cannot free himself from them. He walks in the hospital garden, by himself, retreating to his room if other patients enter the garden while he is there. He asks for "pills" to give him the energy to address audiences of parents of schoolchildren, a chore that he has to perform several times a year. He is scheduled to make one such address next month. He doubts he will be able to do it.
>
> Arthur says that sometimes he feels his heart violently palpitate, when he is forced to be in a crowd. This morning, he says, small acne spots have begun to appear on his face, and he believes that this is evidence that he stands visibly out in the

hospital and is likely to be treated in unwelcome terms. He wonders, too, if the acne has something to do with his heart condition. A dermatology resident examined Arthur later this morning and found no unusual spots, acne or otherwise. Arthur, however, is not persuaded.

Arthur A's case has four clinically prominent features among others.

(1) Arthur has disturbances or interferences in his experience – in his (as it may be put) Intentionality of self and world.
(2) Because of these disturbances, he struggles with one or more necessary activities of daily living, and is stymied or disabled in their performance.
(3) The disturbances are characterized by a variety of negative and imprudent thoughts, feelings and behaviors.
(4) If Arthur is not helped or treated, he may suffer important and continued losses of freedom and social functionality. His condition seems to be worsening.

In its particular symptoms Arthur's case would be diagnosed using DSM as agoraphobia (i.e. acute anxiety associated with being in public places or situations with other people, strangers foremost, and in which escape may be difficult) with panic attacks or disorder (APA 1980: 226; 1987: 235f). (This diagnosis would be supplemented with a diagnosis of hypochondriasis [APA 1980: 249]. Arthur A's heart is healthy, but he is convinced that he has an infirm heart. He has no acne either.)

But why should Arthur A's condition be classified as a mental disorder in the first place? What rationale is there for the DSM assumption that someone like Arthur is disordered, psychiatrically? Let's focus on his acute anxiety about crowds with the proclivity to panic and not on his hypochondriasis.

No doubt, Arthur's emotional response is a deeply upsetting disturbance in his experience of self and world, broadly understood. This does not mean that strictly neurobiological/ neurochemical or brute mechanical processes play no role in Arthur's unfortunate behavior. Of course they do. Nor does it mean that the specific source of his acute anxiety is obvious to him or that it stems, as he believes, from an incident in which he was afraid of failing an exam. But it does mean, as Karl Jaspers puts it in his *General Psychopathology*, "psychopathology has, *as its subject matter*, actual ... psychic events" (Jaspers 1963: 2). The content, character and consequences of Arthur's experience help to explain both why his 'psychic' or mental condition is a disorder and why this particular disorder is of the type that it is – anxiety as opposed to, say, depression or delusional disorder.

Speaking of Jaspers, although some disorders in DSM's all-too-hefty catalogue are compatible with Jaspers's proposition that psychopathologies (mental illnesses/disorders) are disorders in a person's experience, DSM is not in complete and uniform accord with Jaspers on this score. Some conditions mentioned in the manual are not disturbances in experience or Intentionality, although they are classified as mental disorders. This fact is worth a brief digression.

DSM counts or appears to count Down's syndrome as a mental disorder (see e.g. APA 1987: 28ff). If Down's is a mental disorder, then an IQ of 55, depending on its chemical cause, may qualify as a mental disorder irrespective of the presence of conscious distress or behavioral disturbance. Down's can be diagnosed prior to birth by identifying a chromosomal abnormality that is its cause in samples of fetal cells taken from amniotic fluid. The presence of an extra twenty-first chromosome is the source of mental retardation in Down's. No behavior needs to be observed. So, then, why does (assuming it does) DSM classify Down's as a *mental* disorder?

The inclusion of Down's syndrome in DSM may stem from the following two facts: (i) Down's is a neural-developmental disorder and (ii) the distinction between neurological disorders and mental disorders is arbitrary from DSM's perspective given its worry that the category of mental disorder must somehow be pruned of dualist presuppositions.

Taxonomists are mistaken, however, or so I have argued and shall continue to argue, to absorb mental disorders into the category of neurological disorder, even if it is sound to assume that mental disorders are based in physical reality. The authors of DSM may count certain brute brain or somatic disorders (like Down's) as mental disorders, in part, to demonstrate that dualism has been excised from the manual's conceptual or metaphysical foundations. It's odd, however, regardless of the wrongness of the classification, for something like Down's to be listed as a mental disorder, whereas another neurological condition like, say, Parkinsonism, which is a basal ganglia disorder, characterized by tremor, muscular rigidity and loss of postural reflexes, and which may be much more disturbing consciously for a subject, does not appear in DSM. This is despite the fact that some of Parkinsonism's symptoms may be ameliorated with psychological treatments. (Psychotherapy may reduce the anxiety persons often feel over the condition.) No manner of psychotherapy is able to build up a Down's patient's IQ.

Down's certainly is no exemplary *mental* disorder. Down's is not associated with distress or disturbance in a victim's experience, except indirectly through personal adjustment problems that may stem from social circumstances of the condition. Nor do states with Intentionality/Intentional content figure in its propensity or onset conditions. Down's is, however, the sort of condition that some disease-oriented psychiatrists like to count as a mental disorder. Perhaps this is because if Down's qualifies as a mental disorder, then it stands not just as emblematic of DSM's commitment to anti-dualism, but as a case of disorder that is both a disease (with one or few causes, etc.) and an instance of a broken brain. So, classifying Down's as a mental disorder is an application of the biomedical model of mental illness in full aspiration. If all mental disorders could, like forms of mental retardation, be "linked to specific biological abnormalities," writes George Heninger, a psychiatrist at Yale University, "it would greatly simplify matters" (Heninger 1999: 89). "As the biology of a disease becomes more clear so does our understanding of specific dimensions of clinical data" (ibid.: 97). (Note that Heninger speaks of mental disorders as diseases.)

Of course, we do not need to endorse either a disease or a broken brain conception of mental disorder to urge *treating* Down's at least somewhat like a mental disorder. Down's children have a general impairment in intellectual function that pervades all aspects of learning – reading, writing, mathematical computation. Education or training in the skills necessary to compensate for these impairments, such as self-help skills, communication skills, and so on, often fall within the province of the mental health profession. Likewise, social adjustment problems faced by certain victims of Down's, which may be exhibited in aggressive, self-injurious or withdrawal behavior, may stem from trying to lead a life in an environment where a person is unable appropriately to adjust without outside direction and assistance. The mental health profession possesses valuable assistance tools and services for people in distress in different walks of life, even if they are without exemplary mental illnesses or disorders. Victims of Down's sometimes are among them.

Let us return to Arthur A. What about his case? Where is the disorder, the psychiatric condition or mental illness, behind his complaint or symptoms? This is not a question about the particulars of Arthur's diagnosis (of panic attacks), but about his being classified as the subject of a mental disorder period. What makes his case an example of a mental disorder according to DSM?

For DSM a mental disorder is described as a "clinically significant behavioral or psychological syndrome" of a sort that "occurs in a person and that is associated with present distress ... or disability (impairment in one or more important areas of functioning) or with a significantly increased risk of suffering death, pain, disability, or an important loss of freedom" (APA 1994: xxi). In Arthur's case the elements of disability and loss of freedom are parts of the second, third and fourth features of his condition; distress is a first feature. The disorder also is *in* him in the form of the first feature, namely in his distressful or disturbed experience of self and world.

Clearly, the DSM description is not intended to identify a tractable set of necessary and sufficient conditions for qualifying as a mental disorder. That's all to the good of course. But DSM's description also contains a gerrymandered collection of terms, referring to distress, disability, impairment, pain and so on. So, if one is looking for a simple characterization of what makes a disorder a disorder, DSM fails to provide it.

The merits and demerits of DSM's gerrymandered characterization of disorder aside, what I wish to focus on in DSM's description is the following feature. For DSM if a mental or psychological condition consists merely of distress, loss of freedom, and so on, it fails to qualify as a disorder. Remember: Augustine was distressed, but not for that reason clinically depressed. To qualify as a disorder for DSM, a distress or loss must stem from a clinically *significant* disability or impairment. This means that it is not the product of reasoned argumentation (as in the case of the philosophical despair of Augustine, assuming this stems from no disability) or of a mere performance lapse or error.

So what then is that? A clinically significant disability or impairment? It is one thing if I am distressed because I voluntarily expose myself to distress (say, by bungee jumping). It's another if my distress indicates a significant disability or impairment. It is one thing if I am distressed because I am learning how to perform a Beethoven piano sonata and suffer from a lack of self-confidence. It is another if I am distressed because no matter how hard I try I cannot get myself to interact with strangers or to calm myself down from episodes of florid mania.

All that makes intuitive sense, doesn't it? Even without knowing just what it may mean to refer to a *significant* disability or impairment? Consider GOD. Students in this hypothetical condition are precluded because of their grade anxiety from doing as well as they wish on graded academic performances. But although grade anxiety is disturbing, doing extremely well academically is not *that* important or significant. Besides which, it is not a capacity that most of us share. We are not all above average. If I am failing to get top scores, I am missing out on Phi Beta Kappa or academic honors. Life, however, is filled with an immense range of other satisfactions and opportunities, including intellectual challenges, through which to develop and express talents that do not require acing calculus tests or getting top grades on term papers on European history.

It's hard for certain people, especially perhaps for certain students at highly selective colleges or universities, to appreciate all that. In our culture, to quote Erik Erikson (1902–94), from a book now musty on my shelf but a must-read when I was a college student, many "young men and women [are] forced by a compulsion to excel fast, before enough of a sense of being [has been] secured" (Erikson 1968: 151). However, to be truly secure as a person, an individual must learn how to moderate desires and to cope with personal failure. A mature person realizes that sometimes they should seek satisfaction down other avenues or through alternative opportunities. Not in nailing honors.

No such admonition to seek satisfaction elsewhere or to learn to adjust to failure is appropriate for the likes of Arthur. Part of what helps to distinguish his sort of fear or anxiety over being in public from the grade anxiety of students in the grip of GOD, is that avoiding contact with strangers or people in crowded places just is not feasible in normal social environments. Public concourse is necessary for a vast variety of activities and normal forms of human satisfaction.

So, although DSM's description of the disorder of a mental disorder is complex and disjointed, one aspect of it seems both direct and clear. According to DSM to attribute a mental disorder to someone requires evaluating not just the person's capacity (or incapacity) to avoid harms or losses of freedom, but also the importance or nature of those losses and of the capacities that are impaired. And, of course, this raises the following question: Where do we get standards or norms for such judgments or evaluative appraisals? Absent countervailing considerations, "rational persons in all societies" agree that "death, pain, disability and loss of freedom" are undesirable (Gert and Culver 2004: 421). No one denies that. But for DSM an incapacity or impairment does not count as a disorder just because it is painful, risks death, and so on. One can imagine, for instance, being incapable of climbing a mountain in the winter or wrestling with a bear in the woods and this may cause losses for a person (and risk death) if they are in a situation in which they must do these things but can't. But such events for DSM would not mean that the relevant incapacities or inabilities qualify as mental disorders. For a disorder, for DSM, incapacity must ascend to a clinical standard or level of significance. Pain stemming from a significant incapacity? Impairment in avoiding a serious loss? What's that?

The necessity or need for identifying when psychological disabilities are serious enough, clinically speaking, or of sufficient clinical import or relevance, to qualify as disorders arises inevitably, I believe, for any effort to appraise systematically what makes a mental disorder a disorder. Not just for DSM. So, it is no surprise to find that the history of psychopathology has traditionally been concerned simultaneously both with the study of impairments and disabilities and with their degree, nature or type of undesirability, disvalue or harmful impact. A list of impairments would not be of much interest to psychopathology without consideration of standards or norms of seriousness. A list of potential harms would hold no real significance unless associated with a disability.

We could, of course, try to decide on the clinical seriousness or significance of a disability in a normatively flat-footed and unsophisticated way. Social scientists spend a great deal of time gathering statistics. We may try to use statistics to try to identify statistical norms of human psychological functioning. The evaluative seriousness of a psychological incapacity may then just be understood as statistically deviant or abnormal functioning. Being unable to do calculus and therein losing honors would not count, assuming that most people cannot do well at calculus. Whereas being unable to know where one is or what one is doing would qualify. Knowing where one is and what one is doing is quite normal. But we need to ask ourselves whether statistical aberrance should be encoded in a concept of mental illness. Descartes was statistically aberrant, a genius at both science and philosophy. He found himself accepting, imprudently, an invitation to go to Stockholm to give philosophical tutelage to Queen Christina of Sweden, where he behaved foolishly. Christina hoped for instruction in the royal palace in the cold hours of predawn. Descartes assented but caught pneumonia and died just shy of his fifty-fourth birthday. Does this mean he was mentally ill? With Augustine already on the taxonomic cutting block and perhaps now Descartes, one wonders whether any philosopher may escape a diagnosis of mental illness.

Suppose we discover that human beings suffer from all sorts of decision-making errors and cognitive biases. Here is a partial list of potential candidates with their standard names: An out-group homogeneity bias, in which persons describe people in their own group as being relatively more varied in personality and behavior than members of other groups; a fundamental attribution error, in which persons overemphasize the causal role of personality traits in controlling behavior and downplay the power of situational influences on the same behavior; the neglect of prior base rates, in which people fail to incorporate prior known frequencies that are pertinent to a current decision made under conditions of uncertainty; the gambler's fallacy, in which a person assumes that individual random events in a series are influenced by previous random events ("I've flown so many times without accident, that my plane is bound to crash sooner or later"); and hyperbolic discounting, in which people tend to more strongly prefer smaller pay-offs or rewards for their behavior than larger pay-offs if the smaller pay-off is closer in time.

Are any of these biases or errors, which may be quite harmful, mental disorders or symptoms of mental disorder? Not both if they are statistically frequent and if statistical infrequency is necessary for a mental disorder. But that hardly seems right. In somatic medicine, during a massive epidemic nearly everyone has the relevant illness. Frequency does not count against being ill. As for biases, a good concept of mental disorder should spell out just which, if any, biases (assuming that they deserve such a label) are significant. Perhaps none. Perhaps all. Perhaps some. Or perhaps only when associated with certain other impairments or disabilities.

It is one thing to be biased in reasoning or decision-making. It is another for bias to be due to impairment in reasoning as well as significant. Important or significant enough, that is, to qualify as a mental disorder or symptom of a disorder. When is 'enough' enough and clinical significance achieved? Infrequency is a poor norm. So perhaps, for an answer to this enough-question, we should simply leave the relevant standards of importance and significance at a subjective and intuitive level. Forget statistics. Just rely on psychiatrists' judgments of importance, hoping perhaps that they will reach some measure of reliability, unbiased by economic and non-medical considerations. "All this," as one theorist of clinical assessment puts the matter in a related context, "is a question of judgment rather than pure test results" (Powell 2000: 100).

The clinical coalface of mental disorder is human suffering and the need to ameliorate it. Educated compassionate judgment when addressing the needs of particular people with possible disorders may be, in certain instances, not just unavoidable but desirable. Other things being equal, however, if we can find at least a rough-n-ready principled means to make the judgments of importance or significance we need, we should embrace it. Not statistics or frequencies. Not subjective guesswork. But then what? Let us look at some hypotheses for explicit standards of clinical importance or significance.

This brings us, then, to an examination of candidate standards of clinical seriousness or importance. I plan to look briefly at three. One is tied to culture. One relies on evolutionary speculation. One (the one we should prefer, I believe) stems from appreciation of a special feature of Intentionality and of the Intentional attitudes of persons. This is rationality, broadly understood.

CULTURAL CONVENTIONALISM

Suppose the following is true: Different cultures and subcultures possess different standards or conventions for the seriousness or importance of psychological impairments and disabilities and therein for whether a condition is a disorder. In the context of, say, a tribe of Ivy League Phi Beta Kappa scholars, GOD may be classified as a significant disability and count as a disorder. Whereas when in a tribe of general educational malcontents, a syndrome like GOD may have no perceived significance whatsoever. Certainly not that of a mental disorder.

In 1940 in the United States homosexuality was thought to be a "disease" of sexuality or sexual behavior. Today unless is it is believed to be accompanied by a "persistent and marked distress about sexual orientation" it is no longer mentioned as a diagnostic category (Soble 2004: 54–5).

Is clinical seriousness or significance just a matter of social or cultural conventions or norms? The idea that the norms or standards for disorders are nothing but a matter of social conventions may seem appealing. It is appealing if for no other reason than that if conventions say that a particular disability is serious or significant enough to qualify as a mental disorder, then, in a sense, there is a determinate and discoverable fact of the matter as to whether the disability is a disorder. A form of distress is a disorder just in case a relevant disorder-determining cultural convention is in place and says it's a disorder.

Let's put the cultural criterion of seriousness as follows. The possession of the property of being thought, judged, or otherwise treated as serious by a culture both makes a disability important or qualifies it as a disorder, and enables us to recognize it as such. On such a view, for example, "Arthur A's panic attacks are a symptom of a mental disorder" means

"The attacks are symptoms of a disability that is thought serious by Arthur's culture and qualify in that culture as a disorder." Insofar and only insofar as we can identify psychological disabilities thought serious by a culture, we can identify what counts, or should count, as a mental disorder. The cultural criterion, which may be referred to as *cultural conventionalism* about disorder, implies that a disability is not a disorder if a culture fails to judge it as sufficiently serious.

There are different versions of cultural conventionalism about disorder and associated standards of clinical significance. There is also indeterminacy in the concepts of culture and convention, enough, at least, to make it difficult to know, in some cases, whether to count a criterion as a culture's criterion. But these facts do not upset the cultural criterion. Indeed, what most unnerves those who may wish to defend the criterion is when critics misread it.

Consider the statement:

(1) An uncontrollable proclivity to panic attacks is a mental disorder.

Is this statement true, or is it false? For the conventionalist, it is neither true nor false. It is semantically elliptical. It's like saying that 'Boston is next to', but not saying next-to-what. Or saying that 'Sam is tall' but not saying as compared with whom. The truth is, says the conventionalist, that a proclivity to panic attacks is a mental disorder just in those places or situations in which it is culturally judged to be a mental disorder or clinically serious, but not in situations in which it is not. Or consider the statement:

(2) An uncontrollable proclivity to panic attacks in the judgment of Arthur's culture is a mental disorder.

Is that statement true, or is it false? It is true, but not truly a perspicuous expression of the conventionalist criterion. Conventionalism as such is not saying that cultures make judgments about (or have conventions with respect to) mental disorder, which, of course, they do, but that,

(3) An uncontrollable proclivity to panic attacks is a mental disorder in those cultures (like Arthur's) in whose judgment or according to whose conventions it is a mental disorder.

The third claim is a very different claim from the second. The second merely reports a social convention. The third identifies the convention as *the* criterion of a disorder. (The logical or clarifying points I am making here are analogous to some made in defense of moral conventionalism and relativism. See Hocutt 2000 for discussion.)

But is a cultural judgment or convention a sound and sensible criterion of disorder – of clinical seriousness or importance? Suppose we take the criterion to theoretical heart. What are some of the implications?

(1) *Reasoning about whether something is a serious impairment and genuine mental disorder terminates when we reach facts about cultural conventions*. Suppose we know that in Culture C slaves who attempt to flee from their owners are treated as suffering from an

illness known as "drapetomania." Or that gays and lesbians in Culture C* are said to be disabled and in need of a clinical intervention. How do we know this? It may be hard in some cases, but with the aid of anthropologists and sociologists such facts, if they are facts, are discoverable. However, is that where concern about whether a distress or impairment is serious or behavior a disorder should terminate? Is that the end of the investigatory line? Not in psychiatry but in cultural anthropology? One should think not.

(2) *We would lose our notion of cross-cultural medical scientific progress in the study of mental disorder.* Psychiatric medicine has long suffered from what seems to some prominent observers to be an unflattering contrast with somatic illness medical specialties. This is that while advances in somatic medicine tell us more about heart disease, cancer and obesity, medical science is stymied when it comes to understanding an unhealthy mind. Who's to say what constitutes an advance in psychiatry? This alleged unflattering contrast between somatic medicine and psychiatry has tended to provoke either one of two responses. One is to put the very idea of mental disorder (in the manner argued for by Thomas Szasz) into a dismissive category, wherein debates over what counts as a disorder become contests of value judgments rather than inquiries into health-and-illness facts. The other is to identify psychiatric progress with a slower and more complicated history of scientific development than is available for other areas of medicine. This second line of response goes as follows: A psychiatric pathology is, in some ways, a more complicated phenomenon than, say, a malfunctioning heart or diseased kidney. Thus, to take this chapter's example, Arthur's seeking to escape from crowds is distressful for him, but, so the tale goes, just which of his capacities are disabled is open to doubt and debate. There is no clear sense in psychiatry, as there often is in somatic medicine, of just where an impaired performance or symptom has its source. So the line of thought goes.

Cultural conventionalism about disorder would contribute conceptual ammunition to the picture of an unflattering contrast between somatic and psychiatric medicine. For if we adopted the perspective of conventionalism, we would have to admit that one culture could not criticize another for its inferior explanatory understanding of a mental disorder. On the contrary, if one culture condemns masturbation as, say, a mental disorder, this isn't an empirical mistake. The act of judgmental condemnation by a culture makes it a mental disorder in that culture.

Genuine scientific progress means replacing inferior ways of understanding a phenomenon with superior modes of comprehension. Breakthroughs in AIDS research would be one thing; breakthroughs in clinical depression research, if conventionalism is right, would be an oxymoron. A breakthrough? For by what criterion do we judge a new understanding of an illness to be superior? In nineteenth century Anglo-American culture, masturbation was said to be a serious sign of mental illness, which was "characterized by intense self-feeling and conceit ... derangement of thought [and] nocturnal hallucinations" (Maudsley 1867: 452). One unfortunate man in Texas had his penis amputated for treatment of the condition. Two British physicians blistered the prepuce as treatment. A large number of female cases in the office of a London physician were subjected to clitoridectomies (see Reznek 1987). To say that we have made progress in no longer thinking of masturbation as a disorder is precisely the sort of trans-cultural trans-conventional judgment that, according to disorder conventionalism, is illegitimate or without a supportive evidential foundation. It is too non-cultural.

Suppose, contrary to fact of course, that Texans still classify masturbation as a sign of a mental illness or disorder. But natives of California do not. If conventionalism is right, Californians cannot criticize Texans on grounds that they misunderstand the psychiatric status or unhealthy seriousness of masturbation. For conventionalism it matters decisively what a society or culture thinks and, when it comes to a mental disorder, no society is more backward or forward in its thinking than any another. Assuming that the same criterion of social mattering (namely conventionalism) does not hold true for somatic medicine, cardio-vascular medicine makes cross-cultural progress. Masturbation is still stuck, by contrast, hypothetically, in Texas.

(3) *We could make a mental disturbance a mental disorder just by changing the judgmental practices of a culture*. Alcohol abuse is described in DSM as a maladaptive pattern of consumption that leads to impairment and distress (APA 1994: 182–3). But the patterns allowed by DSM to count as maladaptive in a case of alcohol abuse may consist in nothing but censorious cultural/social judgments aimed at an alcohol abuser. So, if you drink heavily, "your spouse [if deemed culturally representative] can give you a mental disorder simply by arguing with you about it," causing you distress and besieging you with marital problems. Then, your spouse [culture] can also "cure you by becoming more tolerant" (Wakefield 1997: 640; see also Horwitz 2002: 102).

Consider, in a related connection, the clinical fate of homosexuality. Homosexuality was listed as a disorder in DSM-II, but following the emergence of the gay rights movement in the late 1960s, and of gay activists lobbying at meetings of the American Psychiatric Association, support shifted in 1974 from saying that it is a disorder to seeing it as a human sexual-preference variation. Homosexuality itself hadn't changed, of course, but what did change were social and cultural judgments about being gay. (Or rather, such judgments changed more or less. Bias against gays has not disappeared entirely from within the psychi-atric profession. See Soble [2004].) If there is little or no significant distress, as it were, associated with a condition, so that whatever significant disturbance is associated with it stems more or less exclusively from a culture's untutored assessment of individuals in the condition, it surely is a mistake, say critics of conventionalism, to classify the condition as a mental disorder. Culturally frowned on, yes. Socially awkward, no doubt. Serious impairment or form of mental disorder? No. My culture's judgment of my behavior may cause me distress, but should not itself constitute the fact that I am the subject of a mental disorder. Saying so does not make it so.

True, some symptoms of a disorder may be culturally or historically unique, occupying niches not replicable across cultures. However, the cultural uniqueness of symptoms is one thing; cultural conventionalism about a disorder is another. Certain disorders may also express unstable historical conditions only to disappear when conditions dissolve. In somatic medicine transient biochemical conditions may cause illnesses to occur for a period but only for a period. (Imagine that diabetes somehow disappears.) The same may wisely be expected of at least some mental disorders. Dissociative fugues or 'travelers' syndrome' – in which sufferers wander roads in trance-like states for months, and which flowered in France at the end of the nineteenth century – seems to have evaporated (see Hacking 1998). But the transience or cultural instability of a condition is not the same phenomenon as the cultural conventionality of standards of disorder. When a disorder is transient or unstable this should make us wonder why it has disappeared or whether it merely is a passing symptom of some more general condition. Conventionalism, by contrast, should make us worry that we may construct or produce disorders just by adopting certain normatively negative conventions toward persons or merely by classifying them as disordered.

The above three italicized consequences plus the existence or purported existence (noted earlier) of exemplars should lead us, I believe, to reject cultural conventionalism about disorder. It makes sound sense, I claim, to think of some disorders as disorders wherever they appear. It makes sound sense to charge DSM with containing some disorder categories that fail to qualify as disorders, because they reflect culturally biased or uninformed conventions. Finally, it makes sound sense to believe that psychiatric medicine has made and hopefully will continue to make scientific progress in the study of mental disorder.

Caution though. Dismissing cultural conventionalism as the criterion for the seriousness or disorder-nature of a psychological incapacity or form of distress by no means implies that we turn a blind eye or deaf ear to other ways in which social and cultural factors are germane to the presence of mental disorder. Conventionalism says that culture and context matter to disorder. The problem with conventionalism is not with taking culture seriously. Culture *should* be taken seriously. Cultures are the contexts in which the harmful behaviors that are indicative or symptomatic of disorder are harmful. But conventionalism ends up saying falsely that cultural conventions are criteria for disorders.

How should culture and context be taken seriously? This is a big topic. I can only speak to it briefly here.

Culture and social context are relevant to the presence or absence of disorders in personal-welfare-impacting ways. The harms with which disorders are associated are socially or culturally situated. A job lost because of an addiction. A family shattered by a parent's depression. No person is a solipsistic island.

Social/cultural factors also contribute to a condition's distinctive complaints or symptoms, vulnerability or propensity conditions, appropriate forms of treatment, and dynamics of recovery and self-reclamation. Eating disorders (like anorexia), for example, surely have something to do with exposure to Westernized norms of thin beautiful women and the fear of being socially disapproved because of being fat. Western norms help to scaffold such a disorder. Or (for another example) as Julian Leff, a professor of social and cultural psychiatry at the Institute of Psychiatry, King's College, London, notes, a disorder diagnosed as conversion hysteria and which used to be common in Europe has now "become a rarity" in Europe, even though it persists in places like Libya and North India (Leff 2000: 13). Why is that? How has the disorder become a rarity in Europe? We don't really know, but perhaps, surmises Leff, patient complaints once interpreted as signs of hysteria have metamorphosed in European cultures into complaints associated with "more cognitive forms of depression and anxiety" (Leff 2000: 13). Cultures also offer different ways of complaining about distress – of, say, describing being depressed. William Styron writes a memoir about depression; a farmer in rural Asia visits a local medical practitioner and complains of sexual impotence.

I like to sum up the above just mentioned points by saying that mental disorder is culturally situated but without being culturally defined. There are no contextually or culturally disembodied disorders. The reason for this is simple. Human mental activity is always situated. It is situated in a body/brain. The body/brain is situated in a natural and social environment. However (and this is the main lesson I wish the current section of the chapter to offer) it does not follow from this that cultural judgments or conventions decide whether a condition is a disorder.

One final point should be mentioned about culture and disorder before leaving the topic. The main reason we find disorders undesirable is not that they are undesirable for us as Americans, Asians, or Africans or just when they are contrary to standards or conventions of the cultures in which we live. The main reason we find disorders undesirable is that they are, in some sense, undesirable period – unwanted in any or virtually any context or cultural environment. They make us worse off when we have them: seriously worse off, no matter when or where we are. They gum us up.

I am tempted to claim that disorders are culturally relational without also being culturally conventional. But I fear that such a manner of speaking would be grossly misunderstood. Again, it's too elliptical. Related to what? Would it mean that mental disorders are not conditions of persons? No, it simply means that disorders are conditions that make us worse off no matter where or when (or virtually no matter where or when) we are. And we have to be *somewhere* and at *some time*. Even a hermit can suffer from obsessive-compulsive disorder. Even a monk can be profoundly depressed. But a hermit may be obsessing over cleaning roaches in a cave. A monk may be sleeping in a painful and self-imposed hair-shirt in a monastery. Each is somewhere at some time.

MIND MALADAPTED

Evolutionary speculation is a prominent feature of cognitive science as well as medicine. (I myself engage in a bit of it in this book, when talking about neurological disorders and hypotheses about standards for proper or normal brain function.) Even self-help books about somatic health and well-being now are beginning to employ evolutionarily inspired theorizing about standards of personal well-being. Here, for example, are some remarks of a physician on the clinical faculty of Columbia University's College of Physicians and Surgeons, admonishing 50-, 60- and 70-year-olds to exercise six days per week and to remain physically active. It's offered as a Darwinian nudge to physical activity and dietary prudence.

> Being sedentary is the most important signal for decay ... In nature, there is no reason to be sedentary except lack of food. Remember we grew up in Africa. No matter how plentiful the game, it rotted in hours ... You had to get up and hunt for hours every single day ... [In order to rot] store every scrap of excess food as fat, dump the immune system, melt off the muscle and let the joints decay. Time to find a cave, huddle in the corner and start shivering. [...] Our ancestors ran for their lives.
> (Crowley and Lodge 2004: 39, 46)

Our taste for sweet and fatty foods may have been adaptive in the nutritional challenges posed by the Pleistocene environment, but has since been rendered unhealthy and maladaptive by the mass availability of ice cream, fries and burgers. Unfortunately selection pressures haven't had time to select for tastes for other and healthier cuisine.

Given the prominence and popularity of evolutionary theorizing, it may appeal to somehow derive judgments about the importance and clinical seriousness of a mental incapacity from results of the theory of evolution. One general method for such a judgment's derivation goes something like this: Assume that the human mind possesses various sorts of psychological faculties and capacities that have been acquired through the mechanisms of natural selection. We have, at least in part, an evolved psychology. Then, argue that a disability is important, a loss of freedom significant, an impairment serious enough for clinical or medical attention, and so on, just when it stems from a mismatch between the activation of an evolved/selected-for faculty or capacity and the novel demands of a current environment. Randolf Nesse of the University of Michigan, and the promoter of an approach to medicine known as Darwinian medicine, has this to say about such a method of disorder-judgment warrant: Much disorder "results from differences between the environment in which we live and the environment in which we evolve." "Natural selection simply has not had the time to adopt [us] to the change in circumstances" (Nesse 2001: 187).

Here is an example or case in point for what Nesse means: anxiety among strangers.

Suppose that under specific evolutionary pressures it is adaptively useful for a person to quickly decide whether to circulate among strangers in a public or unfamiliar but crowded social space. This is perhaps especially true if a person is confronted with serious judgmental challenges that require them to decide whether to trust or rely on strangers. Hunt with them perhaps. Perhaps something perceptually simple like a certain noise level combined with various facial expressions in other persons should be taken as signs to avoid contact with them and to remove oneself from the space.

Consider anxiety of the sort that occurs in Arthur. It may be thought that the current situations that cause people (like Arthur) to be anxious are often similar to those that were dangerous in ancestral environments. Becoming anxious or fearful among noisy strangers, for example, may well have been an adaptive emotional response that guarded "against the many dangers encountered outside the home range" of tribe or family (Marks and Nesse 1994: 251). But, unfortunately, in modern urban environments, people who become anxious (or overly anxious like Arthur) away from their home turf and in noisy spaces among strangers will likely "find it all but impossible to lead a normal life" (Murphy 2006: 284). They may respond to a current environment as if, in matters of public or social intercourse, it is, in effect, similar to the ancestral environment and filled with unfriendly or untrustworthy people. Then, if or when this happens, an anxiety response in the current environment represents an important impairment or disability, not a minor quirk or handicap. It expresses a major misalignment of an old mental mechanism or response pattern in a new environment. The anxiety-response is no longer a reliable guide to intertribal danger.

Can evolutionary mismatch explanations like that just outlined stand up as criteria for disorder? Can evolutionary theory be 'adapted' to help to determine the seriousness of an impairment? The disorder of a disorder?

Answers in the literature to this question vary in a number of different ways. One answer is that evolutionary theorizing is all very intriguing in various manners; but it has little or nothing empirically verifiable or scientific to contribute to the project in psychiatry or the theory of mental illness of plotting the normative contours of a mental disorder. The anxiety-explanation sketched above is highly speculative, to be sure, and is a type of explanation that "is often unverifiable" (Gert and Culver 2004: 420). Our evidence about the details of environments, social structure, and character of human psychology in ancestral times is so meager that any hypothesis about fear or anxiety being adaptive emotional responses in specific ancestral circumstances (say, among strangers with various sorts of facial expressions) is likely to be massively underdetermined by available evidence. True, this does not mean, as the philosopher Robert Richardson wisely notes, that we should "peddle some fatuous form of philosophical skepticism" about evolutionary psychology (Richardson 2007: 381). We may wisely assume, for instance, that there were situations that "put our evolutionary ancestors in danger" and that "fear is the emotion that motivated our ancestors to cope with the dangers that they were likely to face" (Pinker 1997: 386; see also Nesse 1990). In a fit of being too finicky, we should not demand an end to any and all evolutionary speculation about human psychology. But it is mere speculation. We must be skeptical in evolutionary-hypothesis formation. Immensely cautious. The bands of hunter-gatherers who were our Pleistocene ancestors did not leave behind tools and bones that reveal the functionality of avoiding strangers or pinpoint which features of avoid-worthy strangers set off a flight alarm.

Another sort of answer is more accommodating (for helpful discussion see Murphy 2006: 281–305). It maintains that evolutionary speculation can be interwoven with questions about the grounds for speaking of a condition as a mental disorder, especially when wedded to references to what we may independently know of sub-personal or non-conscious information-processing. Just as fear of snakes or heights may have been implanted by natural selection, so apprehensiveness about strangers may have been selected for, but implemented in an anxiety-producing brain mechanism triggered by stimuli or features of the social environment that are not consciously appreciated or self-reflectively processed by a person.

Suppose (caution about speculation aside) we assume that fear of strangers and anxiety over traveling in crowds is an evolved trait, and that Arthur's emotional response is a maladaptive mismatch between this implanted response pattern and one or more features of current circumstance. Would that make his disability serious or clinically significant? A disorder? As part of the mismatch, say, Arthur complains that when he performs or associates with others publicly he becomes hyper-aware of every gesture he makes. His voice becomes high-pitched and reedy, his forehead drips with sweat, and his heart beats rapidly with noticeable palpitations. Unbeknownst to him these may be signs that his autonomic nervous system is preparing for a so-called 'fight or flight response' (perhaps apposite under certain ancestral circumstances). Suppose, in fact, Arthur actually is in a fight/flight mode, just as his primeval ancestors were when confronting an alien tribe or a mysterious group of hunter-gatherers. Suppose, too, that he somehow misinterprets the activation of his body's fight/flight response as evidence of an impending somatic disaster (say, heart attack). In support of this sort of supposition (namely that Arthur misinterprets the activation of his autonomic nervous system) a large and independent body of empirical literature suggests that panic-attack or -disorder victims actually do tend to be hyper-attentive to internal physiological cues (Barlow 1988: 108, 232). As David Barlow and his co-authors write: "Clinical observations over the years have indicated that patients with anxiety disorders, particularly panic disorder, seem to evidence greater awareness of internal bodily states and are constantly vigilant for any somatic changes that might signal the beginning of the next panic attack" (Barlow et al. 1996: 266). Such somatic states 'irrupt' into their experience of themselves as embodied subjects.

Now introduce medication into the story. Suppose that since his hospital admission, Arthur has been receiving treatment with Inderal, a trade name for a beta-blocker. The medication does not directly alter Arthur's conscious distress, but it does block somatic signals of the fight-or-flight response. It keeps the heart from pounding, sweat from dripping, and voice from trembling. It does not by itself make Arthur relax, but it strips his body of signs that he otherwise misreads as signals of impending disaster. The absence or suppression of such signs does, in turn, make him relax. The mode of the drug's action is indirect but effective.

With the help of the example of Arthur are we there yet? Have we identified a source of norms for seriousness or clinical significance? Maladaptation of an evolved response mechanism (namely a fight/flight response in a state of anxiety), which is unsuited to a current environment.

To make mismatch work as a criterion of clinical significance the mismatch must explain what makes the inappropriate response pathological or a disorder. The problem with Arthur is that his response is not just one of anxiety, but so extreme, so pathological. His reaction is not merely a hair-triggered response to avoid strangers but an overreaction, an utter panic. It is one thing for him to become anxious when he should not be, another for him to interpret shopping in a mall or attending a parent-teacher association meeting as an impending catastrophe. His reaction is not merely an expression of inappropriate or 'mismatched' sensitivity, but of anticipated trauma. And *this* feature of his response (the feature that helps to make it a mental disorder) so far is left unexplained by the evolutionary speculation (offered above). Something is not just misplaced in his response but wrong in its depth and resonance.

Presumably the evolutionary view concerns when to avoid strangers or when to go into a fight or flight mode. And there is no doubt, as Dominic Murphy aptly puts it, that "breakdowns in [our] psychology" have something to do with "how evolved minds are organized" (Murphy 2006: 305). But the difficulty is that (if the example of Arthur as discussed here is representative) the mismatch between responses that were adaptive in ancestral environments and responses given changes in current environments has got to pick out the clinical seriousness of an impairment (of a mismatch). Mismatches are not themselves disorders unless responses in the current environment are over-reactive or harmful or deleterious.

In light of this difficulty, we may indulge in additional evolutionary speculation. Perhaps some of our ancestors did panic when in the presence of strangers. Perhaps that was a good thing for them or for their tribe. Perhaps suffering from an excess of anxiety was correct at least sometimes. Perhaps such a variation in anxiety response patterns is heritable. Perhaps Arthur's hyper-reactive autonomic nervous system reveals him to be one of those 'ancestral' panickers. Perhaps.

But now skepticism about evolutionary speculation should begin, I think, to kick in. Inventive evolutionary perhaps-tales can be told. But we can't hope to understand the nature of mismatches unless we understand the problems for which the earlier evolved responses were adaptive. One big worry concerns the massive diversity of behaviors that human beings perform – from culture to culture, circumstance to circumstance, or individual to individual. Do we know or have good reason to believe that some of our ancestors panicked or, if they did, when or what set their alarms off? Whether or not a proclivity to panic (among strangers) was ultimately 'wired up' in specific individuals in ancestral circumstances whose relevant aspects persist in modern urban environments (in similarly 'wired up' individuals, like Arthur) is something we can only guess at. And I mean *guess*. The necessity of such guesswork surely does not augur well for the project of identifying ancestral/current environmental-response mismatches as a warrant base or standard for the attribution of a mental disorder.

So, we still need a standard in terms of which to evaluate the importance or clinical significance of a disability in *current* circumstances. We are still looking for a norm for the seriousness of a disability, something that helps to qualify it as a disorder. Undiscoverable distal sources say nothing about the immediate character and harmful consequences of a disorder.

RATIONALITY AND INTENTIONALITY

Immanuel Kant (1724–1804) asked what distinguishes the harmful behavior of a foolish person or buffoon from that of the "the mentally disordered." He claimed that "they differ not merely in degree but in the distinctive quality of mental discord." What is the distinctive quality of mental discord? The subject of a mental disorder may need to be controlled or directed, he said, "by someone else's reason." A fool or buffoon does not. The reasoning of such people remains intact. Not that of a victim of mental illness (Kant 2000 [1793]: 199).

I would not wish to defend Kant's account of disorder precisely in the form that he himself may have intended (which likely is too intellectualistic, knowing Kant). But, like him, I believe that the best standard or norm for the sort of inability or impairment that is distinctive of a mental disorder is that the subject behaves, and cannot help but behave, in various *irrational*, *unreasonable* or *reason-unresponsive* (or *unwarranted* and so on) ways. Unlike the choices, behaviors, moods or thoughts of thousands of other people who make unreasonable choices or behave in ways that are harmful or imprudent, those of a subject of mental disorder are unreasonable or unwise in ways that they cannot voluntarily or responsibly control. Perhaps they engage in patently inappropriate or deleterious means to try to achieve their purposes or ends, make grossly harmful and unwarranted inferences from their perceptual experiences, or unwisely disengage from otherwise deeply valued personal relationships or ideals. Their best interests are not represented by their behavior, but they themselves are too 'gummed up' to help it or to do anything directly about their deeds. If I (not a subject of a mental disorder) act unreasonably although I am capable of doing otherwise, then my behavior may be imputed to a flawed character or foolhardy temperament, or to vicissitudes of performance (such as simple bad luck, motivational distraction, fatigue or circumstantial constraint). But when Arthur acts irrationally or unreasonably in refusing to enter a mall or to attend a parent/teacher-association meeting, as an individual with a mental disorder, his behavior is no mere performance lapse, mark of fatigue, or blemish of character. Insofar as he is the subject of a mental disorder his 'reason-unresponsiveness' is due to one or more psychological impairments that render him incapable of behaving otherwise. His behavior should be responsive or receptive to the good reasons he has (and is aware that he has) for entering a mall or attending a public meeting. But if we recognize that he is agoraphobic, then we must realize that he cannot enter the mall or attend the meeting, no matter how hard he tries and even though it is in his interest to do so.

The notion that the subject of a mental disorder is impaired in one or more forms of exercise of reason is capable of being developed in a number of different ways. Care must be taken in how it is developed. In this section of the chapter I make some suggestions for how the notion may be used as a norm or standard for a mental disorder or for the seriousness of a condition that qualifies as a mental disorder.

Descriptions of the nature of reason and reasoning vary along various dimensions. Toward one end of one of these dimensions is a position according to which the only aspects of human psychology that are amendable to assessments of their rationality or reason-responsiveness are questions about the consistency or coherence of thought. At the opposite end of this dimension is a position that claims that assessments of reason-responsiveness or rationality are not restricted to thought, or to questions of coherence and consistency, but may be focused on or applied to the full spectrum of human mental states (including moods and emotions) as well as to the overall wisdom or prudence of a person's choices or behavior. These two classes of positions may be said to belong to a *narrow logicist* or intellectualist notion of reason and to a *broadly personal* notion, respectively.

The broadly personal notion is the notion of rationality or reason that I shall be adopting. To gain some traction on the notion and its application to a mental disorder, it is helpful to focus in more detail on how we should think of the Intentionality, aboutness or directedness of the mental.

The philosopher John Searle writes: "Once you have [I]ntentionality ... you already have the phenomena that internally and constitutively possess ... rationality" (Searle 2001: 23). "Rationality," he says, is a "constitutive structural feature of ... Intentionality. When I say that it is constitutive and structural, I do not mean that we always ... think rationally, but rather that ... constraints set by rationality are built in as intrinsic features of intentional states" (Searle 2007: 15). Rationality is not "something added to ... mind" (ibid: 9). Rather: "You cannot have ... Intentionality" without it (ibid: 16).

Donald Davidson (1917–2003) writes: "When thought takes thought as its subject matter, the observer can only identify what he is studying by finding it rational" (Davidson 2004: 98). The ascription (or presence) of thinking, believing, intending and other attitudes (with Intentionality) depends on an assumption of the presence in the person who thinks, believes or intends, of a broad or personal-level rationality.

There are a number of ways of explaining just why the attribution and presence of Intentionality presupposes rationality. For reasons of space I will be brief and confine myself to two sorts of explanation.

One has to do with the very idea of Intentional content or what an attitude (thought, belief, etc.) is about. I will focus on beliefs and their contents.

Contents of beliefs require a medium in which they mean just what they mean. A meaning medium. The medium consists of (what are called) concepts. How is it that we are able to possess beliefs about things that are very far away in space or time (e.g. Abraham Lincoln, Mars) or things that fail to exist (e.g. Santa Claus, unicorns) as well as things close at hand or that do exist (e.g. the bachelor who lives next door, salt)? The simple and intuitive idea is that belief (or Intentional) contents are concepts or conceptual contents. They are *conceptual*. I can believe that Lincoln was assassinated, because I have concepts of Lincoln as well as of assassination. I can believe that the bachelor who is living next door is dating my cousin, because I have concepts of bachelor, living next door, dating and cousin. Inside this conceptual medium all kinds of other beliefs or contents are possible as well. If I believe that a bachelor is dating my cousin, I can also believe that my cousin is dating a bachelor. If I can believe that President Lincoln was assassinated, and that Mars is a planet, I can believe that Lincoln was assassinated but not on Mars.

The conceptual medium of the contents of attitudes helps to distinguish one sort of content or attitude from another. Suppose that Lois Lane believes that she kissed Clark Kent. Clark Kent is Superman. Does this mean that she also believes that she kissed Superman? No, not if she fails to apply the concept of Superman to Clark Kent. Intentional content is distinctive or differential in its conceptual character. So, there is a genuine difference between, for example, Lois believing that Superman can fly and believing that Clark Kent can fly or between my believing that I am attending a parent/teacher-association meeting and my believing that I am attending a meeting in a local high-school auditorium.

Concepts exhibit a property of connectivity one with another. Attribution of conceptual content presupposes other concepts in a person's possession. Suppose when I say "President Lincoln was assassinated," I have grown senile and now suffer from a serious neural disorder evidenced by unusual memory loss (Stich 1983: 55–6). So, if, for example, you ask me whether Lincoln is dead, I reply that I do not know. If asked whether the vice-president took office after the assassination, I ask "Vice-president? What's a vice-president?" In brief, suppose I have no grasp of the notions of either assassination or presidency, although I apparently claim that Lincoln was assassinated. How should we understand this? What is going on in me? What does my saying (or thinking) 'President Lincoln was assassinated' mean to me? Do I believe that Lincoln was assassinated? Is that the content of my thought? Is there a state of my mind that contains the Intentional content *that Lincoln was assassinated*?

Intuitively, it seems that I mean or think no such thing whatsoever. Here is an argument based on assuming that there is a connection between Intentionality and rationality that explains the warrant for that intuitive conviction. It goes like this.

The identity or distinctiveness of an Intentional/conceptual content is positional. Its character depends on its position in a scheme or network of concepts with which it is *rationally* connected. If a person does not realize that assassination constitutes death, or that vice-presidents succeed presidents, and fails in similar recognitions, they do not *really* believe that Lincoln was assassinated. They may say that they believe it, but they don't. They don't because they lack the proper conceptual storehouse, network or medium in which to harbor such a belief. Whatever else such a person believes it's not *that*.

Think, by analogy, of a baseball game. First base is what it is because second base is what it is, and so on. Each of these two bases also is game-wise connected with other bases and appropriate forms of behavior on the part of players, as determined by rules of the game. The identity of each base is positional. A base in a game without any other base is not first base. A game without multiple bases is not a baseball game.

Perhaps when you ask me if Lincoln was assassinated, and I reply that, yes, he was, I am simply remembering a sentence that I read in a high-school American history text. I've forgotten entirely what it means. The concept I am working with is not that of a president or assassination, but of the pictorial image of a sentence on a page. I am on a base, but it's not first base, for there is no second base (see also Graham 1998: 65–86).

As Searle puts it, there is no Intentionality without rationality. Or as I like to put it, there is no Intentionality without Intentional content; and no Intentional content without a rationally interconnected network of concepts.

There are other and related ways of trying to explain why Intentionality presupposes rationality. I said I would mention two. Here is the second explanation.

Thinking of Intentional attitudes (beliefs, desires, and so on) as presupposing the rationality of persons makes it clear that we persons are purposive or goal directed in behavior and that how we act or behave depends on our purposes or reasons for acting. So, for example, suppose I am crossing a busy street, with eyes wide open, and a truck is barreling down toward me. I spot it. Suppose I scurry away from its path. Why do I do so? Here is an explanation: Because I believe that if the truck hits me I will get hurt or killed. I desire not to be hurt or killed. Being rational, I move away from its path. Much of human purposive behavior is, as Daniel Dennett puts it, "simply not interpretable except as being in the rational service of some beliefs and desires or other" (Dennett 2009: 348). One role (a definitive or constitutive role) of Intentional states and attitudes is their serving as a *locus of reason responsive* or purposive or goal directed behavior. Absent seeing the truck or desiring not to get hurt, I would not have scurried. I would not have had a reason to move. There would have been no purpose to scurrying.

As Searle might put it, rationality is not something added to beliefs and desires (or Intentional attitudes). It is central to their role in helping to govern and control purposive or reason responsive behavior.

These explanations of the connectivity between Intentionality and rationality are brief. They also raise questions that I do not pursue here. But they at least give, I hope, the flavor of warrant for the position that Searle and numerous other theorists (including, in different ways, Davidson and Dennett) favor. Wherever there is Intentionality, there is rationality.

It is sometimes charged that this idea or thesis that Intentional states or attitudes are in their nature or character rational (hereafter the *rationality-in-Intentionality thesis* or 'RIT' for short) is defeated by decisive counter-examples. For example, it is said, I may deny some claim that I report believing to be true. I may deny that I have a brother in Cleveland, all the while saying that I believe my brother lives in Cleveland. So, the charge goes, it is false that rationality norms are built into the presence, assumption or concept of Intentionality (see Bortolotti 2004).

There are at least two difficulties with purported counter-examples to RIT, however. One is whether persons described in alleged counter-examples really do assert, think or believe what a counter-example says they do. Do I *really* understand what it means to deny that I have a brother in Cleveland, if I say also that I believe that I have a brother in Cleveland? Isn't it better to question my understanding of the meaning of my denial (or the sincerity of my purported belief report) rather than to assume that I am being inconsistent and irrational? Or perhaps I am ambiguously using the word 'Cleveland' to designate two different locales, one the city in Ohio, the other the small town in Alabama. Perhaps I am denying that I have a brother in Alabama, but affirming his existence in Ohio. The other (and connected) difficulty is that RIT, to some extent, is an elliptical target. How so? A fan of RIT does not have to deny the occurrence of 'irrational' behavior on the part of a person. All of us can be foolish or imprudent. RIT does not assume that we are all *perfectly* rational or responsive to reason (whatever perfection means).

One simple form of accommodation of at least some departures from perfect rationality is to note that sometimes attitudes do not function as genuine attitudes. A purported belief may not behave like a belief. Just as an artifact may not behave as designed, but function in an atypical manner, so a belief or desire may not function as a belief or desire, although it still may help to control behavior in some other and albeit a-rational way. (I shall have more to say about this topic below.) Another form of accommodation is to note that sometimes we behave in ways that are unwise, short-sighted or perverse and irrational in such cases, not in the logic-textbook sense of being inconsistent (although perhaps also that), but because we depart in ways that are not in our best interest or are grossly and overtly incompatible with our well-being or welfare. RIT must respect this fact about the notions of the rational/irrational. There is no simple formula for determining the balance or identifying the presence of rationality or irrationality in the behavior or psychological make-up of a person. Sometimes senselessness is easy to catch, when, for instance, I seem to contradict myself. But at other times the grounds for a proper normative evaluation are more elusive.

If RIT is correct, broadly speaking, a description of the Intentional states and attitudes of a person in no way resembles a list of brute causal connections, correlations or mere 'mechanical' associations between states and behavior. This is because in order for states to be genuine beliefs, honest-to-goodness desires, and so on, or to act as such and not as anomalies of attitudes, they must conform to standards or norms of rationality and reasonableness.

Suppose you learn that your best friend has just died in Boston. You grieve because you love him deeply and know you will never see him again. You feel his death as a profound loss. The world is cold and empty without him. You don't feel his death as if you have just won a lottery. You don't delight in the news. That would be bizarre, senseless. It would mean that your states or attitudes are not connected according to norms of reason. Loss of a loved one ought to spell grief, not frivolity. If you do feel delight, this may mean that your mind somehow is being pushed or pulled into senseless or unreasonable reactions. How can you possibly be pleased as punch that he is dead? That's not how the loss of a loved one *ought* to be received if they are loved but believed lost forever and you are being sensible in your associated attitudes and reactions.

The rational person, in the RIT sense, ideally is not merely devoid of illogical or inconsistent attitudes, but someone with a definite positive description of their character and goals in life (see Feinberg 1989: 107). If possible, they choose after deliberation, avoid acting on unreflective impulses, and maintain a certain level of prudence, self-regard or self-responsibility that balances their present or current preferences against next week's and next year's, those of mid-life and possible old age. They take pains to manage preferences or goals and to connect themselves with the world as well as with other people in important and satisfying ways, so as to try to achieve a measure of satisfaction or fulfillment over the course of a life (of which more in the next chapter). After all, we live in relation with others and so to a significant extent, a person's rationality or reasonableness should be assessed, in part, in terms of their relationships with other persons and the world. Recognizing this is important for the theory of mental disorder, for at the level at which judgments of the presence of a mental disorder are made, a person is not positioned just in relationship to himself, his powers of reason are not characterized just in terms of internal or logic-textbook-type features, but also in terms of what is required in order for them (as William Bechtel puts it) "to operate as a situated organism" (Bechtel 2008: 258). That is, to deal with the world in reason-responsive ways and to lead a purposive and purposeful life in social context and environmental circumstance.

I shall assume hereafter that RIT is true. I do not examine all that needs to be examined to systematically defend this assumption. But I am after the general spirit of the view and anxious to show how it helps to evaluate the seriousness or clinical severity of impairments and harmful incapacities that are distinctive of a mental disorder. I must mention (as noted above), again, though, that Intentional states do not always function as states with Intentionality, just as hammers, keys or other artifacts do not always function as hammers or keys.

Consider the following three explanations of a behavior:

(1) I phoned my friend's wife because I wished to offer her my sympathies.
(2) I got a bad backache because I wanted to see my deceased friend again.
(3) I got a bad backache because I slept on a mattress with hard lumps and broken coils.

The first two explanations look quite similar in that they each make reference to an Intentional state, namely a wishing or wanting, in explanation of behavior. Number (3) makes no such reference. Its form is simply *C caused E* (i.e. sleeping on hard lumps and broken coils caused a backache). But (2) actually is as much like (3) as it is like (1), although in a different sort of way, for (2) also is of the form of C caused E (i.e. wanting to see my deceased friend caused a bad backache). In that sense (namely the C-caused-E sense, the mechanical cause/effect sense), my state of wanting to see my deceased friend acted like broken mattress coils. Even though the state in question was a wanting (an Intentional state and not a sleeping on coils), it did not function as an Intentional state. It functioned somehow just like the coils. Purely mechanically or brute causality. My desire to see my friend did not make sense of, rationalize or warrant my getting a backache, although it somehow was responsible for the ache. (How it may do so I do not surmise. Perhaps through its neurochemical base.) By contrast, the Intentional state referred to in (1) namely of wanting to express sympathy did perform like an Intentional state. It made sense of or provided a rationale for my phoning my friend's wife. Phoning her stemmed from wanting to express sympathy. Phoning her was sensible or warranted – rational. Being rational, I made the call. It was part of my trying to connect with other people in a purposive and satisfying way.

The general lesson here? Intentional states, once an agent is capable of them and once they possess their identity or distinctiveness through rational connectivity with other attitudes and behavior, may not always function like Intentional states. (They may not always express their identity as endowed with Intentional content.) So, reference to them does not always help us to make sense of a person's behavior. Making sense of behavior requires that we discern some rationale or measure of reason-responsiveness in behavior. But there can be brute causal connections between Intentional states and behavior without any rational connection also being in place. When Intentional states or attitudes do function or function properly as Intentional states, as states connected in rational patterns, when, that is, they perform as beliefs and desires and not like coils or elements in brute causal relations, they therein measure up to norms or standards of rationality. That's RIT's point. To be Intentional, to possess aboutness, directionality or Intentionality, and for an Intentional state to guide, direct or control purposive behavior in terms of its Intentional content, it must measure up to norms of reason or reasonableness.

Perhaps an analogy will offer additional help in understanding the notion of the normative or rationality presuppositions of Intentionality. Remember, again, the American baseball game referred to in the fourth chapter. Now think of a player swinging a bat. Consider the following two explanations of his behavior:

(1) The player swung the bat because he was trying to hit a home run.
(2) The player swung the bat because he was trying to chase a rabbit from the field of play.

In each case a bat is swung, but only in the first is it functioning as a bat (as an artifact designed to hit balls in a baseball game). The first case describes the bat functioning both as it can and should. The second speaks of the bat functioning only as it can. Not as it should (or was designed to function). Rabbit chaser? A mere stick would have done as well. The rabbit would not have known the difference. He was not part of the game. Likewise, Intentional states may function as they both can and should (as in explanation [1]) or merely as they can (explanation [2]).

Philosophers who are sympathetic to physicalism or the identity thesis about mentality often worry about the physical make-up or constitution of Intentional states and attitudes and of the nature of the connections among them. How can neurochemical/neurobiological states or conditions compose Intentional states and attitudes and also respect or comport with the reasoning powers of persons? We are not like clay statues, which come into being when a lump of clay is molded in a certain way, and perish, outlived by the lump, when the statue is squashed. Intentionality is no mere matter of the shape of neural cells or particles. It's a matter of Intentional content, of aboutness or directionality, a radically different feature from the statue-likeness of certain lumps of clay. Much of the energy and intellectual efforts of such fields as cognitive neuroscience, sub-personal information-processing psychology, so-called teleosemantic theories of conceptual content and other brain- and behavior-research programs are devoted to figuring out how the material mechanisms of the brain (together with activities outside the skull and skin) enable or generate Intentionality, and permit persons to be rational. I alluded to such a worry in our earlier discussion in Chapter 4 of Intentional-content efficacy and of Fred Dretske's example of a soprano and her aria.

But my interest here in this book is not in deciding how Intentionality or rationality comes into being through neural processing or activity. And it is not in demanding that there must be a physically kosher account (that avoids anti-realism about mental disorder and dualism about mind/body) of the neural composition of Intentional attitudes. My interest here is in deciding whether we can and should deploy a thesis like RIT in classifying mental disorders as disorders and in understanding when an incapacitation or impairment counts as a mental disorder. My question is: Does a disorder's manner or mode of irrationality or unreasonableness help to serve as a standard for a mental disorder? My answer is yes. It does help.

Depending on how an incapacity is understood, if it is an incapacity in reason-responsiveness (that is marked by the autograph of mentality), such a fact helps to constitute a mental disorder. The subject of a mental disorder is disposed to think, feel, or act in unreasonable ways, not because they are fatigued, foolish, or under severe time constraints, or out of ignorance or ill-humor, but because impairments or deficits in rational or reason-responsive functioning are associated with a mental disorder. Those of us who are reasonable may govern our own affairs, feel as we should when a beloved friend dies, and refrain from impulses to act in self-injurious ways. But a subject of agoraphobia, like Arthur, he may be unable to enter a mall to buy a blouse or to be present, as he should, at a parent/teacher-association meeting. He may tell you that he would rather die than have a recurrence of his intense anxiety. From a reason-responsive point of view the disorder keeps him from leading a satisfying life and endangers him.

A drug addict may consume a drug, and decide to take the drug at self-recognized grievous danger to bodily health, and we may ask "how could anyone do that?" or were they "out of their mind" or do they possess "some sort of irrational death wish." We may be mystified by their pattern of self-destructive consumption. If the person knows that the behavior harms them, why engage in it? It just does not seem to make sense. The behavior appears to be utterly uncalled for.

Now complexity or a qualification arises. A distinction needs to be made when we look closer at the unreason associated with a mental disorder. Interestingly, the above general sentiment about mental disorder, namely that the domain of disorder is the domain of sense-lessness or unreason, is a notion that Karl Jaspers endorsed (see Fulford et al. 2006: 170; Bentall 2004: 28). Jaspers offered the standard specifically to apply to the presence of a *severe* mental disorder or psychosis (as in schizophrenia), which he described as un-understandable or as intelligible only in non-mentalistic and neuromechanical coil-like terms and not in terms of an individual's beliefs and desires.

As will be evident later in the book in discussing delusions, I don't agree with Jaspers about the *utter* lack of reason or the complete and swamping presence of a-rationality in mental disorders (even severe ones). In mental disorder and in various other mental conditions, there is causation both without (rational) Intentionality and with (rational) Intentionality. A mixture. Even in severe mental disorders, as long as a disorder is something *mental*, it is not utterly senseless. In it reason is truncated, compromised or impaired, not obliterated. Senselessness is present, to some hefty measure, but not utterly so.

So I like to distinguish between two possible ways (only one of which is the right way) in which to understand the unreason of a mental disorder, which I call the *total* and the *partial* presence of unreason. In neurological disorders reason is totally or utterly un-present (along relevant dimensions of behavior). Consider, for example, the class of such disorders known as neurologically degenerative diseases or diseases associated with degenerative atrophy of the brain (perhaps as a result of pathology of the nerve cells, Andreasen's literal "cells gone bad"). Numerous such disorders produce a diffuse loss of brain function across the cortex and within multiple subcortical structures. Multiple sclerosis. Pick's disease. Progressive epilepsy. In a mental disorder, by contrast, rational and a-rational forces are operative together and unfold in characteristic interactive ways. If we understand a disorder by reference to such forces, we can and must admit to an ongoing role for reason-responsiveness or rationality in the expression of the disorder's symptoms.

To illustrate: Let's return to Arthur. This time we will deploy the notion of the rational Intentional mind that we have been outlining as RIT. On the normative conception of the mental that I am sketching and endorsing, Arthur's impairment in public behavior, his disability, counts as clinically important (as the sort involved in a mental disorder) not just because it robs him of various social freedoms and is a source of conscious distress or harm, but because it makes his behavior, in effect, something quite senseless or mindless and not possible for him to responsibly control. Why should he be panicking? For him to avoid parent/teacher-association meetings as well as other public occasions is inconsistent with his duties as a teacher and discordant with his wish to be a successful professional educator. Yet he cannot help it. No matter how hard he tries. No matter the efforts of others to persuade him. It makes no good sense, we may think, to be gripped by such a fear given the overall circumstances of his life.

It may be wondered why our explanatory understanding of a mental disorder requires reference to a-rational neural activity at all if the brain is undamaged. Why not just deploy the language of Intentionality in a case like Arthur's, together perhaps with discussion of a person's temperament, judgmental biases, biography or learning history – but nary a word about brain activity? Refer only to powers of reason, situated or contextualized to the biographic details of the person. Call such rejection of the need to deploy brain science in the explanation of mental disorder *anti-neuralism*.

If anti-neuralism is to tell us that the subject's mental capacities are reason-intact and unimpaired by a-rational mechanical forces, this seems to imply that mental disorders, so to speak, are not disorders. They are not gummed up. The 'mental' of such a condition (the mental thought of as essentially rational) would rule out the disorder of it (although it may permit other liabilities, wishful thinking, prejudices and so on). This would leave something highly puzzling about a case like Arthur's. We would lack a full understanding of why he, not merely does not favorably respond, but cannot favorably respond, to his reasons for mixing among crowds. His responses are not under appositely rational control. Reference to the gumming-up role of his autonomic nervous system would be unwisely neglected by the explanatory story.

Perhaps a version of anti-neuralism would partition persons into distinct temporally or spatially mental or Intentional agents or selves, each with their own Intentionality or zone of rationality intact, but riddled as sets by intractable conflicts, values or preferences between them, like an ungovernable Faculty Affairs Committee or bellicose nation states, overlapping in mutual coherence on occasion, but otherwise pointing fingers and sometimes swords at each other in irresolvable disagreements. Addictive behavior patterns are sometimes pictured in this manner. One's temporally immediate self, it is said, makes choices that knowingly harm later selves – and therein the immediate self is imperious. It insists that satisfactions fall within its hyper-proximate temporal domain, distant selves be damned. But which temporally or spatially distributed selves make up a whole or single person and how are they individuated or distinguished? Putting a series- or sets-of-selves view together destroys the notion of a single subject or agent – the individual person with a disorder. Your memories and your past tend to interact with your desires and your beliefs to produce actions and activities that stretch out over time. The time of *your* life. Reading this book. Securing a college degree. Marrying a soulmate. It also turns out, I assume, that your mental states and attitudes are realized in (or if dualism is true, interact directly with) your one brain, and only your brain. You are one subject, one embodied person, despite qualitative alterations in your personality over time, despite the dramatic discordances of some disorders. You are *the* addict. You are *the* person who is paranoid or clinically depressed. Though different parts of or episodes of a person's life may conflict with others, there seems no real sense in which, for one and the same person, if broken up into spatially or temporally distributed and partially autonomous selves, a mental disorder could be his or her disorder. It seems to make much more conceptual sense to think of the gum or disorder of disorder, not as a feature of discordant selves or semi-autonomous agents that compose a person (whatever that may mean), but as consisting (in part) of non-rational/a-rational/mechanical/brute neural forces irrupting into the space of a person's reasons or Intentionality and being partly responsible for the truncation or impairment in reason and rational control that helps to constitute a disorder. Not irrupting in the imperious or destructive manner in which a neural disorder may dislocate a person or fasten onto them. But doing so in a hand-in-hand manner with a person's Intentionality or rationality so as to help to produce (what I am calling) the truncated rationality of a disorder (of which more later).

So, according to the view of RIT that I am promoting or in the process of promoting here, there are irruptions of brute a-rationality into the rational operation of this or that faculty or competence or affecting the otherwise more fully sensible behavior of a person. But these leave operative elbow room for reason in the onset and character of a disorder.

An analogy may help with this idea.

Suppose you are picnicking with some family and friends on a beach. You take a nap. While you are napping the tide comes in and irrupts into the space of the picnic. You feel the wetness of the water, awake startled, gather your blankets and food and then retreat to higher ground. The picnic has been disrupted. It's not the same event anymore. It's not what you wanted in a picnic. Certain of its purposes have been blunted. Everyone is disappointed. But the picnic has not totally been wiped out or destroyed. Some corn on the cob and salad remains to be eaten, though the blanket is wet in spots and some family members, especially the cousins from Newark, now want to go home. Call this an analogue of the *disruptive–irruptive way of the neural in a mental disorder*. It helps to produce disorder. It contributes gum. It impairs or helps to incapacitate, but does not obliterate. A picnic of sorts (some measure of reason) remains.

Suppose the very next week you and the others picnic on the same beach again. Again you take a nap. While you are napping the ocean floor is damaged by a huge meteorite. The reverberations cause a tsunami. At the moment it is miles out to sea. You awake. You hear something both sonorous and sinister. A thunderous ocean mass is approaching in the middle distance. You spot nothing yet. But sense it. Leaving all manner and matter of the picnic behind, you and your family hurriedly leave the beach. You run to your motel. Once in the lobby you are directed to the top floor. This does not merely compromise or truncate your picnic, but it enters into the space of the picnic in a destructive way. The beach is cleared. Call this analogue the *destructive–irruptive way of the neural in a neurological disorder* (or a case of brain damage). A person sees; but then his striate cortex is severely damaged; he is rendered blind. A person speaks; but then cysts form on her third ventricle; and she speaks no more. She is rendered mute.

This may sound like a neat distinction: simply drop the thought that all irruptions of neural mechanisms into the exercise of a person's reason, broadly understood, are the same in impact and purport. Simply say that some irruptions of the neural compose neural disorders (the rational function, destructive ones), some not (the rational function, truncating ones; the mental disorder ones). But if this helps to distinguish between the role of the neural in a neurological disorder and the role of the neural in a mental disorder, it creates its own problems, of course. (Alas, no account of either sort of disorder is problem-free.) Some mental disorders help to cause neurological ones. Some disorders are not so neatly classified but constitute borderline cases. Still, I (who wish to live in the Land of Prototypes) am going to stick with it and will try to explain and defend it over the course of the rest of the book. On the approach I am recommending, there is something different about disorders associated with brain damage (neurological disorders) and disorders not associated with brain damage, the difference being that in the former case the (proximate) sources of a disorder can be fully comprehended in mechanistic (brute a-rational neural) terms, whereas in the latter case they cannot. But in the latter case a person's behavior fails in some significant measure to conform to standards of rational or reason-responsive behavior, and this is puzzling. So, we need to look for some a-rational mechanism to be partly responsible, even if we are certain or reasonably certain that the mechanism itself is not broken or fully responsible for the behavior.

LOGIC OF ITS OWN

Given a team of crackerjack neuroscientists, unlimited time and resources, and enough unbiased patience, could this team explain the onset of a mental disorder without recourse to the attribution of states or attitudes with Intentionality (Intentional content, etc.)? I say not. If it is a mental disorder it is not utterly mindless; it reflects in its origins or propensity conditions a role for Intentionality. Perhaps 'mental disorders' are never properly so-called and all disorders listed in DSM are neurological disorders. But we have utterly no reason to believe that that is the case. Even the truth of physicalism does not require that that is the case.

Let's inspect the normative failure of Arthur's panic attacks. Is his behavior *utterly* mindless, senseless? If that particular conclusion is hard to swallow, namely of Arthur's complete senselessness, the following may be the explanation. Isn't the mind *sometimes* infused with at least a sliver or shadow of reason or rationality even when the person appears to be behaving in a rather reason-unresponsive fashion or to be suffering from a mental disorder? Certainly not every behavioral performance in which a mind is at work has to display robust or perfect rational competence or coherence. Sometimes a good reason for someone's behavior is buried in noise, distraction, or gummed up by the unhelpful influence of some a-rational if not impaired brute causal neurological mechanism.

Jonathan Lear refers to the proclivity or vulnerability of the human mind to lapse into partial but not complete unreason as a tendency to exhibit a "strange logic of its own", a "weird intelligibility" or "cunning of unreason" (Lear 1998: 84). The vulnerability in question, he says, does not turn mental disorder into order, "but it does bequeath to [a mental disorder] its own intelligibility" (84). When robust reason is absent, some measure of rationality may still, albeit perhaps in a hidden and complex guise, exhibit its presence, and therein reason is not totally missing in a behavior. So, how may it be present?

Panic attacks, paranoia, addiction, grandiose delusional disorder, each of these and other disorders, possess their own partial rationales. Each contains its own mix of reason and unreason. Just how robust the 'logic' is depends on how close a disorder is to being mentally exemplary and less like a neurological one. The more exemplary, then the more prominent is its presence. In non-mental neurological disorders like Alzheimer's, by contrast, rationality does not figure at all in the immediate propensity conditions or proximate sources of a disorder. Alzheimer's-type dementia is classified by DSM as a mental disorder (APA 1994: 139–43). There is no doubt that states of Intentionality or aboutness play a role in the progression of its symptoms (once the disorder itself is present). Victims may suffer from thoughts of theft and paranoia, which, in the context of the amnesia and confusion associated with the condition, may be misinterpretations of mislaying or misplacing objects (forgetting where they have been placed). Additionally, sadness and depression are often present in individuals with Alzheimer's and may reflect changes in a victim's perception of disturbed social relationships and diminished personal autonomy. A kind of learned helplessness sets in or takes over. Sad but true.

But I do not count (and neither does Kleinman or Bentall) Alzheimer's as a mental disorder. It's certainly no exemplar. This is because, much like, say, Down's, reference to Intentional states or attitudes just does not figure in the best explanation of its origin, source or developmental propensity. The disease (and, yes, it may also be classified as a disease and not just neural impairment) appears due to plagues and neurofibrillary tangles that form in the hippocampus and spread throughout the cerebral cortex, in specific areas or systems of the brain associated with both dementia and amnesia (Andreasen 2001: 263–5; Lovestone 2000: 392). It's a neurological disorder. The mental plays various subsequent or post-onset roles in Alzheimer's (once the pleats of its symptoms start to spread out and influence each other) and is responsible, quite directly, as just noted, for some of its symptoms, emotional disorientation or content. But no form of genuine Intentionality plays a role in the origin of the condition itself. Brute neurological or mechanical forces are the source of its degenerative progression and memory impairment.

In exemplary mental disorders (as I will continue to argue in the book and have often said earlier) Intentionality is a proper part of the conditions of onset or origin of a disorder. Not Intentionality in the full flower of unfettered rationality and apposite connectedness with the world, but with, to use Lear's apt expression, a strange logic or rationality of its own. Rationality truncated by brute a-rational mechanisms, but evident on careful inspection.

Arthur's behavior. Autonomic nervous system activity in Arthur's case, for illustrative purposes I assume, helps to contribute a misplaced rationale to his anxiety. The case is hypothetical and illustrative, but here is a representative kind of explanatory story that I have mind for mental disorders in general.

Suppose that the regulation of the autonomic nervous system occurs (in part) in the hypothalamus, a small region of the brain just below the thalamus. Suppose also that there are reverberating electrical circuits in the hypothalamus that help to modulate emotional responses associated with fear and anxiety. Suppose that in Arthur's case fear and anxiety have become conditioned to locations, smells, discordant noises or other cues associated with crowds of unfamiliar people (in malls, churches and so on) and these are not dampened down by the regulative mechanisms of his hypothalamic circuitry. For some reason, perhaps going back to various reinforcement schedules of his past, he experiences the arousal of his autonomic nervous system as an impending heart attack, and cannot otherwise explain to himself just why he wishes to avoid crowds. It appears so foolish and misshapen of him to avoid them. He knows he cannot properly function in this way. Blips of autonomic nervousness that another person may feel in crowds, but would dismiss as completely harmless, are interpreted by Arthur as signaling the need to consult a cardiologist. It is not utterly unreasonable of him to think this, however, given his reaction to crowds and the meaning of that reaction to him. A kind of logic is there; a rationale of sorts is present. But so, too, is a disorder. Assuming that his hypothalamus is not damaged, dysfunctional or impaired (and there is no particular reason to think that; the circuits were presumably not designed by Mother Nature to permit shopping with strangers), his condition then is a mental disorder and not a neurological one. Having his particular form of anxiety (while not utterly devoid of a rationale) is unreasonable for him – not responsive to his best interests or appraisal of his duties. It also therein is harmful. He can't function socially and may lose his job. But he cannot help it. It reflects an incapacity or impairment.

Barbara Grizzutti Harrison, a recipient of the O. Henry Prize for short fiction, was a victim of panic disorder. "A panic attack has the force of an oncoming train," she writes. It contains a sense of panic "grotesquely heightened" (Harrison 1998: 3–7). That's Arthur's train, too.

Often whatever activities take place within the nervous system, autonomic or otherwise (peripheral, central), both enable and preserve the rationality of behavior. Our nervous system both sponsors and respects reason's sense and sensibility. Rationality sustenance based in brain activity helps to make it possible for us to refer to Intentional states, their contents, and to the rationality inherent in them in the explanation of behavior. It enables us to refer to sources of behavior as *reason responsive*. Such references and explanations, as Dennett wisely notes, do not require that we know "of the ... mechanisms that accomplish" the behavior therein attributed (Dennett 2009: 349). Sometimes, however, neural mechanisms are no respecter or robust sustainer of reason. Sometimes the sheer, raw shifting power of their seismic neurochemical tides or reverberating circuits is inconsistent with maintaining a robust normative character to our beliefs, desires and to links between them and our emotional responses and behavior. When this failure of rationality maintenance occurs (and it occurs along different dimensions and to different degrees) I like (as noted) to refer to such occurrences as 'irruptions' of brute a-rational mechanisms into the domain of the mental or Intentional or the space of reasons. Arthur prepares for flight or fight when a power of reason that is more prudent or more rationally responsive to real threats should command that neither response is warranted. Given, however, that Arthur's bodily activity has gone into a consciously detectable mode (his heart palpitates, he sweats, and so on) and is undaunted by hypothalamic circuitry, and also that he therein misreads his body's preparedness for fight or flight as an impending heart attack, he panics.

Being afraid, it's reasonable for him to be anxious in public circumstances that are associated for him with impending danger. There is a logic or rationale there, although, from a more properly informed or robustly rational perspective, given his woeful ignorance of the nature of his autonomic nervous system and of the absence of a real threat, Arthur's behavior possesses only a truncated logic. He is gummed up by a mechanical process. Crowded elevators and busy malls really are not risky. No need to avoid them. It's unwise or unreasonable to do so.

In Arthur's case, as I have sketched it, the intersection of two sorts of forces lies behind his behavior, one requiring reference to his hippocampus and autonomic nervous system activity and the other to his rationalizing reasons, together lending a sort of strange intelligibility to his retreat from malls. Jonathan Lear notes: "A mind is part of a living organism over which the mind has incomplete [rational] control" (Lear 1998: 85).

In Arthur the two intersecting explanations are not in competition or mutually exclusive. References to thalamic and autonomic nervous system activity and to his own self-interpretation combine to explain his proclivity to panic attacks. But the intersection of these two sorts of forces or sources disables or incapacitates him.

Psychologist Andy Young says that in understanding certain disorders "we need a way of bringing together neurological and psychological factors" (Young 2000: 58). Indeed, that's a central premise behind the conception of mental disorder that I am promoting in this book. I want to bring unreason (mechanism) and reason (rationality, Intentionality) together in our conception of a mental disorder.

Someone is bound to reply to this picture of mental disorder, perhaps having forgotten things that I already have said in the book, that it risks treating any non-mechanical failure or decrement of rationality as a mental disorder. Consider wishful thinking. Cases of wishful thinking stand out as violations of various proposed rationality norms, such as the principle that we should avoid motivationally biased belief, although exactly how motivation may derail rational belief formation in such cases is contestable. Why isn't wishful thinking a disorder? Consider a case.

Betty has good evidence that her son has been killed in the Iraq War. His death was reported by a fellow soldier who accompanied him on a combat mission and by a journalist who said that he saw her son's lifeless body. She has not heard from him in over a month. Yet she remains convinced that her son still is alive. She loves him and refuses to admit that he is dead.

Cases of wishful thinking as such are not disorders, mental or otherwise. This is not because they are harmless. Betty may be harmed by her attitudes. Much depends on how contrary her attitudes are to evidence. But it is because wishful thinking is driven by motivational or affective factors that influence belief formation and therein lead persons to ignore the force of evidence against a favored belief. Nothing is needed to explain such a phenomenon except the language of consciousness and Intentionality. No partial gum-up of reason's works. Reason is in charge (albeit in a motivationally biased manner). In wishful thinking it's nothing but the Intentional mind.

In general, the sort of tale of rationality mixed with brute mechanism, the Arthurian Legend, as it were, if I may be tempted to call it so, is central to the notion of mental disorder that I am promoting or trying to regiment in this book. Intentionalistic (rational) and neurological forces work together in human psychological capacities (or incapacities) and when they do so in a harmful way (depending on the incapacity) mental disorder is present. How they work or intersect depends on the type of condition, the particular case and psychological capacity in question. But, and here certainly is where more work needs to be done in this book, exactly which specific sorts of disabilities or incapacities help to constitute disorders is a topic that has yet to be tackled. GOD no. Not the capacity to ace exams. But then what?

An important but still remaining character in this tale should be obvious. I have not described what counts as the sorts of capacities or faculties that, when disordered, in the manner roughly suggested or outlined above, constitute mental disorders. Reason impaired faculties in general, no less. But which faculties in particular? I plan to answer this question in the next chapter. My answer will consist in saying that exemplary mental disorders are constituted by impairments or incapacities in the rational operation of *basic* or *fundamental* psychological faculties or capacities. But first some closing remarks about the very ideas of incapacity and disability.

A BRIEF ON INCAPACITIES AND DISABILITIES

To end this chapter, I wish to introduce a way of thinking of the incapacities or disabilities that help to constitute a mental disorder, a manner of thinking that is related to the rationality norms or standards introduced and discussed in the immediately preceding sections of this chapter. The question of whether a disability or impairment is significant or serious enough to qualify as a mental disorder (of a prototypical or exemplary sort) is settled not just by whether it is harmful or stems from a decrement in rationality, but, I believe, also by whether the disability or impairment occurs in a *fundamental* psychological competence or *basic* mental faculty. A fundamental competence or basic faculty is something without which it is difficult, and indeed, in most cases, impossible to lead a decent or personally satisfying life (much more on this subject in the next chapter). The impairment is harmful not in the manner in which a mild cut or abrasion is harmful, but in a way analogous to that in which a major limb amputation or serious bone break is. It removes, even if just temporarily, something required if a person is to properly lead a decent life.

Incapacitation is not something that should be confused with a mere failed performance. Humans have an underlying competence for rational decision-making, for instance, despite various common performance errors in reasoning (like committing the gambler's fallacy) and even if most of us cannot describe the rationality norms that govern our decisions. Analogously, we have an underlying competence for producing and understanding grammatical sentences, even if we make ungrammatical utterances and are unable to describe just what makes speech grammatical. Poor performance does not imply disability or incapacity. The key mark of a disability, incapacity or impairment rather than of a mere performance error or lapse is not, pace John Cooper and Margaret Oates, just whether there is an "interference with ... psychological function" (2000: 74). Disabilities and impairments interfere with function, true, but all sorts of other factors may interfere with functions and activities as well but without being disabilities. Distracted attention, environmental overload, motivational inertia, and other forms of 'noise' interrupt proper performance without impugning competence as such.

A distinctive characteristic of a disability or impairment is whether a non-performer (or performer) can be persuaded by reasons for performance (or for non-performance). Are they responsive to incentives/disincentives? If a person can be so persuaded or respond to reasons, there is no need to attribute performance failure to a disability or incapacity. But if a person can be neither moved nor motivated to perform given incentives, expect impairment. Example: I can be persuaded to stop writing this book, by a million-dollar incentive for cessation. But a victim of a movement disorder, like Parkinson's disease, for instance, cannot be persuaded to control their bodily motions by being offered a financial reward for control or by being threatened with punishment for failure to control. An individual with Down's syndrome cannot improve their performance on an intelligence test by being handed a book on the Russian Revolution and told that if they read it their IQ score will improve. Down's and Parkinson's represent disabilities or impairments and constitute forms of incapacitation that inhere neurologically in individuals no matter the manipulation of surrounding contingencies or reasons for action (offers of reward, threats of punishments).

So, too, Arthur's anxiety, as I have imaginatively described matters, also counts as the exemplification of incapacity. If his proclivity or propensity to panic is a mental disorder, it is no mere performance error, but represents a breakdown in his ability to identify genuine dangers posed by other persons. The general faculty or basic capacity impaired in his case is a self-protective measure of successful comprehension of self and others (see next chapter for discussion). However, in crowded public settings, churches, malls, and so on, Arthur just can't comprehend others aright. He distrusts or fears people who should not be distrusted or feared. They pose no real threats to him. Threatening him with disincentives ("Arthur, if you don't get your act together you will be fired") may worsen his panic. Motivating him with bribes ("A thousand dollars for spending an hour at the PTA meeting") may heighten his fear of others, making strangers seem even more ominous in the power of their presence. A breakdown in *that* capacity or competence (comprehension of self and others) is fundamental or basic because without knowing how properly to comprehend others or to recognize the dangers or harms posed by strangers, it is well nigh impossible to form proper attachments or emotionally affiliate with other people.

Contrast Arthur's case with that of GOD. Failure to ace a calculus test, while a student at Brown or Brandeis, may reflect neither impairment nor incapacity. Tell me that you, the dean, will keep my financial scholarship intact so that I don't have to worry about failure and I may do quite well on the test. No incapacity there. But even if I don't do well, there is nothing basically impairing about an inability to do well on calculus (provided this does not reflect some much more pervasive form of incompetence). A person may competently lead an eminently decent life without being able to solve finite and differential equations. No harm done. But understanding in social concourse which persons to trust, fear or mistrust certainly is critical. Without it a decent life not just for Arthur but for virtually anyone is not in the cards.

Incapacities also (it should be noted) are not created equal or possessed of a similar range or purport. Alice may be incapable of getting out of bed given her existing or otherwise normal reasons for rising. That she has to prepare breakfast for her young children does not move her. That she is unwashed or that the postman is at the door may not get her to rise. She is too depressed. But if there was a fire in the house, she may not just rise from her bed but run from her home. A victim of quadriplegia, paralysed in all body regions below the neck, is unable to get out of bed, full stop. No reason *period*, normal or otherwise, can move them. This is part of what I mean by referring to the incapacity or impairment of a mental disorder as a truncation and not obliteration. Not only does some measure of reason, rationale or 'logic' exist in what the subject of a mental disorder does, but a portion of continued or ongoing reason-responsiveness abides as well. If Arthur's wife were kidnapped by hostile terrorists and taken to a shopping mall, he might well enter the mall to help to discover her whereabouts. Mental disorders are like that. Contextual circumstances or parameters frame or affect them, sometimes in quite pronounced or marked ways. The obsessive-compulsive person does not obsess over everything. But a blind person may be unable to see anything, even faint signs of light.

In the next chapter I revisit the total concept of a mental disorder that I prefer. This is the concept that I briefly described in the second chapter and promised to elucidate and defend over the course of the first several chapters of this book. That elucidation and defense is near to closing. I hope I may be forgiven for making the road back to that concept so long and winding. Indeed, there still is one more issue that I have yet to discuss about the idea of a mental disorder, although I mention it just above. This is describing what makes a psychological capacity basic or a mental faculty or form of competence fundamental. I am quite generally suspicious of talking of activities that people are psychologically incapable of performing as symptoms of an exemplary mental disorder unless the incapacity in question helps to preclude leading a decent life. It is this particular harmful mark (and the truncation of reason behind it) that also helps to make a distress or disturbance clinically 'significant' (and not just a decrement in rationality). By this standard I exclude GOD as a mental disorder. People surely have deeply satisfying lives without making Ivy League honor societies. True, how to describe just what sorts of capacities are necessary for a decent life is a tough business, although, whatever the limitations of this project, I see no reason to believe that the attempt is utterly futile.

Perhaps the biggest impediment to identifying psychological competencies or mental capacities as fundamental or basic is that conceptions of the necessities of a decent life appear to be both personally various and culturally variable. But we shouldn't necessarily be unhappy with that result, unless perhaps it backs us into the corner of cultural conventionalism about mental disorder and the denial of medical scientific progress.

CHAPTER SUMMARY AND SUGGESTED READINGS

This chapter was organized around the following single question. What sort of criterion of seriousness or importance is appropriate for a disorder or for the impairment that constitutes a disorder? We explored three possible criteria. Two were found wanting: cultural conventionalism and an ancestral response pattern's being evolutionarily mismatched to current environments. A third is more promising. This is that a mental disability counts as clinically serious, in part, when it constitutes an impairment or truncation in a person's reason or rationality. Much of the energy in this fifth chapter was devoted to describing just why rationality is so central to being minded and to Intentionality. Intentional states refer to objects and states of affairs in the world beyond themselves and they do so subject to various constraints of rationality or reasonableness.

I argued that each of cultural conventionalism about disorder and the hypothesis of evolutionary mismatch are implausible criteria for importance or significance. But this does not mean that cultural context is irrelevant to a mental disorder or that breakdowns in systems of adaptively selected capacities are not part of a disorder.

Appeal to decrements or truncations in rationality as, in part, criteria for disorder requires assessments of the rationality of behavior. I admitted that we do not have a precise account of reason's norms. But even if appeals to reason and unreason are imprecise, they can, if wedded to other elements in a concept of mental disorder, justify or warrant certain attributions of disorder, and help to focus research on the role that brute a-rational forces play in the truncated logic of a disorder. Classifications of mental disorder may then reflect the inability of basic psychological capacities to function properly or fully rationally.

On cultures and psychiatric taxonomies, of interest is Sing Lee's "Cultures in Psychiatric Nosology," *Culture, Medicine, and Psychiatry*, 1996, 20, pp. 421–72. While not directly on the subject of cultural conventionalism and mental disorder, Jennifer Church discusses how social circumstances help to constitute mental disorders in her "Social Constructionist Models: Making Order Out of Disorder – On the Social Construction of Madness." Church also considers the threat that social constitution poses to achieving the scientific consensus about mental disorder that is necessary for making cross-cultural medical progress. Dominic Murphy offers a brief and helpful critical examination of evolutionary criteria for mental disorder in "Darwinian Models of Psychopathology." Both the paper by Church (above mentioned) and this one by Murphy appear in Jennifer Radden's edited, *The Philosophy of Psychiatry: A Companion* (Oxford University Press, 2004).

Darwinian psychiatry attracted the attention of philosophers in a paper that Murphy wrote with Stephen Stich entitled "Darwin in the Madhouse: Evolutionary Psychology and the Classification of Mental Disorders," in P. Carruthers and A. Chamberlin (eds), *Evolution and the Human Mind* (Cambridge University Press, 2000). Introductions to Darwinian or evolutionary psychiatry/psychopathology include A. Stevens and J. Price's *Evolutionary Psychiatry: A New Beginning* (Routledge, 1996) as well as M. McGuire and A. Triosi's *Darwinian Psychiatry* (Oxford University Press, 1998). Also worth consulting is Simon Baron-Cohen's edited collection entitled *The Maladapted Mind: Classic Readings in Evolutionary Psychopathology* (Psychology Press, 1997). Evolutionary psychiatry is not just an approach to psychiatric medicine but a branch of evolutionary psychology. S. Pinker's *How the Mind Works* (Norton, 1997) shows how evolutionary theory may inform psychology. Robert Richardson's *Evolutionary Psychology as Maladapted Psychology* (MIT Press, 2007) offers a detailed negatively critical examination of evolutionary-psychological theory construction.

Daniel Dennett's account of rationality and Intentionality is mined for a model of mental disorder in Derek Bolton's "Problems in the definition of 'mental disorder'," *Philosophical Quarterly*, 2001, 51, pp. 182–99. Bolton's paper also contains a short but helpful discussion of evolutionary-theoretic definitions of mental disorder. Responsiveness to reason is a central theme in John Martin Fischer and Mark Ravizza's *Responsibility and Control* (Cambridge University Press, 1998). Rationality is the topic of Robert Nozick's *The Nature of Rationality* (Princeton University Press, 1993). Skepticism about the rationality assumption behind mentality/Intentionality is defended in Alvin Goldman's *Simulating Minds: The Philosophy, Psychology, and Neuroscience of Mindreading* (Oxford University Press, 2006), pp. 53–68. One of the more popular themes in contemporary philosophy of mind (illustrated in the case of Arthur's somatic flight/fight response to crowds) is the so-called embodied nature of cognition. Shaun Gallagher's *How the Body Shapes the Mind* (Oxford University Press, 1999) is a guide to many of the main issues connected with mind and embodiment. For anyone interested in reasons for thinking that persons are composed of distinct and relatively autonomous subagents, John Heil's "Going to Pieces," in G. Graham and G. Lynn Stephens (eds), *Philosophical Psychopathology* (MIT Press, 1994), is a good paper with which to start.

6   An original position

Reasons – arguments, pro and con considerations, goals, purposes, aspirations – move people to act. Some do so with a bang. Some do so with a whisper. Some run against the tide of other considerations. Others ride within a tribe of complementary reasons. But reasons move.

They don't or can't do so when a person is impaired in acting on them or when the ability to respond to a reason is incapacitated or relevantly truncated. Take the disorder of clinical depression. It may leave a person unable to get out of bed in the morning. So if you ask 'But don't they have good reason to get out of bed?', you have asked why don't those reasons move them to rise, to get dressed, and travel to work. But the condition of their disorder, and the answer to the question, depends on the fact that depression has impaired their ability to respond to such reasons. The reasons, though good, don't move them, and gummed up or 'disordered' as such persons are, they can't positively respond.

There are various capacities whose truncation or impairment explains why subjects of a disorder behave unreasonably or unresponsively. It is a matter of controversy just which capacities these are. Depression is often thought to be a disorder or incapacitation of mood; for instance, it is thought, it's the despondent mood or affect of a depressed person that keeps them from getting out of bed. But that can't be right. People do all sorts of things in all sorts of moods. My depressed mood may lead me to listen to Mahler and drink scotch on the couch all afternoon. Yours may fasten you to your track shoes for a self-punishing run.

Only, I believe, if we know which psychological capacities or faculties are disabled in a disorder may we learn just how or where reason is truncated in a disorder. Disorders are capacity-tethered rationality impairments. Quite specific faculties are 'gummed up' in a disorder. Which faculties of mind are gummed up in disorders?

In this chapter I aim to defend the following thesis: It is the truncation or impairment of *basic* psychological capacities or *fundamental* mental faculties, when brought about through a combination of mental and brute a-rational neural or mechanical forces, which helps to constitute exemplary or prototypical mental disorders.

By 'basic faculties' I don't mean those of a pedagogical textbook sort. We normally possess capacities for memory, emotion, perception, motor movement, and learning. Any entry-level psychology text examines those sorts of faculties. The word 'basic' may be applied to them. But the utility of that sort of taxonomy when offered as a list of basic mental faculties depends on the purposes to which it is put. Pedagogy is one thing; understanding mental disorder another.

William James once noted that if you are wondering what breed of horse is the best, that depends on the purposes to which the horse is put. Racing with alacrity on a track is one thing; moving a heavy plough through a muddy field is another.

It is one task to organize a review of mental faculties to serve pedagogical purposes associated with describing empirical results in cognitive science (see Bechtel and Graham 1998). For such a purpose memory, emotion and so on may be treated as basic capacities. But it is another to develop a useful taxonomy of basic capacities for a theory of mental disorder. For this second and special purpose the identification of basic psychological capacities should be coupled or affixed, I believe, to recognition of the ongoing commitments that we persons make to projects or aspirations that help to give structure, meaning, and purpose to our lives. What do we want a faculty of memory for? What do we wish our emotional responses to do? Why perceive?

Psychological faculties of a standard textbook sort, such as memory, *full stop*, emotion or mood *simpliciter*, and so on, when so listed are not perspicuously pictured as enmeshed in the contexts and purposes of our lives. Stripped of descriptions of our aspirations for a life, and of the wanted or needed operations of our faculties, they appear like existentially desiccated structures, highly generic and too abstract to be fit for a theory of the faculties or competencies impaired in a mental disorder.

Think, by analogy, of bodily limbs and organs. People use their limbs and organs, notes George Henrik von Wright, "to satisfy various wants and needs" (von Wright 1963: 58). Our wants or needs can normally be satisfied only if relevant parts of our bodies perform in *this* or *that* way. To move we need operative legs; to breathe we need functioning lungs. The same general point, I assume, is true of mental faculties or capacities. If certain uses of memory "were not vital to the satisfaction of [certain] needs," it would be a puzzle, von Wright notes, why we should ever refer to a faculty of memory as incapacitated or impaired (von Wright 1963: 59). "Perhaps we can imagine circumstances [in] which remembering would be a [rather] useless activity" (von Wright 1963: 59). If that were to happen, in some distant possible world, no doubt, if, that is, a functioning memory somehow became useless, what would that tell us? It would tell us, I believe, that any 'deficit' in memory would be considered too trivial or inconsequential to count as a disorder.

The capacities for or types of memory that we desire and need are situated in the context of the lives that we aim to lead. Some forms of memory are much more useful in that general context than others; some when impaired help to constitute exemplary mental disorders. The same general points hold true for our other mental 'limbs' and 'organs' – whatever they may be.

SOCIAL ORDER, MENTAL ORDER AND VEILS OF IGNORANCE

How, on earth, can we identify basic mental capacities, life-enmeshed or situated mental 'limbs' and 'organs'? Capacities such that when they are impaired in their rational or reasonable operation help to constitute mental disorders? How so?

I shall assume the following. A basic faculty is essential for lives that we normally or virtually universally want to lead, at least *decent* lives by realistic or normal standards. Not 'basic' faculty dropped from a textbook heaven. Not descriptions primed for the prose of pedagogy. But identifications based on ends or purposes, which, I assume, are of a *general* sort desired by *all* or *virtually all* human beings.

An elusive concept is that of a decent life, to be sure. Capacities necessary for decent lives? Given the elusiveness of this standard, I need help in securing the target list. To assist, I plan to appropriate a thought experiment of John Rawls (1921–2002), the late Harvard social thinker and moral philosopher. In Rawls's thought experiment, which I will describe in a moment, he is concerned with how to distinguish between morally acceptable and unacceptable forms of social order. He wishes to learn what basic structures of a society are principled, just and fair. I, by contrast, am concerned with distinguishing between mental order and disorder. Here in this chapter I wish to identify which basic capacities or faculties of mind are desirable, valuable, and when sufficiently 'well-ordered' enable decent lives to be led. Rawls's thought experiment has social or moral ends. My use of Rawls's experiment has a psychological end.

First some background to Rawls's concern.

Social cooperation makes possible all sorts of goods in life. Schools, hospitals, highways, science and religion. Phones, libraries and movies. Families and friendships. You name it. Without social cooperation little that is truly good or valuable in life can be accomplished or achieved.

Social cooperation of the sorts that help to produce hospitals, sciences, religions and so on requires rules or norms for acceptable social behavior. If social participants are to truly be enthusiastic or engaged and cooperative, the rules or norms of social cooperation must be perceived by reasonable parties to be fair. Ideally, the rules or conventions of social fair play are norms that give each person recognizable status as a respected member of the social order, no matter what their station or lot in life. These are rules that a person may commit themselves to without fearing that they are short changed, devalued or disrespected as compared with other persons with whom they socially cooperate.

Here is a simple domestic example. Suppose: You and I are apartment mates. We throw a big dinner party with many guests. I buy potato chips but neither purchase nor prepare the meal. You buy the main dishes (which are expensive) and prepare a multi-course dinner (which is labor intensive). I arrange the cutlery and answer the doorbell. You slave in the kitchen. "Unfair," you think. You feel short-changed. Your enthusiasm for the party wanes. I fail to carry my proper weight. What we need if we are to help each other cooperatively and enthusiastically is some sort of fair distribution of responsibilities. A measure of impartiality lest either of us carry too much or little weight. Rawls has a hypothesis for how a fair distribution is best understood.

In his magisterial book on socio-political theory, *A Theory of Justice* (1971), Rawls aims to identify which moral rules or norms should govern the basic or foundational structure of a fair social order and therein serve as a framework for enthused and committed social cooperation. Rawls does this by asking which principles of social organization would be chosen by persons from an impartial or unbiased perspective or point of view. To help our imagination to picture that neutral standpoint, he asks his readers to assume that we are "situated behind a veil of ignorance" in a position, an "original position" so-called, prior to commencing our particular individual lives and before the adoption of explicit rules of social order. What makes the veil one of ignorance is that behind it "no one knows his natural assets or abilities." Each person is assumed to know "the laws of human psychology," but not their personal lot or "own plan of life" (Rawls 1971: 136–7).

Rawls asks us to decide, as if from behind the veil, what rules or principles we would desire a society in which we were to live to embrace and institutionally enforce. (He says we would want rules that give each person an abundance of freedom or liberty, but that would also ensure that no one is made intractably worse off by another person's exercise of freedom.) When, then, the imagined veil is lifted and our individual lives or biographies have begun, a society with such rules is one in which, Rawls claims, we would prefer to live, no matter whom we are or what our personal assets and liabilities. Whether we are rich, poor, female, male, old, young, sick or healthy, such is the social order in which people would want to live.

One of Rawls's key assumptions is that the rules or norms that would be chosen in the original position possess an eminent claim to being fair. How so? This is because the rules would impartially balance each person's potentially competing preferences and interests over and against those of other people. The intuition pump of the imagined veil is designed to impose an unbiased standpoint in terms of which to adjudicate between interpersonal preferences when they conflict. In Rawls's terms, it accomplishes this task because it expresses people's "respect for one another" (Rawls 1971: 179). It asks us to project ourselves as possibly being any one of a number of persons of different types, talents and stations – "unencumbered by the singularities of the circumstances in which we find ourselves" (Rawls 1971: 516). We are to assume "a point of view that everyone can adopt on an equal footing" (Rawls 1971: 516). So, no single person is mistreated or disrespected by the chosen rules of social order. Each person and each person's interests or preferences are respected by whatever are the chosen principles.

Consider our dinner party. It's not enough for me just to buy the chips. It's too much for you to do all the work. If I was in your shoes, I would see right away that the situation disrespects your interests. In whatever rules we adopt, persons must be prepared to be in each other's shoes. Such, roughly, is Rawls's notion.

Much has been written about Rawls's thought experiment and much, much more has been said about his book. Rightly so. Some of it has been critical (of, for instance, its sympathy for institutional mechanisms geared, in part, to those who are worse off). Some has been rhapsodically praiseworthy (of, for example, its concern with the benefits and burdens of social cooperation).

I mention Rawls here in a book on mental disorder not because of his theory of fair social order or person-respecting institutional arrangements (or because I endorse the details of the theory). I mention Rawls because of his thought experiment of a Veil of Ignorance in the Original Position and his use of this experiment to uncover desirable rules of social order. A good thought experiment may be used independent of its original clips and chips. A truly good one is, as Daniel Dennett notes, "more robust than any one version of it" (Dennett 1984: 17–18). Rawls's experiment truly is good, I believe. So, let's see if and how we may use it to help to identify our basic psychological capacities.

Suppose, again, we want to talk not about social order/disorder, as Rawls does, but mental order/disorder. Suppose we wish to engage in such talk not as a gratuitous exercise, but because we believe that mental disorders are 'out there'. They are real and undesirable conditions of people. They are *objective* conditions of the, as it were, *subjectivity* (psychology) of persons. Suppose we wish to identify them. We want to explain and predict types of human behavior in terms of them. We want to help people who harbor disorders and to disentangle or release ourselves and others from their unwelcome grip.

It is a challenging project just how we should identify disorders. We've already learned the following. To talk about mental disorder we need a concept or description of mental disorder. To construct such a concept we can focus on mental or psychological disturbances (incapacities, disabilities etc.) that all or most informed observers agree are mental disorders and that attract consensus classification as disorders. This method of informed agreement and extrapolation from agreed-on cases privileges some applications of the expression 'mental disorder' over others. Not every mental disturbance or impairment qualifies as disorder. Not every piece of psychiatric taxonomy in each and every diagnostic manual identifies a sure disorder. Certainly, however, or so I have been assuming, the central or most agreed-on cases qualify as disorders, at least by our current consensual lights. Therein our method, namely, the methodology being followed in this book, has proceeded.

Thus far our search for a concept of mental disorder has helped us to decide whether disorders are best understood as diseases. I say no, but I am not insisting on my negative appraisal. I don't want to be dogmatic about the concept of disease, just cautious. The search has also helped us to appreciate that the concept of a mental disorder is not value or normatively neural. (It is not like the concepts, for instance, of an egg, lump of sugar, or electron.) It is infused (unlike such concepts) with presuppositions about rationality or reasonableness, broadly understood, as well as about norms for the seriousness or clinical significance of a mental incapacity or impairment. We have also discovered that the incapacities distinctive of a mental disorder, in order to be disorders of mentality and not aspects of a broken brain or reflections of neural impairment, should bear the mark or autograph of mind in their propensity conditions and not just in their symptoms and apt treatment methods. But we have learned, in an explanatorily ecumenical spirit, that in a case of mental disorder the fact that it is stamped with mentality does not exclude a substantive causal-explanatory role for forces within the disorder that are non-mental neuro-mechanical or brute a-rational. Quite the contrary, to properly understand a mental disorder, reference should be made not just to Intentional states and attitudes, conscious and otherwise, but also to brute neuro-mechanical processes. Not just to the 'logic' or rationale of a disturbance, but to neural activities that somehow (though without seizing causal-explanatory dominion) truncate, hobble or impair a person's rationality.

So much so far is what we have done. So, I ask now, which mental faculties or capacities are those that when disordered (incapacitated or impaired) help to constitute (depending on their propensity conditions and seriousness) a (prototypical, exemplary) mental disorder? Here is where Rawls becomes relevant to our task.

At the exemplary limit, when harms associated with a condition help to qualify the condition as a disorder, these harms must express impairments or incapacities that disable a person in a profound or serious way: disable people from effectively or reasonably and rationally coping with that might be called (to borrow an apt phrase of Harry Frankfurt) "the universal exigencies of human life" and therein from successfully managing to lead a decent life (Frankfurt 2004: 47). Once disabled (depending on the severity and extent of a disability) a life becomes attenuated, diminished, or worse off. Pain and suffering may occur. Bodily injury or death may take place or be seriously risked. The person may be incapable of caring for themselves or perhaps they may become a menace to others and pose unacceptable social harms or threats. So, psychological disability of the sort constitutive of an exemplary disorder is not a matter of being temporarily frustrated in achieving some idiosyncratic or highly situational personal goal, like playing professional soccer or observing autumn foliage in Vermont, but of failing or risking failure to secure goods and achievements normally thought necessary for a decent life. Goods in language, social relationships, the contexts of a job, love, religion, political autonomy, and a host of universal or virtually universal forms of social and environmental circumstance. One's children may not be cared for; one's powers of friendship or social communion may be undermined; one's decisional powers may oscillate in disturbing forms of dramatically imprudent ambivalence. One's motives may not serve one's considered interests; one's perceptions may fail to locate one spatially; one's autobiographical memories may dissolve into ineffectiveness, making it effectively impossible to learn from past episodes. These are extremes, to be sure, and particular instances of a disorder may, perhaps out of sheer luck, never produce truly severe harms. But disorder exemplars as exemplars occur in plain and painful sight. They hurt.

What, then, should we say about the identity of basic psychological capacities? What are they?

A few pages from now I try to answer this question – from behind a veil of ignorance. But not every part of our answer needs Rawls's thought experiment. Rawls's veil should not be needed for this next thesis. It's a thesis about the importance of consciousness to the lives we wish to lead.

THE IMPORTANCE OF CONSCIOUS EXPERIENCE

I taste an orange, smell a sweet rose, see the purple color on the BMW owned by my neighbor, feel pride on winning an award, and struggle to pronounce a foreign-language word that is phonetically alien to my native speech patterns. In each of these cases, I am the subject of a very different feeling or conscious experience. In the case of conscious experiences, there is always something it is like to undergo them, some phenomenology that they possess. As the what-it's-likenesses or qualities of experience change, the conscious experiences themselves change. If the phenomenal features disappear entirely, no consciousness remains.

Here is a thought experiment. It is owed to Robert Nozick's *Anarchy, State, and Utopia* (1974). "Suppose there [was] an experience machine that would give you any experience you desired" (Nozick 1974: 42). Super-duper neuroscientists could stimulate your brain so that you would think and feel you are climbing a mountain, making love to your soulmate, or preparing to visit Paris. All the while, however, "you would be floating in a tank, with electrodes attached to your head" (ibid.). Should you plug into this machine for life, perhaps having preprogrammed all your future experiences? "While in the tank you won't know that you're there; you'll think it's all actually happening" (Nozick 1974: 43).

You could be musically tone deaf, but think you are composing a wonderfully melodic symphony. Scaling a mountain? Sure, though your feet are floating. Would you take a virtual hike?

I have asked this question of students. Most answer no, but a few say yes. The outliers, the yes-sayers, claim that they would readily plug into an experience machine and do so for life. Why should it otherwise matter to a person, they rhetorically ask, whether he or she is in the dark about the non-veridical origins or falsehood of their experience? Positive or pleasurable experience is the *only* true measure of personal well-being or life satisfaction. As long as you *feel* good why worry about the authenticity of your experience? Consciousness has merit to us as human beings because and only because it makes pleasure possible, not because it offers actual contact with the external world.

I would like to be able to argue such students out of this position of stated utter indifference to authentic connection with the real world. My hope is that if they were actually faced with the choice, they would not make it. They might think twice about never seeing their friends again or being completely cut off from family and school.

Loss of actual contact with the world would worry John Stuart Mill (1806–73). Authenticity or real-world engagement doesn't matter? It's inconsequential whether a person is locked into their own phenomenal world?

At twenty-two years of age Mill underwent what was likely a protracted major depressive episode. He describes it in his *Autobiography* as a "dull state of nerves" in which he "seemed to have nothing left to live for" and experienced "the dry heavy dejection of ... melancholy winter" (Mill 1969: 80, 81, 84). On eventual liberation from his condition Mill claimed the following: "Those only are happy ... who have their minds fixed on some object other than their own happiness." "The only chance is to treat, not happiness, but some end external to it, as the purpose of life" (Mill 1969: 85, 86).

What did Mill mean by such remarks? He meant this. True, people certainly prefer to feel good rather than bad. Pleasurable feelings or positive affects play an essential role in personal well-being and not just in our sense of it. But it is not true that this means that feeling good is ultimately all that really matters in life or that the exclusive and exhaustive merit of our capacity for conscious experience rests in affording pleasures. Periods of pleasure are essential to a good life, but not sufficient.

For Mill pleasures are judged and evaluated on the basis of how they come about, not just on what they are like, as it were, on the subjective inside. Feeling good, if it is to be thought a valuable or good feeling, that is, if it qualifies as the sort of experience that people find nourishing and appealing, has to come about as the by-product of pursuing other goods believed worthwhile. These other goods are not pleasurable feelings per se. They are states of the real world, of one's family, career, friends and so on. "Aiming thus at something else, [one finds] happiness by the way" (Mill 1969: 86). Such are states of affairs in the real world other than merely feeling good that we persons truly care about.

Mill, I believe, makes an excellent point. It is one thing to value consciousness because it can be pleasurable. It is another to value it because of the roles it plays in helping us to secure or produce other good things – good things in the external or real world.

What bothers Mill about the emphasis on mere feeling as the sole measure of the merit or importance of our capacity for conscious experience is that he disbelieves that anyone can really feel good without caring for something other than feeling good, as paradoxical as that proposition may sound. A mother takes pleasure, for instance, in the happiness of her children, because she wants them to flourish. She does not wish them to flourish so that she feels good. True, it makes her feel good to know that her children are flourishing, but she wants them to thrive for their own sakes and not for the sake of something (some positive affect) that takes place solely within the confines of her skull.

Mill is not anti-affect or stoically puritanical. He wishes to be true to facts about human psychology. He is not trying to be derisive about feelings. In his autobiography he bemoans the fact that, as a young man, his own habits of philosophical analysis had a "tendency to wear away [his] feelings" (Mill 1969: 83). But Mill doubts whether a genuinely rational and reflective person can truly be satisfied if they constantly focus just on their own feelings. The best way in which to find meaning and purpose in life is to care about states of affairs other than one's own state of mind. It lies, as it were, in the Intentional objects of conscious experience. Feeling for my child and recognizing that she is flourishing, I feel good. Failing to feel for the politics of Uruguay, I derive neither pleasure nor discomfort in news of its national election. Attending a baseball game, I may be disinterested in its outcome unless I root for a team. Absent caring for a team, I may derive little or no pleasure from the game.

Feeling for something is risky business, of course. Feelings are vulnerable if we commit ourselves to things that fail. I want my former student to be a successful doctor. She does not do well. I am distressed. I want the newly elected president to address perplexing problems of global warming. Suppose, however, that once elected he lapses into indifference about the environment and cares only for the big oil companies. I am upset. A person must learn to feel or consciously care for things or persons that somehow are worth caring about even though one's feelings are not protected against disappointment. The sorts of things we human beings care for, and which help us to lead decent and satisfying lives, include pursuing various sorts of personal accomplishments, sustaining intimate personal relationships, addressing our curiosity about the world, helping other people in need, and so on, not the enterprise of self-absorption in one's own conscious affect. Put again paradoxically, it is only by more or less casting away concern for feelings and conscious states and becoming concerned with something other than one's own state of mind, says Mill, that an individual may be happy – enjoy a good life, a decent life.

So, aside from whatever merits our capacity for conscious experience may have as the vehicle of pleasure, its real merit, if we agree with Mill (and I assume we should), is instrumental. Its main purpose or function is to enable us to attend to things other than conscious experience itself. In it and through it we care about and attend to the world and our life in the world.

One might ask: But can't and don't non-conscious states and attitudes also connect us with the world? Yes, of course, they can and do. But when phenomenal consciousness is absent, impaired or disrupted, the overall character of our contact with or attention to the external world is degraded. When the world enters into consciousness, as it were, all else being equal, intelligence and flexibility of behavior are enhanced. Non-conscious contact, by comparison, "evokes nonselective, nonflexible responses that are relatively insensitive to circumstances," notes Ran Lahav (1993: 79). "[But] conscious experience expresses information available for an entire spectrum of global, integrated, and flexible (non-automatic) behaviors" (ibid.). I may consciously recognize the familiar face of a colleague and shake his hand accordingly. But take away my visual experience of his face, and he will stand on the sidewalk hand unshaken.

We need to be conscious to fully and appropriately connect with the world. That much is beyond doubt. But what else do we need? What other psychological faculties or specific conscious or mental capacities?

If we are successfully to engage in the world, we need more than a capacity for conscious experience. We need capacities for performing activities that, in our being committed to them and aiming for outcomes, make life worthwhile and enable us to lead decent lives. Not capacities to plug into a machine. But powers or faculties that enable us to be accomplished or at least function in the world. What are those capacities? How can we identify them?

Of course, the environments and circumstances of people are variable and variegated. So, in the end, we should not wish for capacities or faculties that are tightly tethered to particular situations or circumstances. We need capacities that enable us to cope with variations and instabilities in the contexts of behavior. These must be capacities of a general and generalized variety: capacities that structure or set the foundations for a worthwhile or decent life. Very fine-grained or particularized capacities or abilities (abilities in soccer, with calculus or olive gardening, etc.) may be developed or constructed, when individual opportunities and situations afford doing so or enable us to learn such-and-such, but only on top of more general, more fundamental or basic capacities.

BASIC PSYCHOLOGICAL CAPACITIES

One candidate means for trying to discover the desired basic capacities is by doing pan-social science. Call this the *hyper-sociological method*. Consider the science or method as a big two-step process.

Step one. Survey all cultures, all societies, at each and every recorded period of history and devise a list of competencies required circumstance by circumstance, culture by culture, society by society. Talent with quantum physics here. The ability to count one's children there.

Step two. Now consider the frequency with which the required competencies occur. If needed talent with physics occurs much less often than other abilities (say, for counting one's offspring), then this is not a capacity that we should classify as fundamental. It's not 'basic'. Some more frequently occurring talent or facility may be basic.

Of course, doing pan-social science is utterly unfeasible, practically or empirically, as well as conceptually pointless. A purely situation-by-situation frequency analysis cannot allay uncertainty about which capacities are necessary or required if we are to face the universal exigencies of life and achieve generally desired outcomes. A long list of frequent capacities is like a long list of business telephone numbers in the Business or Yellow Pages. Impressive but bewildering. Whom should we call? AAA Fix-It Service is listed more times than any other agency. So are Albert and Abe, Attorneys at Law. But are they businesses that demand a call? Or do they merely represent obnoxious advertisements in the phone book. Merely mundane matters are immensely commonplace. Everyone needs a good toothbrush, but this does not mean we need a special talent to purchase one. Perhaps rare is the soul who does not desire a place of religious worship, but this does not imply that a gift for wise and prudent religious affiliation is a fundamental faculty. Which sorts of competencies at what level of generality, grain or description speak to the universal exigencies of life and to outcomes that practically everyone wants, no matter the personal circumstance? To answer *that* question or to identify those sorts of faculties, we need to know what we persons truly care about in our lives independent of situational particulars. Or so I assume.

The hyper-sociological method may appear to have the advantage of solving the problem of identifying basic capacities in two strokes. But it solves the problem by depriving basic capacities of their considered value and importance to us as human beings.

Circumstances, practices, traditions, and forms of life provide the soil in which human life and our particular talents nourish and grow, becoming meaningful and worthwhile. But the general outcomes we want tend to be quite universal. They tend to include such goods or pursuits as meaningful work, making or creating things, being able to express ourselves, gaining the approval and respect of other persons, coping with illness, pain, and death, dealing with the loss of a loved one, sustaining family ties and friendships, and so on. So, the question is: Which sorts of capacities are needed for all that? What psychological faculties are required to secure those sorts of outcomes? No form of competence is sufficient for any of them, of course. (Do we really know what it takes to cope with the tragic death of a loved one? Or to produce the enduring devotion of a friend?) But clearly some capabilities or faculties are necessary for all (or virtually all) of us.

It's time to pump intuitions.

Reasonable, intelligent persons – such as each of us, I assume, if we imagine different but desirable life projects and a likely range of possible circumstances in which we may live, and if we also wish to give ourselves decent life prospects virtually no matter our individual goals and circumstances – are in the best possible position to decide just which capacities are basic (truly and generally valuable). These are capacities or faculties that we care most about insofar as we recognize them to be necessary for much else that we care about. To bring the cared-about capacities out into the analytical open, I propose that we follow Rawls's example and construct a thought experiment of an original position type.

Let's imagine ourselves situated behind a veil of ignorance about our individual talents and particular goals. Assume: We know a good deal about human psychology. We know what people tend to want out of life. We know basic facts of history, anthropology and sociology. We know of the personal and circumstantial challenges that people face and of the tragedies and heartaches that must be endured. We know of various sorts of human achievements and of psychological tools required to secure them. All of this knowledge qualifies as information about 'the universal exigencies of human life'. What we don't know (I assume here) are individuating features of our own goals, capacities and circumstances. We don't know whether we wish to become tailors, tinkers, sailors or spies. We don't know whether we wish to live in city or country, to father or mother, to counsel or command. We don't know whether we wish to affect the lives of others with small graces or to sweep people along with grandiose generosities or acts of heroism. We don't know whether we will be cooks or tennis players, spinsters or spoilers.

Being without particularistic specificity means we should not pick as basic a capacity or faculty tethered to individual particulars. If I am head of the mathematics department at Princeton, I surely need facility with number theory. But I would not pick a capacity at that level of grain or particularity from behind the veil as something required by the universal exigencies of life.

Rawls made an analogous presupposition as part of his standpoint of moral impartiality. A distinctive feature of Rawls's original position is that the parties to his thought experiment do not know of their particular desires or goals. Do they wish to live unmarried in Boston? Or do they prefer to wed a tribal chieftain in central Africa? A presupposition behind Rawls's pump is that people are to choose a principled social order, not derived from their individually variable desires or aims, but based on and warranted by desires that people generally are bound to have, regardless of which particular people they are. Rawls speaks of the aims of such general desires as primary goods (Rawls 1971: 93, 263). Primary goods are conditions required for seeking virtually any other and more particular goals or goods.

Rawls's presupposition about general desires is an assumption similar to the one that I wish to make here. My presupposition is that we people are to identify a set of psychological capacities, not derived from our individually variable desires or capacities, but from competencies that we are bound to value and need, regardless of which specific goals we possess or wish to pursue. So, I am asking about a well-capacitated or well-'facultied' person, not, as Rawls did, about a well-ordered society. What are the primary (basic, fundamental) psychological competencies that are bound to be required or desired, regardless of particulars?

Alongside our capacity for conscious experience, I assume we would pick a non-negligible measure of capacities for or competencies in:

(1) Bodily/spatial self location. We persons must be able to identify our somatic or bodily position in the environment/the world, so that we can utilize our motor capacities in the service of bodily movement and self-maintenance as well as other forms of goal pursuit. To locate myself physically is to know where I am and what my location is vis-à-vis other objects of importance. Am I behind a door or underneath a willow tree? Am I far from a precipice, near a portal, or too close for comfort to a predator?

(2) Historical/temporal self-location. We persons must be able to identify our present position in time and each of us must be able to apprehend ourselves as (what might be

called) an enduring or historically extended agent or individual with a past and future or at least (since people die, of course) a possible impact on the future. Quite apparently no non-human animals possess an understanding of themselves as extended in time. None apparently remembers past events in the sense of being able to relive them in the imagination. But as human beings our sense of where we are, temporally, autobiographically, "extends through time from the past we have experienced to the future we have planned" (Bechtel 2008: 259). I am more than halfway finished writing this book. You are more than halfway through reading it, assuming we each began at the beginning and plan to labor until the end.

(3) General self/world comprehension. We persons must be able to comprehend ourselves and the world to an extent or degree necessary to lead life in at least a moderately well-informed and knowledge-guided fashion. Ignorance of self or world is no bliss. Oftentimes we make mistakes in what we think we know, misremember what we have done, or infer to some false proposition, belief or hypothesis about the world or ourselves. But without some measure of successful comprehension, without knowing whether the food in my refrigerator is poisonous, if my car is safe to drive, whether my neighbors are trustworthy, or if the hot cup of coffee on my kitchen counter is too hot to hold, my ignorance is dangerous and deleterious. (Think of Arthur here, whose generalized and misplaced mistrust of strangers in crowds cripples him socially.) The capacity for self/world comprehension that we desire or need is not angelic; it is situated or contextualized. Knowledge of certain states of affairs is more important to us than knowledge of other facts. If I plan to get theater tickets, I need to know where to get them. If you plan to go with me, you need to know where to meet me and how to get there. Neither of us needs to know the phone numbers of the dozens of strangers sitting behind us in the theater. And there may be no point in either of us attending the performance if we each know ahead of time that neither of us is likely to enjoy the play.

(4) Communication. We persons must be able to communicate about ourselves and the world with others, and this requires sufficient competence in some system of communication (such as our native language). We need both speaker competence and listener competence if we are to be successful communicators. I may be a journalist reporting the atrocities of a political regime under which I lived. A skeptical reader will wonder if I distort the truth, but before assessing the soundness of my testimony, they must at least comprehend or understand what I mean. You may be a pedestrian answering my question about the location of a theater, adding no distracting detail to directions, but wishing to offer me the information I request. Communicative encounters and interactions are a pervasive activity in human life – a source of knowledge and social connectivity or coordination, a bond with others and the world.

(5) Care, commitment and emotional engagement. We persons must be able to care about and be committed to persons and things. To care for and be committed to something is to be invested in it, to identify oneself with it and to regard it as important to oneself, so that we make ourselves "vulnerable to losses and susceptible to benefits depending upon whether what [we care] about is diminished or enhanced" (Frankfurt 1988: 83). It should be noted, too, that normally the capacity for care and commitment requires or

may be constituted in part by emotional or affective engagement in what we care about. "A reliance on logic alone," in the words of Harvard psychologist, Jerome Kagan, "without the capacity to feel … joy, guilt, sadness or anxiety … would lead most people to do many, many foolish things" (1994: 39). Without caring and emotional commitment "the level of [a person's] mental energy and activity diminishes" (Frankfurt 2004: 54). One's responsiveness to the world and to other people "flattens out and shrinks" (ibid.). We have no interest in what happens.

(6) Responsibility for self. There are some things that practically no person can help caring about. This is most true of caring for oneself. A person who cares not for themselves hardly counts as a person at all. Complete indifference to oneself is tantamount to a cessation of caring. And the ability to take responsibility for oneself is utterly essential for self-caring. We must possess some non-negligible measure or level of capacity to take charge of or to govern, guide, manage or control our own behavior if we are to care for ourselves. We must be able to form intentions, evaluate impulses and inhibitions, make practical judgments and self-reflective decisions, and act on those decisions with at least a modicum of freedom from immediately surrounding circumstances (the push/pull of the surrounding environment) as well as from unwelcome or intrusive personal characteristics. A person, for example, who is totally heedless about themselves, promiscuously impulsive in behavior, acting without selectivity or restraint, will not be long for this world.

(7) Recognition of opportunities or 'affordances'. We must be able to recognize opportunities for alternative courses of action or behavior. Circumstances and occasions present themselves as choice or decision points for variable and varying courses of action. Being able to recognize choice points or affordances (as they may be called, co-opting a term of J. J. Gibson out of context [see Reed 1996]) is essential for securing a variety of different human goods and for the development of our own plans and policies, character and personality. Consider the following situation. You visit your doctor with a bothersome bodily symptom. He tells you that it may be a rare and fatal somatic condition, but also that there is a simple and painless skin test that reveals if you have the condition. What should you do? Unless you perceive the opportunity to take the test as a choice point, you may not survive the somatic condition if you harbor it. You will fail to learn of its presence and proper treatment. Many people seem to resist situations in which they have to make decisions. Some people may defer taking such a test under the assumption that Ignorance is Bliss. But presumably we would all want the ability, when anticipated from behind the Veil, to develop our decision-making talents. We would want not to be ignorant of opportunities for alternative courses of action. We would prefer not to live in a straight line, without forks in the road or choices to make, from beginning to end. We would want somehow or to some extent to direct and modify the course of our lives. A major factor in developing that self-responsibility competence is the capacity to recognize and represent for ourselves options for alternative courses of behavior.

It is, I believe, instructive to picture the above capacities or faculties (and they criss-cross, overlap and interpenetrate one other quite obviously) together with the outcomes that they help us to seek or secure as developing, unfolding and being exercised in a manner that, if luck permits and circumstances encourage, enables a person to achieve a satisfying or decent life. Not a painless life. (Remember Freud noted the impossibility of that.) Not a flourishing or utterly self-fulfilling life. Flourishing requires (in addition to sheer good fortune) capacity levels in excess of those presupposed, albeit vaguely, by my talk of 'non-negligible measure'. Flourishing is above and beyond mere satisfaction or decency and flowers into the sort of life that is immensely well worth living and profoundly satisfying. A gift of the gods perhaps. But no such elevated or inflated standard suits the identification of faculties or capacities, such that when impaired or disabled in certain ways, are elements of a mental disorder.

The purpose behind my list is not to propose that each and every one of the above capacities, or impairments or incapacitations in them, is operative in any and all exemplary mental disorders. When the poet Sylvia Plath, who suffered from depression and committed suicide, wrote in her diary in 1952 of "corrosive emotions of insecurity biting away at my sensitive guts," she was speaking of an undermining emotional tone to her life that left her "nerves paralyzed" and her "action nullified" (quoted in Kagan 1994: 288). Such is the disorder of depression that it leaves a person, as T. S. Eliot phrased it in *The Waste Land*, with "a handful of dust." Emotional dust. Without resonance: without the emotional commitments, engagements or forms of caring that enable a person to lead a decent life. Plath, as a victim of depression, was impaired in her capacity for care (of self) and perhaps also in related capacities for self-responsibility and opportunity recognition. She, however, had no trouble, say, in locating herself bodily or in communication (she was a gifted poet). So, to impair one or more capacities certainly is not necessarily to disable others, let alone all.

I am also not proposing that the relevant psychological capacities mentioned above, however incapacitated or impaired, utterly preclude living a decent life. Disability per se does not preclude living a decent life. Perish the thought. Some disabilities may be effectively managed (especially with assistance); others may admit of compensation; still others, in context, may be moderate and relatively inconsequential – like a low-grade fever. As two well-informed clinical observers put matters, "even people experiencing repeated episodes of mildly psychotic symptoms" may do so "without ever becoming floridly unwell" (Frith and Johnstone 2003: 43–4). Disorder, too, is not an all or none affair, any more than the boundary between disorder and non-disorder is clear-cut. Rather my assumption here is that the disabling of one or more basic psychological capacities raises the risks or likelihood of harms or losses of freedom and therein of loss of decency to a life. Such harms or losses, then, depending on how they are brought about, also help to constitute (exemplary) mental disorders. Moderate instances of a disorder are moderate, not by themselves life-shattering. Exemplary instances are serious and severe.

I am also not assuming that the capacities in order to be disabled must be disabled by two kinds of forces, both mental and brute mechanical or somatic. While such a twin pair of sources holds of a mental disorder, both kinds do not operate in all forms of disorder (say, in neurological disorders where only mechanical forces are at work). Just because a psychological capacity is impaired does not mean that mental forces are part of its disabling conditions. Capacities may be disabled purely by brute somatic forces (although when that happens the condition is not, I am urging, a mental disorder).

To continue listing what I am not claiming or proposing: I am not proposing that basic capacities admit of only one sort of impairment or disabled state or condition. Goodness (sadness) no. There are multiple (and for some capacities a bewildering variety of) ways of disabling a basic capacity. Multiple ways, for instance, of disabling a person's ability to locate themselves spatially (blindness is but one) or of impairing the capacity to effectively comprehend oneself or the world (Down's syndrome and schizophrenia are but two). In addition, too, disabilities come in different degrees (as noted), may be restricted to expression in specific situations and, under certain circumstances, may be muted or muffled. Disabilities of different sorts also may affect, influence or interpenetrate each other. Someone with a dramatically diminished power of self-comprehension or historical self-awareness may become so depressed that they are unable to properly care for themselves. I am thinking of various cases of advanced Alzheimer's dementia, for example, in which autobiographical memory loss so disturbs a person that they become frightened, withdrawn and depressed. Or a person may cease being emotionally committed to their personal well-being and suffer a disability in self-care and -commitment. I am thinking of cases of clinical depression here. Someone who is depressed may then be unable to recognize important opportunities for self-change and -transformation (a failure to grasp decisional affordances). So: One type of incapacity may break into another faculty or form of competence, helping to produce a second or even a third dimension to a disorder. "A totally specific [incapacity may] be extremely unlikely" (Karmiloff-Smith 1998: 390).

I am well aware, of course, that the above list of basic capacities contains, quite obviously, vague, loose and imprecise terms. Locating self, comprehending the world, being self-responsible, and so on. These are all capacities that come in different sizes, shapes, colors and varieties and operate along a variety of different fronts, measures or dimensions. Each also has exemplars; each has foils. Failures of rationality may also be quite specific to each. A reckless and ambivalent imprudence in the consumption of drugs may be a sign of addiction. Irrationally miscomprehending others may help to exemplify paranoia. Imprudently choosing to stay in bed rather than report to work may be a sign of clinical depression. Just how one understands and applies notions of impairments in the rational exercise or operation of such capacities (as suggested above) for specific cases or types of mental disorder depends on the needs and contexts of particular applications of the concept of a mental disorder (of which more in the rest of the book).

Although it may be theoretically nerve-racking to base a theory of basic capacity on phenomena that are vaguely and loosely defined and subject to contextual variations and parameters, I know of no way around it. As pointed out earlier in the book, there are some physical diseases (not exemplars of somatic illness perhaps) that also possess vague borders. An illustration is hypertension, an abnormal elevation of blood pressure, which increases the risks of strokes and heart attacks. The boundary between low and high blood pressure is vague, and determined contextually by physicians, who assess a person's risk of vascular disease by including family history, analysis of work stress, and so on. But no one wishes to deny that hypertension is a genuine somatic malady.

What attitude should we take toward vagueness or looseness in capacity designation? Wanting to eliminate vagueness or looseness from the idea of a basic capacity has a scientifically idealistic ring, but eliminating it is an unwise theoretical aspiration for a theory of mental disorder. Remember: In referring to mental disorders we are not talking of conditions with the often relatively more precise descriptive specifications and origins of somatic diseases like malaria or scurvy. Disorders are states that lie on a continuum alongside normal variations in human mental health and well-being, have multiple (not small sets of) symptoms and origins, and lack empirically tractable necessary and sufficient conditions. In speaking of mental disorders we are also referring to conditions that transgress norms of rationality, broadly understood, and therein must be flexibly described given the contextual and rather loose nature of such norms. Reason's rules are not rigid, smothering or algorithmic (as noted in discussing RIT [the rationality-*in*-Intentionality thesis]). The very idea of rationality can and should be adjusted to fit particulars of purpose, time, person and circumstance.

What about particular types or exemplars of mental disorder? How do basic incapacities or impairments figure in the constitution of exemplars? I will begin (in the next chapter) to answer such questions. My discussion will not be complete. There are capacities that I do not mention again in this book. I am sketching or outlining a theory of mental disorder, not detailing it. Lest we forget, however, before proceeding, we've still got some loose and untidy ends that need to be closed up before applying our emerging mental disorder concept to exemplary mental disorders.

Pages have passed since I last confronted in imagination a surgeon with the mismatch between my body and my experience of my body. Body integrity identity disorder. BIID. Which capacity on the list of seven (or eight, with conscious experience) is compromised in this disorder – assuming that it is a disorder? Quite apparently it is a person's sense of just where their body is and how it is poised, posed and feels. But how is such a capacity disabled in BIID?

Well, recall that in the case imagined I claimed to be emotionally dissociated from one of my limbs, namely a leg. I said that the leg does not feel to me as if it is proper to me. Perceptually, I recognize that the limb is attached to me or my torso. I also know that people most certainly tend to feel their limbs as their own. (I do so with my other limbs.) I can and do move the leg as if it is my own. I occasionally feel various pains or discomforts in it. Still, however, I insist that the limb is not properly or truly mine. The limb has an affectively alien or unfamiliar quality. So, I want it removed.

Several hypotheses have been offered in the literature for the source or origin of the alien experience of limb. (I name but do not explore them here.) Emotional flattening. Defective body schema. Defensive reaction in the face of threat to bodily integrity. Depersonalization (a loss of a sense of personal identity). Hallucinatory experience. Bodily image that sees amputation as attractive or sexually arousing.

So, hypothetically, there are a number of explanatory proposals. Alas, we do not know (as best as I can tell from the literature) how to answer the question of BIID's propensity conditions or etiology. Which hypothesis best fits the facts? Perhaps different hypotheses apply to different cases. Right now, it appears, the answer has to be an educated guess. A guess complicated by the fact that we are also in the dark about both the brute neuromechanical conditions that underlie or contribute to BIID and the precise role of Intentionalistic forces if any (assuming that it is a mental disorder). The presence of unanswered questions helps to explain why BIID, at the moment, is in a limbo in medical taxonomy. Is it a true mental disorder or like, for instance, Alzheimer's dementia, a condition with brute somatic conditions of onset and not a mental disorder. Perhaps no autograph of mentality is proper to its originating or propensity conditions.

What of the manner in which my list of the capacities/incapacities proper to a disorder presupposes contestable norms or values? What about my predilection for identifying relevant basic faculties in terms of what people want and desire, albeit under conditions devoid of particular or fine-grained environmental demands? Wants and desires seem like ripe subjects for evaluative contestation. Thomas Szasz may take ironic delight in the 'original' position strategy that I use, recognizing in it the recurrence of the sorts of presuppositions that render the very idea of a mental disorder medically otiose to him. I can hear his voice if not see his face behind the veil. "I told you so." "The notion of a mental disorder is a conceptual sham."

Recall that Szasz and certain other anti-psychiatry critics pick out the presupposition of values (or especially of allegedly contestable values) as an insurmountable obstacle to counting mental disorders as genuine illnesses. Values presupposition strips the idea of a mental disorder, such critics charge, of medical-scientific legitimacy or objective factual authority. Of course, legitimacy or authority may have a foundation other than absolute freedom from values presupposition. In the fourth chapter, we were encouraged to think of certain mental conditions as mental disorders by virtue of the following fact. Presupposing values (albeit perhaps often hidden) hasn't stopped bodily diseases from being described as genuine or objective illnesses. So, it should not prohibit a mental disorder from counting as a *bone fide* disorder either. What's dignifying for the somatic goose is respectful of the mental gander. When someone is physically ill, there necessarily is something *wrong* with them. No surprise, then, if when something is mentally *wrong* with a person, the person may be the subject of a mental disorder.

But still the Szaszian objection annoyingly persists. As one sympathetic admirer of his position puts it, "Szasz got mired in questions of the meaning of terms." "But his conclusions [are] in many ways correct" (Pickard 2009: 98). The relevant norms for the diagnosis of a mental disorder may seem so much more contestable than those that undergird the attribution of a somatic illness. They are, if I am right, norms that depend on assessments of the rational (or irrational) and reason-responsive exercise of basic capacities. Often they are also norms that presuppose the acceptance of standards of positive or commendable character traits and desirable patterns of behavior. To make this explicit, think of the example of our capacity for care and commitment. It is natural to think that some things are worth caring for and others not. It is worth caring for one's children, not the wrinkles in one's sheets or the freckles on the face of one's dead uncle. Whatever the precise nature of such norms may be, and whatever sort or degree of irrationality caring for wrinkles or freckles rather than children exemplifies, such norms can appear highly controversial, eminently contestable. The relevant norms in somatic illness seem not so contestable. They consist of standards of proper bodily function. They are thought less controversial and markedly less debatable than mental disorder norms. It is one thing to say that a heart or kidney is not functioning as it should, another to say something similar about a person's capacity for emotional care or commitment.

One response to this reintroduction of Szaszian worry is to claim that the normative or evaluative differences between standards for somatic and mental disorder are differences of degree only and not of kind. Each notion of disorder relies on norms for the sorts of persons we wish to be or want to become and which faculties or capacities are needed to realize those aspirations. Also, we should not pretend that culturally situated aspirations and situational variables don't influence bodily-illness attribution.

Complementary to that response is the following response. It is customary in discussions of the existence of a mental disorder to worry over whether there is such a thing as the objective truth about a diagnosis. This worry has two parts. First, are our beliefs and assertions about a diagnosis of mental disorder true? If a psychiatrist says that someone is, say, clinically depressed or delusional, is such a statement true? Does the patient have the ascribed condition or not? It is, as a physician might put it, up to our diagnostic judgments to get a diagnosis right. Second, is a mental disorder something that exists independently of our diagnostic classifications or judgments? If someone has a mental disorder only because we think that they have it, it's not the disorder (the real and independent existence of the disorder) that conveys truth on our diagnosis, but the act of diagnosis itself that makes it true that the person 'has' the disorder. It's a matter of diagnostic fiat. A performance, not an inference. Saying so makes it so, as it were. Nothing could be less medically or objectively real for a condition or disorder.

As noted in the first chapter to this book, I am a realist about mental disorder. I affirm the existence of objective truths about mental disorder attributions and diagnoses. Anti-realists or radical skeptics about disorder often base their anti-realisms on such things as the values contestation of mental disorder norms (such as rationality norms) and the allegedly suspect tests or assessments for a mental disorder diagnosis (no skin tests, no blood tests or X-rays). One might be tempted to straddle the fence here and say that the jury is still out on whether mental disorders are real conditions of persons. But I don't believe that the jury is out. At least at a coarse-grained level of analysis, which allows for ragged borders between disorders and non-disorders, mental disorders are real. I see no deep or ultimate difference as a harmful condition between that of a clinically depressed person who cannot get out of bed in the morning and tragically ends the day by committing suicide and that of an individual who dies of a heart attack in their office. What is present in both cases are the effects of something wrong with a person, something that they cannot manage, something that is undesirable and harmful – an emotional incapacity, a hobbled heart.

So: we come back now to the central theme of this chapter. Let's return to the issue of basic capacities. For a heart to be capable of circulating blood is one condition. For self-care and commitment to keep a person from harm is another. Unbiased by particularistic personal desires, we have described a list above of psychological capacities that people value or would want to possess given the general character of life. These are faculties that no one, I assume, would wish to be without or to have seriously compromised or impaired.

It may also be noted that the impartial identification of capacities conducted from behind the veil of imagined ignorance excludes as well as includes capacities as germane to classifying a mental disorder. GOD (grade obsessive disorder) is not a mental disorder. There is no reason to confer medical respectability on GOD as a diagnosis. Failure to achieve high academic performance in a stress-free manner reflects no basic impairment or incapacity (assuming, of course, that GOD is not a specific symptom of a more general impairment). Particular desires of particular individuals may be hampered by GOD. No doubt, they are. But life is like that. Not everyone can succeed at everything.

GOD is a problem or difficulty in living, a circumstantial or academic liability, and not the disabling of a fundamental capacity. It stymies in quite specific circumstances certain desired accomplishments or forms of success only. Panic attacks with agoraphobia, by dramatic contrast, infect and disable much more broadly or profoundly. Suppose: If someone asks me to walk with them through a mall, I decline. I cannot get to work in a bus or subway. My office is on the twenty-fifth floor, but I cannot ride an elevator. Unmarried I am eager to find a spouse but cannot attend church services, join a club, or vacation at a singles resort. Such circumstances are crowded with strangers. All to the good are such places if a person is looking for a spouse. But I get hyper-anxious. All to the bad if I am hoping myself to find one. So, it has become practically impossible for me to meet new people. Practically, no one could live well under such circumstances. The propensity to stranger-induced panic locks me in a closet socially. It reflects a reason-responsive truncation in a capacity to comprehend others (if I am right) as well as perhaps in self-responsibility. People matter to me. I've read Mill and labored through Augustine. I want someone to love to give meaning to my life, but can't control myself well enough to meet them. I need to maintain my job but struggle to do so. Such would be the case if I was a victim of agoraphobia.

Finally, just mentioned and lest we forget him, St Augustine. Augustine yearned for salvation. Dispirited he wanted communion with the divine. In his dispiritedness no basic capacity was impaired. He pulled himself out of his philosophical or spiritual despair by the bootstraps of prayer and theological reflection. Most certainly, too, there was nothing irrational in Augustine's desired outcome. One may question or debate the reality of God, of course, but all sorts of eager souls hunger and thirst for Him. A spiritual yearning for other-worldly transcendence through allegiance to a divine agent, even if objectively aimed at a myth or phantom, is, it appears, a near universal human proclivity. Augustine, to his credit, recognized the theological affordances of his Christian cultural milieu. He brought powerful and arresting conceptualization to the Christian vision.

Can we fault him? Suspect his reason? We can, I believe, only hold people to standards of reason and rationality that reflect historical or cultural circumstances. A meditating monk, who is sitting naked on a New York City subway and humming unintelligible mantras, may raise proper suspicions of schizophrenia or delusional disorder, but we cannot blame Augustine for failing to consider, say, Buddhist naturalistic principles in his quest for a life-defining purpose. "The naturalistic picture of persons is not inherently deflating or disenchanting," writes Owen Flanagan (2007: 107). With Flanagan we may agree, but it would be absurd to demand such insight from someone born in Numidia in AD 354. "Our norms and values are designed to serve our purposes as social mammals living in different social worlds" (Flanagan 2007: 107). Geniuses or the deluded may break their current linkages between the social world and rationality, but attitudes outside the scope of cultural possibilities are too much to expect of people even if on occasion and otherwise they may be preferable.

Let me now sum things up and bring this chapter to a close by describing the concept of mental disorder that I have constructed. It is designed to apply to prototypes or exemplars of disorder. The concept was mentioned in the second chapter. It has since, I hope, been soundly derived and sensibly extended with additional detail. So the statement below is not exactly like the one in the second chapter. (This one mentions rationality, for instance, rather than just, as in the second chapter, mentality.)

A CONCEPT OF MENTAL DISORDER

Here is the concept. Using the language of theses to describe it, it contains four theses. The concept of a mental disorder, prototypically understood and regimentally clarified, is the concept of a (i) (*rationality-disability thesis*) disability, incapacity or impairment in the rational or reason-responsive operation or exercise of one or more fundamental mental faculties or basic psychological capacities of a person, that (ii) (*harm thesis*) causes harmful or potentially harmful symptoms/consequences for the person (and perhaps also for others). The disability also possesses a special sort of source, genesis or set of propensity conditions. It is (iii) (*mixed-source thesis*) brought about by a balance or mix of Intentionalistic activity, on the one hand, and brute a-rational neural causes or mechanisms, on the other, and (iv) (*some preservation of rationality thesis*) the combination or intersection of such activities infuses a mental disorder with a truncated 'logic' or compromised rationale of its own i.e. when a capacity is impaired or disabled in a mental disorder it is compromised in its reason-responsive operation but not destroyed. (The incapacitation or impairment – which, remember, is subject to contextual parameters – is not an obliteration of reason or reason-responsiveness.)

Each thesis has been introduced and explored in the preceding chapters of this book, but each requires further elaboration and clarification. I plan to offer some of that in the rest of the book, but I am under no illusion that what I say will be sufficient or complete. It will not be.

Considerations of particular disorders will figure prominently in the continued course of the argument, and they will appeal to specific parts of the above concept. But oftentimes I will be interested not so much in the neural activity behind or underpinning a disorder as in the assumptions being made about the rational or desirable operation of a basic capacity.

CHAPTER SUMMARY AND SUGGESTED READINGS

This chapter outlined how to identify the psychological or mental capacities impaired in exemplary mental disorders by appeal to a thought experiment appropriated from John Rawls. Critics like Thomas Szasz of the idea of mental disorder on grounds that it presupposes contestable values ask too much of the notion of mental disorder. The concept should not be faulted for presupposing values (even contestable ones). The concept can survive if it presupposes values that all or most of us hold dear and appeals to psychological capacities that all or most of us deeply value. Is there room for contestation about the identity of such capacities or the nature of such values? Yes, to be sure, there is. But complete and utter immunity to contestation is not a feasible desideratum. There is conceptual elbow room for disagreement about the nature or relative importance of each of the capacities identified in this chapter, just as there is for various judgments about the parameters of physical illness. And, no doubt, there may be other potential points of contention. But we took Rawls's experiment to be applicable to psychological order because it helps to flag the basic capacities impaired in prototypical mental disorders.

It is also important for a theory of mental disorder to recall that our capacity for conscious experience is held dear and to appreciate why. Not for its pleasures only (Mill's lesson) but for the sake of other things in the world that we value or care about or to which we consciously attend. Grounding the value of consciousness in externalities (commitment to family, concern for personal achievement, etc.) engages us in the world in ways that may make life painful for us, but would make it pointless to be conscious without such commitments.

What of Rawls? Rawls's conceptions of social order and the veil of ignorance are effectively summarized in C. Kukathas and P. Pettit's *Rawls: A "Theory of Justice" and Its Critics* (Stanford University Press, 1990). A short but useful summary is available in Norman Daniels's "John Rawls (1921–2002)," in A. Martinich and D. Sosa (eds), *A Companion to Analytic Philosophy* (Blackwell, 2001).

The usual manner in which to classify or individuate psychological capacities is in terms of such generic faculties as memory, perception, learning, reasoning, decision-making and the like. Numerous chapters in Part II of W. Bechtel and G. Graham (eds), *A Companion to Cognitive Science* (Blackwell, 1998), outline much recent work on those capacities. The approach taken to basic faculty identification in the present chapter is in terms of capacities or capabilities that are embedded in individuals' desired forms of life. The wisdom of the approach as applied to the topic of mental disorder must speak for itself, of course, and there is no research source that I know of that offers an alternative outline and defense of it. But there are authors who adopt a similar approach to capability classification, although for different purposes (in ethics, for example). James Rachels's discussion of the moral relevance of the capacities of non-human animals relies on the approach and may actually have introduced it into the field of ethics. See his *Created from Animals: The Moral Implications of Darwinism* (Oxford University Press, 1990) as well as "Do Animals Have a Right to Liberty?" in T. Regan and P. Singer (eds), *Animal Rights and Human Obligations* (Prentice-Hall, 1976). With credit to Rachels as well as to Rawls, Martha Nussbaum deploys the approach in *Frontiers of Justice: Disability, Nationality, Species Membership* (Harvard University Press, 2006).

Emphasis on identifying capacities necessary for good or satisfying forms of life may be found in the Aristotelian tradition in ethics. The main idea behind the tradition is that what counts as good personal conditions for a person depends on the maturation and development of their natural human powers and not necessarily on what people may actually desire or want (whether from behind a veil or over the actual course of life). For an exercise in the Aristotelian tradition, see Richard Kraut's *What Is Good and Why: The Ethics of Well-Being* (Harvard University Press, 2007). Offhand, Kraut's approach seems quite different from the quasi-Rawlsian picture of capacity identification outlined in this chapter. This chapter stresses what properly informed and culturally or situationally neutralized people purpose or want. The Aristotelian approach targets what people should want if their talents are properly to develop. Just whether my approach is different in what it actually identifies as good for a person requires inspection. Rawls expresses some sympathy for the Aristotelian approach in the seventh chapter of *A Theory of Justice*.

A probing essay on the capacity for emotional commitment and concern is Harry Frankfurt's "The Importance of What We Care About," in his *The Importance of What We Care About* (Cambridge University Press, 1988). Frankfurt believes that at the center of our power for emotional commitment and concern is a capacity for unconditional love. It is by loving unconditionally, he says, that we shape the aims and concerns around which to lead our lives. For discussion of this idea, see his engaging little book *The Reasons of Love* (Princeton University Press, 2004).

On the role of autobiographical memory (locating oneself historically or in time) in a satisfying life, much can be learned from failures of this capacity and how loss of memory is a burden to a person. Thomas DeBaggio has written a memoir on his early diagnosis of Alzheimer's that is both insightful and well-written, entitled *Losing My Mind: An Intimate Look at Life with Alzheimer's* (Free Press, 2003).

Discussions of the utility of consciousness include U. T. Place's "Consciousness and the 'Zombie-Within': A Functional Analysis of the Blindsight Evidence," in G. Graham and E. Valentine (eds), *Identifying the Mind: Selected Papers of U. T. Place* (Oxford University Press, 2004); Michael Tye's "The Function of Consciousness," *Noûs*, 1996, 30, pp. 287–305; and Robert Van Gulick's "Deficit Studies and the Function of Phenomenal Consciousness," in G. Graham and G. L. Stephens (eds), *Philosophical Psychopathology* (MIT Press, 1994).

Diagnostic vicissitudes and moral quandaries posed by BIID are explored (as I have mentioned before) in Tim Bayne and Neil Levy, "Amputees by Choice: Body Integrity Identity Disorder and the Ethics of Amputation," *Journal of Applied Philosophy*, 2005, 22, pp. 75–86. On disorders of embodiment, more generally, see S. Gallagher and M. Vaever, "Body: Disorders of Embodiment," in J. Radden (ed.), *The Philosophy of Psychiatry: A Companion* (Oxford University Press, 2004).

7 Addiction and responsibility for self

Often we persons do things because we expect them to be rewarding or to confer benefits, although we may simultaneously know of and be willing to accept various negative aspects or consequences of what we do. I shop for a car. I need one. My old car is on its last cylinders. I discover one that I decide to purchase. It has a good consumer rating, reliably infrequent repairs, excellent gas mileage, and I can afford it. It's not made in colors I like. Nothing but Precambrian Pink or Geothermal Green. But I believe I can put up with incredulous stares from neighbors and the occasional snide remarks of pedestrians. Situation is: Among the options for a good car that I think are open to me, this one strikes me as the best at the time.

Are addictive patterns of behavior like that? When we spot a gambler living in financial debt up to his neck, having wasted away his life savings, divorced from his spouse, separated from his children, living in a rundown efficiency apartment in a dangerous part of town, waiting on tables in an all-night diner, is this the lifestyle he has chosen? Among the options that he actually believed were open to him, did habitual gambling strike him as the best at the time? Is it wrong to suppose that there is something wrong with him? That he is the subject of a disorder?

Gary Becker and Kevin Murphy (1988) propose just such a 'no disorder' model of addiction. An addict, they say, may act self-destructively or objectionably by social or moral standards. Or they may be ignorant of certain harmful consequences of their behavior. But, they say, addictive behavior is the upshot of rational efforts to satisfy desires or preferences for various goods given circumstantial and temporal constraints. So, while addictive behavior is something mental, for it's a choice and deliberate, it is not a disorder. An addict's behavioral preference for drugs or wagers at a horse track just is a decision, and like any other decision-maker addicts try to get as much preference satisfaction overall as any other agent. Out of bad luck or ignorance or an ill-considered or fearless devaluation of the future, they may not succeed, of course, just as we may fail to be satisfied by our behavior. When, however, an addict consumes a drug or places a series of wagers at a track, at the time, this is a good choice from their subjective point of view. Yes, an addict may harm themselves, and, yes, we may try to help them to avoid situations in which they do so. But we should not help under the faulty assumption that addiction is a disorder or that something is wrong with them.

So say some theorists. Of course, denying that addiction is a disorder depends on just how addiction is understood. If we assume that addiction, properly so-called, puts a person's health or welfare at serious risk, that an addict's preferences or desires may be unsettled or in conflict, and that addicts are not indifferent to or ignorant of the harmful consequences of their behavior but often have difficulty (an impairment in rational impulse control perhaps) avoiding such behavior even though they wish to and sometimes do succeed (albeit temporarily), then the case for classifying addictive behavior as a type of disorder starts to become strong. Certainly it is stronger than depicting it as a mere preference satisfaction. So, too, I hasten to add, is the warrant for classifying addiction as a *mental* disorder and not a neurological disorder.

Is addiction a disorder? Is it a mental disorder? The terms of this question – 'mental' and 'disorder' – are all subject to interpretative disagreements. In previous chapters in this book I have tried to describe or explicate their proper meaning. I have spoken, for example, in connection with the first term, of Intentionality, and in connection with the second, of a-rationally gumming up the rational works. If all or much of what I have said is agreed on, we are in a position to decide whether addiction is not just a disorder but a mental disorder. No mere preference satisfaction but something wrong with a person.

I shall begin by coming to fuller terms with a term.

'Addiction' is used by ordinary folks as well as most behavioral scientists to identify excessive and deleterious behavior, behavior that is repeatedly engaged in despite its negative consequences, often prefaced by impulses or motives that the addict wishes to control but finds difficult to consistently master or govern. The term 'addiction' hasn't always had such an unfortunate reference. At one time (in Britain in the early seventeenth century) the word referred to a devotional or obligatory attachment to a particular pattern of activity (Ross et al. 2008: 4). In that sense of the word, I am addicted to philosophy, for I am devotedly attached to it. That's not, needless to say, the reference of the term on which I plan to focus here in this chapter.

Lest in this chapter we be unsure of how 'addiction' is being used, I offer the following outline of the stages of addiction or addictive patterns of behavior. I take there to be eight main stages or steps in a typical clinical coalface case of addiction. In referring to addiction's clinical coalface, I mean the behavior pattern of an addict who appears in an addiction clinic or professional mental-health-care setting and seeks and receives treatment for addiction. Clinics for alcohol addicts, cocaine addicts, and so on, are "largely populated by people who are in the process of making a serious attempt to stop their behavior" (West 2006: 128). We may speak of such addicts as unwilling addicts as opposed to those who may, in some sense or other of 'addiction', be addicted but willingly or preferably so (if perhaps because they are unaware of the deleterious consequences of their behavior or somehow indifferent to them). Here are the eight stages or steps:

(1) A person commences a behavior that is harmful or deleterious (consumes a deleterious drug or other chemical substance or gambles).
(2) The behavior becomes an object of focal attention and periodically repeated activity.
(3) The behavior produces consequences that are not just harmful or that seriously risk harm to self (and/or others) but are perceived as harmful or destructive by the agent.
(4) The perception or direct experience of harmful consequences leads the addict on certain critical and reflective occasions to negatively self-evaluate the behavior and to attempt to refrain or quit.
(5) The addict refrains, quits, or inhibits the behavior during certain periods (perhaps without assistance, perhaps only with assistance – individual cases and occasions vary).
(6) Quitting or cessation ultimately (timing and intervals vary) proves unsuccessful, however. The addict relapses. They 'fall back' into the detrimental behavior after a period of temporary stoppage. The behavior returns together with its negative consequences or risks.
(7) Relapse is interpreted by the agent as a form of personal disappointment or failure, not just as something destructive or risky, but as a source of shame, regret, self-blame, embarrassment or diminished self-confidence or self-esteem.
(8) The steps or phases of harmful behavior, temporary abstention, and relapse cycle repeatedly. The recycling, in some cases, may cease permanently, perhaps without harmful long-term residue. (Thousands of addicts just plain quit for good at some point, although sometimes not until much has been lost or destroyed.) Or the addictive pattern may lead to an addict's personal demise.

The eight steps that I am assuming to constitute an addictive pattern are not present in all cases of behavior that may be classified as addictive. They are not present in willing addictions, for instance. But in order to make progress on the topic of addiction a theorist has to make certain background classificatory assumptions. So I assume that addiction, at least in prototypical cases where treatment is sought or received, possesses or cycles through the full steps.

There has been much discussion in the clinical and therapeutic literature of the actual and possible objects (substances, forms of activity) of addictive behavior. Drugs. Gambling. Smoking. Food. Sex. Shopping. Internet. Shoplifting. In this chapter I have nothing directly to say about the possible range of substances or activities to which people may be addicted or why. I plan to focus on activities such as the consumption of drugs (like alcohol and cocaine) and gambling. These are the prototypes of addiction. The exemplars.

Some steps in addictive behavior are more or less well understood. We certainly know that people behave imprudently and engage in risky behaviors (Step [1]). We know that such behaviors have variable motives. Sometimes risky behavior is engaged in simply as a form of entertainment; other times it possesses more serious or dramatic motives. We also know that non-human animal models of addiction help to explain some forms of habitual but deleterious or risky behavior, as does explanatory reference to certain well-known features of human psychology such as the fact that imprudent risk-taking may be pleasurable or reinforced by peers or promoted in one's subculture. But other steps in addictive patterns are not well understood.

Relapse (Step [6]) and some of the negative attitudes experienced after or during relapse (Step [7]) are poorly understood and so herein in this chapter I plan to concentrate not just on addiction but on relapse, namely the episode of relapse itself and the agent's interpretation of relapse (the sixth and seventh stages of addictive patterns). I also plan to examine just what makes addiction qualify as a *mental* disorder rather than a disorder of the brain or neurological disorder.

IMPULSE, INHIBITION AND RESPONSIBILITY FOR SELF

Addictive patterns are constituted, in part, although only in part, by "impaired control over behavior" or by an incapacity to inhibit behavioral impulses that lead "to significant harm" (West 2006: 10). (DSM talks not of addictions but of "disorders of impulse control.") I say 'only in part' because the full-bodied tale of the cognitive-motivational dynamics behind addiction is, I claim, a story of an incapacity or impairment in taking evaluative stock of oneself and of exerting self-control. Following a practice introduced into contemporary philosophy by Charles Taylor (1976) and others, I call taking stock and exerting control taking 'responsibility for self'. No small chore that: taking responsibility for self. Telling a tale of the failure of self-responsibility in addiction requires going well beyond trying to understand addiction just in terms of impulse control or inhibition failure or deleterious habit formation.

Consider impulse and inhibition first, though. William James tells us: "Impulses [push] us one way and obstructions and inhibitions [hold] us back" (James 2002 [1901–2]: 287).

References to impulses and inhibitions help to explain why people do what they do. Adam smokes cigarettes because he enjoys lighting up. He has an impulse to light up. Eve doesn't indulge because she is worried about her health. She is inhibited.

To correctly attribute an impulse or inhibition to a person means that they are inclined or disinclined, respectively, to behave in a certain manner on certain occasions. A person may push forward (impulse) or pull back (inhibition). Offer me a delicious piece of chocolate cake in a four-star restaurant. I will take it. Offer me the same piece off the back of a garbage truck. I will refuse. The first situation reflects impulse. The second reflects inhibition.

We human beings, of course, are not mere creatures of impulse and inhibition. Normally, we have and exercise a power or capacity to reflect on our impulses or inhibitions and to decide whether we should, or should not, possess or act on an impulse or inhibition. Our capacity for evaluative self-appraisal and -assessment (taking stock of oneself) the philosopher Harry Frankfurt aptly calls a "capacity for reflective self-evaluation" (Frankfurt 1988: 12).

As reflective self-evaluators we persons try to put in place self-appraised, reflexive motivational relations to our impulses and inhibitions, our acts and abstentions. If I positively evaluate or appraise a disposition, say, judge it to be good or approve of it, I may attempt to stand by this judgment and act in terms of it. If I negatively evaluate a disposition, disapprove of it, I may try to inhibit the impulse. Tempted to steal or cheat, but judging the behavior to be base, degrading or incompatible with cherished character traits or with the life I wish to lead, I may decide that I don't wish to be tempted. I may yearn to be free of the disturbing impulse. Inclined to sample a recreational but potentially unhealthy drug and appreciating that consuming it jeopardizes plans or projects that I hold dear, I may try to restrain myself. Perhaps I will turn away from the site or sight of temptation.

The twin or related powers or capacities, the one of evaluative self-reflection, the other of behavioral self-control, are constituents or elements in responsibility for self (as I will explain momentarily). It's a clear-cut linguistic distinction between them, to be sure, but any hard-and-fast separation in practice between the two powers can be tricky. Behavioral self-control or mastery is often a feature of reflective self-evaluation. The intensity or seriousness of mental effort behind evaluative attention, for example, through which a person appraises their own impulses or inhibitions, is not a purely cognitive matter, not a matter of a spectator-like intellect. It is not always easy to control one's ruminations and mental activities.

A persistent theme in the literature on the manic episodes distinctive of bipolar disorder is the enormous surge of energy that a person in manic states acquires. Nancy Andreasen speaks of mania as like "riding a horse that is out of control" (Andreasen 2001: 233). "If the increased energy and richness of thought could be harnessed and focused, a time of mania could be a time of great creativity and productivity" (Andreasen 2001: 232–3). But, sadly, people in manic states typically lack prudent inhibition and respond to all sorts of indiscriminate thoughts. When mania is acute or severe, a person may experience a 'flight of ideas', thoughts or feelings whose wealth and abundance skips so rapidly from topic to topic that they cannot self-reflectively step back and effectively evaluate their impulses. The person may be incapable of asking themselves whether their behaviors are deeds in which they should be engaged. They may not even experience their agitated or excessive impulses as disruptive or upsetting. All of which seems best described as difficulties of self-control within the very effort of self-evaluation. Focusing prudently on consequences of anticipated behavior, directing one's thoughts to desired traits of character, not allowing one's ideas of possible behaviors to be swayed by attractive temptations to dangerous activity, and so on, all may require exerting a sizeable measure of self-rule or self-governance over one's mental processes and not just over one's physical movements.

The possible and more than occasional need for self-control within self-evaluation aside, still the two dimensions of self-responsibility are distinguishable. Philosophers have been intrigued by the roles of the capacities for self-evaluation and self-control in human agency and personhood. "Is there a sense in which the human agent," Charles Taylor asks in a classic paper on responsibility for self, "is responsible for himself which is part of our very conception of the self?" (C. Taylor 1976: 281). Taylor answers, yes, a human person is "not just a de facto kind of being, with certain given desires, but it is somehow 'up to him' what kind of being he is going to be" (ibid.). He writes:

> Human subjects are capable of evaluating what they are, and to the extent that they can shape themselves on this evaluation, are responsible for what they are in a way

that other subjects of action and desire (the higher animals for instance) cannot be said to be. ... My dog 'evaluates' [a piece of] beefsteak positively. But the kind of evaluation implicit in the above [remarks] is a reflective kind where we evaluate our desires themselves.

(C. Taylor 1976: 282)

The evaluative power of which Taylor speaks is the capacity for reflective self-evaluation. The corresponding power to shape, sculpt or mold oneself along the lines of one's evaluation is the capacity for reflective self-control. Both powers are proper parts of self-responsibility. To possess a power of self-responsibility, a person must not only be capable of evaluating which desires, impulses, or inhibitions she acts on or possesses, but "of controlling ... behavior in the light of such reflections" (Kane 2005: 165).

Robert West, a professor of health psychology at University College London and the editor-in-chief of the flagship journal on addiction aptly called *Addiction*, has noted that when addicts evaluate themselves, appraise who they are and how they should behave or act, often they want to stop their deleterious behavior or quit for good (West 2006: 128). (Indeed, thousands of addicts ultimately do give up their addictions voluntarily and often without assistance from others.) Of course an addicted person's desire to quit may not be sustained in effective purport and may undergo alteration or reversal. Motivational alteration should not surprise us, however. People quite ordinarily change tastes. Sometimes we adopt completely new and contrary preferences or aspirations. West remarks: "[I]t is unrealistic to assume that the situation would be any different for addiction" (West 2006: 128).

Some forms of motivational alteration are normal and not deleterious. They raise no judgmental eyebrows. Their effects are not harmful or destructive. But one can hardly take a casual attitude to reversal or alteration when harm to self as well as perhaps to others is a consequence and a subject's self-evaluation urges inhibition or restraint. One of the core elements of addiction, in cases of persons undergoing voluntary clinical treatment, and unlike much more pedestrian forms of behavioral inconsistency, is that the agent knows that a behavior is deleterious and may make genuine and successful, albeit not enduringly successful, attempts to refrain. When things are going well and self-responsibly, I (suppose I am an alcoholic) don't enter a bar and order a drink. When something goes wrong, abstention fails, and there is a self-responsibility problem. "A shot of Scotch, please." Taking a drink, if desired and close at temporal hand, may be an impulse to which I succumb, when the deleterious consequences are far ahead or "the recollection of having suffered them in the past is ... already fading" (von Wright 1963: 113).

The phenomenon of failed abstention and return to deleterious behavior in a case of addiction is known, as noted, as relapse. Relapse is a psychologically puzzling state of imprudent affairs. It is difficult to explain how something that is negatively evaluated or believed by the agent to be harmful retains a grip on behavior. Unwanted behavior, rather than being a docile and easily mastered servant, may possess a motivationally salient grip on action.

Why does relapse occur despite the fact than an addict knows or feels that it represents a subversion of their efforts to refrain? If there is a single answer to this question (and I am not sure whether there is) it is not simple. Perhaps it has something to do with the fact that addiction is a form of compulsion. That's what numerous theorists and clinicians claim. So: Is relapse due to the fact that addictive patterns are compulsive? And, if so, what exactly is meant by calling it compulsive?

Some of the most striking statements in the literature about addiction and relapse are about drug addiction and the perils of certain drugs. Several scientists speak of drug seeking and consumption as compulsive. Alan Leshner, in a special issue of *Science* devoted to addiction, writes that the essence of drug addiction is "compulsive drug seeking and use, even in the face of negative health and social consequences" (Leshner 1997: 46). A publication of the Institute of Medicine claims that drug addiction consists of "drug seeking behavior involving compulsion [and] resulting in substantial impairments of health and social functioning" (Institute of Medicine 1996: 19).

Is addiction a species of compulsion? Not just drug addiction but addiction period? Reading the memoirs or autobiographies of addicts may suggest that it is.

Jack London was a prolific American novelist and short-story writer. He wrote *The Call of the Wild* and other books. London apparently struggled with alcohol dependence or addiction. "It is the penalty," London wrote, that a person's "friendship with John Barleycorn [beer and whiskey] sends [them into] the pitiless spectral syllogisms of ... white logic." A person "sleeps a drugged sleep" and "looks upon life ... with the jaundiced eye" of a pessimist to be "flung into the scrap-heap at the end" (London 1982: 940).

Caroline Knapp (1959–2002), columnist and editor, also battled with alcohol dependence. (She died in 2002 of lung cancer.) She drank cognac, double shots of Johnny Walker Black, expensive red wine, and silky Merlots – among other types of alcohol. In a post-recovery memoir entitled *Drinking: A Love Story* (1995) Knapp reports that drinking occurred "when I was happy and ... when I was anxious and ... when I was bored and ... when I was depressed" (Knapp 1998: 167). This meant Knapp drank, as she puts it in one simple ironic word, "often." Knapp says she now experiences "pangs of horror" when she thinks back to what she did to herself (169). Alcohol had become "a kind of liquid glue that gums up all the internal gears" (168).

Cocaine, too, of course, may be immensely addictive. Consider the case of a woman named Helen. Paramedics found her "sitting alone on the floor in a corner of the kitchen." "Her legs ... pulled up underneath her chin and her arms ... wrapped tightly around her knees." "She was too agitated and disorientated to comply" with their request to lie down (Flynn 1998: 181–2). Helen now reports that during the cocaine addicted period of her life "the only thing ... important ... was cocaine" (184).

Not just substances but activities, too, may be addictive. Consider sports wagering or casino gambling. "What did gambling do to me?," asks one victim (Heineman 1998: 163). He answers: "It removed all the positive characteristics my parents worked so hard to foster within me." "I cursed them, blamed them, stole from them, and, in the end, I attacked them physically" (163–4).

Compulsives, although certainly there is more to compulsion than this, fail to refrain from the 'compelled' behavior even though knowingly possessing good reasons to refrain. They somehow get derailed from responding to reasons to refrain. The addicts described above seem to fall under this description. To save her physical health, Helen had good reason to abstain. To avoid attacking his parents, the gambler had good reason to quit gambling. So as not to be mired in the 'glue' of alcohol, Knapp had good reason to stop drinking. London, speaking from personal experience (as I assume he was), knew better than to end up in a scrap heap. But neither person consistently or unfalteringly did what they possessed self-acknowledged good reason for doing. Quitting. Refraining.

COMPULSION AND ADDICTION

Frankly, I am not sure whether it makes good sense to classify addiction as a form of compulsion. Much depends on what counts or should count as compulsion.

Compulsive motivations are sometimes referred to as irresistible impulses. So, addictions are sometimes pictured as compulsive because said to stem from irresistible impulses. Relapse, in particular, it is said, amounts to yielding to irresistible impulses. Addiction, remarks Carl Elliott, "holds the leash" (Elliott 2002: 48). Attribution of irresistibility or leash-holding, however, is in general not an illuminating way in which to depict addiction. If addictive behavior generally was irresistible, no addict could quit for good. Addicts do refrain, of course, and sometimes without help. Many addicts also exhibit a sizeable measure of circumstantial self-control, periodic self-regulation or modulated abstention over the character or tempo of their impulse to behave (e.g. to consume a drug, to gamble). If the price, say, of a drug is too high, or a preferred dealer is inaccessible, a drug addict may temporarily curtail consumption and re-seek their drug of personal choice only when its price falls or the special supplier returns. An alcoholic office worker may abstain from drinking when her boss or colleagues are visibly present. It is not as if the impulse itself is irresistible.

Compulsions are sometimes said to be insatiable. So, some clinicians, who are fond of classifying addiction as a form of compulsion, claim that certain substances or activities induce insatiable appetites or desires and this, so they claim, means that addictive behavior is a species of compulsion. Relapse, it is said, stems from a failure to be satiated or to effectively eliminate a craving or insatiably intense desire for a drug or form of behavior.

The portrait of addiction as insatiable craving is also not illuminating, however. Attribution of insatiability is not in general a veridical way in which to picture the impulse or motivation behind either a general addictive pattern or the particular stage of relapse, although it does depict certain individual episodes or cases. If certain drugs (say, alcohol) or behaviors (say, gambling) by their very nature induced insatiable cravings, then seemingly everyone who drank alcohol or gambled presumably would become an addict. But relatively few people who consume drugs or gamble end up as addicts. Even with a drug like cocaine less than 20 per cent of users become addicted (Robinson and Berridge 2003: 26). The desire to consume or engage is not so stable, intense and all-encompassing that, as West notes, it necessarily "sweeps all other considerations before it in a myopic and single-minded search for the object of desire" (West 2006: 77). People become addicted at different rates and under diverse circumstances, some in states of single-minded craving or insatiability, but most not. Some addicts do not even experience unpleasant withdrawal discomfort or negative or aversive affect prior to relapse.

So then, what explains why addicts do not lastingly abstain, but relapse and then persist in addictive patterns? If not insatiability or irresistibility, what? Is it time to give up on the very idea of addiction as a form of compulsion? Some commentators urge that we should abandon the idea (see Levy 2006). But perhaps that's too hasty. Perhaps we should think of addictive behavior as compulsive, *provided* that the concept of compulsion is free of reference to irresistibility or insatiability. Is there a sound alternative notion of compulsion that lacks such a semantic commitment?

Aristotle was emphatic in insisting that compulsions are not voluntary, but his notion of being non-voluntary is not a form of compulsion that addictions share. Aristotle's influential characterization of compulsion occurs in the *Nichomachean Ethics*. (The quotes that follow are taken from *The Nicomachean Ethics of Aristotle*, translated by Sir David Ross [1971]. See Book III, chapter 1, pp. 48–52. See also Stephens and Graham 2009b from which the next several paragraphs are adapted.) Aristotle claims:

> Those things, then, are thought involuntary which take place under compulsion or owing to ignorance: and that is compulsory of which the moving principle is outside, being a principle in which nothing is contributed by the person who is acting ... [for example] if he were carried somewhere by a wind or by men who had him in their power.
>
> (Ross 1971: 48)

> What sorts of acts, then, should be called compulsory? We answer that without quali- fication actions are so when the cause is in the external circumstances and the agent contributes nothing.
>
> (Ibid.: 48–9)

According to Aristotle, behavior is compelled only when its causes or sources are physically "external" to the agent and dominate their internal state or suffice to produce the behavior irrespective of the agent's internal state or cognitive-motivational economy. An example is that of a sailor whose boat is caught by a powerful wind and driven onto the shore of an island. From the moment the wind takes hold of the boat, the sailor contributes nothing to determining the boat's course. What he wants, believes, decides or intends is irrelevant to explaining what happens to him. The outcome of ending up on the shore is entirely deter- mined by external forces.

Aristotle stresses the externality of causes of compulsive behavior, but internal forces, internal to an agent's body, may also dominate the agent's desires and expectations. Suppose, for instance, that a cerebrovascular accident in my left hemisphere renders me mute. My failure to respond to a question about the city of my birth is entirely due to the brain damage I suffered. I know of my native city and wish to pronounce it as requested, but it matters not what I desire. My stroke has rendered my desire irrelevant. I am, we might say, compelled to remain mute. Suppose, then, that what counts for compulsion, in the spirit if not letter of Aristotle, is not that it puts my behavior under the control of forces outside my body, but that it removes it from the control of my cognitive-motivational states or of my mind period. It puts it outside my Intentionality dynamics or reason-responsiveness – not by virtue of being motivationally irresistible or insatiable but somehow by other means.

What then? If 'compulsion' implies bypassing the control of one's cognitive-motivational dynamics, this, too, is not a useful notion for understanding addiction. Here's why.

Terry Robinson and Kent Berridge, two biopsychologists at the University of Michigan, who have written extensively on drug addiction, offer the reason.

> An addict who steals, another who scams, another who has money and simply must negotiate a drug purchase – all face new and unique challenges with each new ... negotiation. Instrumental ingenuity and variation are central to addictive drug pursuit in real life. ... We believe that the flexible and compulsive nature of drug-seeking behavior in the addict requires ... motivational explanation.
>
> (Robinson and Berridge 2003: 34)

Addicts are motivated to obtain certain objectives and they exercise cognitive capacities to devise flexible strategies for achieving them, appropriate to challenges presented by changing circumstances. If addiction is compulsive, then it must be a form of compulsion that works *through* or taps into the addict's cognitive-motivational dynamics or Intentional attitudes, not operating outside them. Behaving addictively is something a person does, not something that happens to or befalls them. The cognitive-motivational structures involved in addiction no doubt differ from those of the non-addicted, but they are not bypassed or rendered impotent in an internal manner analogous to the wind that strikes Aristotle's sailor.

OK? So, what now? Should we *still* use 'compulsive' to refer to addictive behavior patterns? Perhaps. But we've not yet hit on a sound and applicable analysis of the meaning of the term.

Robinson and Berridge describe addiction (or drug addiction, their interest) as compulsive. They write:

> Addiction is more than mere drug use. It is ... a compulsive pattern of drug-seeking and drug-taking. ... The key questions in addiction, therefore, are why do some susceptible individuals undergo a transition from causal drug use to compulsive patterns of drug use, and why do addicts find it so difficult to stop using drugs.
>
> (Robinson and Berridge 2003: 26)

Addictive behavior is compulsive behavior. So they say. But what do they mean by this? In a remark made more offhand than addressed explicitly to the character of compulsion, they mention a promising (if undeveloped by them) possibility for understanding compulsion. They say that even if an addict "has a stable rational resolution to refrain from taking drugs," the motivation to take a drug may compete with and "momentarily surpass rational intentions, precipitating a binge of relapse" (Robinson and Berridge 2003: 45).

Perhaps what they have in mind by thinking of addictions as compulsions goes something like this. Addictive behavior is risky, destructive or harmful. Addictive behavior is habitual or repetitive. But the typical addict (remember, of the type who passes through the eight stages), also periodically reflectively negatively self-evaluates the behavior and may, on various occasions, resolve, decide or intend to break the pattern and inhibit the impulse. A decision ('rational resolve') to break is evident in their efforts to refrain and in experiences of shame, regret, remorse and similar self-critical reflexive attitudes on relapse. Call these experiential elements of shame and so on parts of the conscious phenomenology of relapse. When some rational choice theorists (like those mentioned at the beginning of this chapter) deny, in effect, that addiction is a disorder, they seem blind to the conscious phenomenology of relapse and to conflicts or forms of ambivalence that addicts often feel or experience toward their behavior. Deciding to quit, quitting, which may be or feel difficult, but then lapsing and being disappointed in oneself. Such are the consciously unstable wages of addiction.

I propose that we refer to the desire to break an addictive pattern and avoid relapse as an instance of wanting to take responsibility for self. What the addict lacks, as evident in relapse and in what Robinson and Berridge refer to as a failure of rational resolve, is the power or ability to *consistently* act in a reflectively self-responsible way. Addicts may try to correct themselves and strive for more consistent self-control, but, while addicted, they cycle through periodic failure. They break, as I wish to put it, promises to self to refrain, promises that stem from what otherwise (to use Robinson and Berridge's term) is a matter of stable rational resolve.

I will return to this idea of breaking resolve in a moment but first, before doing so, I wish to examine what is meant by referring to the *self* for which an individual wants to take responsibility and to whom a person may make promises to refrain. The psychiatrist George Ainslie's work on alternation and time-inconsistency of impulses and inhibitions provides a useful vehicle for commentary on the reference of the term 'self' in a context like that of addiction and addictive relapse (Ainslie 2001).

On Ainslie's picture preferences or impulses to engage in certain behaviors in pursuit of perceived rewards or goods may *dramatically* oscillate or reverse themselves over time. Reversals may be harmful to a person and an individual may regret the behavior that stems from them. But the closer in time a particular perceived good (no matter how small) is to a person the more likely they may be to follow the impulse to seek or consume it. As a result of proximity, an individual's evaluation of the merit of future goods may be inconsistent and therein 'irrationally unstable' and not in the person's best or prudent interests over time.

Suppose X and Y are mutually exclusive goods, one large-scale, the other small-scale, respectively. Say, X is protecting health and well-being. Y is snorting cocaine. When each of X and Y is far off in time, I may believe that the value or desirability of X far outweighs the value of Y, but as Y gets closer or becomes temporally more immediate, I may convert to thinking of Y (consuming the drug) as more valuable or desirable. If the 'self' of responsibility for self refers just to the time slice of me at the moment of my decision to consume, then there is nothing rationally inconsistent or unstable in deciding to take the drug. Clearly I want it here and now. The drug, just like the slice of me at a time, is here and now. Health and well-being belong to a distant and possibly never existing slice or segment of my life. (I may die in the interim.) Self resolutions are not surpassed; promises to self are not broken. The self is wholly and only present. Consumption helps to satisfy the stronger preference of the time slice. What *I* want just is what here-and-now-me wants.

It's not easy to have an articulated grasp of what a time slice of a person is. The idea is not just metaphysical (nothing is wrong with that, of course) but esoterically so. So much of who we are as persons is connected with past acts and future possibilities. A slice may seem like a dissociated or all too merely molecular fragment. Hopefully, too, I am not so foolish as to judge that all that matters to me is here and now. Hopefully, impatience to consume does not overwhelm whatever judgment I may make about the value to me of my long-term future. Hopefully, as a rational agent, I may prefer current rewards but not at all costs. My reflective or considered intentions call for a temporal distribution or blending of benefits, not of 'more now is better', as if I am a slice, but of balancing and coordinating short- and long-run interests or preferences. Not so an addict in relapse, whose 'impatience' surpasses whatever desire for across-time benefits they may harbor or self-reflectively endorse.

Preferring present to future benefit is not utterly and absolutely indefensible or unreasonable even when the future good markedly is greater, of course, for in the meantime misfortune (as just noted) may overwhelm a person. Better something now than nothing later. We cannot be certain we will live to experience a future benefit. But self-responsible people both acknowledge the possibility of unkind future fates and commit to across-time projects, aspirations and goals. After all, we are *historical* beings pursuing enduring and sometimes far-off achievements. Self-responsible people care about the future.

The self-evaluation that is constitutive of being a self-responsible person is tied to being an individual who has a "sense of ... historical continuity," to use a helpful phrase of Erik Erikson (1968: 16). One of the most important ways in which we as persons think of ourselves is as persistent things or as creatures with biographies or stories of our own. Without an historical or autobiographical sense of one's own person and temporal endurance as a person, there is no self for which to be self-reflectively responsible. There are no long-term plans, projects or commitments to hold dear. Without a sense of persistent selfhood there are no aspirations to care about in the sense that a person makes themselves (in Frankfurt's words) "vulnerable to loses and susceptible to benefits depending upon whether what [they care] about is diminished or enhanced" in an outlook that is "inherently prospective" and that "both entails and is entailed by [their] own continuing concern with ... what goes on in [their] life" (Frankfurt 1988: 83–4).

For persons as self-reflective creatures the fact that some rewards induce preference reversals does not mean that other preferences (desires for the distant or less proximate) are obliterated or set at motivational or phenomenal naught. Our self-reflective evaluations and aspirations may remain active even when they are behaviorally ineffective. Failure to act in conformity with them in relapse is often painful and regretful precisely because such forces remain subjectively and affectively alive.

The lapse of relapse is a measure of the power of addictive impulses. But relapse should not be seen as a mark of the total impotence or evisceration of an inhibition or reflective desire to refrain. The desire may still be in place, true, not exercised in the act of consumption, but experienced in the shame and personal disappointment of drinking in a bar or snorting cocaine.

The philosopher Neil Levy has a crisp and effective way of making the point that I am making here that we are not time slices but creatures persistent in time and that addiction reflects a failure to take responsibility for ourselves as historical beings with across-time commitments and concerns. Levy speaks in terms of personal autonomy and of a faculty of will or volition rather than of responsibility for self, but the spirit of his message is similar to mine despite its difference in conceptual letter. Levy writes:

> Addiction impairs autonomy ... because it fragments the agent, preventing her from extending her will across time. ... Her preference is temporary, and does not reflect her will.

> (Levy 2006: 12)

One striking feature of addiction, which is sometimes observed in clinics, is that while a preference to consume a drug or gamble might win a battle with self-evaluation in guiding an agent's behavior, this is not so much because the agent's evaluation is impotent or has evaporated, but because (despite its being negatively evaluated) the impulse to consume or to engage is life-defining for an addict. It's a part of a person's subjective persona: their self-conscious sense of themselves and what they are like as a person. And this fact can in turn imbue non-addiction with an element of risk or unwanted indeterminacy. The impulse may not be effectively counter-balanced or inhibited by an affectively articulated or emotionally rich conception of life without addiction. Addictive consumption or engagement may be felt to express, for an addict, who they are, fundamentally. It may be their way of locating themselves in their social and cultural environment. An addict may have trouble imagining how they could reinvent, redesign or reconstruct themselves, no matter how much they may regret the failure to do so, as someone who does not gamble or consume. So, the failure of successful abstention may have less to do with its being temporally discounted than with an inability to imaginatively feel for or affectively engage with what it would be like to be someone who does *not* enter a bar and consume a drink. The motivation to refrain may be stunted by a failure to grasp new life-defining affordances. "This is who I am, the person in the bar or snorting cocaine, not someone who returns to his air conditioned room to watch CNN and sip a Diet Coke." An addiction-free future may seem as barren to a person as that of the desiccated time slice, albeit immensely more extended.

The problem for some addicts may be, in short, with the whole lifestyle of non-addiction and the project of reconstruction that is required to live it. Andrew Garner and Valerie Hardcastle put this problem succinctly. An addict may "remain addicted because they don't know, in a profound and fundamental way, how else to be" (Garner and Hardcastle 2004: 377). "Becoming someone else is hard to do, and most of us simply cannot do it." An addict may "feel no kinship with the world of recovery," the world of non-addiction (377). If so, rational resolve or promise to self is compromised or surpassed not or not just because of oscillating or changing impulses, but because a person is unable to imaginatively compensate for the perceived emotional emptiness or detailed vacuity of an addiction-free selfhood.

So the role of our self-reflective historicity or across-time personhood in addiction is complicated psychologically and emotionally. As persons (and not just as addicts) we may not only reverse or alternate in preferences, as Ainslie notes, but simultaneously hold onto preferences of two literally different orders or types. The one urging inhibition, while the other impulsively overrides reflective self-control. The failure of inhibition may become a source of shame or regret when self-control is overridden. But the psychological force of inhibition by itself may be unable to fill in the imagined blanks of an addiction-free selfhood or of successful efforts to refrain.

So then, what about the term 'compulsion'? What might this word aptly mean if it is to apply to addictive behavior? In light of the notions of reflective self-evaluation and responsibility for self, another way of understanding the category of compulsive behavior suggests itself. This is not the notion of behavior under physically external or motivationally bypassed control. Not the notion of repetitively dangerous behavior. Not that of behavior driven by essentially insatiable or irresistible desires. But of behavior that contravenes an agent's efforts to take responsibility for self. Such a notion of compulsion may be put this way: A person behaves compulsively when they act against the motivational grain of their aspirations for responsible selfhood. In so doing, they exhibit a failure in their own reflective terms to take control of themselves namely a failure of, as Robinson and Berridge put it, stable rational resolve. This failure takes place when acting on desires or impulses that are incompatible with their appraisals of how segments of their life should hang together. I enter a bar and order a drink, even though I know full well that I have good reason for not doing so and likely will regret it afterward. Impulse to drink wins out over my more or less persistent and reflectively desired inhibition.

Claire, a hospital administrator, music lover and accomplished amateur pianist, likes to play Chopin after stressful days at work. Such days occur often. In such a mood, she is likely also to drink several glasses of scotch, although she has spent thousands of dollars in alcohol-abuse clinics. Claire sometimes describes herself as "perfectly fine," but she seems not to believe it. Often she thinks to herself "enough is enough." "If only I could refrain from this impulse to drink." "I don't want to end up wasted away."

By urging us to look beyond the limits of the present, efforts at responsible selfhood ask us to be, in a sense, visionary, and to bend efforts toward across-time aspirations. It is the whole historical person on whom is aimed the enterprise of self-responsibility, not just today's self. Tomorrow, it is hoped, I will behave responsibly, contrary to today's barroom or cocaine-snorting defection.

Claire? Perhaps it is unthinkable to her how *she* could refrain from drink. "I regret drinking." "I sometimes drink to dull regret." "But, look, if you ask me do I wish to avoid drink, of course my answer is yes." "Trouble is, though, if I were a non-drinker that person would not be or feel like *me*." "I can easily imagine playing one of the Chopin Études rather than a prelude, but that is who I am." "I can play either and still be me." "Without alcohol, though, I would not be myself."

ANIMAL MODELS

It is widely believed that work on non-human animal models of addiction provides helpful insight into the behavioral grip of addiction. It does, no doubt. But if addiction is understood as behavior that contravenes efforts to take responsibility for self, animal models can't tell the full story of addiction even if they tell important parts or speak to non-reflective forms of addiction.

Suppose that a subject is addicted (and perhaps compelled, in relevant clinical cases) only if their behavior runs against the grain of efforts to take responsibility for self. This self-evaluation or reflexive attitudinal component of addiction cannot be addressed by animal models. Animal models may help us to understand addictive phenomena such as behavioral persistence in spite of harmful consequences, sudden preference reversal or continued seeking for a substance even when it is visibly missing from the environment (Robinson 2004). (Seeking visibly missing substances is called "chasing ghosts.") Without, however, a component of negative self-assessment or disapproval, it is difficult to draw a line between dangerous and dramatic preference reversals, on the one hand, and patterns of behavior that deserve to be described as addictive (in the relevant clinical sense), on the other hand. Can a rat try to abstain from taking a drug, regret relapse and then pass negative judgment on itself? It can't, of course. Rodents lack the cognitive or conceptual resources required to make self-reflexive judgments. Rats may dramatically and dangerously reverse preferences over time, from the naturally prudent to the grossly imprudent. But reference to a mere change of preference fails to capture the content or character of an addict's self-evaluation.

Addicts, in their self-evaluation, as witness the cases of Caroline Knapp and others, don't report after relapse that they regret reversals in their wants, desires or preferences. No, they report shame or regret over acting on preferences (for drugs, for gambling) that they themselves wish not to possess or to be moved by, namely preferences that represent failures of responsible selfhood. Theirs is not a complaint about oscillation or across-time inconsistency. It's a complaint about letting themselves down, breaking promises to themselves, selves understood as historical entities. It's a complaint about sacrificing health and well-being to drug consumption or wagers at a track.

A non-human animal, a rat, for example, may exhibit habitually destructive behavior. It may also, of course, change sharply from prudent to imprudent preferences. It may self-administer in an experimental setting a dangerous drug, when otherwise it would pursue more natural rewards such as food and water. But a rat or rodent does not judge or feel itself to be a failure for those behaviors. It does not feel depleted in self-esteem. Relapsed addicts met in an addiction clinic harbor just such feelings. They feel depleted (ashamed, disappointed and so on). They have broken a contract or promise with themselves or violated a form of evaluative commitment in which they, at times at least, have invested quite successfully by refraining or abstaining, albeit if only temporarily.

Robert West writes of such an addict:

> When ... restraint fails, there is ... no sense of having changed (one's) mind and deciding to engage in behavior as a positive step; rather the sense is of a failure to exert control followed by regret and a feeling of having let oneself down.
>
> (West 2006: 133)

West's observation rings true. Addicts fail to control impulses. True. Addicts engage in harmful or risky behavior. True. Addicts engage in such behavior knowing that it is deleterious. True also. But what really marks a pattern of behavior as addictive (in the clinical coalface sense) is the inability to muster consistent motivational energy or strength around the effort to take responsibility for one's own person coupled with the feeling of, as it were, letting oneself down.

To sum up matters thus far: I am not trying to insist that addiction is compulsive. I have, however, tried to render plausible the claim or intuition, shared by many theorists, that addiction is a species of compulsion. The much more important thesis for me that I am after here, which also, I believe, is more useful in understanding addiction, is that addictive patterns are linked to incapacity in responsible selfhood. Addiction is not just or only an impulse-control disorder. It is a form of impairment or truncation in the rationality or reason-responsiveness of one of the capacities that we would pick from behind a veil of ignorance (as listed in the previous chapter). This is responsibility for self. (In addiction the ability to recognize and act on affordances may also, of course, be impaired.) Just such impairment is also the crux of why addiction is a *mental* disorder, since an agent's cognitive-motivational dynamics and self-appraisals are central to the propensity conditions of addiction. I mean 'central' not in the sense of excluding explanatory references, as will be seen in the next two sections of this chapter, to the irruption of brute mechanical forces into the space of reasons (rational resolve, reason responsiveness). But I mean 'central' in the sense of stamping the autograph of mentality on addictive patterns.

NEURAL MODELS

The neurological bases of addiction and of drug addiction, in particular, lie, in part, in the brain's internal reward system, primarily in the mesolimbic dopamine system. This is a system of neurons projecting from the ventral tegmental area to the nucleus accumbens (NAcc) that use dopamine as their neurotransmitter (Malenka 2004). So, one hypothesis for addiction that a broken-brain theorist may offer is that addiction is a breakdown or impairment in the reward system of the brain. Addiction is a disorder *of* the system and not just *in* it. If such a hypothesis is correct, this means that addiction is, contrary to my explication of the concept of mental disorder not, strictly speaking, a mental disorder. It is a neurological disorder. Addictive behavior stems strictly and purely from damaged neural hardware.

A lot of theorists endorse that particular assumption. Tempting and neurologically stalwart as the assumption may be, however, it is not a truly warranted hypothesis. To justify interpreting a disorder like addiction as neurological and not just as a disorder that is physically based, one must demonstrate that the base itself is damaged or impaired. It's one thing to possess a physical base. It's another for the base to be damaged or disordered.

Consider the following analogy. No one would assert that a thermometer is anything but a physical artifact. If, however, a human oral thermometer is mistakenly placed in an oven-hot loaf of bread and it breaks, then this does not mean that the thermometer broke because it was physically 'disordered' or 'dysfunctional'. The thermometer's failure is physically based certainly, but it is a situational failure. The break is due to the fact that the artifact was situated in an environment in which it was not designed to function and therein was unwisely placed. So, likewise, a person vulnerable to addiction may engage in behavior in the 'wrong situation', at a horse track, growing up in a family with alcoholic parents, and so on, where the basic processes of learning, memory and preference-development and -satisfaction produce objectively harmful or imprudent results. This is not to say that the brain of such a person is broken, disordered or impaired. The brain may be doing just what it should be doing, neurologically speaking, but in circumstances in which it shouldn't be doing what it should be doing, so to speak.

To demonstrate that the neural base of addiction is broken or impaired, it would be useful if there are findings independent of addictive behavior that neural damage has occurred. This is because if the only evidence for the presence of brain damage is addictive behavior (which itself has a lot of Intentionalistic or cognitive-motivational activity within it), then the concept of addiction as a disorder of the brain would be conceptually or semantically parasitic on standards for addiction as a *mental* disorder and on norms (of reason-responsiveness, rationality and negative self-evaluation) for determining the presence of *mental* disorder. Addiction, in such a case, would be a disorder, not in virtue of an independently speci-fiable neurological impairment or dysfunction, but because relevant neurological activities contribute to undesirable behavior. The addict's brain may be, as it were, improperly situated, functioning properly but in an unhealthy learning environment or misdirected manner.

In general, there is no explanatory utility in offering the thesis that addiction is a neural disorder (or a disorder of the brain) as a replacement for referring to addiction as a mental disorder, if we then must refer back to its status as a mental disorder in order to understand what makes it a brain disorder. To use an earlier example, imagine if the only way in which to know that a computer has a hardware problem is to know it has a software problem and if the hardware problem must ultimately be described in software terms. The alleged hardware problem would then hardly count as a hardware problem. The difficulty, though hardware based or realized, is in the software.

How are neural impairments or neurological disorders demonstrated in clinical neurology? There is no simple answer to this question. Various experimental procedures are used, studies of anatomical sites, searches for toxins (e.g. carbon-monoxide poisoning), and so on. I do not hope to shed light on the methods or demonstrations of clinical neurology in this book. But I will briefly focus on two sorts of impairments for the lessons that they contain. My intent is to help to explain why I believe that addiction as such is not a neurological disorder.

It has been known since the nineteenth century that damage to the striate cortex and to the region known as V1 produces a blind field or scotoma, such that patients normally report not seeing anything when stimuli are presented to that portion of their visual field (Weiskrantz 1986). Quite fascinatingly, some patients with the scotoma possess a form of competence of their visual system in which consciously *invisible* stimuli influence (reliably above chance) judgments about the location, brightness, orientation and even shape of those stimuli. For instance, if asked to "just guess" whether a presented stimulus is of vertical or horizontal grating, subjects may respond rather accurately, despite denying that they see anything at all. The subjects themselves are completely unaware consciously of what they are looking at or that they are able to give rather accurate reports of a limited range of features of a surrounding environment. This phenomenon of limited and personally unrecognized success is known as "blindsight." The brains of blindsighted subjects are damaged cortically. Just how or where they are damaged is a matter of empirical contention, but there is no doubt that blindsight is a disorder of (and not just in) the brain. Reference to damage in the striate cortex aims to explain the performance (and decrements or limits) in visual judgment. Note, too, blindsight is not a mental disorder, although it has mental consequences (namely scotomas), for nothing Intentionalistic (cognitive or motivational or reason-responsive) figures in a scotoma's propensity conditions. No reference is made to a person's beliefs, desires or to other attitudes in the description of its origins. Explanation is conducted in terms of a failure or decrement in the machinery of conscious vision and that's it. Emphasis is placed on finding an explanation in terms of the various cortical regions and brain systems that are involved in processing retinal inputs to discriminate specific aspects of a visual stimulus, such as its color, motion, shape, location and orientation.

It is important to appreciate that making blindsight possible is not what the brain should be doing. In blindsighted subjects the path for processing visual information about an external stimulus in 'blind' portions of the visual field fails to influence behavior in needed and proper ways. Suppose while shaving Sam reaches for an aspirin bottle on his medicine shelf because he feels headachy and visually recognizes the bottle on the shelf. But suppose Sal his next-door neighbor, also headachy, also shaving, and also with an aspirin bottle on his shelf, doesn't reach for his bottle, for Sal is a victim of blindsight and the bottle appears in the 'blind' portion of his visual field. True, in a forced-choice questionnaire in which Sal is asked to pick from a limited number of alternative replies to questions, he will report, for example, whether the bottle is marked with vertical or horizontal lines. But helping people to answer questions on a forced-choice questionnaire about non-conscious visual information is not what the brain is supposed to be about, any more than a baseball bat is supposed to be used to chase rabbits from a field of play. The brain's proper function is, in part, to control or regulate motor activity based on visual information. Sam's brain does as it should; Sal's does not.

There are all-to-numerous examples of behavioral dysfunctions that possess exclusively a-rational brute causal (non-cognitive, non-motivational, non-Intentionalistic) neural sources. The field of clinical neurology is filled with references to them. Consider, for another example, ideomotor apraxia. This is a disability in carrying out simple voluntary gestures such as saluting or waving goodbye. When, for example, given a request to salute, a patient with the condition may be unawares that his hand needs to be raised in an appropriate fashion. They may appear confused, "being unable to either complete the movement or place the hand correctly" (Rogers 1999: 101).

When testing for ideomotor apraxia (as in analogous testing for blindsight) it is critical that the patient's non-performance is not under voluntary control and that the misplacement of, say, the saluting hand is not a purposive action. Neurologists debate just where damage or injury to the nervous system must occur to produce the condition, but presumably "lesions in the posterior regions of the dominant hemisphere, specifically the parietal or temporoparietal region, are essential" (Rogers 1999: 101). Again, once voluntary or cognitive-motivational control has been ruled out and a lesion is said to be responsible, nothing Intentionalistic is thought to figure in ideomotor apraxia's sources or causes.

To be sure, each and every behavioral upshot or consequence of a neurological disorder is not necessarily completely and utterly non-Intentionalistic. When brain damage or a neurological disorder is present, as Derek Bolton notes, "there is a fundamental ... dysfunction caused by damage to neural structures" but the person with the disorder may still "seek to act despite this." In such a case, what may be observed in behavior "will be strategies for coping, as well as ... direct signs" of the brain damage itself (Bolton 2001: 196). Perhaps, for instance, the repetitive, isolated play of an autistic child reflects avoidance of situations that require understanding other persons. Neural damage presumably is responsible for the incapacity to understand, but the child's repetitive and isolated play may be a purposive and compensatory strategy. Perhaps playing is aimed at or reinforced by reduction of the disorientation associated with social incomprehension (see later the discussion of Jonathan Glover's friend, who is a victim of Asperger's syndrome). Signs of a brain disorder may therein not be immediately open, as the example of autism illustrates, to an unencumbered clinical view. Such signs may be "disguised in some way by coping strategies, and will need special tasks, circumventing the coping strategies, to elicit them" (Bolton 2001: 196). Special investigatory clinical tasks may be needed to learn if Intentionality (beliefs, desires, and so on) is not a proper part of a disorder's propensity conditions and if brute neural processes are the sole sources of a condition.

Clinicians may vary in their approach to neurological examination and diagnosis. But the search is for non-Intentionalistic mechanical damage – infections, tumors, traumas, toxins, metabolic disorders, strokes, lesions, developmental abnormalities and the like – and a subject's inability to control the manifestation or expression of direct symptoms of a condition (not the compensatory behaviors that Bolton mentions).

Is addiction like that? Is it the result of brute neural or mechanical damage? No doubt, as just noted above, the neurological base of addiction (or drug addiction in particular) lies (in part) in the brain's mesolimbic system and concentrations of dopamine in the extracellular space in the nucleus accumbens and NAcc-related circuitry. No doubt, too, addiction is a disorder: an unhealthy or harmful disability. But is it a disorder not just based in the brain but also, like blind-sight or ideomotor apraxia, of the brain? Does it result from neural impairment? I have said 'no'.

In thinking of the brain as damaged and of such damage as responsible for a behavior or set of harmful or undesirable behaviors, it isn't enough that neural activity, in some broad sense, is responsible for the behavior. No, the behavior must depend on the brain in a particularly impairment-specific way. Something must be wrong not just in the behavior but with the brain itself. Think, by analogy, of the ringing of a door bell. Suppose my door bell rings at odd times of the day or night, and when I answer it, no one is ever there. Is it broken? This depends not just on the fact that it rings at odd times or that no one is at the door, but on whether the bell is failing to operate as it should because of something wrong with the bell itself. If squirrels are pushing the doorbell button, there is nothing wrong with the bell. If the bell was installed surreptitiously by my unfriendly next-door neighbor, purchased to give me hard time, and designed with a random ringing mechanism for just that sort of annoying purpose, then the bell is in perfect working order. Unfortunately for me, it works.

What about the brain and addiction? Note that the very same reward system that is responsible for addiction serves a whole variety of psychological and biological functions, such as endowing safety, food, water and sexual partners with reinforcing properties. Facilitating prudent consumption of a recreational drug or temperate betting at a horse track presumably is not what Mother Nature designed the neural reward system to do, however, any more than she constructed the brain to help individuals to study ballet at the Juilliard School of Music – itself risky behavior. If the brain reward system regulated drug consumption or gambling (or ballet dancing) well, it might do a lot of more significant and prudentially important tasks poorly. So, imprudent drug consumption or deleterious horse wagering is no reliable sign or trustworthy criterion of a damaged brain. The brain, in general, is not hard-wired for personal prudence. Neural activity may systematically underwrite unwise behaviors without exemplifying a breakdown or something wrong or damaged in its wetware or machinery.

Of course, addictive behavior may *produce* a brain disorder given, say, the prolonged consumption of an alcoholic substance or other drug. Toxins may destroy relevant neural circuitry making it impossible for a person to control a wide range of responses. Parkinson's, for example, is a degenerative disorder in the dopamine system. Dopamine signals entrain motor habits and one of the symptoms of Parkinson's is loss of motor control. Chemical antagonists found in certain drugs (such as cocaine) may do something comparable in certain cases of addiction, causing difficulties of concentration, learning, planning and motivation. But it is one thing for a pattern of behavior to cause brain damage and another for it to be a neural disorder. So, my claim is that addiction (gambling, cocaine consumption and so on) is not a neural disorder, as such, although it may harm the brain and become an effect or mark of brain disorder over time.

The claim that addiction, although (as I am assuming) brain based, is not *per se* a disorder of the brain, combined with the proposition that addiction qualifies as a disorder because of its harmfulness or undesirability, has implications for the proper role of neuroscience in the study of addiction. Investigators should not presume that the brain reward system is broken in a case of addiction, although neuroscientific investigation still should play a prominent role in our explanatory understanding of addiction. Various important questions about addiction's origins and behavior patterns cannot be answered just by reference to states possessed of Intentional content or to an addict's cognitive-motivational dynamics (beliefs, desires and so on). I plan to outline one specific possible contribution of neuroscience to the study of addiction in a moment. It's a contribution offered by Robinson and Berridge (see also Berridge and Robinson 1995). First, though, I wish to make a short autobiographical digression.

Once, while writing a draft of this chapter, I delivered a presentation on addiction before a group of neuroscientists. They were perplexed (or worse, in some cases made verbally dizzy) by what I have said just above, namely that addiction is or may be a disorder based in but not of the brain. One scientist complained that I was playing with prepositions ('in' and 'of') that lacked empirical traction or clinical significance. (Such are the perils of being a professional philosopher. A person may be charged with indulging in word games or explanatorily useless terminological distinctions.) Others expressed more worrisome challenges. Some suspected

I was embracing a devious (devious to them) form of mind/body dualism. (Readers of this book, I hope, know that I am not doing that.) Others feared that I was objecting to the presumptive utility of pharmacological therapy for addiction. They assumed that only if a disorder is of the brain or reflects something wrong with the brain, i.e. a neural disorder, is it a suitable candidate for a drug remedy. This is not an assumption that I wish to make. In certain cases of addiction, drug therapies may be all to the good if they help people to resist relapse and regain self-responsibility. Of course, it is another matter entirely to deploy pharmacology because, medically speaking, an addict's brain is presumed to be broken and in need of chemical repair. 'Fixing' the brain under the assumption that it is damaged, when it fact it is behaving properly, may well (given the type of medication) further disable a person by interfering with other desirable functions, such as learning and exploratory behavior – or dancing in a favored ballet company.

In general, the neuroscientists themselves had difficulty appreciating that the mind of a person may be derailed even if the brain continues to run on its proper neural activity track. The brain processes in mental disorders do not, at the explanatory and taxonomic level of neuroscience, constitute disorders of those particular processes themselves. Such is my view. So, suppose we grant, with me, that addiction is not a disorder of the brain. An addict as such does not possess a broken brain. How may neuroscience still help us to understand the condition?

An Intentionalistic or psychological understanding of addiction just in terms of an agent's cognitive and motivational dynamics and self-appraisal never reaches a completeness point. Some key questions about addiction and about the truncation or impairment in rational resolve or reason-responsiveness in relapse seem answerable only by deployment of the explanatory framework of neuroscience. Reference to brute a-rational neural mechanisms may help, for example, to explain why addicts suffer from relapse in spite of themselves. This is because somatic mechanisms may gum up the rational works of quitting. Addicts just can't soak up sufficient motivational power from their acknowledged reasons or aspirations to refrain and persistently act on their basis. How so? Let's look more carefully at the relapse stage.

ONE WAY IN WHICH THE BRAIN MAY GUM UP THE WORKS

Why, in particular, do addicts relapse? A number of different hypotheses about the irruptive role of a-rational neurobiological/neurochemical mechanisms into the space of reasons in relapse are available in the literature. These range from attributions of fluctuations of glucose levels in fronto-cortical blood flow to chemically impeded learning from punishment (West 2006; Levy 2006; Robinson and Berridge 2003). I am not going to sort through them. Rather, I plan briefly to describe one hypothesis that strikes me as a potentially fecund suggestion for how neurological mechanisms may contribute, in part, to relapse contrary to an agent's considered disapproval of addictive behavior and attempts at self control. (Remember, we are talking of addicts of the sort who seek or at least consent to treatment.) The explanatory hypothesis in question focuses on the onset of relapse i.e. on its first or incipient steps, not on the full-blown behavior pattern, which may be immensely complicated and, of course, is infused with Intentionalistic activity. The hypothesis, which is owed to Robinson and Berridge, comes in three main parts or progressive steps (see Stephens and Graham 2009b for related discussion). It goes like this.

Step one. The impulses or dispositions behind addiction and relapse are not forces necessarily irresistible. They are (often, as noted above) resistible. Indeed, some addicts successfully abstain for long periods. Addictive impulse may also be independent of pleasure-seeking motivation. Gambling or drug consumption is not necessarily associated either with expectations regarding pleasurable effects of behavior, for there may be no pleasurable effects in some instances, or with a desire to make withdrawal less painful, for addictive patterns may recur long after withdrawal discomfort has disappeared. (See Stephens and Graham 2009b; West 2006.) As Robinson and Berridge note:

> The truth is that addicts continue to seek drugs even when no pleasure can be obtained, and even when no withdrawal exists. For instance, addicts seek drugs when they know those available will be insufficient for pleasure. Further, addicts crave drugs again even before withdrawal begins: ... And addicts continue to crave drugs long after withdrawal is finished.
>
> (Berridge and Robinson 1995: 71)

(Parenthetically, I am not sure why Robinson and Berridge speak of addicts 'craving' drugs when no pleasure or withdrawal discomfort is involved, but I shall let their use of the term pass unexamined here.)

Rather, according to Robinson and Berridge, addicts find it difficult to avoid relapse because they do not remove themselves, or fail to appreciate the need to remove themselves, from environmental cues or circumstances that evoke impulses to seek drugs (or to gamble) – to pursue harmful or risky rewards. Environmental cues help to determine the emergence of the impulse to indulge. They signal the prospect of reward.

So, wherein resides the behavior-gripping strength of environmental cues? Why is it important to remove oneself from the premises (their presence)?

Step two. The strength of cue–response–reward connections is based in a distinct neural substrate from the one that underlies liked or pleasurable goals as well as conscious representations of environmental situations as occasions for pleasurable reward (Robinson and Berridge 2003; Berridge and Robinson 1995). NAcc-related circuitry underlies cue–response–reward connection strengths, whereas prefrontal and other cortical areas help to serve as substrates for conscious intentions as well as for anticipations of pleasure associated with behavior. These two substrates can dissociate or begin to control behavior independently of each other. When that happens 'wanting' (that is, whether a person has an impulse or disposition to behave) splits off from 'liking' (that is, whether a person expects to gain pleasure from the behavior). Robinson and Berridge cite a combination of, in their words, "neurobiological and behavioral evidence that ... suggest that ... dopamine-related systems [incentivize] rewards by a ... process that is separable from ... pleasure" (Berridge and Robinson 1995: 73).

Robinson and Berridge do not insist that pleasure seeking and reduction of withdrawal discomfort never play a role in addiction. Such phenomena sometimes do play important roles, especially perhaps in the early stages of development of addiction (as in e.g. recreational drug taking). Berridge and Robinson insist, however, that "after one has accounted for all instances of drug use by addicts motivated by pleasure or withdrawal, a vast amount of compulsive drug use remains to be explained" (1995: 73). They conclude, then, that there must be some other form or system of motivation at work in addiction that is distinct from pleasure seeking ("liking"). This other system is (what they call) "wanting."

> The sensitized neural systems responsible for ... incentive salience can be dissociated from the neural systems that mediate the hedonic effects of drugs, how much they are "liked." In other words, "wanting" is not "liking." ["Liking"] is a different psychological process that has its own neural substrates.
>
> (Robinson and Berridge 2003: 36)

Step three. Dissociation between wanted or incentivized and liked or pleasurable behavior or reward means that the environmental cues that signal reward may help to trigger the onset of relapse via a process that, because it is not consciously associated with the expectation of pleasure, is difficult or impossible for an agent to introspectively recognize and therein inhibit. Wanting *per se* does not make addictive highs more pleasurable or withdrawals more painful. If it did conscious affective (pain-going/pleasure-coming) signals would reveal to an agent the presence of initial impulse to seek a drug or to re-begin a pattern of deleterious behavior. Rather, it's as if there are two ways of being motivated to engage or re-engage in addictive behavior, two motivational systems. One uses pleasurable or affectively salient signals or incentives to re-motivate. The other deploys wanted incentives. The two systems (as noted) can operate independently. A person may want what they don't like (or indeed like what they don't want). So, even if a person's self-declared goal and self-reflective judgment is to refrain from a behavior, wanting to indulge or consume might momentarily slip past personal aspirations to inhibit, constituting the first movements or time slices of an imprudent behavior pattern. Such a tilt is not itself a lapse, but a lapse cannot occur without some tilting whose full or ultimate import may ultimately be hard to inhibit.

Robinson and Berridge's three-step approach to the onset of relapse offers a neurological explanation for the impulse to re-engage in a form of negatively self-evaluated behavior. It helps to explain the onset of what may be called the tilt to lapse. Once the impulse or want is activated then what happens? To re-secure a drug or to place a wager consciously flexible and deliberate behaviors are required. Not just an initial 'lapse tilt' in behavior but the activity of purchasing a substance, avoiding the law, and so on. I offer no surmise here (and neither do Robinson and Berridge) about the neural processes that underlie these more complicated behaviors (all of which may take place during relapse and whose explanation requires reference to an agent's cognitive-motivational dynamics). Planning, decision-making, emotional variables, and long-term memory processes all play a role in full-scale relapse. So, for me (and apparently also for Robinson and Berridge), at post-tilt points, Intentionalistic explanation (reference to an addict's cognitive and motivational dynamics) is required for our explanatory understanding of relapse. Of course, again, reference to Intentionality does not kick-in to the exclusion of continued reference to neural activity or to its irruptive role. (Berridge notes that references to mechanisms of protein folding, monoamine production, as well as to various other neural processes must also be part of the full neural story of addictive motivation and reward [Berridge 2004: 205].) But it does operate to the exclusion of a fully or purely neurobiological/neurochemical explanation of relapse.

Here is a complementary suggestion for an explanatory role for neuroscience in understanding relapse. It is known that concerted or strenuous efforts at inhibition may cause falls in glucose levels and a general loss of what is sometimes referred to as mental energy (Levy 2006; Bayne and Levy 2006). So, one additional possibility, to that noted by Robinson and Berridge, is that the resources in the brain that are required to resist or inhibit emerging impulses or wants are depleted or may be exhausted by prior efforts to sustain abstinence, and that such 'exhaustion' may make resistance to the full complement of relapsing Intentionalistic behaviors difficult. Some addicts may engage in full-scale complex drug-seeking or gambling behavior in part because the 'willpower' or motivational energy needed to inhibit the behavior has become weak or depleted by past efforts to refrain. This depletion may occur despite the fact that they sincerely negatively evaluate their addictive behavior and anticipate regretting relapse. They may then take a drug or gamble in a "compulsive degree" (Robinson and Berridge 2003: 44). This would be contrary to their otherwise self-responsible resolve.

I am not here, as noted above, prepared to offer anything like fulsome speculation about the place of reference to brute neural mechanisms alongside reference to Intentionalistic and reason responsive forces in the total story of relapse or addiction generally. I assume that the complete story will give a more or less balanced place to both strictly neural and mentalistic/Intentionalistic or motivational elements and that reference to neural elements will be useful in understanding how addiction gums up the attempt to take responsibility for self. Above I have merely sketched some neural speculation that may be relevant to understanding the initial onset of relapse behavior.

I should add that we should not underestimate the potential explanatory utility of reference to the wanting/liking distinction in understanding various mental disorders, not just addiction. It is a helpful distinction, despite the fact that there is a confusing tendency in ordinary language to equate talk of reward with talk of nothing but conscious pleasure (as will be recalled from discussion of the merits of consciousness in the last chapter). People as well as perhaps non-human animals often engage in behavior that is wanted without being liked or associated with pleasurable experience. Understanding the effort to be responsible for self exhibits the utility of the distinction in more contexts than that of addiction.

A person's likes and dislikes can be at odds with their evaluation of how they should feel and not just act. Agoraphobic Arthur realizes that certain of his anxious and fearful feelings are unhelpful responses to being among strangers. He knows that he would be better off without such feelings in such circumstances. One dimension of responsibility for self is self-control of pleasant and unpleasant feelings. Suppose Anita, one day in the very same shopping mall as Arthur, exerts self-control over certain aversive feelings. She, too, dislikes shopping among strangers and feels apprehensive at the prospect. But Anita deliberately eliminates her unpleasant feelings by vividly imagining shoppers in the mall in floral ballet tights and pink slippers. She reduces her anxiety with comedic images. She shops comfortably in the mall. She enters one of the stores in the mall and purchases a shirt for her husband.

Anxiously hovering near the disliked threshold of the same store, but trying to summon the courage to enter, Arthur, by contrast, is at a loss for self-control. He wants to enter. It's near Christmas and he needs to purchase a gift for his wife. He intensely dislikes entering. Unlike Anita, however, he just can't control his anxiety. There really is no chance that he will stick to his intention and enter the store. Within moments he leaves the entire mall.

But back now to the topic of neural models. A mental disorder's particular form of impairment asks for explanation in terms, in part, of brute somatic mechanisms. Absent knowledge of the underlying neurobiology or neurochemistry, we do not *fully* know why a person behaves in a manner distinctive of a disorder. It's not that psychological explanation by reference to Intentionality or consciousness is displaced or usurped by neurobiology or neurochemistry. Quite the contrary, references to the psychological play critical roles in understanding a mental disorder. It's just that 'mindful but brainless explanation' is incomplete. Why, for example, does addictive behavior cycle through relapse contrary to a person's good reasons to refrain? Mere mechanisms may be responsible for at least the initial tendency to relapse. Cognitive and motivational forces perhaps then play a predominant role once inhibition has started to fail.

If I might use a metaphor, the productive elements of a mental disorder may be conceived as like a pale gray fabric woven tightly of thin black threads representing a-rational (non-Intentionalisitic) processes described in strictly brain-science terms and white ones representing a subject's cognitive and motivational dynamics and described in Intentionalistic or psychological idiom. Were a disorder all black in descriptive onset and persistence, it would be a brain disorder or neurological illness. It is at just this point (deciding what type of disorder a disorder is) that some neuroscientific theorists of mental disorder end up painting themselves into a tight explanatory corner. They say we should drop reference to the role of mind or mentality from a disorder's architectural specifications. They assume that a disorder with a physical basis is therein a non-mental physical disorder. Down that monothematically mechanical explanatory path lies not only anti-realism about mental disorder, I believe, but the inability to properly understand and appreciate the sources of a mental disorder. The contrary theoretical disposition, which is to view a disorder in all white or Intentionalistic terms, puts reason too much in charge and neglects the subtle and complex ways in which neural activity and brute mechanical processes help to gum up reason's works. Down that rationalistic or all-white explanatory path lies the inability to grasp both the physical forces underlying a disorder and a proper understanding of various 'mechanical' treatments or forms of clinical address that may be necessary to dissolve or control a disorder.

The addict? True, like any rational agent an addict acts on preferences and makes choices. Addicts are not utterly irrational in their addictive behavior. But the life of an addict is dangerous and hard. Addicts become less and less well off in spite of their choices and often need help.

CHAPTER SUMMARY AND SUGGESTED READINGS

As explained earlier in the book, I advocate a complementary attitude toward the explanatory understanding of a mental disorder. By this I mean that reference to mentality (Intentionality) as well as to neurobiology/neurochemistry is necessary for our comprehension of a mental disorder. Addiction illustrates how this complementary attitude operates. There are features of addiction, perhaps foremost the initial stages of relapse, for which neuroscientific explanation is helpful, and other features of the disorder, such as the reasoning deployed in engaging in addictive behavior and the phenomenology of relapse, for which reference to states with Intentionality is unavoidable.

Addiction, on the analysis offered in this chapter, is an incapacity for taking effective responsibility for self. It is a deficit of rational resolve or in effective responsiveness to one's aspiration to be self-responsible. Saying this is not meant to obscure or neglect other related capacity failures that may take place in addiction (such as the inability to affectively engage with affordances for a non-addictive life). But addicts, I suppose, are peculiarly and harmfully periodically unresponsive to their own evaluation of reasons to refrain. This fact about addiction cannot be exhaustively understood in terms of non-human animal models. It requires also a metaphysical assumption about persons. This is that we persons persist through time and experience ourselves as bearers of a history or biography. Our lives possess parts or phases. There are parts or phases in which an addict refrains, aspiring to be free of addiction and successfully responsible for self, and parts in which they relapse. Whether or not addiction is a species of compulsion is left ultimately undecided in this chapter, but a tentative defense is offered for the assumption.

Robert West's *A Theory of Addiction* (Blackwell, 2006) offers a good overview of theories of addiction. The philosopher Gideon Yaffe provides a nuanced survey of the various theories of the nature of addiction in "Recent Work on Addiction and Responsible Agency," *Philosophy and Public Affairs*, 2002, 30, pp. 178–221.

Herbert Fingarette's *Heavy Drinking: The Myth of Alcoholism as a Disease* (University of California Press, 1988) is a classic monograph on alcohol abuse. Ferdinand Schoeman's paper, "Alcohol Addiction and Responsibility Attribution," in G. Graham and G. Lynn Stephens (eds), *Philosophical Psychopathology* (MIT Press, 1994) urges helpful caution about the depth and scope of Fingarette's analysis.

George Ainslie's work on hyperbolic discounting lies behind a concerted multidisciplinary study of gambling behavior co-authored by D. Ross, C. Sharp, R. Vuchinich and D. Spurrett, and entitled *Midbrain Mutiny: The Picoeconomics and Neuroeconomics of Disordered Gambling* (MIT Press, 2008). The Ross and company book also constitutes an informative case study in the new field of neuroeconomics, which appeals to economic theory and the modeling of rational agency to understand the relation between valuation and behavioral control at the level of sub-personal neural systems and activities.

Many of Harry Frankfurt's important essays are available in his *The Importance of What We Care About* (Cambridge University Press, 1988). A probing analysis of Charles Taylor's theory of responsibility for self is Owen Flanagan's "Identity and Strong and Weak Evaluation," in O.

Flanagan and A. O. Rorty (eds), *Identity, Character, and Morality: Essays in Moral Psychology* (MIT Press, 1990). A short introduction to K. Berridge and T. Robinson's work is their "The Mind of the Addicted Brain: Neural Sensitization of Wanting Versus Liking," *Current Directions in Psychological Science*, 1995, 4, pp. 71–6. An appreciation of their work on the wanting/liking distinction in the larger context of understanding the neural mechanisms of motivation and reward may be found in Cory Wright and William Bechtel, "Mechanisms and Psychological Explanation," in P. Thagard (ed.), *Philosophy of Psychology and Cognitive Science* (Elsevier, 2007).

On the phenomenon of self-control Alfred Mele's *Autonomous Agents: From Self-Control to Autonomy* (Oxford University Press, 1995) is well worth reading. On some lessons of mental and neurological disorders for difficulties posed by the need for critical self-evaluation, see J. Anderson and W. Lux, "Knowing Your Own Strength: Accurate Self-Assessment as a Requirement for Personal Autonomy," *Philosophy, Psychiatry, and Psychology*, 2004, 11, pp. 279–94.

8 Reality lost and found

"Schizophrenia," says Hanna Pickard, may not be "a category that carves the world at its joints" (Pickard 2009: 91). What Pickard means by this remark is that schizophrenia seems to her not to be a genuine or distinguishable mental disorder. 'Schizophrenia' does not refer to a type of mental illness. An alleged type, yes. A real type, no. However, if schizophrenia, she notes, is not as such a mental disorder, this fact does not mean that various symptoms or behaviors associated with a *diagnosis* of schizophrenia are not real or matters of impairment, disturbance and undesirability. Its symptoms can and should be studied ("scientifically explained" is the expression she uses). A clinical and investigatory focus on symptoms, which is independent of the veridicality of an overall diagnostic category, opens up empirical doors even if the current categorization of a disturbance or set of conditions does not.

Pickard is not alone in trying to push a-categorical doors open. Jeffrey Poland, a philosopher, for years has been trying to open up symptom-orientated portals for the study of mental disorders (especially schizophrenia) (see Poland 2007). So, too, has Richard Bentall, as noted in our discussion of exemplars of mental disorder (Bentall 2004).

I know, first-hand, of what they speak. The importance and stand-alone interest of symptoms.

SYMPTOM AND SCHIZOPHRENIA

During the Vietnam War I performed two years of Civilian Alternate Work Service for the US Selective Service. I was a Conscientious Objector. I worked as a nurse's aide in a Harvard teaching hospital. During the first year I served in a medical-surgical unit. During the second I served in the psychiatric unit.

In the psychiatric facility one of the patients for whom I cared was a Roman Catholic priest. One day I entered the priest's room early in the morning shift. I found him underneath his bed on the chilly linoleum floor in his pajamas. He grinned as he grasped his hands around the underside of the metal bed frame. I had at most a few minutes to see that he was robed and escorted to the unit's dining room for breakfast. Most of the other patients in the unit had eaten. Many already were back in their rooms or in one of the recreational areas. A lingering three or four were just finishing their meals.

The priest appeared to have been awake all night. He spoke to me.

"Graham," he said, "you are the worst kind of a devil." "You seem like a good angel." "But you're bad." "*Really* bad."

I had had encounters with him previously that were similar, marked by his disorientation and distrust. In them I had little or no control over his behavior. So, I thought I would be unable to fulfill my dining-hall escort assignment. The priest spoke to me of feeling the "tidal pull" of evil, of communion wafers being an "ordeal" to swallow, and of his wish for no "contrivance" with the devil.

"You contrive me, Graham," he said.

Contrive him?

What, if anything, was he meaning or intending to say? I could only guess. Perhaps he wished to dissuade me from seeing to it that he had breakfast. Or perhaps he was offering a jibe or joke, possibly a humorous neologism with a touch of theological irony. However, he did not seem to be in a humorous mood. His grin was more anxious than friendly. Or perhaps he was hearing voices, the verbal auditory hallucinations common in someone with his diagnosis. Perhaps he was sharing their content or his interpretation with me.

His diagnosis? Schizophrenia. Christopher Frith, a neuropsychologist at the University of London, refers to it as "the most devastating" disorder "seen by psychiatrists" (Frith 1998: 388). It certainly is so in severe cases. Or if one wishes to put a point in Pickard's terms, the symptoms of the alleged condition, by any other name, would still disrupt as much. It's a disorder or symptom cluster in which a person often loses cognitive "touch with reality" (Frith and Johnstone 2003: 24). Touch with themselves, touch with the world, touch with the Land of the Public and Real.

I'm not sure myself whether schizophrenia is a genuine disorder or if its category merely reflects current diagnostic conventions. But clearly the priest was delusional. He had a penchant for losing contact with reality. I may have been no angel, but I was no devil.

People diagnosed with schizophrenia often strike other people as at times out of contact or touch with the world or themselves, not just in what they say, but in how they say it and in their non-verbal behavior. They may hold to an odd posture or gait, stare at odd times or laugh inappropriately. They may utter strange and contextually bizarre things such as:

- My food is being poisoned by the police.
- I have the power to forgive sins.
- I am infected by insects crawling under my skin.
- My uncle's thoughts are being carried on snowflakes that fall on my head.
- My wife has been replaced by an impostor.

- I exist in two separate places at the same time.
- Barack Obama's thoughts are being inserted into my mind.
- I am dead. I do not exist.
- I have been metamorphosed into a beast.

The possible intentions behind such utterances are hard to fathom. They do not express claims that one can easily imagine oneself sincerely making. They are alien. How alien? Karl Jaspers surmised:

> The profoundest difference ... seems to exist between that type of psychic life which we can intuit and understand, and that type which, in its own way, is not understandable and which is truly distorted and schizophrenic. ... [W]e cannot empathize, we cannot make them immediately understandable, although we try to grasp them somehow from the outside.
> (As quoted in Frith and Johnstone 2003: 124; see also Jaspers 1963)

If Jaspers is right, then the utterances of schizophrenics or persons diagnosed with schizophrenia often are so alien and bizarre that they defy empathetic understanding. Empathy, when successful, consists of taking the mental perspective of another person, i.e. imaginatively assuming another's frame of mind or conscious mental attitudes. If Jaspers is right, then certain symptomatic utterances of a schizophrenic just cannot be rendered imaginatively or intuitively understandable. We cannot imagine our speech being congruent with theirs. We cannot imagine what sort of meaning their speech acts may have. We may say of such people "It's not as if she really does believe that Obama's thoughts are being inserted into her mind" or "It's not as if he thinks that his wife has been replaced by an impostor." "It's only a malfunction of their nervous systems speaking," or "They are exhibiting neurochemical impairments and not genuine speech acts infused with Intentionality." So, it's no wonder, again, if Jaspers is right, that we may comprehend such episodes only from the outside. Only impersonally. There is nothing Intentionalistic or reasonable going on inside such subjects when such symptoms are expressed. No general frame of a rational mind into which to project ourselves. Their disorder is a neural disorder or set of neural disorders flat out.

Is Jaspers right? In thinking of Jaspers, I think of my priest patient. I liked him a lot. At times he was quick, candid, ironic – traits in his speech and of his person that I enjoyed. So did he really mean *nothing* in calling me a devil?

One must be cautious in making a Jaspers-like judgment of un-understandability, 'unprojectability', or non-meaning, for, as Bentall warns, if we fail to empathize "hard enough, we may fail to recognize the intelligible aspects of [another] person's experiences" (Bentall 2004: 29). The affected person may have, on the whole, a very different conscious or mental life from our own, to be sure. But to their disorder we should not add the loneliness and isolation that comes from our not making a concerted effort to understand them. If we make that effort, if we attempt to empathize, here is an idea that may help to orientate our effort.

In a paper that appeared in *Mind & Language* in 1997, Tony Stone and Andrew Young outline an account of the intelligibility of delusions, of the sorts exhibited in the speech acts above, that proposes that such persons have unusual or anomalous perceptual experiences that help to give rise to delusional beliefs and to genuine speech act intentions (Stone and Young 1997). Stone and Young regard linkages between unusual perceptual experiences and delusions as, in effect, from-the-inside imaginable or empathetically understandable. Here is part of what they say:

> [Some] delusions can be best explained in terms of the person suffering from the delusion trying to make sense of or explain a disturbing perceptual experience that is brought about by ... brain injury. On this view, the brain injury does not alter beliefs directly, but only indirectly by affecting the person's perceptual experiences.
>
> (Stone and Young 1997: 330)

On Stone and Young's view, some delusions may actually be subjectively reasonable responses, in some manner, to unusual perceptual experiences (which Stone and Young attribute to brain damage or injury, of which more below). Brain damage may be responsible for the anomalous experiences. But the unusual experiences and the need to interpret them are responsible for the delusion. If this hypothesis is true, empathetic understanding of delusions and associated speech acts may be achieved if we can somehow mimic or imagine undergoing relevantly similar unusual perceptual experiences. Claims about Obama's thoughts being inserted and of one's spouse being an impostor are not like psychic coughs or sneezes. They are spontaneous efforts at trying to make sense of experiential anomalies.

That's an intriguing conception of delusion. It's one that may open up an empathetic window inside at least some symptoms of schizophrenia (delusions in particular). As we will see momentarily, it's not an idea that is original to Stone and Young, as they readily admit.

On the question of empathetic understanding compare schizophrenia with autism. Autism is a neurodevelopmental or brain disorder, although the precise neurological details are not known. Its central symptom is, in two words, social aloneness – an obsession with objects (not persons), a paucity of imaginative play, a lack of normally expressive social engagement (such as eye contact with others), and engagement in monotonous, repetitive activities with, say, numbers or the material innards of physical objects. Presumably, there is something it is like to a person to undergo at least some of its symptoms. But what is that like, to be autistic?

Understanding autism from the inside or empathetically presents a serious intellectual challenge to the imagination of family members, clinicians and other persons engaged with autistic people, although by drawing on the memoirs of high-functioning autistics, a variety of clinical and experimental studies, and other sources, it has proven possible to describe various aspects of the inner life of autism. Indeed, attempts to describe the experience of autism offer a method for describing what it may be like to suffer from at least certain elements in schizophrenia. This is to focus not on the total condition, assuming that there is one, but on particular symptoms or types of complaints and to ask what those particulars may be like to a person. Symptom-focus in the case of understanding autism does not necessarily presuppose that some symptoms (say, paucity of imaginative play) are neatly walled off from others (say, repetitive activities). Various symptoms may affect and be affected by others. But focusing on symptoms does require not lumping or 'gluing' all sorts of symptomatic behaviors together. Whether a symptom can be understood empathetically and apart from other symptoms is, in the broadest sense, an empirical question. Not to be decided in advance or *a priori*.

Symptom focus is a common orientation among clinicians who treat disorders. Sally Satel, a psychiatrist and lecturer at Yale, remarks that often "it is symptoms, [and] not formal diagnoses, that direct the clinician" (Satel 2008: 42). She's right, of course. Symptoms constitute the evidence base for a diagnosis and are the primary behaviors marked for initial clinical attention.

A symptom-orientated approach may help us to inside-understand the conscious states that underlie the lack of expressive social engagement in persons with autism. It may make 'rational' or 'logical' sense of their lack of engagement. Normally, when we see a happy face, our smile muscles react, and when we see the face of someone who is suffering or in pain, our face may react in the way in which we ourselves would if we were in pain. One quite common result of our power for spontaneous facial mimicry is that we come to feel the same emotion that we are observing. A person does not need to be an astute clinician or tenured social psychologist to notice this phenomenon. We are all familiar with it. Attempts at deliberate affective mimicry were imaginatively made by the nineteenth-century poet Edgar Allan Poe (1809–49):

> When I wish to find out how wise, or how stupid, or how good, or how wicked is any one, or what are his thoughts at the moment, I fashion the expression of my face, as accurately as possible, in accordance with the expression of his, and then wait to see what thoughts or sentiments arise in my mind or heart, as if to match or correspond with the expression.
>
> (Quoted in Goldman 2006: 17–18)

Capacities or abilities for facial or affective mimicry are often impaired or absent altogether in autistics and this suggests that autistic persons may miss much of what the philosopher Jonathan Glover aptly dubs "the small change of everyday life" (Glover 2003: 513). The possibility that autistics miss the communicative meaning of face-to-face encounters, namely Glover's small change of daily life, may help to explain why autistic individuals become socially confused and withdraw or become preoccupied with impersonal objects. One high-functioning autistic friend of Glover (a woman with Asperger's syndrome) asked him to imagine what his social interactions would be like if other persons actually had no faces whatsoever. This thought experiment offered Glover an empathetic glimpse of her inner world (Glover 2003: 514). Absent non-facial cues, social contact with other people would appear mysterious in the extreme. What person would not withdraw or become confused under such 'faceless' circumstances?

But just what are the symptoms of schizophrenia? According to DSM (APA 2000: 312; see also Frith and Johnstone 2003: 34) to qualify for a diagnosis of schizophrenia a person must exhibit at least two from a list of five so-called characteristic symptoms. The characteristic symptoms are delusions, hallucinations, disorganized speech (e.g. frequent derailment or incoherence, word salad), grossly disorganized or catatonic motor behavior, and negative symptoms (e.g. absence of interest, avolition or emotional unconcern). The symptoms of the condition, says DSM, should also be associated with social or occupational dysfunction or serious personal imprudence and persist for at least half a year, with two or more appearing during a single month-long period.

Patients with one or more of the first four sorts of characteristic symptoms (sometimes called 'positive' symptoms as opposed to the 'negative' symptom set) typically exhibit not just various reason- or evidence-unresponsiveness to facts about the external world, but in self-knowledge and self-comprehension as well. A person with the diagnosis may think, for example, that "her thoughts, emotions, bodily sensations, or movements are under the control of some alien being or force" (Sass and Parnas 2007: 71). Or an individual may be withdrawn and lacking in expressive levels of affect. They may be depressed. Bentall notes: "Depression is ... commonly experienced by [schizophrenics], both during acute episodes and also during the prodormal phase that precedes the appearance of positive symptoms" (Bentall 2004: 234).

The capacity to comprehend self and world is an immensely multiplex and elusive competence to describe. (My talk of 'the' capacity should be taken as a gross oversimplification.) It's one of the most general and complex capacities mentioned in the chosen list of basic psychological competencies in Chapter 6. Self/world comprehension is not all of one kind either, of course, and different types or forms require different analyses or descriptions. Our capacity for comprehension is also always a bounded or situated capacity. By this I mean that our powers of knowledge and understanding are framed or limited by all sorts of background variables, not just our native intelligence, but practical aims, personal learning history and judgmental temperaments. Fortunately, however, for the specific task of understanding a condition like schizophrenia, and the delusions that are among its prominent symptoms, we don't need a grand theory of human comprehension. We 'just' need an account of whatever impairments or incapacities in comprehension are distinctive of a disorder's symptoms. For someone diagnosed with schizophrenia, this means, first and foremost, an account of the phenomenon of delusion.

All sorts of delusions occur in disturbed people. Just to name a few: grandiose delusions (e.g. that one is divine or divinely inspired), delusions about the state of one's body (e.g. that it is diseased or infected with parasites), sexual delusions, and delusions that one's ideas, impulses and intentions are under the control of or being broadcast to other persons or agents.

Laura, a young woman diagnosed as schizophrenic and the subject of a case study by McKay et al. (1996), helps to illustrate a range of delusions that may occur in people. Laura reported that the hospital staff was plotting against her (persecutory delusions). She complained of being forced to urinate on herself and to pace the ward (delusions of control). She said that other people sometimes invaded her mind, banishing her other thoughts (delusions of thought withdrawal) or projecting their thoughts into her stream of consciousness (delusions of thought insertion). She also lamented that other persons were directly aware of her thoughts as soon as they occurred to her (delusions of thought broadcasting).

How can we understand what it is like consciously to undergo a delusion? Delusory ideas, feelings or beliefs may seem, as noted, utterly weird and unintelligible. Normally, when we describe another's thoughts, we can imagine (or think we can imagine) them harbored within ourselves. But how can we imagine what it is like to think Laura's thoughts or those of the priest for whom I cared in Boston? I am forced to urinate on myself? The nurse's aide literally is a devil? What is the subjective or conscious Intentional content of such attitudes like? What do they mean to their victim? Do subjects of delusions possess any kind of warrant or reason behind them? Where did *this* or *that* delusion come from? Did it come from an anomalous experience? Regardless of where it came from, why does the person persist in and not reject it?

To get a handle on all this, which is a set of topics that will occupy various, not all, parts of this and the final chapter, I am going to begin with a pair of speculatively possible cases of delusion taken from the Bible. Yes, that's right: Scripture. One is Abraham; the other is Christ. Yes, that's right: Christ. I plan to draw on these two candidate cases, in part because the psychiatric literature occupies itself mostly with pre-established clinical cases (like that of Laura) and typically under a sponsorship of the diagnosis of schizophrenia.

I wish to begin with possible examples of delusion that are not pre-classified for psychiatric treatment and not assumed to be cases of schizophrenia. I wish to do this so as to learn without pre-existing conceptual fetters or biases just what the concept of delusion means or should entail, if we are to regiment it. I plan to argue that a common way in which delusions are understood in the literature on delusion is, if not mistaken, at least partial, incomplete or misplaced in its emphasis. This usual way is, as it were, largely focused on the supposed upstream causes of attitudes or states that count as delusions rather than, as I believe it (also) should be aimed, at the downstream effects that a delusion or state may have on the behavior and self-conception of a deluded individual. The usual way emphasizes how delusional attitudes are acquired and why they may count as bizarre in content or grossly false, rather than the place or impact that a condition possesses in a person's overall psychological economy, self-comprehension and behavior.

GRAND DELUSIONS

The Bible reports a case promoted by the Church as a triumph of religious faith, although it may be a better fit for classification as delusional. It's the story of Abraham and Isaac. The tale goes as follows: God orders Abraham to sacrifice his only son Isaac. To add poignancy to Abraham's situation, Isaac had been born after Abraham's wife was past her years of child-rearing. Abraham is told by God to "Take now thy son ... and offer him ... for a burnt offering upon one of the mountains that I will tell thee of" (Genesis 22).

Here is a quick and imaginary version of the tale that the Christian philosopher Robert Adams says he presents to his students:

What would you think if you asked your neighbor why he was building a large stone table in his backyard, and he said, "I'm building an altar because God has commanded me to sacrifice my son as a whole burnt offering. Won't you come to the ceremony tomorrow morning?" All [Adams's students] agree that the neighbor should be committed to a mental hospital.

(Adams 1999: 284)

Should we say the same thing about Abraham? He was deluded. He had lost contact with reality. He should be committed to a mental hospital. But, if so, why classify him as deluded?

Suppose the following assumption is true of subjects of delusion. Delusional thinkers are unrestrained by common sense or relevant background knowledge that they should possess. Laura should know better. People don't force other people to urinate. As for Abraham? Abraham fails to filter the command of an apparent divine voice through "his knowledge of right and wrong" (Adler 2007: 282). The philosopher Immanuel Kant says of Abraham's experience of an apparent divine voice: "Abraham should have replied to this supposedly divine voice: 'That I ought not to kill my son is quite certain'." "But that you, this apparition, are God – of that I am not certain, and never can be, not even if this voice rings down to me from [visible] heaven" (quoted in Adler 2007: 271). Allowing an apparent divine voice to overrule one's background ethical knowledge is not triumphal faith. It's delusional.

But we must be careful here. Is a delusional state or attitude necessarily unwarranted or evidentially unrestrained? Even if, objectively speaking, Abraham should not have taken the voice experience seriously, perhaps, were we in his situational shoes, it is understandable that he thought of God as communicating with him. Such a belief may have helped him to make sense of the bizarre voice experience.

Harvard psychologist Brendan Maher (1974, 1988 and 1999) has argued (in a manner that has influenced Stone and Young and numerous others who think and write about delusion) that delusions are sometimes attempts to make personal sense of bizarre or unusual perceptual experiences. Maher writes: "the processes by which deluded persons reason from experience to belief are not significantly different from the processes by which non-deluded persons do" (Maher 1999: 550). Not significantly different? Maher's hypothesis is that delusional attitude generation may be as rational or reasonable as certain forms of attitude formation in non-delusional people. The pathology or wrongness of a delusion, then, for Maher lies not in the bizarreness of a delusional attitude or conviction as such, but in the experiential aberration that helps to generate it. From a deluded subject's point of view, such an experience cries out for an explanation, in a manner that suggests not that something minor has happened to its subject, but that "everything [has] changed in a fundamental way" (Maher 1999: 560).

If anomalous experiences figure in the generation of delusions, perhaps we should not be surprised if the phenomenal content of an experience is often close to the Intentional or conceptual content of the corresponding delusion. In such a case the content of the anomalous experience may be taken at face value and the deluded subject more or less just endorses it (Bayne and Pacherie 2004). For example, the experience might be an experience as if God is speaking, and although the content of the experience is utterly bizarre and not to be expected, the experience is taken as reliable and trustworthy.

If the Bible is to be believed, just such an anomalous (bizarre, unusual, and endorsed as veridical) perceptual experience occurred to Abraham. Kant, however, still would insist that Maher would be mistaken if he was to claim, in, say, Abraham's case, that "I should kill Isaac" is an instance of a normal reasonable response to a supposedly divine voice. A divine call to kill one's son? That sort of interpretation of experience dramatically outstrips the norms or limits of common sense or warranted assertability, subjective constraints and the failure to ignore base rates and all. Abraham should have surmised that something was wrong with him, not that he was struggling with a genuinely divine imperative. Maher may be right about the subjective warrant of *some* delusions, but he would be wrong about *that* one. No parent should believe that God wants him to kill his child. The experience as of hearing a nurse's voice commanding you to urinate is one thing. Perhaps on a hospital ward it might make sense to believe that a medical authority is barking orders to you. But kill your son? God no. God would never ask for *that*. Such is Kant's position.

So, was Abraham deluded? I believe there is much to be said for the proposition that, yes, he was. But I do not wish to pursue an interpretation of his case here. My target is the phenomenon of delusion, not Abraham.

So what, then, is a delusion? Is it merely something bizarre and objectively unacceptable or without proper evidential support and out of touch with reality as the case of Abraham perhaps teaches us? APA (1994) offers the following gloss on the notion of a delusion.

> A false personal belief based on incorrect inference about external reality that is firmly sustained despite what almost everyone else believes and despite what constitutes incontrovertible and obvious proof or evidence to the contrary. The belief is not one ordinarily accepted by other members of the person's culture or subculture (e.g., it is not an article of religious faith). When a false belief involves a value judgment, it is regarded as a delusion only when the judgment is so extreme as to defy credibility. Delusional conviction occurs on a continuum and can sometimes be inferred from an individual's behavior. It is often difficult to distinguish between a delusion and an overvalued idea (in which case the individual has an unreasonable belief or idea but does not hold it as firmly as is the case with delusion).
>
> (APA 1994: 765)

The DSM gloss is not completely helpful. It describes delusional thinking in terms, in part, of falsity of a belief. But delusional attitudes may sometimes be true. Some paranoid people are persecuted. When she was charged by Henry Kissinger with being distrustful about her Arab neighbors, Golda Meir, then prime minister of Israel, is supposed to have quipped: "Even paranoids have enemies."

DSM leaves conceptual elbow room for such possibilities. Here is its description of the jealous type of delusional disorder: "This subtype applies when the central theme of the person's delusion is that his or her spouse or lover is unfaithful." "This belief is arrived at without due cause and is based on incorrect inference supported by small bits of 'evidence' (e.g. disarrayed clothing or spots on the sheets), which are collected and used to justify the delusion" (APA 1994: 297). All of which leaves open the possibility that a delusional conviction of jealousy may be true albeit insufficiently supported by a subject's own evidence or warrant base.

Are delusions firmly sustained? Some are. But delusional conviction may fluctuate. Clinicians report that some of their delusional patients entertain the possibility that they are mistaken in their beliefs (Bentall 2004: 324).

How about the notion that delusions are inferable from a deluded person's behavior? Such inferences are possible, of course, oftentimes, but not always. There may be "'double or multiple bookkeeping', whereby the delusional [belief] is kept separate from the rest of experience" (Sass 1992: 275). A man may say, "My wife has been replaced by an impostor" and then let her fix his meal or sleep next to him in bed. Or a "patient who insists that her coffee is poisoned with sperm still drinks it without concern" (Sass 1992: 274). A delusional 'belief' may be so shorn off from apt behavior as barely to appear belief-like. Indeed, coincident with this unbelief-like possibility, a body of opinion has begun to emerge in the literature that delusions need not be beliefs at all, strictly speaking (see Stephens and Graham 2004; Stephens and Graham 2007). A delusional set of attitudes may consist of thoughts, feelings and other unbelief-like elements.

Then, too, why should articles of religious faith secure exemption from the category of delusion? Perhaps license for exemption depends on the social or cultural contexts in which religious attitudes are typically embraced. Articles of religious faith are parts of people's normal cultural equipment and among the belief stocks acquired from a surrounding community. "It is undeniable," Dominic Murphy writes, "that normal maturing brains do pick up on religion, along with many other ... theories of the world" (Murphy 2006: 181). So "religion is not delusional even if religious beliefs are false" (181). But Murphy adds: "Numbers matter with delusions." "If only a tiny minority of humans were religious we might be more tempted to call them delusional" (Murphy 2006: 182). If Murphy is right, if religious attitudes may count as delusional when numbers of religious believers are small, then where does such a possibility leave, say, a religious leader like Jesus Christ, who believes that he is God Incarnate? Was Christ deluded? The initial number of Christians was small.

One quite common type of delusion is of a grandiose variety in which an individual is convinced that they possess special powers or are on a special mission. Was Christ possessed of grandiose delusions? If he and only a tiny minority of others (immediate followers, Doubting Thomas aside) believed that he was God Incarnate, then perhaps the more delusional his attitudes towards himself should appear to be.

The temptation to picture Christ as deluded, of course, demands clarification. Reflection on the temptation is helpful, I believe, in understanding delusion more generally.

Grandiose delusions occur in several different types of disorder, including mania, so-called delusional disorder, and schizophrenia (Munro 1999: 140–2). Grandiosity consists of inflated and evidentially unwarranted estimations of one's power, worth, knowledge or importance. Did Christ suffer from it?

Perhaps ironically, given the imprimatur, a number of Christian apologists have worried about this question. Here is C. S. Lewis in *Mere Christianity*:

A man who was merely a man and said the sort of things that Jesus said would not be a great moral teacher. He [might be] a lunatic – on a level with a man who says he is a poached egg.

(1952: 55)

But Lewis raises the possibility of Christ being deluded only to dismiss it. "It seems obvious to me," writes Lewis, "that he was [not] a lunatic" (56). (See also Davis 2002.)

The physician, musician, theologian, and Nobel Prize winner, Albert Schweitzer in a book with the fascinating title of *The Psychiatric Study of Jesus*, considered whether Christ was a victim of delusion. But he denied it. Schweitzer summed up his appraisal as follows: "The high estimate that Jesus [had] of himself ... fall[s] far short of proving the existence of mental illness" (1948 [1913]: 72).

If we take aspects of the Gospels at face value, however, a plausible case can perhaps be made that Jesus was truly or genuinely delusional. Let's see how such a case may be constructed. It will, I believe, teach us something about delusion itself. Or at least that is my aim.

Numerous eyewitnesses who were familiar with his activities and teachings claimed that he was "raving mad" (John 10:19) and "out of his mind" (Mark 3:21). He said bizarre and grandiose things such as:

*   I am the Way, the Truth, and the Life; no man cometh unto the Father, but by me. (John 14:6)
*   I and my Father are One. (John 10:30)
*   Before Abraham was, I am. (John 8:58)
*   I am the light of the world. (John 8:12)
*   Whoever acknowledges me before others, I will acknowledge before my Father in heaven. (Matthew 10: 32)

According to historical orthodoxy, shared by both Christians and non-Christians alike, Jesus claimed to be an equal to God or to be God in incarnate form. (Not every scholar, it may be noted, agrees with this orthodox interpretation of Jesus. Bart D. Ehrman, a distinguished historian of the Gospel period, claims that "the historical Jesus did not believe in his own divinity." "His concerns were those of a first-century Jewish apocalypticist" [1999: 243]. Here, however, I merely report and assume orthodoxy, not defend it.) Christ believed himself to be carrying out various divine prerogatives like forgiving sins, not just wrongs against his own person, but wrongs to others, as if he himself had been wronged in the harms done to other people. He also thought himself to exemplify the best or most secure or reliable way in which to have a proper relationship with God.

Imagine, borrowing a thought experiment from the philosopher Daniel Howard-Snyder, that you have a pious neighbor by the name of 'Florence' (Howard-Snyder 2004). She claims to be divine and offers to forgive your sins. Florence is a nice person. Kind and generous, in fact. Wouldn't you be tempted to believe that she is delusional? Howard-Snyder suggests he certainly would.

Our question, again, though, is as follows: Is it plausible to claim that Jesus was deluded in believing, assuming he did so, that he was equal to God or God in incarnate human form?

Remember Jesus could have been both deluded in believing such things and not utterly irrational or without subjective warrant or reason for doing so, if Maher is right. Perhaps "I and my Father are one" was a reasonable proposition for him to embrace even if he was deluded about it. Remember Maher's (and Stone and Young's) claim that some delusions are subjectively reasonable responses to anomalous perceptual experiences. Consider the following hypothetical story.

> *The Maher Story of Jesus*: Jesus had all sorts of bizarre and anomalous experiences. He perceived himself to be able to cure various ailments (fever, leprosy, lameness, blindness, and so on) and to raise people from the dead (see Mark 5:35–43 and John 11:38–44). He appeared to himself to be able to walk on water, still storms, multiply loaves (see Mark 6:30–44). While many contemporaries rejected him, and although he himself lamented that though foxes and birds have places to stay he has nowhere (Matthew 8:20; Luke 9:58), his 'miracle-performances' had numerous purported eyewitnesses. So it came to pass: Jesus explained these bizarre perceptual experiences to himself by believing that he was the kingly Messiah, the fusion of God and Man – divine, the Son of God.

The psychiatrist Alistair Munro writes of delusional grandiosity as follows: "An interesting element in grandiosity is that of centrality." "Highly unusual and improbable things happen to him, yet he does not question these." "Centrality is often associated with ideas of ... persecution" (Munro 1999: 142).

Suppose we add the following ingredients to the Maher Story. Jesus' self-attribution of divinity was reinforced by his interpretation of the Messianic Story in the Scriptures and by the messianic culture of first-century Palestine. Christ viewed his suffering and persecution not as a miscarriage of justice, but as having been foreshadowed by and endowed with apocalyptic significance in the writings of the prophet Isaiah. The persecution is God's plan, he thought. True, during Jesus' time, a lot of other persons claimed to be messiahs. Scores of people believed in them without empirical confirmation. But Jesus' own I-am-God belief continued to grip his personal imagination. It helped him to account for the otherwise unusual and improbable things that appeared to happen to him at the end of his life. These were perceptual experiences that possessed for him a deep "feeling of significance [so that] everything must have changed in some fundamental way" (Maher 1999: 560). "There is something profoundly different about me," he may have thought. "I must be the Son of God." Such would be a rather full-bodied Maher-like tale. It may not be good Christology, but it is useful, I think, in understanding a psychopathology.

So, again, *was* Christ deluded?

Some examinations of Jesus' delusional or non-delusional status confuse the question of whether his belief in his divinity was true with whether he was deluded. Here, for example, is the psychiatrist O. Quentin Hyder on whether Jesus was deluded. It begins with a quote from a diagnostic manual.

"A delusion is a persistent false belief not in keeping with a person's cultural and educational background or level of knowledge." Jesus' belief that he was the Messiah was by contrast totally in keeping with his background. The whole of the Old Testament Scriptures look forward to and actually spell out the coming of a Messiah together with his characteristics and qualifications. Jesus was thoroughly familiar with the Old Testament and knew that his birth and early life had already fulfilled many prophesies. "Search the Scriptures – for – they are they which testify to Me" (John 5:39). His own prophesies about his own death and resurrection, later literally fulfilled, indicate further that he *knew* [italics added] that he was the Messiah that Israel was waiting for.

(Hyder 1977: 8)

I certainly do not wish to examine here whether, in fact, Christ was the Messiah. If he was divine, he could not have been deluded, of course. An omniscient deity does not make that sort of mistake. But, again, it's delusion I am after, not Christology. For my target, which is understanding delusion, I am going to assume that Christ was not God incarnate (or died and was literally resurrected). I am going to presuppose he was not divine. What then?

Munro notes that "some individuals with grandiose beliefs can adopt a lifestyle which accommodates and sanctions their delusions and their behavior" (Munro 2006: 141). One obvious way in which this may happen is by propagating a kind of extreme apocalyptic religious ideology "which allows the person to share and even propagate his strange beliefs" with a group of "equally deluded individuals" (Munro 2006: 141). Such group sharing may help to explain the testimony of alleged eyewitnesses to Christ's miraculous performances and other 'evidences' of his divinity. None of the observers may have been truly reliable or trustworthy. Perhaps they were as deluded as he may have been.

Let us, however, take another approach to delusion, not in terms of the actual truth or falsity of its content, as with Hyder, or in terms of the subjective warrant for its acquisition, as with Maher, or even in terms of reference to a group delusion, but in terms of its persistent and self-represented role in and consequences for a person's (like Christ's) overall psychological economy. Consider claims by psychologist Mike Jackson about what he calls "benign psychosis" (Jackson 2007).

Benign psychosis? I am not pleased with this locution. It seems oxymoronic, like referring to a desirable disorder. But there is an important point behind it that I wish to extract. This is its emphasis on downstream or forward-looking considerations in classifying delusions.

Some people's religious convictions and experiences, Jackson notes, are neither disruptive nor intrusive, but inspirational, "involving a sense of authority and meaning" and exemplifying "creative thinking" (2007: 245). By contrast a delusion as such (or a 'malignant' psychosis, adopting Jackson's terminology) harbors or risks a "devastating impact on [a person's] well-being and ability to function" (2007: 247). "Rather than resolving ... existential concerns, a situation of radical and threatening social dislocation is likely to exacerbate them" (2007: 248). Jackson notes: "People ... tend to be isolated by their delusional beliefs" (248).

Jesus was neither socially isolated nor emotionally devastated by conviction in his own divinity (assuming that that's exactly what he, in fact, did believe). Hyder, in a passage devoid of the question-begging assumption that Jesus *knew* that he was the Messiah, writes of how Christ's belief in his own divinity may have helped to inspire his moral insights:

> The Sermon on the Mount is still the best ever summary of principles of living in this life (Matthew 5–7). Psychotherapy today uses many of the principles he first enunciated. The principle of self-love means having a good sense of self-worth, esteem, or respect for oneself which is the vital prerequisite to obeying the commandment, "Thou shalt love thy neighbor as thyself" (Matthew 22:39). The principle of forgiveness is essential to all healthy interpersonal relationships (Matthew 18: 21–22), as is also the so-called Golden Rule of doing to others what you desire that they would do to you (Luke 6:31).
>
> (Hyder 1977: 11)

The historian Philip Schaff offers praise of Christ's acuity when he asks the following rhetorical question (meaning to answer it affirmatively):

> Is such an intellect – clear as the sky, bracing as the mountain air, sharp and penetrating as a sword, thoroughly healthy and vigorous, always ready and always self-possessed – liable to a radical and most serious delusion concerning his own character and mission?
>
> (Schaff 1918: 97)

Suppose Jesus was grossly mistaken in thinking himself to be divine. Suppose also that his attitude was not just bizarre and grandiose but objectively unwarranted by the evidence. Christ may have had unusual perceptual experiences, which felt very significant to him and in need of explanation, but suppose, too, that even these did not truly warrant his believing that he was God. Suppose that they were hallucinatory or in some other severe manner epistemically or evidentially deficient. Suppose Christ, much like Kant's Abraham, should have filtered them out and not used them to ground belief in his own divinity, if that is just what he did. Jackson assumes that such a belief (despite its lack of pedigree) qualifies as delusional (or 'malignantly' psychotic) only if it results in pragmatic distress or has a destructive personal impact. But if Hyder and Schaff are correct, Jesus' conviction in his divinity had no such impact. If they are right, the conviction contributed to Christ's sense of meaning, purpose, moral insight, and capacity for benevolent and productive social engagement.

Jackson urges that we adopt such a forward-looking criterion for a (for him 'malignant') delusion. If so, a belief or attitude fails to qualify as delusional if it contributes positively to leading a worthwhile life and is integrated helpfully into a person's overall psychological economy. Such an attitude may still qualify as some other sort of normative error – a superstition, an instance of wishful thinking or self-deception, whatever. But if Jackson is right, and if our standard for delusion should include reference to its harmful consequences (and also, of course, if Hyder and Schaff are correct about the positive consequences for Christ of his conviction), Jesus was not deluded. He was not deluded, because his belief played a positive role in his life.

My interest in the case of Jesus is not in him per se, as noted earlier, but in what may be inferred from his situation about the nature of delusion and the differences between delusional and non-delusional attitudes. Jackson's plea for examining consequences helps to explain how beliefs like that of Jesus in his own divinity, which are bizarre and grandiose, nonetheless may not deserve to be categorized as delusional. Even if Jesus' claim to be God was false, it may have been precisely the element of his psychology that helped him to achieve moral insight. The conviction did not drive him into despair or wreak havoc on his powers of reasoning and communicative expression. Quite the contrary, if Schall and Hyder are correct, it contributed to his intellect and moral vision. Pragmatically speaking, it was eminently responsive to reason.

The moral I want to draw from examining the case of Christ is this. Consequences matter for delusions.

I am reminded of a remark about the relevance of consequences to mental abnormalities of a religious nature that William James makes in his masterpiece on religious psychology, *The Varieties of Religious Experience*: "What then," to quote James, whom Jackson acknowledges as an influence on this own thinking, "is more natural than that this temperament should introduce one to regions of ... truth, to corners of the universe, which your robust Philistine type of nervous system, forever offering its biceps to be felt, thumping its breast, and thanking Heaven that it hasn't a single morbid fiber in its composition, would be sure to hide forever from its self-satisfied possessors?" (James 2002 [1901–2]: 29).

James's and Jackson's point is well-taken. Harmful consequences matter for delusions. Helpful or beneficial consequences matter for non-delusions. Even if a belief or attitude is false, bizarre or otherwise immensely suspect, as long as it seriously enhances a person's adjustment to or contribution for the world, and causes no severe undesirable harm, this leaves room for classifying it as non-delusional. Not faultless to be sure. But not delusional.

So what then does make a belief or attitude delusional?

Karl Jaspers claimed, perhaps in a manner not totally consistent with his skepticism about empathetic understanding of schizophrenia, that being deluded involves being in a special mood or frame of mind, which possesses both affective and cognitive components, namely a "delusional mood," and that even true beliefs may count as delusional, if they occur enveloped in such a mood (Jaspers 1963). What this mood amounts to, Jaspers claimed, is difficult to describe with precision other than that it (among other things) invests a belief or attitude with great personal consequence or importance, dominated by its atmospherics (its 'centrality', to use Munro's term, or 'significance', to use Maher's), so that to deny it (and here is one of a delusion's negative consequences) would be perceived or interpreted by the person as shattering their sense of self or world. Jaspers writes: "Delusion proper ... implies a transformation in ... total awareness of reality" (Jaspers 1963: 94). It is something that, as the philosopher Shaun Gallagher notes, a "deluded subject experiences and lives through" (Gallagher 2009: 257). A deluded individual lives 'in and through' their delusion.

The psychiatrist and philosopher K. W. M. Fulford (like Jackson, James and Jaspers) also offers a consequence-oriented approach to understanding what makes a delusion a delusion. He writes that "the irrationality of delusions should be understood in terms not of defective cognitive functioning but rather of impaired reasons for action" (1993: 14). That is, what makes a delusion a delusion is not how the patient acquires the attitude, but the manner in which they self-represent, appeal to, or rely on it in reason giving and action guidance. How it makes them live in the world. The pathology or disorder of delusion is practical (related to choice and action). It is prospective, namely, what a person does with or because of a belief, thought or attitude. Not retrospective, namely, how a person acquired the belief or attitude.

Consider the priest for whom I cared in Boston. Thinking of me as the devil was bizarre. Who knows how this particular idea may have arisen or the basis of its personal appeal? Perhaps, if the Maher–Stone–Young-line is correct, it helped the priest to explain something experientially anomalous and yet perceived by him to be important. But walling this belief off from contrary evidence, being wedded to it in spite of being under his bed in bedclothes, and not properly evaluating or appreciating its imprudent impact on his behavior is, for Jackson, Jaspers and Fulford, what helps to make the priest's conviction delusional. Not how he acquired it or came to believe it. Not whether it is false. But how he lives within it.

Consider Laura. She believes that unseen speakers are urging her to pace up and down the ward and to urinate on herself. Whether she is deluded does not hinge on whether this belief is bizarre (surely, it is) or radically unsupported by available evidence on the hallway (certainly, it is). It depends on her deployment of the attitude and its effect on her. Does it lead her to deeper insights or to effective social intercourse with other people? Or does she over-identify with it, failing to appreciate the negative impact it has on her behavior? When prior to treatment Laura is asked if she was sick, she replied that she was suffering from things that bothered her. When asked why she was in the hospital, she replied "I do not know." She failed to appreciate that something was genuinely wrong with her. After a year of treatment, however, in a prescient sign of recovery, when asked about her delusions, she offered the following telling response: "I think I was getting sick at this point" (Young and Leafblood 1996: 107). Negative consequences were self-recognized and halted the persistence of her delusions in a moment of diagnostic insight. Her delusional world began to dissolve.

Crack the acquisition code, the generation of a delusional attitude, some say, and one should be able to determine whether an attitude is delusional. Dominic Murphy writes for the majority of theorists that "we need to appeal to some general ideas about belief acquisition to explain why certain beliefs count as delusions in the first place" (Murphy 2006: 180). In the first place? I am unconvinced (and Murphy himself also seems unconvinced; see below). Certainly that is not the way in which clinicians commonly identify delusions. Clinicians normally are not directly privy to acquisition or generation conditions. They are a party only to effects or consequences of a person's attitude. When confronted with a patient who seems to hold unusually distorted or bizarre beliefs, it is not the origin that confronts the observer, but the manner in which the attitudes are dealt with by the subject and the person's failure to properly respond to challenges that such beliefs or attitudes present to them as persons or rational agents. G. Lynn Stephens and I put matters as follows: "As bizarre as it may be to think that, for example, worms are devouring one's bones, delusion consists not in [the contents of] such thoughts but in the pathological manner in which we respond to them as persons" (Stephens and Graham 2004: 241). It is one thing to learn how a belief or attitude that becomes delusional is initially acquired. It is another to understand "why it is maintained and not rejected in the light of everything else that the patient knows" or believes or experiences – including exposure to its harmful or imprudent consequences (see Bell et al. 2006: 221). This last feature of delusions, namely their persistence or maintenance in spite of bad and even self-perceived bad consequences, is typically the focus of clinical concern and treatment. And well it should be. Living through a delusion hurts a person.

DELUSION AND SELF-COMPREHENSION

Sally's son Sam is a classical pianist. Sally is a widely admired music critic for *Gramophone*. As a talent Sam is strictly second tier, although Sally lavishes praise on his performances and promotes his few recordings as stellar. She tells one of her colleagues that Sam is the new Vladimir Horowitz. She sincerely believes this. Why does she do so? Two explanatory hypotheses suggest themselves.

One is that, although absent affection for her son, Sally would recognize the genuine limits of Sam's talent, given the presence of parental affection she believes as she does out of love. Her belief is motivated by a desire for its truth rather than grounded in solid evidence for it. She wants it to be the case that Sam is a marvelous talent. So, she believes that he is.

Bertrand Russell (1872–1970) observes:

> We desire many things which it is not in our power to achieve ... But it is found that a considerable portion of the satisfaction that those things would bring us if they were realized is achieved by the much easier operation of believing that they are or will be realized.
>
> (Russell 1921: 74; see Graham 1986 for discussion)

So it is with Sally, or so says a first explanatory hypothesis. Wanting her son to be the new Horowitz, she somehow has gotten herself to believe that he is. Self-deception? Wishful thinking? Either way her belief is motivated. Motivated belief is not belief over which one has direct voluntary control. That's not what talk of its being motivated means. But it is a belief, as it were, under the influence of emotions or desires which skew the belief-forming process. Motivated belief is also not necessarily a bad thing. We are all prone to it and sometimes it helps. When faced with a catastrophe, for instance, a person may take solace in a wishful estimation of the future. But wishing something to be true is no indication whatsoever that it is true.

A second hypothesis is that, with motivation irrelevant, Sally actually misreads the evidence of Sam's playing as solid evidence that her son is a spectacular talent. Given her reading or interpretation of the evidence, she believes that he is a superb pianist.

The second hypothesis admits of two variations. One is that Sally's reading of the evidence of her son's talent is connected with a cognitive bias. Call this the *doting-parent bias*. The bias causes her preferentially to attend to information about Sam's playing that is positive, not negative. The doting-parent bias is such that reasoning about one's children is skewed in favor of being child-serving. Parents may misidentify all manner of behavior in their offspring, like playing the piano well, as evidence of a child's truly immense talent. Just why parents harbor this bias may admit of some sort of evolutionary psychological explanation (so says the variation). Perhaps parents who harbor it produce more self-confident offspring. Perhaps that is a good thing for one's genes. But it has nothing immediately to do with personal love or affectionate motive. It's in the affectless mechanism of genetic transport, as it were.

The other variation on the second hypothesis is that Sally's belief in Sam's immense talent is connected with a deficit or gap (rather than a bias) in her manner of evidence gathering and construal. Sally suffers from an observational blind spot when it comes to her children. Call this the *seeing-child defect*. Certain less than sterling features of Sam's piano performances just are missed. Her (what might be called) child-appraisal system is impaired in a manner that is specific to a person's own children. Perhaps (so surmises our imagined advocates of the second variation) a specific sort of parietal–temporal lesion is responsible for this. Sally hears her son play but she just does not acoustically attend to his misreading of the Chopin nocturnes.

I've made up the story of Sally and Sam, of course, as well as the two explanatory hypotheses and variations of the second. But they bear similarities to the two main approaches to theorizing about delusion generation or acquisition in the literature. One is a motivational approach that regards delusions as serving personal motives for a deluded person, perhaps defensive or palliative in nature. The other is an unmotivated-belief or cognitive-processing approach, which regards delusions as constituted by cognitive biases in belief formation or deficits in reasoning or evidence interpretation.

Freud favored a motivational picture of the generation of delusion. He claimed that "a delusion is found applied like a patch over the place where originally a rent had appeared in the ego's relation to the external world" (1986 [1924]: 565). Freud is not alone in turning to an account in motivational terms of the origin of a delusion (see also Bentall 2004: 330–46). Here's a sketch of a motivational picture for a delusion.

Consider the Capgras delusion. Capgras is a delusion in which a person believes (thinks, feels) that a loved one, perhaps a spouse or close relative, has been replaced by a physically identical replica, although the deluded person may otherwise be mentally lucid and sound. Such a delusion, since it is typically tightly themed or circumscribed (around a loved one or ones), is sometimes called, for that reason, monothematic. (More multidimensional delusions that involve more widespread misappraisals of reality are sometimes called, for that very reason, polythematic.) Enoch and Trethowan (1991) offer a motivational analysis of the condition. It goes something like this.

A person with Capgras possesses conflicting feelings towards an intimate (spouse or family member), feeling both love and affection together with hate and spiteful aversion. But by believing that the loved one is an impostor the tension between these two conflicting feelings is more or less dissolved. The person with Capgras may feel hate and aversion towards the intimate (after all, they are an impostor), without the guilt or shame associated with such feelings if recognized as directed towards a real spouse or family member. The

Capgras delusion therein serves a function, a palliative function. Of course, it does so at practical and perhaps ultimately unwanted personal costs. One is that it complicates the subject's everyday responses to the 'impostor'. How can I comfortably eat a meal that my impostor-spouse has prepared for me or enjoyably visit with my in-laws? In each case, if I genuinely believe that the person whom I am with is an impostor, I must somehow avoid letting this belief affect my behavior negatively, otherwise its palliative function will be undermined. If I reveal to my spouse or to her parents that I think that she is an impostor, the tensions present within my conflicting feelings will surface, dramatically, no doubt. Palliation will not be secured.

Capgras in the psychiatric literature has also been accounted for in a manner that conforms to an unmotivated-belief picture. Here is an example of one such description. It is an example of the cognitive-deficit variation (like the seeing-child defect in Sally).

Normally, when we recognize an intimate (a spouse or family member), we experience a brief emotional response, a feeling of familiarity. The response helps to reveal to us whether we are encountering friend or foe. We may also recall specific information about the person, for example, what the person looks like – say, the pattern of their face.

Suppose the following is true: These two types of recognition are performed by or implemented in different information-processing pathways in the brain (see Bauer 1984). Face recognition is performed in the ventral visual-processing pathway, whereas the affective (emotional) aspect results from activation of pathways connecting the ventral pathway and the limbic system. The Capgras delusion arises in cases where the pathways connecting the face-recognition unit with the limbic system are damaged, leaving ventral processing unimpaired. The subject sees someone who appears, in all visual respects, identical to the familiar person. But the subject does not experience the normal affective 'familiarity' response. Rather, they experience a feeling of estrangement or unfamiliarity. So, victims of Capgras in order to explain to themselves why the intimate does not feel right (remember Maher's thesis about some delusional attitudes being subjectively explanatory of anomalous experiences) form the belief that they are interacting with someone who looks very much like, but nonetheless is not, the intimate. An impostor, replica, dummy, robot or whatever operative technology a surrounding culture may perhaps suggest. Full and proper recognition of the intimate would occur only if the intimate both looks right (pattern matches) and feels right (feels familiar). In Capgras belief acquisition is impaired by a feels-right-recognition deficit (see Ellis and Young 1990; see also Langdon and Coltheart 2000: 186).

Again, though, such an analysis of delusion acquisition has costs. One cost is theoretical, having to do with its limits as an explanation. It harbors explanatory gaps. One of these is that if a deluded person really does possess a recognition deficit (or for that matter a reasoning bias), then why don't they simply appreciate that in conceiving of the person as an impostor something must be wrong with them and not with the loved one? The impostor hypothesis is bizarre. One does not see impostors (dummies and so on) very often, if at all. The background base rates or prior probabilities for such a possibility are at or close to zero. Some people with anomalous or hallucinatory experiences of an intimate family member actually do acknowledge or believe just that. Some brain-damaged individuals who are impaired in the ability to recognize faces understand that they have a perceptual problem, and they do not acquire the bizarre belief that they are encountering impostors. Since some individuals don't make or perhaps even dream of making that assumption, something extra must be added to the deficit (or bias) hypothesis, for Capgras cases, if the hypothesis is to help to explain why 'Capgrasians' acquire impostor-beliefs. The mere presence of a looks right/feels wrong experience is insufficient to explain impostor-belief acquisition.

A theorist of delusion may, of course, try to mix both non-motivational and motivational approaches (and some do) in accounting for the origins of a delusional attitude. Imagine that a Capgras patient is paranoid. Their paranoid (persecutory) mood or attributional style is such that they deeply and generally distrust others, but not themselves. Adding paranoia to the background mix of the delusion may help to explain why they believe themselves to be living with an impostor rather than that something is wrong with them or their perceptual experiences. They don't fault themselves. They self-protectively blame the other, namely the impostor.

Our imagined case of Sally is in need of a similar explanatory fix. We must ask the following question about her case. Why doesn't Sally recognize that she is a doting mother who simply is mistaken about her son? Not hear her son as the new Horowitz, but as the truly fine but still less than superlative talent that he is. Perhaps the more complete answer behind her belief formation goes like this. Sally has a temperamental tendency to entertain grandiose ideas. This tendency is socially reinforced by her being a highly regarded critic whose words make or break performance careers. If so, perhaps it is no wonder, then, that she thinks of Sam as like Horowitz rather than that she is wrong in her own judgment. Nothing but a Steinway Grand Piano for Sam and a seat as his page turner for Sally.

I have no wish to deny that various sorts of hypotheses, like those mentioned, may help to explain the origin of bizarre beliefs (like the impostor-belief). I remain skeptical, however, about the significance or force of acquisition accounts for what makes a delusion delusional. For even if we identify the processes or propensities responsible for bizarre or anomalous beliefs, we still need to characterize the consequential norms that delusions violate that help to make them delusions. Belief-acquisition conditions may and often do lead people into error, but, I am claiming, it's what a person does with or because of the attitude, or fails to do, that makes for a delusion. Acquisition is one thing; upshot or consequence another.

If an attitude like the Capgras belief is enveloped in a delusional mood (to use Jaspers's notion), then it acquires a distinctively pathological or harmful character. It moves from being aberrant, unusual and/or objectively unwarranted (but perhaps otherwise harmless or even of positive influence) to something deleterious and incompatible with mental health. Again: I contend that it is not the falsity, bizarreness or irrational origin of an attitude that makes delusion. Delusions constitute, I propose, a failure of prudent self-comprehension and responsible epistemic self-management and it is *that* sort of failure and its impact on a person that makes for a delusion, not or not just the bizarre, erring or inept manner in which a person represents self or world.

So why then cling to an attitude in the face of negative consequences? Why be so unresponsive to good reasons for abandoning it? Perhaps it is time to consider whether a rational personal-level or Intentionalistic language description of the sources of a delusion's maintenance needs to be supplemented or complemented by reference to a-rational brute causal neural forces described in a non-Intentionalistic idiom. It is hard to see why a victim of, say, Capgras, persists in it. What is keeping him from abandoning the conviction that his wife is an imposter, given that he is now being asked to cover the funeral expenses of her dead father or to deal with several hostile siblings each claiming to be primary heirs to the man's estate?

In *Content and Consciousness* (1969), one of the classics of twentieth-century philosophy of mind, Daniel Dennett offers a suggestion for when to move from an Intentionalistic, rational-person-presupposing type of explanation of behavior to a "scientific story about synapses, electrical potentials and so forth that would explain, describe and predict all that goes on in the nervous system" (78). This is when a person's "response to the environment 'makes no sense', and, since it makes no sense, no Intentional (putatively sense-making) account of the [behavior] will be justified" (78). A behavior then "should be susceptible to explanation and prediction without any recourse to ... Intentionality" (78).

Dennett's idea goes roughly like this: Whatever procedure we use to ascribe Intentional states or attitudes to a person in order to explain this or that aspect or feature of behavior, if the explanation just does not seem to explain it, then shift to neurobiology/neurochemisty. Shift to the language of brain science when not all features of behavior appear to be rational or controlled by the reason-responsiveness of a subject. Look for a brute causal mechanism as responsible for such behavior. True, it is not as if Intentionalistic explanation is *a priori* excluded from such cases. Though straining credulity, we may continue to cite palliation in explaining the persistence of a Capgras delusion. But nevertheless such an explanation may just not fully or plausibly explain the behavior. Recall, for example, the discussion of addiction in the previous chapter. It is quite obvious that there are stages or steps in addiction about which our explanatory understanding should be complemented by using the language or perspective of neurobiology/neurochemistry. There appear to be causal links between non-Intentionalistic or a-rational neural activity and the first signs of relapse, for instance, stages not mediated by the rationality of an addict or by the reason-responsive operation of his deliberative-response patterns. In such a case, we may assume that there is neural mechanism that links the impulse or disposition to drug consumption with a failure of rational resolve.

Likewise, there are features that are highly perplexing about delusional disorders and that the rational-person language of Intentionality has trouble understanding. We may wonder why a person fails to wrest themselves from the grip of a delusional mood. In such a case we may suspend the language of palliative or defensive motivation and shift to "the sub-personal [explanatory level] of brains and events in the nervous system" (Dennett 1969: 93). At this sub-personal or a-rational level of analysis and explanation, the sources responsible for the persistence of a delusion receive descriptions in brute causal terms.

One recent and widely discussed proposal along sub-personal/non-Intentionalistic lines is that dopamine release in the brain – reinforced perhaps by a subject's temperament, situational stressors or mood – invests certain thoughts (through their neurological realization or base) with a personal importance, salience or centrality that makes a subject feel as if these thoughts are more insightful or veridical than otherwise they would seem to be (Kapur 2003). They rouse a person and awaken feelings of significance. Even the most banal and otherwise neglected thought or attitude may become hyper-salient when excited by dopaminergic activity (see also Broome et al. 2005). When this happens the brain reward system a-rationally irrupts into the space of reasons. It irrupts into the causal linkages between Intentional attitudes or states and behavior. This sort of irruptive activity may be quite normal. Perhaps it occurs in dreams. It may occur in various forms of creative imagination. It may occur under conditions of emotional stress. It may also be quite specific. Certain sorts of thoughts (say, distrusting or grandiose ones), depending on the individuals involved and their temperaments or learning histories, may be affected rather than others.

Again, as in the analogous case of addiction, it would be a mistake to automatically assume that such irruption means that there is something wrong with a person's brain. Perhaps there is. But more likely, I think, not. Some neuroscientists who talk of a sense of importance or heightened significance in delusion or psychosis being modulated by dopaminergic activity do speak of the neural activity as aberrant. Kapur, for instance, refers to it as a form of "neurochemical dysregulation" (Kapur 2003: 15). Dysregulation? But perfectly normal people have bizarre and unusual thoughts, too, all the time. Sometimes these are taken seriously; sometimes not. Sometimes they change one's orientation to life; sometimes they are reflectively dismissed as unimportant and inconsequential. Sometimes evidence excises them from a person's belief or attitude stock; sometimes not. Moreover, the mere fact that an attitude or condition may persist in the face of contrary evidence or evidence of harm to self does not by itself demonstrate that some sort of neural 'dysregulation' or chemical defect is responsible. Perhaps such neurochemical activity has the effect in ordinary life of focusing attention, memory and imagination in ways that are resistant to certain sorts of contrary evidence. Perhaps this is or can be, normally, a good thing. If a man is convinced that he has found his soulmate, for example, it would be unwise to abandon this conviction just because he spots animosity in her father or stinginess among her siblings. If one plans to seek therapy for drug addiction, it may be a good thing to believe that this plan is central to one's self or preferred form of life, if it means that the prods or encouragements of one's dealer to re-consume are robustly resisted. A person's insensitivity to contrary considerations may be suffused with a feeling of immunity to disconfirmation. Not a good feature of one's psychological economy on occasion, to be sure. But not always a bad thing pragmatically either.

So: Might the hypothesis of a dopamine-induced sense of salience, importance or veridicality help to explain why a conviction of a delusional sort is not abandoned? It might. Such a hypothesis could help to frame, if true, a proper and fuller explanatory account of delusional persistence than an account offered just in Intentionalistic terms. Perhaps, for delusional subjects, being in the presence of certain persons or situations, and confronted with an anxiety or fear, may trigger an activation of dopamine activity that helps to endow certain thoughts or beliefs with resistance to forces otherwise pressing for abandonment. Contrary evidence may be rendered impotent. Doubts may be muted. A person may over-identify with a thought or conviction. A disorder is here. A mental disorder. But not a brain disorder, although reference to neural activity helps to explain one or more features of the disorder. (Or at least, not a brain disorder in certain cases of delusion. Some delusions may be associated with and due to brain damage, of course.)

I say 'helps to explain'. Dominic Murphy wisely remarks that if "the key variable is just dopamine activity ... there is a missing level of explanation" (Murphy 2006: 179). "We still need to characterize the role that [the bizarre or unusual thoughts] play in the patient's mental life" (Murphy 2006: 179). Murphy is exactly right. We need to know of an attitude's consequences (which is what I take him to mean by 'role'), not or not just of its neurochemically modulated salience. But how should we characterize the role, the consequences, of an attitude that qualifies as a delusion?

If I am deluded I may regard a thought like e.g. 'I am infected by insects crawling underneath my skin' as insightful, inspirational or intuitively certain, despite its being utterly bizarre or unusual. If I am deluded, no matter how unlikely such a thought is to be true, I may accept it relatively unquestioningly. Or I may become humorless or oversensitive about it or turn secretive or evasive when questioned about its source, rationale or provenance. I may represent or classify the thought to myself as a belief or conviction, with a propositional content that I represent as true and worth stating sincerely. (Some such hyper-salient thoughts actually may become beliefs, even if they do not start their epistemic life in this manner, if, for example, I classify or represent them to myself in a belief-like way.) Or I may cling to certain thoughts with a kind of non-belief-like ironic detachment or double-bookkeeping that is not indicative of a belief as such, but still is compatible with my being classified as deluded (Sass 1994: 21). A deluded person who says that her coffee is poisoned with sperm may drink it without concern. Or if there is a degrees-of-belief continuum, her behavior may be too wide of the behavioral mark to count as believing that her coffee is poisoned. She drinks it with relish and abandon. But still a psychiatrist may wisely classify her thought or frame of mind as delusional.

Thinking or experiencing one's thoughts (beliefs, attitudes, etc.) in such ways is thinking of them in the manner that, I believe, Jaspers had mind when he referred to delusions as enveloped in a delusional mood. G. Lynn Stephens and I speak similarly of such thoughts qualifying as delusions or parts of delusional states insofar as they are harmful or imprudent in the manner in which they are self-understood and self-appraised. Such thoughts are, as we put it, in the grips of a *delusional stance* (of which more in the next chapter) (see Stephens and Graham 2004; Stephens and Graham 2007). Once gripped by the delusional stance or enveloped in a delusional mood they qualify as delusions. Or such is our claim.

The enveloping mood is incapacitating. The delusional stance is disabling. The gripped attitude may become incorrigible and impervious to proper contrarian considerations. A delusion may be socially or therapeutically challenged by questions aimed at making the deluded individual describe the belief (or thought) more explicitly or cite reasons or warrant for it. If so, the deluded individual may confabulate or make reasons up. There may be associated features of the thought or its content like its hauteur, paranoia or grandiosity, accompanying or precipitating abnormal experiences or hallucinations or a deluded subject's rapid as well as inexplicable mood changes. Such features may reinforce its classification as delusional. When unwelcome costs or harmful personal consequences are pointed out to a deluded person, the individual may not question or aptly modify the thought. The deluded subject's sense of self and world may be unperturbed by such deleterious behavior. The grip of a thought or belief on them is too strong. As a deluded subject one cannot 'step aside' and consider it more prudently or rationally. They cannot ask themselves whether they should truly harbor or embrace it.

Of course, as may be obvious from how I describe matters, reference to a delusional mood or stance as constitutive of a delusional attitude (belief, thought, feeling, etc.) does not cleanly or precisely distinguish delusional from non-delusional attitudes. Moods and stances are vague sorts of things. Many convictions in politics or religion appear bizarre or unusual to non-believers, are held with intuitive certainty or a deep sense of significance and high levels of affect, treated humorlessly by 'true believers', and so on, and carry harmful or injurious effects in their train. Think of some intensely patriotic people who volunteer to risk their lives fighting in grossly unjust wars, all the while unquestioning dictatorial political or military rule. Efforts to discourage them may be met with anger. Attempts to disabuse them may be perceived as a threat to their moral or ideological integrity. But the mood that surrounds their convictions may lack the character or full force of a delusional mood or stance perhaps, in part, because the convictions are culturally quite normal or heavily socially reinforced, encouraged or shared. A patriot cannot be expected to step aside to examine his authoritarian convictions given that so few if any people in his society do step aside. His inability to question himself may lie not in a mind stuck in pathological gum (not in a personal incapacity or disability) but in a culture mired in misbegotten allegiances and historically or ethnically entrenched loyalties. (Remember: There is more to a disability than a performance lapse and disabilities or incapacities are contextually framed.) His attitudes are not so much delusions as signs of indoctrination.

Neuroscientific clues about the organic mechanisms, like the brain reward system, behind the self-protective seriousness or centrality within which a thought may be enveloped may come from the study of dreams, which combine random thought generation and the toleration of content bizarreness along with feelings of deep personal significance (see Hobson and Leonard 2001). Dostoevsky writes in *The Idiot* of a dream in which a killer turns into a woman, and then morphs from the woman into a sly and hideous little dwarf, and this is accepted, in the dream, without the slightest hesitation. A dreamer, he says, may feel that their reason is "at a pitch of ... power, shrewdness, perception and logic" (quoted in Glover 2003: 528).

Of course, in everyday life, we embrace and persist in beliefs that we would never seriously imagine giving up and with which we emotionally identify. "They are beliefs so heavy," remarks Jonathan Glover, "that we cannot pick them up and move them" (2003: 530). Four of them for me (for all of us, indeed, relevantly rephrased) are: I exist, I am not alone in the world, a world exists external to my senses, and I have a past. I feel a central and authoritative commitment to them. So, too, a deluded person clings to their thoughts or beliefs. There is a quality of personal or self-definitional centrality to them. But for a deluded subject in the grips of the delusional stance this quality takes unhealthy and imprudent or irrational forms.

To abandon my four heavy beliefs would be irrational or immensely unwise. Not so the thought that my spouse has been replaced by an impostor or that I am infected by insects crawling underneath my skin. If I properly comprehend self and situation, and appreciate the imprudent impact that such bizarre thoughts exert on my behavior and prospects, then

I must recognize (if I am more fully rational) that they are unworthy of assent. I should be receptive to liberating myself from them and examining contrary evidence. Medication and drug-therapeutic interventions may be useful or required for this purpose (especially if the brain reward system is involved). Indeed, a common element in the pharmacological treatment of persons diagnosed with schizophrenia and its associated delusions consists in drug effects on dopamine and the blockage of dopamine D_2 receptors. (If a medication reduces the affective salience of thoughts and stymies the elaboration of further delusions, various forms of psychotherapy may be deployed.)

The authors of a recent literature review of the cognitive science of delusion claim that the theory of delusion should draw a distinction between "beliefs resulting in pragmatic distress and impairment" that are delusional, and "those that are simply ... anomalous [and] unusual or 'magical', but otherwise benign" (Bell et al. 2006: 224). Why so? Because, as I have been urging, consequences matter for delusions; not a delusion's cause or origin, bizarreness, falsehood or lack of warrant (unless such matters themselves affect consequence).

True, knowing that some delusions possess certain origins may assist in their proper therapeutic address and in offering apt and helpful competing non-delusional explanations of the experiences that may be a delusion's subjective source. In the full light of the evidential and therapeutic day an unusual attitude may disappear. But questions of origin and of pathology are in principle separable.

I will have more to say about the topic of delusion at the end of this chapter (in a discussion of paranoia) and in the next chapter. But right now I wish to address some questions about cognitive contact with reality raised by the case of depression. The ways of losing contact with reality are multiform. Delusions, alas, are but one of them.

REALISM AMONG THE RUINS?

It is obvious that sometimes we succeed in comprehending the world correctly and sometimes we do not. Take the case of beliefs, for example. They are true if the world is as the believer believes and false otherwise. Our beliefs are accurate or in proper cognitive contact or touch with the world in some circumstances and inaccurate or false in others.

There are, of course, so many possible factors that affect a person's ability to be in proper cognitive contact with the world. Suppose depressed people, not persons who are so profoundly despondent that they never get out of bed, but persons who experience persistently depressed moods and emotional outlooks while trying to lead normal lives, are in more accurate cognitive contact with the world than non-depressed people. Suppose that depressed people make more realistic appraisals of events and describe themselves and their ability (or inability) to control events with greater accuracy and less self-serving bias or error than do non-depressed people. Suppose also that whatever it is that depressed people believe about the world more closely or even-handedly corresponds to the actual facts than whatever ordinary non-depressed persons do recognize. This set of suppositions, together with various observations about human psychology and the circumstances that allegedly back them up, is known as the thesis of *depressive realism* or the *sadder-but-wiser* thesis (see Alloy and Abramson 1979 and 1988).

Here is some more supposing. Suppose that in order to maintain one's physical and mental energy and to be capable of moral and socially useful action as well as perhaps to avoid being depressed and unhappy, people need to make overly optimistic assessments about the probability that good things will take place in the future as well as about their own power or ability to bring about good events. A person may need, for example, to make self-serving or personally biased assessments that they are much less likely to suffer calamities than other people. Or a person may need, again, for another example, to overestimate the degree to which they will do well in life especially concerning matters that require personal effort and judgment. Suppose, in short and in one way or another, people need 'positive illusions' (as such falsehoods are called in the literature) if they are to cope effectively with life and to engage in productive and creative work (see S. Taylor and Brown 1988; S. Taylor 1991).

How should we react to each of these two sets of suppositions or hypotheses? They pose an awkward dilemma, do they not? Depressive realism versus positive illusions. Sadder but wiser versus happier but less wise. Here's the dilemma. In facing the world be either (a) (as depressive realism says) realistic or cognitively in touch with reality but, alas, depressed or (b) (as the thesis of positive illusions urges) optimistic but, alas, unrealistic and inaccurate or out of proper cognitive contact with reality.

To avoid a protracted discussion, though at the risk of oversimplification, I want to quickly bundle a variety of considerations into something that may be called a 'passing glance' estimate of the warrant base for each of the two hypotheses. I wish to reach judgments about each hypothesis that come filtered through concern with what each hypothesis tells us about being in touch, or in proper or comprehending cognitive contact, with reality.

The (b)-hypothesis that we need positive illusions to live by is in conflict with the ideal of truth-seeking and reality-monitoring, sometimes with disastrous consequences, especially in contexts (like investing in the stock market [see Odean 1998]) in which overconfidence tends to undermine one's ability to achieve important goals. Although, with luck on one's side, you may be happier believing that your spouse is faithful, loves you, and is not having an affair, when they unexpectedly depart with their adulterous intimate for Paris, Texas, and empty your mutual bank account, you may regret that you were never told the truth. Illusions, I assume, people had better try to live without. Of course, too, just what is an illusion? The fact that our beliefs (our cognitive contacts with the world) often are tied up with hopes, wishes and aspirations doesn't mean that we turn off your reality detectors when belief-forming mechanisms are in gear. And it certainly does not mean that hopeful beliefs, just because they are hopeful, are false. Belief formation may be framed by motivational or affective influences which, on the negative side, may lead people astray from the truth (witness Sally on Sam). But, on the positive side, it may result in a pragmatically effective being-in-the-world realism that is formed by facing the ambiguities of this world (when it is ambiguous) with a hopeful or positive motivation-influenced interpretation of the evidence.

One general situation in which it seems perfectly wise, sensible and rational to adopt beliefs that turn pivotally on hopes or aspirations is when doing so is permitted by the evidential indeterminacy of a situation and when the energetic pursuit of a goal or valued purpose demands a goodly measure of optimism. If the power of pessimistic evidence massively exceeds any room for optimism, of course, it's time to face the sullen facts. But the world often is an ambiguous place. Sometimes terribly ambiguous. Not just in the ambiguity it presents to our perceptual systems, but more profoundly in the indeterminacy if offers to our attitudes and moods.

Consider a doctor who is trying to save a patient's life in a desperate situation in which she does not *know* whether his life can be saved, but her ability to help is indissolubly bound up with her believing that she can. The question of the 'realism' or accuracy of her conviction or belief depends crucially on how things look from the standpoint not just of the evidential situation (medical track record, patient's age, and so on) but in terms of such a conviction's practical consequences. If the gods could speak they might whisper in her ear: "Proceed in the belief that you will save this person and you will therein improve your chances of saving his life." "The evidence that he will die is far from decisive." To win the battle against the patient's illness, given the epistemic latitude or evidential ambiguity of the clinical situation, the norm or rule that what the doctor believes should correspond to (or be in touch with) reality ought to presuppose a loose and contextualized sense of the real, reality and the world. What is real often is not known or knowable. Setting one's beliefs against what utterly is obvious is, of course, unrealistic and foolish. An illusion perhaps. But when a person adopts a belief that is hopeful or purpose-serving, we should not disparage this as an illusion. It may be a helpful and proper response to ambiguous circumstance.

Nicholas Rescher expresses the point well:

> We face a fundamental contrast. [T]he future [is] factual. ... But our warranted attitudes can be practical. ... [T]hey can reflect our appropriate hopes as we assess them pragmatically with reference to their potential consequences.
>
> (Rescher 1987: 106)

So, what then, in turn, about the (a)-assumption that depressed people are more realistic or in more accurate or veridical cognitive contact with the world than those who are non-depressed? This assumption, too, rests on controversial premises about just what it means to be realistic or in contact with reality. Consider the attitude of paranoia. An excessively paranoid co-worker may be able to give a more detailed and accurate description of her boss's comings and goings than a more trusting office mate. It scarcely follows, however, that she is a better worker, more rational or "for that matter more in touch with reality" (Garrett 1994: 88). Richard Garrett notes:

> People who trust the world, trust in themselves, trust their spouses, and in general trust others may get duped in many small ways. But people who trust little or not at all get duped in very big ways. [They may] happen to see the individual trees better, [but] lose sight of the forest. And this leads them to do and say things that frustrate their deepest longings and hopes.
>
> (Garrett 1994: 88)

Garrett's general point about paranoia applies to depression as well. Even if it should turn out that depressed people are more accurate in certain observations than normal non-depressives, it does not follow that they are in superior cognitive contact with reality. What a depressed individual may miss is "the larger picture, the larger truth that in general it is better" to possess a "positive and constructive" picture of the world and of the future (Garrett 1994: 88, 89). This is not just because trustful or hopeful attitudes may be self-fulfilling or self-confirming. But it also is because people often objectively are worthy of being trusted, and the world, too, is, in some measure, oftentimes good. So, arguably, often the deepest and most useful or helpful cognitive contact with the world is achieved only if we harbor or maintain for ourselves a moderately positive image of things, not illusory, and certainly not desultory, but as pragmatically sensible and evidentially sound as purpose and circumstance permits.

Bertrand Russell once announced that "the life of Man is a long march through the night" as one by one we are "seized by the silent orders of omnipotent Death" (1989 [1917]: 172). Some philosophers have argued that the fact that we will all be dead in two hundred years and that millions of years from now the solar system will cool or wind down and collapse, and all remnant of human effort will vanish or be ruined, means that a positive or optimistic image of anything (no matter how moderate) is unwarranted. But such a deep and dark cosmic pessimism is very hard to take seriously as a rational response to things. Or it should be. Even if there ultimately is no point to everything, there are points to the many immediate or smaller dimensions of life. When we care about particular things and persons and are committed to them, "the feeling with which we do so is not ... one of dispirited impotence" (Frankfurt 1988: 89). We find ourselves most fully realized and fulfilled when we focus not on global solar death but on the smaller-scale aspects of human life and appreciate that our capacity for care and commitment is one of our most cherished faculties as persons. In rejecting a measured or moderate optimism, and embracing a global pessimism, a person is contending not so much with trying to live in a ruined world (if unbeknownst to us it truly is ruined) as against themselves and their own best interests, hopes and aspirations.

PARANOIA, BENEVOLENCE AND IMAGINATION

Above I mentioned paranoia. I want to say more about it. Such thoughts will help to remind us that the understanding of a mental disorder is a morally contentious place and that in attending to delusions, in particular, we should invest more of our energies in the behavioral outcomes and proper management and elimination of delusional attitudes rather than striving to develop accounts of their origins. I begin with a remark about morality.

Morality often requires us to be kind and benevolent towards other people and perhaps, too, to make compassionate efforts to control or intervene in another's behavior for their own sake or on their own behalf. Morality also requires us, in helping others, to be respectful of their dignity as persons, assisting only in the most unobtrusive or essential ways or only when our assistance is urgently or drastically needed or asked for explicitly.

Caring for victims of delusional disorders poses special difficulties for the discharge of our duty of benevolence. To begin with, deluded persons may actively resist our help. The effects of assistance or intervention also may be the opposite of those that we compassionately intend. To a victim of persecutory delusions or paranoia, for instance, attempting to help them may reinforce their distrust of other people's motives. A paranoid may misinterpret another's efforts at assistance as a cover for manipulative designs or intentions. As Munro notes: "Delusional disorder sufferers are notoriously difficult to engage in treatment and persecutory ones especially so" (Munro 2006: 131). In addition, assuming that we ought to help a victim of delusion, it may not be possible to feel the compassion or sympathy that motivates and modulates help. Perhaps our moral imagination or ability to empathetically project ourselves into the shoes or situation of a deluded person may be blunted. When caring for a victim of a flood, one can imagine "all one's possessions being washed away" (Torrey 1995: 29). But, by contrast, what about caring for someone with full-blown schizophrenia or florid delusions? What then?

E. Fuller Torrey, a psychiatrist specializing in schizophrenia, writes:

> Sympathy for those afflicted with schizophrenia is sparse because it is difficult to put oneself in the place of the sufferer. ... Those who are afflicted act bizarrely, say strange things, withdraw from us, and may even try to hurt us. ... We don't understand why they say what they say and do what they do. ... [And] the paucity of sympathy for those with schizophrenia makes it that much more of a disaster.
>
> (Torrey 1995: 29)

Sympathy is empathy extended or filtered through compassion. Arthur Schopenhauer (1788–1860) requires of compassionate motivation that we successfully put ourselves in the place or shoes of the sufferer and that we must be sympathetic. "How is it possible," he asks, "for another's weal and woe to move my will immediately?" His answer: "Only through [my feeling] his woe just as I ordinarily feel my own" (Schopenhauer 1965 [1841]: 143–4). Schopenhauer regards the ability to emotionally identify with another's subjective situation as the source of our benevolent impulses and the main "incentive to morality" (170). But is empathetic mixed with sympathetic identification truly required if we are to properly help? In order to treat another benevolently, must we empathize with their weal? Sympathize with their woe? Compassionately project ourselves into their shoes or straits?

One has to be careful in insisting on the psychological-moral standard of effective projection. Suppose, as it is often assumed in ethical theory, that 'ought' implies 'can'. Suppose, that is, that the presence of a moral obligation presupposes a capacity for relevant action (for fulfilling the content or directive of the obligation). You ought to repay a debt, for example, but only if you possess the capacity to repay. You ought to keep a promise, but only when you are able to keep it. If 'ought' truly does imply 'can', and if, in addition, Schopenhauer is correct about the proper motivational source of morally benevolent impulses and duties, then there is no good reason to say that you ought to help another person, unless, in fact, you are able to imagine yourself in their place, in their shoes.

The simulated experience of another's state of mind requires assuming one or more of the other's mental states. It requires 'mimicking' aspects of the subjective world of the other. Is this always possible? Nomy Arpaly cautions that there is a lot to be said for the empirical possibility that another person's inner world or what it is like to be in their subjective situation, may be "very, very different from our own" (Arpaly 2005: 298). Another's mind may be too different from our own to project ourselves into. Certainly attempts to project ourselves into another's situation may come up empty.

Of course, a claim of 'cannot' as in "cannot successfully project" or "unable to imagine" may reflect a misreading of the evidence for one's own simulationist powers. It may be hard to tell apart the presence of an incapacity, about which the agent can do nothing, from that of a mere performance failure or transient inability, which, after proper learning or additional experience, may convert to competent performance. A developing ability to project oneself into another's situation may outrun the reach of current evidence for one's imaginative powers or potential.

Imagine, then, a case of imaginative projection into a paranoid person's delusion. Everything in a paranoid's psychology crystallizes around distrust of others and "an intense preoccupation with an individual's [own] position in the social universe" (Kinderman and Bentall 2007: 280; see also Bentall 2004: 330–46). Let's briefly consider the challenge of trying to be benevolent towards a paranoid via, in part, projection into their subjective circumstances.

> Individuals [with the disorder] are known for their hypersensitivity, mistrust, and suspiciousness of other people's motivations. They are always on guard, easily slighted, and quick to take offense. They believe that others are trying to trick or harm them, and will go to great lengths to prove it. They question the loyalty of others and often see plots where nobody else can see them. They are often rigid, argumentative, and litigious. ... They appear to have few tender feelings, disdain weak people, and lack any sense of humor.
>
> (Torrey 1995: 92)

Is that the sort of person whose weal and woe, whose distrust of others, I can feel or imagine harboring in myself? With what exactly must I empathize in the distrust harbored by an individual who is a victim of paranoid delusions?

Kinderman and Bentall remark that "patients who are diagnosed as suffering from that kind of delusion [typically] say that they are the target of some kind of organized conspiracy to cause them harm, although patients vary in the agencies to [which] they attribute this intention (which may be specific persons, religious or ethnic groups, or organizations such as the CIA or MI5)" (2007: 281). Kinderman and Bentall's comment is a helpful hint about the inner world of paranoia. Let's pursue it by talking briefly about the epistemology or evidence base of conspiracy theories.

In a discussion of the epistemology of conspiracy theories, the philosopher Brian Keeley claims that one of the more striking features of conspiracy theories is that evidence against a conspiratorial explanation is construed by its advocate as evidence in the explanation's favor (Keeley 1999). Contrary evidence is presumed to intentionally misdirect or mislead the effort at its proper interpretation or explanation. Consider the following vignettes:

> Charles says that his co-workers discriminate against him because he is a Roman Catholic. Charles refers to the fact that he has not gotten a pay raise in two years as

proof that he is the object of a discriminatory conspiracy. When it is pointed out that his boss is active in a local Catholic parish, he says that "he," the boss, just wants Charles to believe that he (Charles) is not being mistreated by the firm. "My boss really is not a Catholic."

Darlene is an 18-year-old college student who sought treatment at the student health center at the request of her dormitory supervisor. A shy and rather "rigid" looking young woman, who had never been involved in any counseling before, she complains of being uncomfortable and unhappy because of the noise and lack of privacy in the dorm. She told the dormitory supervisor that other students are watching her using hidden cameras plugged into her bedroom light fixtures. "They are attempting to catch me in cheating or sleeping with my under-age boyfriend, so that they can have me expelled from the school." When asked why other students care about expelling her, when she has just been admitted to a popular sorority, Darlene retorts that her admission to the sorority is part of a plot to keep the expulsion plan a secret. The more popular she thinks she is the more likely she is to let her guard down.

David, a successful Toronto engineer, is agitated and upset. He says that a paramilitary Canadian national agency is out to get him, and that some powerful data that he has gathered, about which he speaks only in vague terms, will prove that fact. David says that a number of his friends in the firm where he works have been killed in recent weeks in mysterious accidents. When it is noted that no colleagues of his have died within the last two years, he replies that the recent deaths have been disguised as leaves of absence or terminations of employment and that he himself has just recently been offered a vacation leave.

Partly because conspiratorial hypotheses require an increasing and increasingly complex amount of skepticism about contrary data and falsifying evidence, a paranoid's delusions embody a deep pessimism or skepticism about the behavior and motivations of other people (the boss, sorority sisters, the firm). As Jennifer Radden points out, "while it is neither prudent, nor virtuous, nor mentally healthy to trust too much, or injudiciously," it is, of course, also unhealthy to "trust too little as the paranoid does" (Radden 2007: 267). But so what, then, is it to trust too little as the paranoid does? Whatever a victim of paranoia does as a paranoid, in their relations with other people, even if they try to minimize their reliance on others, a paranoid person trusts and does so injudiciously their distrust of others. They over-trust their ability to recognize the untrustworthiness of other people. In trusting others too little, they trust themselves too much and are insufficiently epistemically humble or appositely critical about themselves.

A simple example from ordinary life, that comes from Annette Baier, makes an insightful observation about the inseparable connection between trust of others and self-trust (see Baier 1989: 278). I trust my mailman not to discard my mail on days in which he may feel too fatigued to deliver it. I trust myself in this judgment to trust him. I realize I may be disappointed, however. So, suppose that one rainy day in a melancholic frame of mind, I try to guard myself emotionally against the disappointment that the mailman may not deliver my mail by distrusting him. Suppose I become suspicious of him. Such an attitude if widely extended to other ordinary forms of reliance on others would make social life utterly unbearable. Trusting neither mailman, nor bank clerk, nor waiter, I am precluded from all sorts of necessary or desirable patterns of social engagement. True, in trusting others I am vulnerable to being neglected, manipulated and used. The mailman may hurt me in various ways. He may read my private correspondence or encourage the neighbor's dog to defecate under my mailbox. If, however, I wish my mail to be delivered, and to engage in other normal social behavior and mutual reliance, I must develop a taste in people, and then trust it (Baier 1989: 279). I must trust in my judgment or trust of others. If my taste or judgment fails, others (among them a mailman, waitress or whomever) will let me down. But that's a small risk to be undertaken for entering into beneficial relations of social cooperation and coordination.

Trusting usually is not the product of a deliberate predictive cost/benefit calculation about other people's behavior. It is something more akin "to a kind of faith in the other" (Radden 2007: 267). It's a form of faith that may require imagining the other as in certain relevant respects like me. Guided by the thought that I myself would deliver the mail if I was both a mailman and fatigued, I imaginatively simulate his delivering the mail. Tired or not, I would deliver it. I assume he will do so as well.

A deficiency in the capacity for projection, empathy or simulation may be part of what impairs the paranoid's capacity for trusting others and comprehending the actual motives of other people. A paranoid may over-trust their own self and distrust others, perhaps because the subject cannot extend or project their implicit (self) trust to the other. This failure to extend, project or mimic produces a blindness or evidential tunnel vision towards the paranoid's own self-trust. It deprives them of evidential feedback from others about their own attitudes or feedback from a "second self, to give [them] sight" (Baier 1989: 279). If I am paranoid, others are not allowed to teach or model for me whom to trust, how to trust or whether or when distrust of others is well- or ill-founded.

However note: The difficult challenge, stated earlier, of imagining the inner world of a paranoid person appears to be dissolving the more we think about it. We are developing a sense of what it is like to be a subject of paranoid delusions. Paranoia represents a deformity in self-comprehension (of when to trust one's very own person) as much as categorical skepticism about the motives of others. Additional analysis may continue to help in this task of inside-understanding paranoia, too, of course. But our suggestions for describing the 'inside' of paranoia are also raising a difficult therapeutic or treatment issue.

At first blush, it may appear obvious that in order to therapeutically intervene in a benevolent and genuinely respectful manner in the outlook and behavior of a deluded person, we must be able to imagine their inner world. Perhaps compassion requires it. In a case of paranoia, this means having empathy for a paranoid's distrust of others. The better inside-understood the better is the patient cared for. Such is the clinical-moral maxim. But we are also revisiting a misgiving about helping certain sorts of deluded persons, that was mentioned earlier. When it comes to treating paranoia, Munro says, "pessimism pervades the literature" (Munro 2006: 135). Not only may paranoids resist treatment, but they may be reinforced in their paranoid attitudes by treatments that require caregivers to enter their world imaginatively. Such entry may be received as manipulation and deception. David may read a therapist's expression of misgiving over the former's misreading of the offer of a vacation leave as an effort to soften his suspicions about the firm. Darlene or Charles may make comparable distrustful interpretations of relevantly analogous therapeutic responses. So, entry must be cautious and unobtrusive. As Munro counsels, "a patient, low-key, nonjudgmental approach by the psychiatrist is necessary" (ibid.). But just what might cautious entry involve? No doubt, there is more art than science here. If one can't blurt out "I feel your pain," what can one do?

If a person, although a subject of paranoid delusions, has some (however weak) warrant or rationale for some of their distrustful attitudes (remember, the mere fact that a person is delusional does not automatically mean that each and every aspect of their delusion is utterly unreasonable or even false), there may be room to reason with them. There is increasing evidence that a delusion *per se*, although perhaps not the total illness (like schizophrenia) in which a delusion is embedded, may be modified by cognitive-behavioral therapy (CBT) if conducted with sensitivity, skill and diplomacy. CBT recognizes that a deluded person has difficulty interpreting evidence against their delusional convictions. But if a supportive non-confrontational relationship is established with a therapist, the therapist may then apply practical logic, rules of evidence, and Socratic questioning in a manner that encourages the deluded person to expose, question and moderate or modify their delusional outlook, mood or stance (see Munro 2006: 227 for references; see also the Suggested Readings for this chapter). Knowing when or whom to trust is knowing when or whom to distrust. And both trust and distrust are attitudes that possess a composite nature, neither solely cognitive nor judgmental, nor exclusively affective or volitional. Judicious therapeutic focusing within a CBT or comparable framework on the affective or volitional components of paranoia should also be part of the therapeutic mix. Why is the person refusing to abandon their persecutory convictions? What is required is that the patient or client should assess competing hypotheses (trustful ones), while questioning the veridicality of less than trusting and more than suspicious moods, thoughts or convictions.

CBT is one of a type or form of therapy that I call *pass through reason* treatment. Numerous varieties of this form of treatment are practiced in the mental health profession including Freudian psychotherapy, rational emotive therapy, interpersonal therapy, and reality therapy, among others. Pass-through-reason treatments share one common goal: they aim to redirect and improve a person's self-knowledge and understanding or comprehension of their situation (see Graham and Stephens 2007: 359–63 for related discussion). Different forms of the general type of therapy differ in how this goal is best achieved as well as the manner in which proper comprehension and cognitive contact with the world or with others is understood. A cognitive behavioral therapist, for instance, puts emphasis on a person's knowledge of how to cope with current circumstances and unwelcome or distressful behavior. A Freudian explores a patient's understanding of their disorder's supposed etiology, perhaps as far back as childhood trauma. It would make sense, for example, for a person, who as a child was surrounded by threats and attendant and genuine harms, "to become gradually more hyper-vigilant for threat-related information" when an adult, although "this kind of bias in processing information [may] tend to the maintenance of paranoid beliefs once established" (Kinderman and Bentall 2007: 285–6).

In cases of disorder in which a person is explicitly resistant to intervention (as may happen in paranoia) or in which delusions are too florid or bound up with other symptoms to be questioned or conversationally examined, what then? How should we treat them? The most popular alternative forms of intervention or treatment are a-rational somatic, namely psychopharmacological (neuroleptics, antidepressant drugs, mood-stabilizers, anticonvulsants) and non-pharmacological (electroconvulsive therapy). I call such types *bypass-reason* treatments.

Bypass-reason treatments also share a common goal: they try to reduce or suppress the symptoms of a disorder or delusion. Except in cases in which reduction or suppression is deemed an end in itself (as sometimes does happen), the assumption behind them is that a patient may be better able to manage or understand their own behavior and ultimately to respond to pass-through-reason therapy only when they are no longer in the overbearing grip of the delusional stance or emotional distress.

Big Issues of both a moral and therapeutic nature loom large over the comparative pros and cons of reason-pass-through and -bypass treatments for mental disorder (see Elliott 2003). How we interpret and think about ourselves, the kinds of treatments we design for ourselves, affect how we are.

Some mental health professionals are reluctant to countenance psychopharmacological or bypass-reason treatments for delusions even in cases of paranoid schizophrenia. There may be good reasons for this reluctance. These include worries about a patient's immediate personal safety, concern about long-term health effects, apprehension over drug dependencies that may somehow undermine self-comprehension and personal autonomy, recognition that delusions may remit on their own without any sort of intervention, the charge that bypass interventions tend to treat or suppress symptoms only and not the illness itself, and so on. Of course pass-through treatments also harbor problems. Some pass-through treatments enhance rational capacities, but others are manipulative, aimed at creating long-term profit-motivated dependence on therapy, delivered by incompetent therapists, or based on erroneous and misinformed assumptions about the nature of a mental disorder. Neil Levy wisely cautions: "Psychotherapy is not a synonym for truth-seeking" (Levy 2007: 111). Pass-through treatments may also be more labor-intensive, time-consuming, and expensive than bypass interventions. On each side of the treatment ledger, therefore, bypass or pass-through, the risks or potential liabilities are real, even if their desired and possible or frequent benefits are also real.

How may bypass treatment be morally or benevolently justified in a case of paranoia? There are different ways of answering this complex ethical question, depending on the actual circumstances or reasons for resistance. One possibility is to assume a moral principle of *future-orientated consent* to assist in the justification (Battin 1982: 155). Here briefly is the principle: Although a person may now object to whatever bypassing interference is made on their behalf, later (when they discover what harm they were doing to themselves) they "will be grateful that the interference was made" (ibid.). So, for example, in a case of paranoid delusions, although a subject of paranoid delusions may now reject whatever bypass intervention is made on their behalf, later (when the person has come to their better senses or discovers that they had when paranoid broken off from social reality) they will be glad that a bypass was conducted. Their future self will embrace or retrospectively endorse what was done to and for them. Or so we may hope. If so, we can justify, say, some forms of involuntary drug treatment.

Future-orientated consent justification, of course, presupposes that there will be future consent, rather than that the post-paranoid person will express anger or regret over the fact that they were subjected to mechanical intervention or involuntary medication in an effort to eliminate or dampen their distrustful world view. Frith and Johnstone note: "After recovery, many patients, although not all, will accept that treatment has helped them" (Frith and Johnstone 2003: 168). Note the 'not all'. Some persons wish not to have been 'helped'.

Of course, it should be noted, not all interventions in cases of mental disorder in general or of paranoid delusion in particular are aimed at serving just the interests of the individual involved. Bypass treatments may also serve the interests of other persons (e.g. family members who must care for the deluded person) or the public at large (e.g. those who are victims of violent sociopaths or alcohol-addicted automobile drivers). So, although it may not always be recognized, there are moral complexities to intervention that are not focused just on the dignity or self-respect of the patient or paranoid person themselves. But, as remarked, even focusing just on the individual is no small moral chore. What happens if someone desires to remain categorically distrustful and suspicious of others, resents taking a drug that turns them into a less-vigilant person and claims that a non-paranoid world view is inaccurate and precludes the sorts of success that they want in life – despite the harms of paranoia? (Kinderman and Bentall quote a tongue-n-cheek quip of the CEO of a major computer technology firm that "only the paranoid survive" [Kinderman and Bentall 2007: 275].)

The moral-rights-based notion that a person's life is one's own is widely endorsed in the thinking of many anti-psychiatry critics like Szasz. One component of one's life being one's own is deciding for oneself. Even if I constantly worsen my life, and even if you would do better if you took charge, I would not wish you to do so. Take, for example, Darlene. She may vigorously protest if she is sent home and forced to take medication. A person's right to cut themselves off from treatment (even when this makes a mess for them) is recognized in cases of somatic illness. Why not in cases of a mental disorder, especially when the distinctiveness of a mental disorder and the ragged edges between mental health and illness produce heated forms of contestability?

The feeling that each person should decide for themselves how to live their own life is among the deepest moral convictions that we have. But I believe that there is a powerful reason for doubting that this feeling is morally legitimate in cases in which a paranoid patient resists necessary treatment and is in danger of harming themselves or being cut off from social relations. The reason has to do with responsibility for self.

Day-to-day self-responsibility involves a kind of commitment to one's welfare and best interests that a paranoid person just cannot self-provide. Frankfurt notes that there are a number of respects in which the care and concern that a person ought to have for their selves and their personal well-being is closely analogous to the care and concern that parents ought to have for their small children. Parents generally do care about the good of their children and are "concerned to protect and to pursue [a child's] true interests" (Frankfurt 2004: 83).

Suppose that a parent is attempting sincerely to add to the training of their child the formation of character traits and habits. Suppose that one of these is trust. Children need to be told when and whom to trust; they need this as a character trait or habit. It would seem that whatever the detailed guidance would be, a child must feel pleasure in trusting – otherwise it will not become a character trait. It would also appear that a child needs to be the recipient of trust – that (to co-opt from a helpful discussion of Hanna Pickard of sharing [see Pickard 2009: 95]) "he or she needs to experience how nice it is to be [trusted]." But when we consider the unhappy complexities of generalized distrust of others or paranoia, this seems not at all the sort of habit or character trait that a parent would wish possessed by one's child. A persecutory world view is often accompanied by feelings of victimization and powerlessness, pleasure-less engagement with other people, depressed mood, as everywhere there seems to be for the paranoid, in the words of Kraepelin, "hounding and backbiting, jeering and chicanery" (quoted in Radden 2007: 266).

We should hope that a post-paranoid individual is appreciative of and grateful for the treatment that they receive. But if, by chance, they aren't, then that fact, by itself, counts as a failure of proper self-responsibility and concern. "Barricading ourselves against all possible attackers," to quote Baier, so that the social world and our need for other people cannot break in, is not what a parent would wish for their child if the parent loves them (Baier 1989: 279). Intervention, then, may be morally justified independent of a post-paranoid's positive appraisal of the effort to help. Suffering persecutory paranoia is not what I would wish for my child. It is not what I should wish for myself. Not to underestimate the moral complexities of treatment, others may do me no moral wrong if they try to direct me down a trusting path, even if I resist and end up resenting them for doing so.

CHAPTER SUMMARY AND SUGGESTED READINGS

In this chapter we explored various disorders or symptoms in which a person may be said to disconnect from or lose cognitive contact with reality. We paid particular attention to the presence of delusions in schizophrenia and to the thesis that delusions consist of false and bizarre beliefs. We argued that there may be subjective warrant for a delusional attitude and that a delusional attitude may not be false. So, we sought for another mark or aspect of delusion. We found it not in whether a subject of delusion falsely represents the world or in other upstream aspects of an attitude, but in the failure 'downstream' to understand the nature and manage the harmful consequences of one's own mental activities. Understanding the phenomenon of delusion requires understanding a deluded subject's failure to control or direct their own cognitive activities in a satisfactory and prudent or reason-responsive manner.

In this chapter we also examined just what it means to accurately represent reality as well as to empathetically understand the conceptions of the world and other people that some delusional subjects harbor, paranoids in particular. Why do some people over-identify with imprudent attitudes? Why are some individuals unduly pessimistic or distrusting of others? We noted that often what we should believe of the world or of others is quite indeterminate cognitively. This leaves elbow room for shaping our cognitive attitudes in a manner that enables us to properly care for ourselves and to protect our own best interests or true good. This does not mean that people should freely embrace or welcome so-called 'positive illusions'. But it means that given the evidential ambiguities of the world, moderately positive attitudes towards real world situations and other people may constitute proper and reasonable cognitive contact with the world.

In this chapter we also introduced a distinction between two types of therapy for a disorder. One works through a person's reasoning capacity, while the other bypasses it. Working through reason is not always effective or even possible (depending on the disorder). Perhaps a person is paranoid and bent on distrusting others. A disorder may also pose a stiff challenge to a caregiver to imaginatively simulate the mindset of such a person. Proper therapeutic care may turn out to be a mix of pass-through and bypass treatment.

A brief yet surprisingly full discussion of schizophrenia may be found in Christopher Frith and Eve Johnstone's *Schizophrenia: A Very Short Introduction* (Oxford University Press, 2003). Skepticism about the taxonomic category of schizophrenia is defended by Jeffrey Poland in "How to Move beyond the Concept of Schizophrenia," in M. Chung, K. Fulford and G. Graham (eds), *Reconceiving Schizophrenia* (Oxford University Press, 2007). A fine collection of papers on delusion is Max Coltheart and Martin Davies's edited, *Pathologies of Belief* (Blackwell, 2000). Vaughan Bell, Peter Halligan and Hadyn Ellis have written a helpful overview of recent work on cognition and delusion entitled "Explaining Delusions: A Cognitive Perspective," *Trends in Cognitive Sciences*, 2006, 10, 219–26. Tim Bayne and Jordi Fernandez have edited a collection that includes a number of papers on delusion and belief formation. It is entitled *Delusion and Self-Deception: Affective and Motivational Influences on Belief Formation* (Psychology Press, 2009). For speculation about the role of mesolimbic dopamine in endowing certain thoughts with aberrant or contextually inappropriate salience, see L. Bartolotti and M. Broome, "Delusional Beliefs and Reason Giving," *Philosophical Psychology*, 2008, 21, pp. 821–41.

Positions about when to shift from Intentionalistic/rationality-presupposing explanations of behavior and attitudes to non-Intentionalistic ones can be distinguished along many dimensions. Martin Davies has written a helpful paper on the topic of explanation shifting entitled "Persons and their Underpinnings," which appears in the journal *Philosophical Explorations*, 2000, 3, pp. 43–62. See also William Bechtel's *Mental Mechanisms: Philosophical Perspectives on Cognitive Science* (Erlbaum, 2008), especially pp. 143–57.

On whether positive illusions serve mental health and well-being, see C. Colvin and J. Block, "Do Personal Illusions Foster Mental Health? An Examination of the Taylor and Brown Formulation," *Psychological Bulletin*, 1994, 116, pp. 3–20. Depressive realism is examined in R. Ackermann and R. DeRubeis, "Is Depressive Realism Real?," *Clinical Psychology Review*, 1991, 11, pp. 565–84. Martin Seligman, the personal force behind the original (non-reformulated) learned-helplessness model of depression, has recently become an advocate of something he calls 'learned optimism'. To help to spread the positive-psychology gospel, he has written a number of books on the subject. One is *Learned Optimism: How to Change Your Mind and Your Life* (Vintage, 2006).

On paranoia two recent and probing papers are Jennifer Radden's "Defining Persecutory Paranoia" and Peter Kinderman and Richard Bentall's "The Functions of Delusional Beliefs," each of which appears in *Reconceiving Schizophrenia* (Oxford University Press, 2007) (mentioned in citing the Poland paper above). Cognitive behavioral therapy (CBT) for paranoia is considered in P. Chadwick, M. Birchwood and P. Trower's *Cognitive Therapy for Delusions, Voices, and Paranoia* (Wiley, 1999). Pioneers in the application of CBT to schizophrenia are David Kingdon and Douglas Turkington. See D. Kingdon, D. Turkington and C. John, "Cognitive Behavior Therapy of Schizophrenia," *British Journal of Psychiatry*, 1994, 164, pp. 581–7. For a brief overview of their and related work, together with a helpful bibliography, see Richard Bentall's *Madness Explained* (Penguin, 2003), pp. 504–12. On rethinking the clinical-therapeutic enterprise so as not to force fit the symptoms or complaints variously associated with schizophrenia (and other related disorders) into determinate taxonomic categories, W. Spaulding, M. Sullivan and J. Poland's *Treatment and Rehabilitation of Severe Mental Illness* (Guilford Press, 2003) is well worth reading.

The premier theorist on the role of simulation (i.e. assuming other people's positions or points of view imaginatively) in human psychology and social life is the philosopher Alvin Goldman. His book *Simulating Minds: The Philosophy, Psychology, and Neuroscience of Mindreading* (Oxford University Press, 2006) is not just a detailed treatment of the topic but offers insightful discussion of autism along the way. Heidi Maibom's "The Presence of Others," in *Philosophical Studies*, 2007, 132, pp. 161–90, is a valuable contribution to the literature on simulation. Well worth reading on what it may be like to be autistic (or a high-functioning autistic person) is a memoir of Temple Grandin about her autistic childhood. Co-authored with Margaret Scariano, it is entitled *Emergence: Labeled Autistic* (Warner Books, 1986).

9 Minding the missing me

ME, MYSELF AND MY SELVES

Children all too easily scratch, cut or scrape their skin. Abrasions and surface wounds overpopulate the accidental territory of childhood.

As a young boy, I had more than my share of cuts and bruises. Climbing trees or exploring thick thorny bushes caused minor wounds. Playing stick ball or touch tag on the Brooklyn city street where my family lived produced numerous temporary scars.

Minor and surface wounds disappeared quickly, of course. But they left an indelible impression on me of the body's ability to reconstitute its borders. So, I was delighted, when, in the summer of my eighth year, while vacationing in the mountains of Pennsylvania with my parents and siblings, I discovered something marvelous about the tiny, lowly salamander. (In the evening I collected salamanders, some injured, in shoeboxes and jars.) This is that the adult salamander is blessed with a miraculous power. It can regenerate an entire lost limb over and over again, no matter how often the limb is shorn or amputated from its body. Just how this is done was utterly mysterious to me at the time. One key, I since have learned, is that when a salamander's limb is amputated blood vessels in the remaining stump contract quickly so that bleeding is limited. A loose arrangement of stem-like cells in the area of the stump then begins to serve as progenitor of the replacement limb (Muneoka et al. 2008: 56–63).

Wouldn't it be wonderful if our mental health or emotional well-being, when scarred or damaged, similarly healed autonomously, immediately and fully? Suppose a wounded mind would 'know' of the right repair for its damaged capacity or faculty, access the extent of injury, initiate a regenerative response, clean the emotional scar, restore the contour of cognitive or psychological function, and heal itself. Just as we may watch a lowly salamander grow back a missing leg, we may observe the subject of a severe depression or crippling paranoia quickly and efficiently reconstitute their person.

It would be wonderful, indeed. And, on occasion, something very roughly like that actually does happen after certain episodes or experiences of mental ill-health. At least in this sense: people remit, self-regenerate, self-reconstruct. Not quickly perhaps, but efficiently. Psychiatric self-regeneration, however, is not something on which surely to count. We aren't salamanders. We often need the help of other persons and mental health professionals and cannot properly constitute or reconstitute ourselves without assistance.

'We aren't salamanders.' So, what are we, then?

I intend this 'What are we, then?' to be a deep question. A very deep question. A metaphysical question. A question about our fundamental or essential nature or identity as persons. A straightforward answer like 'author or reader of this book' will not do. A salamander fundamentally or essentially is a type of non-human animal. But what fundamentally or essentially are we?

As bizarre or counter-intuitive as this may seem, numerous philosophers have claimed that, as a matter of strict metaphysical fact, we are nothing at all. We don't exist. Fundamentally, we are unreal. Thomas Metzinger in a note to his aptly titled *Being No One* announces that "strictly speaking, no one ever was born and no one ever dies" (Metzinger 2004: 633n7). "No such things as selves exist in the world," he says (626). Daniel Dennett announces that we are a "theorist's fiction" (Dennett 1991: 429). If Dennett is right, what I am rather is like, say, Santa Claus, Holden Caufield or Moby Dick: a figure of myth, tale or story. I am a pretend thing, not a real thing.

There surely is something, as noted, bizarre about such claims. Two bizarre things, really, although they are connected. Metzinger and Dennett (and others) say we don't exist. But you cannot say you do not exist without existing, can you? The thesis seems hopelessly self-contradictory. Furthermore, you'd think you would *want* not to say such a thing. What can such a thesis contribute? What problem does it solve? The proposition seems not just self-contradictory but pointless.

The incredibly counter-intuitive idea that we are fictional and unreal has a long and checkered history in the philosophical literature on the metaphysics of selfhood or personhood. Occasionally, fictionalism or anti-realism about ourselves (as the idea sometimes is called) is mistakenly generated by violating a sensible caution admonished by the philosopher Anthony Kenny. Kenny's warning goes like this: Do not allow the syntactic space that distinguishes the expression 'my self' from the word 'myself' to produce the illusive appearance of reference to a special metaphysical entity, namely the self, and then ask if selves exist, arguing that selves per se do not exist. And then conclude that therefore we our*selves* do not exist (see Kenny 1988; see also Kennedy and Graham 2007). Or that we are creatures of fiction, not fact. Such reasoning serves as a foundation for a form of fictionalism or anti-realism about our selves (read 'ourselves'). But it rests on a false distinction between me and my self (or, analogously, between you and your self). I am not a self, though I am, of course, nothing other than myself.

Fictionalism about selves (again read, 'ourselves') has been promoted on more philosophically subtle and dialectically nuanced grounds, however. Such grounds give it a point if not obvious freedom from self-contradiction. These grounds vary in structure, content and contour. Relevant to this book are promotions of fictionalism that rest on examination of mental disorder. MPD (multiple personality disorder) has been an especially prominent extrapolation base for the fictionalist case (Dennett and Humphrey 1989; Dennett 1991; Wilkes 1988 and 1991).

Though short on history as a taxonomic category MPD, now known as DID (dissociative identity disorder), is long on metaphysical controversy. Some clinical observers deny the sheer existence or reality of the condition. Nicholas Spanos in a book-length analysis of MPD charges that it is not a real honest-to-goodness disorder but an artifact or construct of clinic and therapy. A pseudo-disorder. Spanos writes:

> Patients learn to construe themselves as possessing multiple selves, learn to present themselves in terms of this construal, and learn to recognize and elaborate on the personal biography so as to make it congruent with their understanding of what it means to be multiple. ... Psychotherapists play a particularly important part in the generation and maintenance of MPD. Some therapists routinely encourage patients to construe themselves as having multiple selves ... and provide official legitimation for the different identities that their patients enact.
>
> (Spanos 1996: 3)

The philosopher Ian Hacking (1995) appears (and I say 'appears') to offer a similar charge against MPD to Spanos. He argues as follows.

Popular conceptions of MPD exert looping effects on potential subjects of the diagnosis, causing them to behave in manners that conform to the category or concept and therein to think of themselves as multiples. Certain clinicians and therapists notice possible candidates of the condition among their patients and respond by explicitly or implicitly encouraging them to represent themselves to themselves and others as possessed of different personalities, alters or identities. The MPD/DID concept is constituted in part by predictions and proscriptions for what counts as appropriate behavior for people who are diagnosed with MPD (hereafter I drop the 'DID'). Attribution of the MPD classification leads certain people to conform to norms for the disorder. For such subjects the disorder may serve any number of conscious or more likely unconscious palliative or defensive purposes. Perhaps foremost, Hacking suspects, it frees a person from the unbearable suffering or anxiety of real or imagined memories of childhood sexual or physical abuse.

Hacking's position is not that of Spanos, however. For Hacking the role of looping in MPD does not necessarily mean that MPD is not an honest-to-goodness disorder. It means merely that the reality of MPD is confined to an unstable or transient cultural, therapeutic or clinical niche. It is socially constructed, as it were, in that niche. If so, it is a disorder of a sub-culturally embedded or particularized sort and not of the type captured by the cross-cultural prototype of a mental disorder.

As fascinating as Hacking's depiction of the origins of MPD is, however, I must skip past his discussion of MPD here (see Graham 1996 for additional examination of Hacking). (Also: I am not going to commit myself one way or another on whether MPD is a genuine condition. But I will focus on claims about it for its alleged metaphysical implications.) This first section of the chapter has another target concern with MPD. Not the reality, existence or presence of the condition, but the unreality or non-existence of its participants or subjects, namely the 'selves' of MPD. So here is this different worry about MPD. It is a personal existence concern. One that has to do not with Spanos-like skepticism or with whether MPD itself is real, but with what, if anything, MPD tells us about our own existence, assuming that MPD or something like it actually does occur.

On the clinical coalface of it, a good part of what is supposed to be wrong with victims of MPD is that their personal memory or autobiographical self-consciousness is deeply and multiply disturbed. Keeping conscious track of ourselves is crucial to who we are as persons. "Self," wrote John Locke (1632–1704), "is that conscious thinking thing . . . as far as the consciousness extends" (1975 [1690]: Book II, chapter 27, §19). Possession of an autobiographical memory that extends ourselves into the past is a key aspect of one of the basic psychological capacities that I suggested (in Chapter 6) we would pick from behind the veil of ignorance. This is the capacity for historical/temporal self-location. From an 'original position' we would want and perceive ourselves to need a capacity to remember past personal experiences. We would want the ability to harbor conscious memories of earlier episodes in our life. Why so? Well, we cannot lead a truly satisfying or decent life without such historical self-awareness or extension of our consciousness into our past.

Locating ourselves historically or in time requires a particular form of self-awareness or self-recognition. It requires in addition to temporally locating some person, recognizing that the person so located is none other than oneself. It requires, in backward-looking cases, personal or autobiographical memories, and, in forward-looking cases, what is sometimes called prospection, in which a person mentally rehearses or imagines a situation in which they may or will be involved. It is also frequently accompanied by resonant emotional or affective experiences. In reading a book, planning a vacation, remembering the death of a childhood friend, such across-time mental time-travel, as it is sometimes called, is often filled with affective attitudes and feelings. Pride. Shame. Guilt. Pleasure. Disappointment. Fear.

> "I remember, much to my shame, that I amputated the limb of a salamander."
> "I held my PhD thesis in my hands, much too nervous to deliver it to the chair's office for my defense."

Personal/historical or autobiographical memory is often cast as a type of narrative construction, not as "a causally imprinted trace on a passive receiving system forming a 'spool like' cumulative record of self-standing [past] events" (Gillett 2008: 95). But as a product whose content and contour is constantly developed and updated, reinterpreted or re-woven together often in the light of current concerns and emotional associations and edited.

> When you recall an episode in your life, you [often] reconstruct it in much the same way as you would reconstruct an episode in a story. However, your own life story is much richer and contains many more details important to you than any story you

might read. So you need a much finer system of cues and rules to reconstruct your life than to construct a story.

(Glass and Holyoak 1986: 244)

Thomas DeBaggio, once a professional herb grower and newspaper journalist, in *Losing My Mind* (2003), has written a remarkable memoir of living with the effects of early onset Alzheimer's. De Baggio ends the main part of the memoir with the following testament to the importance of personal historical self-awareness:

> I must now wait for the silence to engulf me and take me to the place where there is no memory left and there remains no reflexive will to live. It is lonely here waiting for memory to stop and I am afraid and tired. Hug me, Joyce [his wife], and then let me sleep.
>
> (207)

DeBaggio wrote his memoir, in part, because he wanted to be understood by others as someone possessing a past rather than as product of his deficits and in need of custodial care.

Autobiographical memory seems to suffer a double disturbance in MPD. One concerns a person's ability to recall or retrieve events in their past history. At given moments, various stretches of a multiple's history appear hidden from them in blank spots or behind so-called 'amnesia barriers'. These juxtaposed patterns of accessibility and inaccessibility may be quite complex. Confer and Ables's (1983) patient, Rene, for instance, originally recalled nothing in her life from age 11 to age 13, despite detailed memories of events both before and after the period. Under hypnosis her powers of retrieval seemed to improve. She was able to offer vivid recollections of formerly blank periods. How this was described or evidenced by her (see below) exhibits the second disturbance of personal memory in MPD.

The second disturbance is an often bizarre and unexpected, given the drama of recollected events, proclivity to recall various events in an otherwise blank period, not as something that happened to or involved oneself, but as having happened to another person (self, alter), who shared the body of the remembering individual. Rene, for example, recalled in vivid detail her rape by her father, but spoke of the rape while clinically presenting under the therapeutic persona of Stella. She/Stella referred to the victim of the rape as someone else – Rene.

> It was Easter. And she was 11. ... I was watching ... but she didn't know it. ... I've been with men, but I wouldn't do nothing like that with my own father. ... She was a wreck. A complete wreck. ... Well, I can see that it was ... hard for her to take.
> (Confer and Ables 1983: 127)

What are we to make of recollections like that (assuming their veridicality)? As I have remarked elsewhere in a discussion of MPD and fictionalism:

> These self-conscious recollections described by the patient are typical of MPD. They are cases in which a multiple recalls events from her personal history: things she

has done, said, thought, felt, and things that have happened to her. However she recalls these as things that were done by or happened to another person or agent. Her autobiographical perspective on exactly what parts of her history belong to her and which to someone else varies with her current state. As Stella, Rene has access to some of this forgotten history, but is alienated from it in the sense that she fails to experience it as her own.

(Graham 1999: 161–2)

What do such MPD-like disturbances of personal memory reveal about our existence? Do they help to demonstrate that we are fictions, unreal, myths? If so, just how might they warrant such extraordinary claims? These questions demand more discussion than I can provide here. I cannot compose a detailed response. But here is a reconstruction with simplifications of what Daniel Dennett says about the metaphysical lesson of MPD.

For Dennett the distorted complexities of autobiographical retrieval in MPD dim any realistic hope of getting a decisive empirical measure or bead on 'who remembers', and hence any standard for what counts as the subjects of MPD. Indeed, the general metaphysical moral, for Dennett, to be drawn from MPD is that we ourselves are a figment, an illusion, of the cognitive system's or brain's mode of operation. We are virtual or fictional rather than real entities. How so?

Suppose we assume, in the manner of common sense, that for a person to be real he or she must be distinct from other persons. In MPD, however, there is no precise or determinate boundary between one person or individual (say, Rene) and another (say, Stella). The lines or psychological boundaries or distinctions between persons (selves, personalities or alters) are intractably fuzzy and vague. So, to announce that Rene is one person and that Stella is another ultimately is a matter of arbitrary decision or practical fiat. There is no independent or objective fact of the matter about just who is who in the condition. *This* person rather than *that* person is a distinction we make up if or when we interact with someone as a multiple.

Some MPD-observers talk, contrarily, as if one and only one individual (rather than an indeterminate or indistinct set) is present in MPD. Not multiples, fuzzy or otherwise. Thus Hugh Silverman remarks:

> MPD is an attempt of a beleaguered individual, unable to ... defend against external adversity, to flee inwardly and create alternative selves and alternative constructs of reality that allow the possibility of psychological survival.

(Silverman 1995: 589)

Stephen Braude exclaims that MPD is the "dominant coping mechanism of ... one subject" (Braude 1991: 179). Grant Gillett writes that "the subject uses different names to collect different clusters of attitudes ... ways of thinking, and styles of learning" (Gillett 1991: 107).

According to such 'one person/one body' conceptions, single subjects or selves are the agents, structural and motivational supports of the disorder. Indeed, just above, I, too, spoke in terms of the singularity of a person by referring to Confer and Ables's 'patient'. It's hard to avoid speaking in that way. But, says Dennett, strictly speaking, we should avoid it, namely the assumption of a single self underlying MPD. For Dennett, however, this is not because there actually are a definite or distinct number of multiple selves in the disorder. Rather, it is because no one is in or behind the disorder. Single selves underlying MPD are no more real than the personas identified as Stella or Rene.

Indeed for Dennett: No one is us or in us normal folk either. Dennett himself is no more real than either Stella or Rene. "By calling *me* Dan," writes Dennett, we are referring to "the theorist's fiction created by . . . well, not by me but by my brain" (Dennett 1991: 429). None of us is a real item or entity.

> Some people [make] a simple arithmetical mistake: they have failed to notice that two or three or seventeen selves per body is really no more metaphysically extravagant than one self per body. One is bad enough!
>
> (Dennett 1991: 419)

You and I are no more real than Stella or Rene? For Dennett the cumulative metaphysical impact of MPD is to put intense weight on how to distinguish or differentiate between selves or persons and to individuate or identify them, to despair of being able to do so, and then to infer that the reason it is so difficult to differentiate between selves is that there really is nothing there to individuate or differentiate between in the first place.

Consider the following analogy. Imagine that you are asked to picture a tiger before your mind's eye. Then imagine being asked, without doing anything whatsoever to your initial image, to count the number of its stripes. (Filling in a number is cheating. You cannot enhance the image.) The stripes, for Dennett, are like we ourselves or the selves that are allegedly present in a multiple. We may pretend that the imagined tiger has a certain definite number of stripes, but it does not. We may pretend that there is one of us or (in MPD) two, three, or seventeen of us, but there is not. To suppose that we are real is like supposing that the imagined tiger has a certain definite number of stripes. In a fit of fictive fiat we may claim it's got its determinate stripes. It is a tiger image after all. But no specific number of stripes is truly present in the image. Likewise: No specific number of us is us. There are no stripes there. There is no self here.

Clever argument? Perhaps. But I take it that the conclusion that we don't exist should be resisted. If so, how so? How resist fictionalism about ourselves?

Well, one possibility is to claim that fictionalism is a kind of realism but in disguise. Better to exist as a fiction than not to exist at all. But fictional objects do not exist, period. A fictional person is not a type of person. It is a type of non-person. Or: we may claim that denying that we exist is so grossly counter-intuitive that it defies belief. But Dennett may consider that fact, namely the proposition's counter-intuitiveness, as an iconoclastic plus rather than an unwelcome minus. Much that is true is counter-intuitive, as he would point out. (Just stare at the earth's horizon at dawn. It appears that the earth is flat, but, of course, it's not.) Or: we may claim that

- We ourselves are nothing but –.

Then fill in the blank with mention of something that does exist (say, a brain or a biologically alive human animal). If we ourselves are nothing but, say, biologically living human animals, then, assuming that animals exist, we exist (see Olson 1997). The animal that is Rene may carry different names (say, 'Stella') on different occasions or for different purposes, but she is still one particular human animal.

I have some sympathy for the proposition that we are biologically living human animals fundamentally or essentially. This proposal is known in the philosophical literature on personal or self-identity as *animalism*. If animalism is true, you and I are nothing but particular living human animals. I am a living human animal. You are a living human animal. But there are difficulties with the position. One difficulty is that a merely biologically alive human animal can exist, albeit only with assistance, without possessing any conscious life whatsoever, autobiographical memories or otherwise. But can you and I really exist or persist in such a literally 'thought-less' condition? If animalism is true, I could exist in a permanent vegetative state. To me this consequence of animalism – namely that I could exist permanently non-consciously, just biologically – strips what we fundamentally are from the capacities or powers that, as Lynne Rudder Baker aptly puts it, "matter most deeply to ourselves" (Baker 2000: 227). It matters most deeply to me that I am conscious or possess a capacity for conscious experience, for example, and therein am able to lead a life. (Remember our discussion of the importance of the capacity for conscious experience in Chapter 6.) Biology may be a precondition for all that (being conscious, leading a life, locating oneself historically and so on), but biology isn't what truly matters to me about myself. Being stripped down to mere biological features seems like a fate indistinguishable from personal death.

Consider the case of Terri Schiavo, who in 1990, at the age of 26, had a heart attack (apparently from a potassium deficiency associated with an eating disorder) and suffered a severe anoxic brain injury. She gradually descended into a permanent vegetative state (PVS) with credible evidence, which eventually included the results of an autopsy, of an irreversible loss of consciousness. If so, while biologically she remained alive, biographically she was dead. If such a state befalls me or my body, it would make no difference to me for me to be in the state. So, I speak of a 'fate indistinguishable' from death. If I don't and never can know that I am alive or exist, why be alive? It hardly matters.

So, then, why speak of my 'some sympathy' for animalism? The animalist position does pick out something real and non-fictionally single as me, namely an animal. Moreover, in order to account for periods in which I exist but am temporarily unconscious, say, while asleep or in a non-permanent coma, we have to suppose that there is a single entity that is conscious at one time, unconscious at another later time, and persists through time and engages in various sorts of conscious activities at still later times. This entity that is me could then well be a particular human animal. Just as there is one animal writing this chapter, so there is one me authoring the book, from start to finish, if I am that animal. Writing the chapter is something that I, a particular organism, do.

If I am an animal I 'share' with this particular organism all sorts of other metaphysical virtues, virtues connected with the animal's biophysical singularity. I am separate and distinct from other persons and things. I am publicly observable. I am embedded in a social and cultural world. Various sciences may examine me. My autobiographical memories may be confirmed or disconfirmed by eyewitnesses of my presence. If I am an animal I also share a common essence or nature with other human animals. This means that all sorts of empirical regularities and inductive generalizations that hold of other human animals also hold of me. Patterns of sleep; matters of motion; means of commingling; tangled trajectories of development and decay; and so on.

Regardless of the merits or demerits of animalism, however, it should be noted that conventional therapeutic treatment for MPD normally pushes and pulls in favor of picturing 'victims' as single individuals, namely as one distinguishable thing (Putnam 1989 and Kluft 1986). Treatment of persons with MPD often consists of taking a healthy presenting personality and enlisting its services in flushing out and rejecting or unifying with other personalities. A single subject is presupposed as the target therapeutic destination of a multiple and as a healthy gain or improvement from evidence of a beleaguered multiplicity in the initial appearance of a patient in therapy.

However, back now to my original query, whose upcoming 'answer' has just been framed by brief discussion of MPD, fictionalism, animalism and selfhood. What is our fundamental essence? Of what nature am I?

Fundamental essences are powerful. They constitute us. They define us. They, when present, mean we exist. They, when absent, mean we fail to exist. Suppose, for example, that my essence is such that I am a particular non-physical or immaterial mind or substance. If that particular immaterial substance exists, I exist; if it fails to exist, I, too, fail to exist. Or suppose, for example, that my essence is such that I am a particular living human animal. If that particular animal exists, I exist; if it does not, I do not.

Despite some personal sympathy for animalism, I don't want to insist that the doctrine is true. In good faith I can't. The arguments for animalism don't roll over misgivings about it. For the later purposes of this chapter, however, we do not require a definitive or settled answer to the essence question. Instead, I wish to make an assumption. This is that we are not in a position to prove or demonstrate *what* fundamentally we are, although we know in self-consciousness *that* we are. Built into our experience of being self-conscious is recognition of our own existence (of which more below). However, being aware of our own existence does not require or presuppose that we possess explicit knowledge of our fundamental essence (again, of which more below). That I am what I am is one thing. That I know what I am is another. I like to call this position – namely that we know that we exist but not what essentially we are – *self-serving agnosticism*. I know that I exist. You know that you exist. But it is left open or metaphysically topic-neutral precisely in *what* sort of metaphysical class we matriculate. We are not fictions; we exist, we are real, not imaginary. But for essence-speculation beyond that, we are in a metaphysically ignorant mode. We do not know whether we are best understood as brains, animals or whatever, though we do know that we are real.

Naturally, we may and do make educated guesses about what we are. Some educated guesses may be superior to others (animalism is my guess). But knowledge, after all, is "a thick epistemological concept" (Goldman 2006: 223). It's more than just an educated guess. It is a true belief possessed of demonstrable reliability or provable justification. The epistemological bar for knowledge is high, too high, I assume for knowing precisely what sort of being we are. However, failing to know what we are does not mean, again, that we fail to know that we are. It is evident to me that I exist. When my finger, for example, is accidentally smashed, I feel pain. The pain is experienced as mine, as in my finger. My. Me. When I feel anxious about climbing a ladder on a cold and windy winter day to get to the roof of my home to remove a fallen tree limb, it's anxiety in me that I know I feel. I do not feel an episode of anxiety and then ask whether it is my own. I experience the anxiety as, as it were, adjectival on or as a modification of me: as my own apprehensiveness.

The philosopher Colin McGinn advocates a form of self-serving agnosticism. (I am not sure whether McGinn would appreciate the label or name of 'self-serving agnosticism'. Perhaps not.) McGinn writes:

> We know [of our] existence with a special kind of assurance, but we know next to nothing about [our metaphysical] nature. We know with certainty *that* [we are], but we are grievously ignorant of *what* [we are].
>
> (McGinn 1999: 163–4)

I wish to rephrase and add to McGinn's claim as follows: Strictly speaking, we do not know exactly what our essential thing-hood is. We may embrace a hypothesis about the matter, but we should not talk confidently of its truth. The essence of our selves (remember, I mean 'ourselves') is one thing. Our comprehension of that essence is another matter entirely. We just do not know what that essence is. Why is that?

McGinn has an explanation for why we don't, and indeed, on his view, can't know our essence. It has to do with the absence of scientific, objective or impersonal criteria for the existence of ourselves as well as, for that matter, of our termination or annihilation. We don't know what ultimately constitutes our existence. He asks:

> Does severe Alzheimer's disease put an end to the self or just modify it? What about deep coma? . . . There is the body, recognizably the same; but is it the same *person* in there?
>
> (McGinn 1999: 162)

Why don't we have an impersonal criterion for the existence of ourselves? Because, he says, we don't have it for the existence of consciousness, and "if we cannot understand states of consciousness [scientifically], then it is hardly likely that we will be able to understand the nature of the *subject* of those states" – namely ourselves (McGinn 1999: 157).

Terri Schiavo's parents believed that their daughter continued to exist and perhaps was conscious of them during certain periods of the wake phase of her sleep–wake cycle. (Diagnosis of PVS is made when a patient exhibits preserved sleep/wake cycles but appears unaware, in the wake phases of such cycles, of self and immediate environment.) We may lament that the truth of her parents' perhaps wishful thought or belief was massively unlikely, but, if McGinn is right, we don't *know* that Terri Schiavo was not conscious or did not exist. This point – namely, that the absence of a behavioral or impersonal sign of consciousness may not be reliably indicative of non-consciousness – is acknowledged or conceded by a number of neuroscientists. Some patients, Martha Farah notes, "continue to experience full awareness of themselves and their surroundings while being unable to indicate their awareness behaviorally" (Farah 2008: 12). Silence may envelop behavior without the thinker themselves being annihilated.

I am not going to commit to an interpretation of the Schiavo case. I also am not going to commit to McGinn's particular defense of the assumption of a self-serving agnosticism. But I share in its assumption. The assumption, the conclusion, is that we don't know the truth about our fundamentality. We don't know what makes for ourselves. What is the particular me? – an animal? Whatever?

Now I do not interpret self-serving agnosticism (and neither does McGinn in the case of his own position) to imply that we are completely and utterly in the dark about some of our critically important characteristics. Radical skepticism about our constitution ill-suits a book on mental disorder that relies on and urges deep respect for empirical evidence. Besides which, grievous ignorance about our essence is one thing. Absolute blindness to important features of our selves is another. So, I am going to add to the assumption of metaphysical ignorance or self-serving agnosticism about ourselves (henceforth call that 'A1' for a first assumption) six additional assumptions or sets of assumptions that certainly do commit to claims about us and what we are like. So, this means that there will be, in all, seven sets of assumptions about us. Each of the following six assumptions I assume to be sensible and indeed commonsensical. Each is freighted with metaphysical presuppositions and consequences, to be sure, but none explicitly require that we be, say, animals, immaterial minds, souls or sets of material particles or whatever. The assumptions are as follows:

(A2) There is a complex and subjectively important difference for each of us between our being consciously alive (or existing as conscious subjects) and our consciously leading a life or directing and being responsible for it. If we imagine ourselves as subjects of experience only, as nothing but spectators who exert no influence or control whatsoever over our lives, many of us would not wish to live for long like that. It would be repellent. We would crave the ability to lead a life – to take responsibility for ourselves. Leading a life (and not just living it) by comparison is, as James Rachels has put it, "immensely important; it is the sum of one's aspirations, decisions, activities, projects and human relationships" (Rachels 1986: 5). You and I aspire, decide, and are active. We are no mere spectators nor do we wish to be.

(A3) Over the course of a life, we gain and lose features or characteristics; we may change in size, weight, physical appearance or shape; we may lose and acquire beliefs, desires, values and other attitudes. But we persist. We endure. We are not ephemeral. Here today; gone tomorrow. Some changes affect our ability to lead a life; others do not. Being unable to control a grossly imprudent behavior pattern, say, a drug addiction, does affect one's ability to lead a life. It may destroy a person. But losing a single hair on one's thickly haired head or a freckle on one's ankle does not.

(A4) We are not individually scattered or dispersed creatures but unified or integrated. A city, like, say, New York City, is scattered all over the place. We are not. Our bodies are not disintegrated sets of toenails, eyelashes and a tongue, but integrated (one term from philosophy of science that may be useful here is 'homeostatically clustered') systems of organs and borders. Our bodies possess what might be called a 'hang-togetherness'. Mentally also we possess a hang-togetherness: interlocking memories, projects, beliefs and commitments. Our unity or clustered integration is not an all or nothing affair. It comes in degrees and ramifies along different dimensions, at times surviving disintegrating periods or episodes, at times not, but at its gravitational center as persons is our possession of a conscious point of view, namely our first-person perspective on self and world. Our first-person perspective enables us to look backward (to where we have been or to what we have done) as well as to project ourselves forward (to possible future circumstances). The possession of perspective means that episodes in our life "bear relations to one another that must be understood if any part of the life is to be understood" (Rachels 1986: 51). So, for example, I am unable to fully understand what you are doing at present in reading this book, if I fail to appreciate how reading it fits into your plans or intentions. Suppose, for example, you wish to be a professional psychiatrist, and to possess sufficient literacy in philosophy of mind to help you to read Dennett or McGinn and to participate in meetings of the Association for the Advancement of Philosophy and Psychiatry (USA) or the Philosophy Group in the Royal College of Psychiatrists (UK). Absent such knowledge of this 'inside' point of view or of information taken from your personal perspective, your present activity may make little or no sense to me.

(A5) A conscious first-person point of view may be thought of, by illustration, as follows. There is something it is like to be thinking of Paris, there is something it is like to see a dog, there is something it is like to taste bitter-sweet dark chocolate, and there is something it is like to read this book or to go for a walk. There also is something it is like to have these experiences together either at a time or in a series or stream of conscious episodes. A personal point of view is the relation that such experiences have to each other when they occur to a single individual person or subject as components of a single conscious state or series of such states. To the extent it is unified or integrated, a conscious point of view or perspective enables a person's beliefs to be updated or revised, memories to be consolidated, values and commitments to be evaluated and made consistent, intentional actions to be performed and appraised, and so on. Disunity of view disrupts or impairs such activities. A disintegrated flux of conscious episodes prohibits or stymies belief revision, memory consolidation, evaluative self-appraisal, and deliberate behavior. It prohibits truly leading a life, comprehending one's self, and taking responsibility for self.

(A6) The unity or integration of a conscious point of view is not just the unity of a mere locus of consciousness or of experiences had by oneself as their subject. Given that we lead lives as agents, it is also the unity of conscious first-personal agency: of bringing things about and causing things to happen in the world. As Terence Horgan, John Tienson, and I put it: "Your phenomenology ... presents your own behavior to you as having [you] yourself as its source" (Horgan et al. 2003: 225). We persons appear to ourselves as sources, doers, initiators, directors, and executors. When the world resists our attempts to act, this "may give rise to the feeling of effort – the experience of needing to invest energy and willpower in our actions" (Bayne and Levy 2006: 57). We try. Sometimes we succeed. Sometimes we fail. In trying, too, we experience ourselves not as mere subjects but, again, as agents; not just as possessed of a conscious life but as trying to lead it.

Six complex assumption sets down. One final set, the seventh, to go. So, what's the seventh assumption? Stating it must wait a moment. First, I wish briefly to look at how the word 'I', the singular first-person pronoun, behaves in ordinary speech.

In using 'I' to refer to myself (and the same analogously may be said for you, of course) I am not alone, even if no one else is in the room and the room is otherwise empty except for a chair. By this I mean that when I use 'I' (to self-refer), a whole class of physical objects is coincident with me. Suppose, for example, I am sitting on the chair and I announce:

- I am thinking of Paris.

Then, there is a living human animal sitting in my chair. There is a mass of matter in the chair (made up of body parts and the molecular components of those parts). There is a brain with a certain shape, size and mass in the chair (atop the mass of matter), together with other regions of the mass of matter (kidney, lungs and so on). There also is a left and perhaps verbally dominant hemisphere in the brain. And so on. But presumably there is only one thought and one thinker of this one thought. Or more precisely, in *my* thinking of Paris, there is only one thought (of Paris) and one thinker (namely me). So, it cannot be that the animal is the thinker, and the brain (or left hemisphere) is the thinker, and the mass of matter is the thinker, and so on. If any one of these things is the thinker and each of these things is distinct, then *only* one is the thinker. This is because I myself the thinker am one. Other entities may be coincident with me or overlap with or help to constitute me, but only one (if any) is me. Which one?

Perhaps none that I have just mentioned. Perhaps none of those objects (animal, material mass, brain), being material, is the thinker. Perhaps I am merely fortuitously housed in a portion of matter (animal, brain or mass of matter) but am not myself material. Perhaps some form of dualism is true. Since there is only one of me, one thinker, but a variety of different portions of matter (animal, brain, etc.) in the room, no one of which jumps onto the Metaphysical Stage as me, perhaps we need to revisit the mind/body problem as well as the problem of mental causation. Perhaps we need to embrace the dualist side in the dualism/physicalism debate. Perhaps we should treat the reference of 'I' as denoting, say, an immaterial mind or non-physical entity. It will be recalled, however, that there are grave reasons for doubt about whether dualism is true. It is difficult (as Kim has argued, among others) to understand how an entity without mass or shape can causally interact with something that is physical – with mass and shape. So, do we really want to embrace dualism? Dualism may be a decently educated guess about our metaphysical position in the world, but, in the end, it is just a guess. Much can be said against it.

I do not wish to deny that some guesses are better or worse than others (e.g. we are not nothing, not fictions), but I am going to continue to abstain from speculation about the best guess here. My second through seventh assumptions about our selves (that's 'ourselves') should be more than enough for purposes of this chapter.

So, here then is the seventh and final assumption or set of assumptions. It is owed, in part, to the philosopher P. F. Strawson (1919–2006). Strawson claims that each of us is: "An undeniably persistent object ... who perceptibly traces a physical, spatio-temporal route through the world" (P. Strawson 1966: 164). The assumption goes as follows:

(A7) Our knowledge of our bodies and brains does not disclose a clear or precise physical locus for us to be in or at (left hemisphere, whole brain, whole body, with this or that molecular edge etc.?). So, again, it may be tempting to agree with a species of dualism that we are non-physical entities, only fortuitously conjoined with matter. We should be suspicious, however, of presupposing the detachability of ourselves from our bodies. Any such temptation may derive solely from the failure to recognize the necessary physical realization or constitution of ourselves. Regardless, we do know the following about ourselves (and here now is the idea of P. F. Strawson). We are things or entities that can be traced through space–time (even if we are not just such things). We are perceivable, tractable or observable in the public physical world. So, for example, if I refer to myself being *here* but having been *there*, you can trace me from locale to locale. If *then* I did such-and-such (e.g. purchase a loaf of bread), you may have spotted me. If *now* I am composing this chapter, you may observe me currently hard at work, eyes focused on my laptop, fingertips darting along the keyboard. Utterly fine-grained in locus or not, a perceivable locus I do nonetheless possess.

Let's offer a quick and partial summary of the above assumption making. We are more or less unified or integrated leaders of a conscious life. Our lives cannot be wholly understood without appreciating 'inside' or subjective point of view connections between various episodes or stages in a life, namely connections understood from a person's own perspective. We are not all 'inside' creatures, however. We are publicly observable. We possess a public presence and behave in and have a causal impact on the physical world.

Those certainly are hefty thoughts. In their own ways, of course, they are deeply metaphysical, although not of the specific sort that decisively identifies our 'essence' as animals, brains or whatever. I plan to use them as a background or framework for the topics to be discussed in the rest of this chapter. What will those topics be?

Galen Strawson, the son of P. F., and himself (like his father) a philosopher, writes of

> A friend who recently ... found that the thought 'I don't exist' kept occurring to him. It seemed to him that this exactly expressed his experience of himself, although he ... knew, of course, that there had to be a locus of consciousness where the thought 'I don't exist' occurred.
>
> (G. Strawson 1997: 418)

No ordinary friend is that, of course, for the proposition that there has to be a locus of consciousness where a thought like 'I don't exist' occurs is a quite sophisticated act of conceptual recognition (see Kennedy and Graham 2007). As Strawson-the-father once noted, "it would make no sense to think or say: This ... experience is occurring but is it occurring to *me*?" (P. Strawson 1966: 166). If I am directly aware of a thought and linguistically designating it with a demonstrative like the word 'this' (even a thought like 'I don't exist'), the thought must be occurring to me, and I must be the locus in which or the subject to whom it occurs.

> That's why I am in position to refer to it as *this* experience. Its distinctive identity as represented by the demonstrative is inseparable from my own presence or existence as the subject modified by the experience.
>
> (Kennedy and Graham 2007: 237)

Well and good. But what then of persons who seem to have lost their ability to recognize their own selves as subjects of conscious experience or as responsible agents and who undergo various dramatic forms of 'inner' point-of-view disunity or disintegration? Consider a life in which there is no real possibility of integrating one's memories or revising one's beliefs or a life hobbled by an otherwise discordant or disintegrated point of view. There is a puzzling class of mental disorders or symptoms of conscious disunity and disintegration that vary along numerous complicated dimensions. I want to look at two disorders in the class. In the next two sections of this closing chapter I plan to explore them. In so doing I wish to test the illuminating power or wisdom of some of our framework assumptions, such as that our consciousness tends (or normally tends) to be unified along two dimensions (that of subjectivity and agency/life-leading). I plan to begin with a disorder akin to the expressed sentiment of Galen Strawson's friend. It is known as the Cotard delusion.

'I AM DEAD' BUT DON'T MEAN IT

In the early 1880s Jules Cotard, a French psychiatrist, encountered a 43-year-old female patient who claimed that she had "no brains, chests or entrails and was just skin and bone" (Cotard 1882; see also Bentall 2004: 299, and Young and Leafhead 1996). Cotard introduced the term *délire de negation* to refer to the delusion and, after the French doctor's death, it was widely assumed that he had identified a particular type of nihilistic depressive delusion. Its central defining characteristic? A person denies that they are alive or claims that they are dead. Some individuals with the syndrome may claim not just that they are dead, but that they don't exist at all. Subjects may say things like (see Enoch and Trethowan 1991):

- I have no blood.
- I used to have a heart. I have something which beats in its place.
- I am a corpse that already stinks.
- I have no body.

If there is a distinctive delusion here, which I assume there is, considerable variation characterizes its claims and symptoms (see Berrios and Luque 1995). I plan to focus on two truly striking expressions just mentioned of the syndrome, namely, the claims that:

- I do not exist.
- I am dead.

Each may be made by subjects of the delusion.

Early observers of the Cotard condition, it appears, were correct that the delusion tends to be indicative of or associated with depression. Of 100 cases, for instance, in one representative study, severe depression was reported in 89 per cent of these (Berrios and Luque 1995).

So, what may lead a depressed person to say (and believe?) that they don't exist or are dead? If I tell you that I am dead, mustn't I appreciate that I am speaking, hence that I am alive? Or if I say that I don't exist, mustn't I recognize this proposition to be utterly false? If I say or think "I don't exist," I must exist. Fictionalism should be dismissed.

A famous assumption of Descartes about the metaphysics of selfhood was driven by his conviction that personal existence denial is incoherent. He wrote:

> I saw that while I could pretend that I had no body and there was no world and no place for me to be in, I could not for all that pretend that I did not exist.
>
> (Descartes 1984: 127)

The Cotard delusion seems like ripe territory for Jaspers's caution that delusions are not rationally intelligible or empathetically sensible or coherent. Perhaps, though, the Cotard delusion is intelligible, at least up to a Maherian point. Perhaps empathetic sense may be made of its outlandish claims or of what they mean to a person, if we can pinpoint aberrant experiences or affective disturbances that underlie it.

The philosopher Philip Gerrans offers a venturesome solution to the 'making sense of' puzzle of the Cotard delusion that is in the Maher mold. Gerrans surmises: "The Cotard delusion, in its extreme form, is a rationalization," by which Gerrans means a Maher-type subjective explanation, "of a feeling of disembodiment based on global suppression of affect resulting from extreme depression" (Gerrans 2000: 112). Gerrans describes the connection between Cotard and depression as follows.

> Nothing that occurs [to the Cotard patient] evokes the normal emotional response. The Cotard patient experiences her perceptions and cognitions, not as changes in herself, but [as] changes in the states of the universe, one component of which is her body, which now feels like an inanimate physical substance, first decomposing and finally disappearing. The lack of affective experience ... produces a feeling of [corporeal] insubstantiality.
>
> (Gerrans 2002: 50; expressions in brackets inserted by me)

In an independent and unrelated discussion Nancy Andreasen fleshes this sort of depressed state descriptively out a bit:

> A person who is depressed can have cognitive symptoms so severe that he ... has delusions. ... Sometimes the delusions are turned inward, so that the person [feels as if] his internal organs are rotting away.
>
> (Andreasen 2001: 228)

William James, too, offers an apt description of certain aspects of a relevant depression. He writes that while severely depressed a person may feel as if "they are sheathed in India-rubber," as if there "were a wall between" the individual "and the outer world" (1890: 298). The affective possibility of making emotional contact or engagement with the world and of engaging in its opportunities or affordances is absent from experience.

Gerrans's picture appears to be the following. Patients suffering from the Cotard delusion are shorn or stripped of feelings, on their part, of being in the world and of affective concern for how they behave in the world as well as of their own corporeality. In bodily action or intentional behavior, normally emotions or feelings are associated with specific motivations and dispositions to act. I care what I do. I care whether my actions turn out successfully. In people with the Cotard syndrome such care-emotions fail to occur. What do occur are feelings of insubstantiality or of (no pun is intended) not mattering.

The Gerrans-type picture of the Cotard delusion is that dead-feeling (feeling insubstantial and absent affective connectedness with the world) produces and, in a sense, subjectively warrants believing that one is dead or does not exist. The belief that one is dead is formed by the subject in explaining the dead-feeling. I feel dead because, well, I am dead. Or so I think of myself.

Is this a plausible tale? We should be careful with it. As noted, the story presupposes the Maher premise that delusional attitudes such as those expressed in the Cotard delusion and understood in belief-like terms are generated as explanations by subjects of unusual or aberrant feelings or perceptual experiences. The Cotard delusion that the subject is dead or does not exist (Gerrans is primarily interested in the claim of being dead) is adopted to account for why the person feels (or fails to feel) as they do. The subject feels insubstantial. So, they believe or assume that they are dead or do not exist. They *are* insubstantial.

It is true then, if Gerrans is right, that the assertions of the subject of the Cotard delusion are partially rational. Or is it? The trouble is that although this Maher-like tale of Gerrans looks like it helps to preserve the rationality of the subject of the Cotard delusion, insofar as it reflects an effort to make sense of certain feelings, it is, as noted above, notoriously difficult to deny one's own existence or, for that matter, to assert that one is dead without being aware of the gross inconsistency of such speech acts with one's living or existing as speaker. No one who denies his existence, for example, can use such words without, it would appear, knowing the statement to be false and knowing that one continues to exist.

Suppose I am a victim of the Cotard delusion. Is it that I, while a subject of the delusion, don't even realize or recognize that I am speaking or saying something that contradicts my very speech act? Gerrans surmises that "the depression is [so] deeply entrenched ... it produces a deficit in reasoning which makes it impossible for the subject to bring counter-vailing knowledge to bear" (Gerrans 2000: 120). Does Gerrans mean by 'countervailing knowledge' the recognition that I exist or am alive when I speak? But how, then, does the mere entrenchment of depression screen me off from recognition of my speech acts as my own or of their implications for my being alive or existing? It stretches credulity to say that such speech reflects even partially rational beliefs.

Gerrans seems to assume the following about the delusion. While the subject is quite aware that she feels dead or insubstantial, and is also sufficiently aware of herself to claim "I am dead," she fails to understand that in making this claim she actually is and must be alive. There is awareness of a claiming as well as of feeling insubstantial, but no awareness of one's life or existence as speaker? Gerrans's account of why subjects of the Cotard delusion utter existence denials seems explanatorily inadequate or incomplete, does it not? If I believe that I am dead or do not exist, it must be explained how I may believe this all the while knowing that I am saying these things.

I admire Gerrans for trying both to describe the phenomenal inside of the Cotard delusion and to make it empathetically understandable. But let's see if we can substitute another hypothesis for his analysis in a productive way. How can I say something that is utterly incompatible with understanding that I am saying it? One possibility is that the speech acts in question are semantically empty and Intentionality-less, like coughs or sneezes. No intention, no rationality, no reason fuels the sound. But such a construal strips the subject of the Cotard delusion of the speech, as it were, of his speech, namely of intending to mean something by saying something. It would be grossly incompatible with Gerrans's effort of reconstruction in the Maher-mold to strip the act of its Intentionality. So, it is worth considering an alternative approach to the Cotard delusion. One with a speech-act semantics different from that presupposed by Gerrans. What's missing in the Gerrans account is an explanation for why a belief such as that I am dead or do not exist is generated rather than some more readily intelligible or non-contradictory expression of a victim's sentiments, such as reports like the following: "I feel insubstantial" or "I don't feel as if I am having an impact in the world."

Here is a brief sketch of an alternative proposal aimed at dissolving the appearance of incoherence or irrationality on the part of the Cotard victim's attitudes. It is offered in a speculative spirit and from the interpretational perspective of the delusional stance conception of delusion mentioned in the last chapter (and available in Stephens and Graham 2004 and 2007). The proposal rests on an interpretation of claims like "I do not exist" or "I am dead" as they occur in cases of the Cotard delusion. It goes like this.

Utterances of "I am dead" or "I don't exist" are not reflective of a subject's beliefs (that they are dead or do not exist), for these are not (the proposal says) propositions that they actually or really do believe. Rather, such claims are misleading expressions of the subject's feelings of insubstantiality or of the absence of affective connectedness with the world. What a subject of the delusion basically is doing, when he says that he is dead or does not exist, is ventilating or *expressing* the fact that he just does not feel anything like his normally engaged and corporeal self. He feels *as if* he is dead or does not exist and this feeling has become central or hyper-salient to him. His utterance is a tangled and misleading way of expressing such feelings or emotional experiences.

Call this proposal an *expressivist* interpretation of Cotard claims. It says: The utterances in question are expressions of feelings (or of the lack of them), not (also) of beliefs. Just why a subject reports feelings as if they are beliefs (e.g. that I am dead) may be explained in a number of ways. One possibility is that the person means to convey the subjective centrality of the feelings. I feel vividly as if I am insubstantial. I feel vividly as if I am disconnected from the world. In order to express that, I use belief-talk. Another possibility is that subjects misunderstand the difference between speaking of feelings and beliefs. I've had many a student claim that Descartes *felt* that there is a contradiction between his doubting whether he exists, on the one hand, and his possibly not existing, on the other.

Delusional subjects do not distance or wall themselves off from the attitudes (beliefs, feelings, thoughts and so on) that are the elements of their delusion. They are entangled in them. This contrasts with the stance or attitude of subjects who suffer from obsessions. Subjects who suffer from obsessions often struggle against their condition and appreciate that their obsessive thoughts draw energy and attention from more prudent and useful activities. Delusions often are more insidious than obsessions in that delusional subjects may be incorrigibly committed to maintaining them and make no effort to be free of them. They over-identify with their delusions, blind to their harmful consequences. Deluded subjects fail to realize that the persistence of a certain thought or feeling indicates that something is wrong with them and that their disinclination to abandon the content of a delusion should reveal to them that they are not thinking or feeling properly. (Such is the grip of the Intentional Stance on a thought, feeling or belief that it keeps a person from distancing themselves from such attitudes.) In the case of Cotard such subjective centrality or over-identification may mistakenly, at least in some of a subject's delusional claims, be expressed in the language of belief.

I shall not press for this expressivist interpretation. Kinderman and Bentall warn that "by denying that delusions are beliefs ... patients [may be] treated with disrespect, and [this may deny] them a voice in determining their treatment" (Kinderman and Bentall 2007: 288) (expressions in brackets inserted by me). By working with a Cotard's patient's delusion, understood as a 'mere' feeling but reported as if a belief, do we risk clinical mistreatment? I think not. Besides which, my proposal is meant to be speculative and to address a problem with Gerrans's account. It is also intended to offer the semantics of the relevant speech acts of a person with Cotard's. Whether this semantics is shared diagnostically with the person is a distinct treatment issue.

Much of the clinical and neuropsychiatric literature on delusion focuses on a-rational neural or brute somatic sources or causes behind delusions (like the Cotard delusion and others): brain tumors, aneurysms, strokes, epilepsy, Alzheimer's disease and others. One report is of a man who following a hematoma in his right basal ganglia, somehow believed that he had acquired an extra arm, protruding from the middle of his body (Halligan and Marshall 1996). *Prima facie* same symptoms, of course, may have different sources or distinct propensity conditions (and not truly be the same), which fact is worth remembering if we wish to preserve a reasonably well-behaved notion of a mental disorder. Just because a disturbance may seem to be a mental disorder given its syndromal cluster does not mean that it is a mental disorder. If the symptoms directly stem from brain damage, it is not. It is a neurological disorder and the symptoms themselves bear no (however even partial) rationale.

One of the difficulties with a merely symptom-orientated criterion for a mental disorder is that it classifies disorders independently of causes. Without reference to causes, as I have argued before, one cannot classify a condition as a mental disorder or know exactly what sort of disorder it is.

Dominic Murphy writes:

> Common sense denies that you have a mental disorder if you are in a diabetic coma, or have no cortical activity because you are on a life-support machine and with only a brain-stem intact. Yet mental functioning is impaired in these cases, so I have to call them instances of mental disorder.
>
> (Murphy 2006: 62)

'Have to?' Comas have mental symptoms (absence of consciousness), no doubt. But did Terri Schiavo suffer from a mental disorder? Just because her consciousness was 'disordered' does not mean that she was the subject of a mental disorder. Murphy conflates, I believe, whether a person has a condition that mentally impairs them with whether they are the subject of a disorder that is mental in type or kind.

So here is my prescription: If you want to know whether something is a delusion, look downstream. Look at its consequences. But if you want to know if something is a mental disorder or if a delusion is a symptom of a mental disorder, then look upstream as well. Find out about its generation or conditions of onset. Absent an autograph of mentality on those conditions, it's not mental.

SELF-SERVING IN A SUPERMARKET

Suppose. I am in front of a supermarket. I intend to walk into the market to buy a sack of sugar and a loaf of bread, and, of course, I know this. But how do I know that I possess this intention? It can't be inferred from my current behavior. I am standing outside the market and have not taken a single step inside. Nor can I appeal to my history of walking to this particular store or buying just bread and sugar. I have never shopped in that market. I have never purchased just bread and sugar. So, my past behavior is no guide for me as to what I now intend. The obvious answer is that the intention is immediately evident to me. My intention is self-evident to me. It wears its presence as well as its 'mineness' or adjectival quality, namely its being mine, on its conscious sleeve.

Now consider the following extension to the story (see John Perry [1979]). I step into the market and grab a shopping cart. I push my cart down an aisle that contains sacks of sugar, pick a sack, and place it in my cart. Then, I set off for a loaf of bread. After exploring two or three aisles, neither of which holds bread, I spot the bread aisle. While pushing the cart, however, I notice that someone is producing a trail of sugar, presumably from a leaky bag in their cart. It's all over the floor. It has formed a distinct line on various aisles. I backtrack to explore a neighboring aisle in search of the culprit whose bag is making a mess. Although the trail gets thicker, I seem unable to catch up to the person. Then, it dawns on me. *I* am the person with the leaky bag. I look down at my cart and sure enough, my bag leaks. My behavior changes accordingly. I stop looking for an unknown person with a bad bag. I cuff my bag to try to keep it from leaking further and return to the aisle that holds the sugar in hopes of finding a better bag. I find one. I put it in my cart. Then, I deposit the leaky bag at the service counter, explaining to the clerk that it has a hole in it, and follow a sign to the bread aisle.

A key feature of this sugar story is that I changed from believing that *someone* has a leaky bag (but not knowing whom) to knowing that I am that someone. It's my bag that leaks. Initially, I failed to make this inference. It certainly was not self-evident to me that I had the defective bag. By contrast, it was self-evident to me that I had the intention to shop in the store. Not just that someone intended shopping. I intended. No inference required. Indeed, how could it be otherwise? It seems impossible for me to misidentify the intention as someone else's intention. To appropriate from remarks of P. F. Strawson in another context: "It would make no sense to say or think: *this* conscious intention is occurring but is it occurring to *me*?"

But hold on. Not so fast. Our little self-serving story continues.

Suppose, sound sack in cart, I visit the bread aisle. I spot the loaves. The following thoughts occur to me: "Good." "Here is a nice loaf of fresh multigrain bread." "I must purchase this loaf." "It's a brand that my wife and I love." Oddly, though, suppose that instead of experiencing those thoughts as *mine*, I experience them as if they somehow are made for me or done to me by an external agent or individual: as if an intelligent force or person other than me somehow is thinking them inside my own stream of consciousness. I am thinking of their thoughts as somehow in my stream? Yes, suppose the thoughts 'I' and 'my' occur, but I don't interpret them as referring specifically to me. I don't take myself to be thinking that I must purchase this loaf. I don't interpret the reference to 'my wife' as a reference to my wife. It's as if I overhear another person thinking – another's cogitative activity going on inside me.

Two matters appear to be wrong with me or in my conscious experience in the bizarre market circumstance just described. One is that I seem to fail to identify myself as the thinker when it should be immediately evident to me that *I* am thinking. How could thoughts occurring to me be other than mine? A bag of leaky sugar, yes, that may belong to a stranger. But thoughts? In me? How could I experience them as anyone else's but mine? The other matter is that rather than simply judging that something is amiss with my own thinking processes, I come up with the incredible belief or notion that someone else, some 'alien' or other agent, is doing their thinking inside me. I attribute the thinking to another person. Why, on earth, do that?

In attributing thoughts to another I don't think of the other as exerting a mere causal influence on me. I am not making a claim about another's thought-control over me. (I am not saying, for instance, that by whispering in my ear another person is priming me to pick a multigrain loaf.) I am also not making a judgment, as I would if I were a victim of MPD, that another person or alter once entertained thoughts in my body. No, I am making a judgment about another's thinking occurring in me right here and now, as I stare at the bread.

Without meaning to be too dramatic, given the above details, imagine that I have become a victim of an occurrence of what is known in the literature on mental disorder and schizophrenia as *thought insertion* (see Graham 2004 and Stephens and Graham 2000). Thought insertion is a type of delusion. It's not the literal insertion of a thought in me (whatever that could mean). Rather, it is experience of one's own thoughts as if they somehow or in some manner belonged to another and had been inserted into one's stream of consciousness. Witness the consequences of this attitude. If, for instance, I am questioned in a case of thought insertion as to how a thought in my stream of consciousness could possibly belong to another person, I may offer outlandish explanations such as:

- He treats my mind like a screen and flashes his thoughts onto it like you flash a picture. (Mellor 1970: 17)

- Thoughts come into my head like ['Get the bread']. It's just like my mind working, but it isn't. They come from this chap, Chris. They're his thoughts. (Adapted from Frith 1992: 660)

Cahill and Frith describe the phenomenon of thought insertion:

> Patients report that ... the thoughts which occur in their heads [are] not actually their own. It is as if another's thoughts have been ... inserted in them. One of our patients reported physically feeling the alien thoughts as they entered his head and claimed that he could pin-point the point of entry!
>
> (Cahill and Frith 1996: 278)

Evident similarities exist in clinical presentation between thought insertion and various other anomalies of self-ascription in self-awareness (see Stephens and Graham 2000). Inner or sub-vocal speech may be experienced as the voice of an external agent, for instance, even when there is no acoustic or phenomenal quality to the voice. So-called made feelings or emotions also are described similarly by patients as inserted thoughts.

- They project upon me laughter, for no reason, and you have no idea how terrible it is to laugh and look happy and know it is not you, but their emotions. (Mellor 1970: 17)

In cases of schizophrenia, such strange misidentifications or misattributions between the experience of self and of one's own activity occur not just with respect to mental but also bodily motions and activities. Some patients complain that their body is moved by alien or external and irresistible intelligent forces. Others assert that a moving limb that they actually do or may self-control is not a part of their body. It's no wonder, then, that clinical observers of schizophrenia (or of persons classified as schizophrenic) comment as follows: "One of the essential features of" schizophrenia is the disturbances of the experiencing 'I'" (Bovet and Parnas 1993: 589). Or: "Schizophrenics tend to lose their sense of integrated selfhood" (Sass 1999: 319). Indeed.

Perhaps the most harmful general consequence of schizophrenia is that the condition is incompatible, during disturbances of the experiencing 'I', with properly leading a life and assuming effective responsibility for self. The ability to be self-responsible requires that we identify ourselves as ourselves and know that our conscious mental and bodily activity is our own. It requires self-comprehension (another one of the basic capacities mentioned in Chapter 6) or proper self-attribution or self-identification. Lynne Rudder Baker describes the requirement of proper self-identification in terms of what is necessary to qualify as a person. She says: "A being that cannot think of itself in a ... first-personal way is not a person" (Baker 1997: 443). Baker's point is that in order to be a (as she puts it) person (or as I would wish also to put it, someone who leads or is responsible for their own life) I must comprehend my thoughts or deeds as mine, as modifications or activities of me. I must experience my conscious mental and physical activity as mine. I need to do this if I am, for example, to act on my intentions or aspirations. I must be able to compare what I do or fail to do with what I intend to do. I must also be able to keep track of myself over time. (This capacity, too, namely keeping track of oneself, it will be recalled, is also one of those classified as basic in Chapter 6.)

Let's look more carefully at the phenomenon of thought insertion. How is this puzzling phenomenon best understood? Does it really and truly consist of the self-misattribution of thoughts? The answer is yes and no. Yes and no? How so?

William James once wrote that "whatever I may be thinking of, I am always at the same time more or less aware of myself, of my personal existence" (James 1961 [1892]: 42). Alvin Goldman makes a similar claim: "The process of thinking ... carries with it a non-reflective self-awareness" (Goldman 1970: 96). James and Goldman are saying that conscious thoughts present themselves to their subjects as modifications or alterations of themselves. Modifications of the 'experiencing "I"'. This fact does not mean that if I am thinking of something I *judge* or *infer* that I am thinking of it, say, as I may judge or infer on the basis of visible evidence that the leaky bag of sugar is mine. That would be a case of reflective or propositional self-awareness and Goldman, for one, denies that the presentation of self in thought is inferential or judgmental. 'Mineness' is a proper part or constituent of the experience or phenomenology of thinking. It is not a higher-order or self-reflexive comment on it in the form of a belief or propositional judgment. But the experience of self-modification does mean that I know when a thought occurs to me and I experience it as a modification of or episode in me.

So, thought insertion does not consist of misidentifying my self as *subject* of conscious thoughts. Subjects of thought insertion, like me on the bread aisle, recognize that certain thoughts occur to them. "Thoughts come into my head," I say. What, though, of their attribution to another person or agent? How are we to understand that?

In order to construct an answer to this question, first let us consider an analogy. Suppose a man is looking for a suit in a large clothing store. After trying on four or five suits, the man says to the sales assistant:

- I am fat. I am skinny.

Perhaps he says this to vent his frustration at being unable to find the right suit. On the surface, though, it seems that he is also contradicting himself. But suppose there are people much thinner as well as other people much heavier than him in the store. If so, the man is not necessarily contradicting himself. Perhaps he is just being ambiguous or equivocal. Relative to the thin people whom he observes, he is fat. Relative to heavy people, he is skinny.

Something similar, I claim, occurs in thought insertion. Reports of inserted thoughts are instances of equivocation or ambiguity. Relative to one sense or reference point for 'being mine', the thoughts occurring to me on the bread aisle are experienced as mine. This is the sense in which I experience myself as the subject to whom they occur. This is what I wish to call the *subjectivity* sense of being mine. But relative to another sense of being mine, I experience them as another's thoughts. What sense is that? I will come to it in a moment, but first a bit more about subjectivity.

No special act of judgment (as noted) is required to experience one's thoughts as one's own in the subjectivity sense. When you undergo an experience, as noted, its manifest character as yours holds true even if you are hallucinating or dreaming, and thus even if the thought otherwise is dissociated from reality (bizarre, false, whatever). Just how vivid this adjectival or modificational quality of 'mineness' is depends on at least two factors. One is the type of thought or conscious mental episode in question. The other is the role played by surrounding activity and circumstance.

On the topic of type, consider a toothache. Consider your last toothache. Was there ever any question about to whom the ache occurred? No distinctive mechanism for determining that a toothache is one's own should be posited. The ache *self*-intimates or manifests to its subject as one's own. My ache appears to me as mine. Yours appears as yours. Or consider feeling cold, feeling warm or feeling sad. Such feelings or episodes wear their *being-one's-own* character on their conscious sleeves. So, too, in the case of thoughts of a cognitive nature. "This is the bread to buy." Such a thought occurs to me and I know it, even if I report it as an inserted thought. It is 'inserted', as I seem to experience it, but in *me*.

Surrounding circumstance is another factor affecting self-intimation of thought. A person may have thoughts running through their stream of consciousness, all the while concentrating on another task. Suppose that I am visiting with a close friend in a neighborhood bar discussing his pending move to another city. The prospect of his move saddens me. I am aware of my feeling sad, but my sadness hovers in the moody background. I am not attending to it. My focus is on the conversation. But suppose that two days later I learn of his death in an untimely and tragic automobile accident. I grieve terribly. My mourning is vividly self-intimating. Nothing else distracts from my attention to it. It's grief I feel; *I* feel it – and know it.

But what is the other sense? If a thought is experienced as one's own in the subjectivity sense, but, in thought insertion, attributed to another person or agent, what is this second sense? How can a thought be experienced as someone else's if it occurs to a person and he or she knows it?

The theory to which I am attracted I wish to call the *sense of agency theory* (see J. Campbell 1999; Frith 1992; Gallagher 2000; Graham 2004; Stephens and Graham 2000). A thought, such as my thought about a loaf of bread, may be attributed to oneself in either of two ways or senses. It may be attributed to oneself as the subject to whom it occurs. Or it may be attributed to oneself as the agent who does the thinking. Thought insertion represents a misinterpretation of the agency behind a thought (and not its subjectivity). Before describing this sense of agency theory, I need to mention three background assumptions behind it.

The first assumption is the reminder that first-person reports of inserted thoughts are equivocal or ambiguous. In one sense (the subjectivity sense), subjects can just tell that a thought occurs to them. But in another sense, they ascribe it to another. Just what this second sense is I am about to describe.

The second assumption is that thinking or conscious activity in general often is an active voluntary process. At the semantic level, 'thinking' is an activity verb. "Activity verbs," U. T. Place (1924–2000) noted, "refer to an ongoing activity in which an individual can be engaged and on which he or she can spend time" (Place 1999: 381). Forms of being engaged in thought are various and multitudinous: studying, theorizing, scrutinizing, planning, deliberating, wondering, concentrating, pondering and so on.

The third assumption is that thinking (the activity) possesses a distinctive what-it's-likeness or conscious character. This what-it's-likeness includes experiences as of controlling one's thinking; as of initiating, directing, redirecting and terminating one's lines of thought; as of coping with impediments or distractions while trying to think; and so on. To illustrate: Suppose that for years, I have had a number of accounts in a certain bank. But the bank shows signs of impending financial collapse. Suppose I am trying to decide how to tell my banker that I wish to withdraw my accounts from the institution. I experience myself as not just deciding to withdraw but also of directing germane patterns of thought. I have money concerns. I am looking for a way of disengaging from a bank that has been good to me in the past. I may think to myself: "My relationship with the bank has become too personal." "It's just business." But I also may fault myself for being "an unfeeling capitalist" who entertains the prospect of closing accounts in these immensely difficult financial times.

Perhaps I find myself giving into my guilt feelings over terminating my relationship with the bank. Or I may feel weakened by the effort of deliberation. Just as my legs may feel on the verge of collapse after a long hike or run, my mind may feel on the edge of collapse or depletion after an activity of stressful deliberation and emotional decision-making.

A word of caution is needed before proceeding. One should be careful not to conceptually misstep in describing the what-it's-likeness of the activity of thinking. Frith remarks: "Thinking ... is normally accompanied by a sense of effort and deliberate choice as we move from one thought to the next" (Frith 1992: 81). Effort or choice? One thought to the next? I am not sure what Frith means by such a remark. One interpretation is that he means that, in the activity of thinking, we form intentions or decisions to think *particular* thoughts. But do we have such intentions? To think particular thoughts? Hardly. Particular lines of thought, yes. We do form lines-of-thought intentions. But an intention for a particular thought content itself, no.

Compare with bodily action, where we may form and act on particularistic intentions. Suppose I am at a town-hall meeting. I arrive desiring to vote for Eunice Clay for town council. I've known Eunice for years. She's a good person and caring citizen. Suppose the people in attendance are asked to vote by raising their hand when the name of the person for whom they wish to vote is mentioned. Eunice's name is mentioned. I intend to vote for her here and now. So, I raise my hand to vote. Is thinking like that? First: the intention to do X? Then: the doing of X? First: the intention to think of Y. Then: the thinking of Y. Again no. Nothing like that happens in the world of thought.

We may form intentions to think about problems or themes, to solve puzzles, to make thoughtful decisions, to discontinue unwelcome lines of thought, to resist mental fatigue, and so on. But in so doing there is no intention for particular thoughts as one thought progresses to the next. Imagine the following. I form the intention to think of Paris. *Then* I think of Paris? Note that if I merely form the intention to think of Paris, a Paris thought occurs in the very intention. So, there would be no distinction between the intention to do X (vote for Eunice, think of Paris) and the doing (voting for Eunice, thinking of Paris). Nor, likewise, is there a choice or decision as I move from one thought to the next. Suppose I am undecided as to whether to raise my hand for Eunice or for her neighbor Tom. I deliberate and decide to vote for Eunice. Nothing like that happens with thoughts. If I am undecided as to whether to think of Paris or of Berlin, I *already* am thinking both of Paris and Berlin.

In the activity of thinking as well as in bodily activity, effort may be needed and energy expended. In certain mental chores, such as trying to solve a mathematical problem or deliberating about a tough career choice, thinking may be effortful and infused with choice, but this is not, as said, choosing *specific* thoughts. The choices may be of themes or desired lines of thought, outcomes or directions of content. "Hard decisions are experienced as requiring effort," Tim Bayne and Neil Levy note, "perhaps as a consequence of the cognitive resources we need to devote to them" (Bayne and Levy 2006: 58). They aptly add:

> Mental effort is also experienced when we actively direct our thoughts. Anyone who has struggled with a difficult conceptual issue has experienced the effort involved in thinking a problem through. It gives rise to characteristic feelings of tiredness and a growing urge to stop. When we do stop for a break, it seems to require real effort to return to the task.
>
> (Bayne and Levy 2006: 58)

So, then, what's going on in thought insertion if this phenomenon is understood as involving not the sense of subjectivity, but a distinguishable sense? Here is the hypothesis of sense of agency theory.

In thought insertion, thinking is experienced as an activity. However, although particular thoughts or episodes of thought are experienced as occurring in or to oneself (as subject), the activity itself *qua* or as an activity is experienced as if it is conducted or engaged in by someone else. Another is represented as the agent or author of the activity. An analogous phenomenon occurs in verbal auditory hallucinations common in schizophrenia in which I (as subject) seem to myself to hear another person's voice. I experience a voice not as a random or willy-nilly bit of doggerel, but as the intelligent speech act of another person. No other person is, in fact, speaking to me, of course, but I believe that another is speaking. "Donald Trump is urging me to turn a deaf ear and blind eye to my emotional relationship with the bank and to move my accounts to another bank," I report as the message of a voice. "It's just business." In thought insertion experiencing oneself as thinker (or as the thinking activity's agent) is displaced by experiencing the thoughtful activity as if conducted by another.

Just as there is a distinctive what-it's-likeness to thinking as an activity, there is a distinctive what-it's-likeness to thought insertion. It's as if another is doing the thinking in me. The representation of another as doing the thinking may be voiced in a silent, running introspective narrative on my thinking. "These thoughts belong to Chris, not me." "He loves multigrain bread." "I don't." "I am strictly a white bread person." "He projects his thoughts into me and treats me like a screen."

Thought insertion, so understood, also reveals that the "sense of subjectivity can survive when the sense of agency is lost" (Proust 2006: 89). Thus, when a person claims that certain thoughts occurring in them are not their own, they don't mean this in the sense that the episodes of thought do not occur to them. They maintain their sense of subjectivity (else they would not know of the thoughts). Rather, they mean that thinking (which is in fact theirs) appears to them as if it is being conducted by another agent. Their sense of self as agent is disrupted, which raises a question that is nicely posed by Joëlle Proust:

> Supposing that a patient with schizophrenia is impaired in monitoring her own ... thoughts, why does she not simply recognize that something is wrong with her ability to keep track of what *she* ... thinks? Why does she instead come up with odd judgments, such as that her neighbor, or some unknown person she met in the street, [is thinking in her]?
>
> (Proust 2006: 89)

Victims of schizophrenia (and I am talking here as if schizophrenia is an illness, though I may rephrase matters just in terms of the individuals who receive the diagnosis) have notorious problems keeping track of themselves. They may, for example, be deluded that other people are watching them (delusions of reference) or plotting against them (delusions of persecution). They may be deluded that their thought processes are being broadcast to others (delusions of thought broadcasting).

Various proposals have been offered in the literature for explaining the generation of the 'odd judgment' of attribution to another and of failing to keep track of one's own activity in schizophrenia. G. Lynn Stephens and I, for example, have suggested that inserted thoughts may be experienced as (what may be called) agentically dystonic, that is, as inconsistent with the subject's background beliefs about themselves or of what they are like as a person (Stephens and Graham 2000). If so, the 'inserted' thoughts occurring in a person's stream of consciousness are felt to be intelligent and seem to be guided or directed, but the person (given background beliefs about themselves) takes them to be personally anomalous. So, they automatically assume that another's 'psychology' must be at work in them. ("Someone like me would never think stuff like this." "Someone else is the thinker.")

A second and complementary proposal would account for the 'alien' ascription of thoughts as due to a failure in working memory. Working memory is a type of short-term declarative memory. It stores and manipulates information needed for "the execution of complex cognitive tasks, such as deliberating, making decisions, and foreseeing consequences of decisions" (Glannon 2007: 62). Perhaps victims of thought insertion suffer from information overload at certain critical moments, with perhaps too many cognitive activities to plan for and execute. This may lead to their temporary forgetfulness about activities or about the intentions behind activities in which they are voluntarily engaged. A person may lose track of their plans or patterns of thought, so that when thinking does occur it is not experienced as their own but, given its direction and intelligence, as if it is another's.

A motor-behavior analogy may help. Suppose I find myself taking up a pencil and rapidly inscribing marks on a piece of paper (see Graham and Stephens 1994: 106). The words and sentences express love to a woman named Beatrice. Suppose I recollect no one named Beatrice and that I have no idea of how the letter will end or of the purpose behind it. Given the intelligent momentum of the letter, however, suppose I experience the activity of writing as if another person or agent is writing to Beatrice through me. I am 'possessed', as it were. But now move the Beatrice-phenomenon inside the head, so to speak, from overt writing to covert thinking: from the activity of writing to the activity of thinking. Suppose that rather than finding myself writing to Beatrice, I find myself thinking of a woman named Beatrice and entertaining loving thoughts about her, although I have no idea who she is. I may think of the movements of my mind, my thoughts or inner speech, as belonging to that of another agent. Not that someone is merely influencing me to think of Beatrice (by, for instance, whispering her name in my ear), but that the conscious mental activity itself literally is that of another person or agent. Another is doing it 'inside' me. If so, if this is what happens in thought insertion, perhaps it is not so much that a victim of thought insertion thinks thoughts that are unfamiliar or personally dystonic (though that may be a factor). It is rather that they have trouble maintaining their goals or intentions in working memory (and perhaps suffer from other attention deficits as well). Whereas normally the sense of being the mental agent or in control of one's thinking activity is automatic, and perhaps self-evident, the self-comprehension involved in short-term memory of one's intentions may fail in a case of thought insertion. Thinking, in such a case, carries no sense of authorial 'mineness'. Thoughts occur to me independent of my sense of my own Intentionality. But I represent them to myself as another's activity, since they still possess, to me, an authorial quality.

I am sure we don't know yet how best to fully explain attribution-to-other in thought insertion. I believe that the sense of agency theory is part of the story. But it is not the whole tale. There are several questions that need to be answered about the phenomenon. Why do inserted thoughts occur on some occasions but not others? Is this because on certain occasions working memory is overloaded (under conditions of stress, for example) in a manner that compromises keeping track of one's intentions? Are some people prone to be flooded with thoughts in certain circumstances, because, for them, too much mental effort is required to keep track of what *they* are thinking? Just how or where does neurobiology/neurochemistry help to gum up self-attribution? Does the neural gumming up that is part of thought insertion occur in the prefrontal cortex, which enables a person to hold an intention 'on line' and perform self-monitored intentional activity? Is the gumming up best described as an irruption into the space of reasons but of the destructive sort due to a neural disorder or brain damage?

Despite the presence of many still-unanswered questions, there is an important lesson about self-experience and our capacity for self-comprehension to extract from the phenomenon of thought insertion. This is that while we are, as it were, the absolute authorities over the contents of our thoughts as well as whether these contents occur to us, we are not equally authoritative about our agentive role in thinking. It is quite possible to get one's agency, as it were, lost in thought. Indeed, for someone seriously mistaken about the role of their own mental agency, the thinking in which they engage may come apart to such an extent that it is implausible to say that they are responsible for their own ideas.

Grant Gillett writes:

> A person exercises a quite particular skill [as they] weave together a conscious narrative [of themselves] in a way that locates him or her ... in a world of objects and events presented amidst an abundance of ... information.
>
> (Gillett 2008: 97; expressions in brackets inserted by me)

For some persons thoughts occur to themselves that they don't properly self-attribute. If there is a narrative here, it needs more than a mere taleteller. It needs a good editor: someone to keep track of who is thinking. An editor-less thinker is no author at all.

CHAPTER SUMMARY AND SUGGESTED READINGS

I stand in a special relation to myself in which no other person stands. I am myself. No one else is me. This special relation poses questions. What sort of being am I? An animal? An immaterial soul or ego? The metaphysical implications of mental disorder for our understanding of our nature are among its most widely discussed and philosophically puzzling features. The goal of this chapter was to find out whether the evidence of mental disorder points to this, that or another metaphysical hypothesis or implication about ourselves.

Does MPD (multiple personality disorder) constitute evidence that we are unreal? No, it does not. It shows that we may not know *what* we are. But it does not show that we fail to know *that* we are. Does the Cotard delusion reveal that a person can coherently believe that they do not exist? No, it does not. It helps to show that feelings may be misread as beliefs as well as that a delusion is a complex multilayered state which exemplifies a failure of self-comprehension and cognitive self-management. But nothing in that particular delusion makes the speech act of self-denial intelligible. Does thought insertion show that self-attribution is ambiguous and that a distinction must be drawn between two forms of self-experience, namely of oneself as subject, of oneself as agent? Yes, it does. We have already seen (in Chapter 7) that experiencing oneself as agent and evaluating one's actions are central to our psychological capacity for self-responsibility. Experiencing oneself as a subject can dissociate from self-experience as an agent.

Daniel Dennett has introduced a popular way among philosophers of mind of referring to the self as a 'center of narrative gravity'. One of Dennett's many papers on the topic is "The Self as a Center of Narrative Gravity," which appears in B. Gertler and L. Shapiro (eds), *Arguing About the Mind* (Routledge, 2007). Eric Olson's "There is No Problem of the Self," which originally appeared in the *Journal of Consciousness Studies*, 1998, 5, pp. 645–57, also appears in Gertler and Shapiro. Olson is skeptical about a lot of self talk, though perhaps not all of it.

Colin McGinn's *The Mysterious Flame: Conscious Minds in a Material World* (Basic Books, 1999), in a chapter entitled "Secrets of the Self" (chapter 5), defends the proposition that knowing "that the self has the property of existence is not at all the same thing as knowing what *other* properties it has" (p. 164).

MPD (aka DID, dissociative identity disorder) is the focus of detailed philosophical analysis in Stephen Braude's *First Person Plural: Multiple Personality and the Philosophy of Mind* (Rowman & Littlefield, 1995, rev. edn). Owen Flanagan discusses narrative self-construction in recovery from MPD in "Multiple Identity, Character Transformation, and Self-Reclamation," which appears in G. Graham and G. L. Stephens (eds), *Philosophical Psychopathology* (MIT Press, 1994). A good introduction by Dennett to his anti-realist/fictionalist thesis that, strictly speaking, we don't exist (conducted partly through examination of

MPD) is "The Reality of Selves," which is chapter 13 in his *Consciousness Explained* (Little, Brown & Company, 1991). Skepticism about the role of autobiographical narrative in self-understanding is defended in Galen Strawson's "Against Narrative," reprinted in Gertler and Shapiro. A case for the desirability and virtual unavoidably of constructing narratives about ourselves as vehicles of self-comprehension is offered in Grant Gillett's *Subjectivity and Being Somebody: Human Identity and Neuroethics* (Imprint Academic, 2008).

For a consideration of the Cotard delusion through case studies, Andy Young and A. W. Leafhead have written a helpful paper entitled "Betwixt Life and Death: Case Studies in the Cotard Delusion," which appears in P. Halligan and J. Marshall (eds), *Method in Madness: Case Studies in Cognitive Neuropsychiatry* (Psychology Press, 1996).

The delusional-stance conception of delusion is outlined in G. L. Stephens and my "The Delusional Stance" and "Reconceiving Delusion." The first paper appears in M. Chung, K. Fulford and G. Graham (eds), *Reconceiving Schizophrenia* (Oxford University Press, 2007). The second first appeared in the *International Review of Psychiatry*, 2004, 16, pp. 236–41, and has been reprinted in the collection (cited above) of Gertler and Shapiro. In those papers the introduction of the delusional stance approach to delusion takes place in reaction to the received view that delusions are a species of belief.

Christopher Frith's now classic 1992 book on schizophrenia, entitled *The Cognitive Neuropsychology of Schizophrenia* (Erlbaum) is well worth a read. So, too, is his recent work on disorders of volition in schizophrenia, such as his "Interpersonal Factors in the Disorders of Volition Associated with Schizophrenia," which appears in N. Sebanz and W. Prinz (eds), *Disorders of Volition* (MIT Press, 2006), and reveals a new interest, on his part, in the *social* context of failures in agency attribution.

Epilogue

The final affliction –
Copenhagen interpretation

I was desperate enough to give old Kierkegaard another go.
                    Laurence 'Tubby' Passmore, in David Lodge's *Therapy*, p. 100

Reading Kierkegaard is like flying through a heavy cloud. Every now and again there's
a break and you get a brief, brilliantly lit view of the ground, and then you're back in
the swirling grey mist again, with not a ... clue where you are.
                    Laurence 'Tubby' Passmore, in David Lodge's *Therapy*, p. 109

There is a condition of *being a mental disorder*. GOD (grade obsessive disorder) is not
such a condition. Neither is blindness resulting from a lesion. Depending on their causes:
Delusional paranoia is. So, too, are addiction, panic disorder and major depression.

Being a mental disorder, as I here understand it, is a feature of the minds of persons,
of our reason-responsive and capacity-tethered Intentionality, or situated rationality, broadly
understood. It is harmful to possessors, not under voluntary control (it is an incapacity),
and carries (unlike strictly neurological disorders) both mental and neural autographs on its
causes.

Naturally, I anticipate criticisms of my theory of mental disorder. To mention two: One
is that the concept of rationality that it deploys is vague and marks no real difference
between mental disorders and 'mere' problems in living or mental disturbances. Another
is that vagueness smudges its distinction between neurological and mental disorders. The

distinction is imprecise and marks no true difference between disorders that are due to brain damage and those not due to brain damage.

I concede (and have readily acknowledged all along) that some of the theory's key distinctions are vague. Vagueness is such a perplexing topic. One thing that a critic might say about it, in the context of denying some of the theses of this book, is that there are perfectly sharp cut-off points between "being a mental disorder" and "not being a mental disorder" or between "being a neurological disorder" and "being a mental disorder," although no one knows, and no one will ever find out, precisely where such demarcation points lie. These distinctions are unknowably precise, rather than known to be imprecise. Vagueness is in the cataract-ridden lenses of the beholder, not in the distinctions themselves.

In the Gray and Murky World of Mental Disorder and human health and illness, however, *that* just stated position is not one to which anyone should be attracted. However much time we end up spending on the study of mental disorder, we will never escape, I am convinced, the recognition of imprecise cut-off points and the necessity of drawing lines or making distinctions that, in contestable zones or areas, are arbitrary. Whether, as a theoretical and alternative matter, such vagueness means that the distinctions in question fail to make for real or significant differences seems to me to be much less clear, of course. For vagueness to make for slippery borders is one thing; for it to eliminate differences between disorder/ non-disorder and neurological/mental disorder is another.

The reader will recall that the distinctions (as made in this book) are tied to exemplary or prototypical cases. What I have argued is that if we follow various non-capricious or exemplary contours of rational/irrational behavior, this sets limits on what counts as a mental disorder. Something similar is true of neural activity. Theories of disorder that invoke cells gone bad as the physical basis of a mental disorder need to find good evidence of bad cells that is independent of the presupposition that just because something is a mental disorder and physical means that it is a neural disorder.

I assume as a matter of method that in developing a theory of mental disorder, mixed with a philosophy of mind, we are not attempting to report or describe a well-entrenched, well-defined pre-existing concept of a mental disorder. There is no such concept. We are trying to enact rectitude in the concept. We are trying to build a theory that respects consensus among mental health professionals when or where it wisely occurs. But sometimes (when there is no consensus or when a particular form of consensus appears to be unwise) it may happen that the needs of theory must override the opinions of others. We need to construct a theory that will play positive roles in the science and clinical and humane treatment of a mental disorder.

One consequence of the theory offered in this book is that when it comes to deciding whether a condition is a mental disorder or requires clinical or professional attention, and especially in non-prototypical or non-exemplary cases, personal decisions made by subjects of the condition are an irreplaceable feature of concerns about mental illness. It is no more likely that there is a best way in which to address some mental disturbances or distresses (especially those at the borderlines) than there is a best horse, best child-to-parent ratio, or best manner of mounting a production of *Hamlet*. From the perspective of the theory of mental disorder offered in this book, it's to be expected that different decisions about classification, care and treatment may prove desirable for different people in the same general condition of disturbance or distress, given different personalities, levels of confidence, learning histories, and personal goals. This is not because mental disorder is a matter of acts of human classification or because saying so makes things so (which would breed anti-realism about disorder). It is because (as I note below) of certain general features of human nature and the human condition.

What features? I have used Augustine, Rawls, Dennett and others to help to make some of my earlier points. Here again I need assistance.

Some of the most penetrating and insightful passages in the history of philosophy appear, on multiple readings, to be difficult to grasp or understand. Notoriously, some are *really* hard to comprehend. A favorite passage of mine of the hard type sits a few paragraphs below. It's about self and sickness (spiritual sickness) and comes from the pen of the Danish philosopher Søren Kierkegaard's (1813–55) *The Sickness unto Death*. Before examining the passage, though, I wish to make a brief and cautionary terminological note.

The caution is about a word. Above I put the term 'spiritual' in parenthesis. In *Sickness* Kierkegaard aims to discuss a spiritual malaise for which he claims that there is one best solution. For him the solution is a form of Christian theism. Spirituality, however, does not need to be understood theistically or even supernaturally (see Flanagan 2007). It may be 'naturalized', so that spiritual questions such as "How ought I to live?," "What sort of activity should I pursue in this world to try to secure meaning and fulfillment?," and related others, are given thoroughly this-worldly and non-theistic answers. In what follows I do not plan to address the theistic aspirations behind Kierkegaard's thought. So, lest a word like 'spiritual' impress some readers as awkward given possible supernatural connotations, I will let terms like 'existential' or 'human' substitute in its stead. An existential malaise. A human malaise. Such is my rereading of Kierkegaard's intended topic.

So, what is the tough paragraph or passage to which I refer? It's about the self. It is this.

> A self is the last thing the world cares about and the most dangerous thing of all for a person to show signs of having. The greatest hazard of all, losing the self, can occur very quietly in the world, as if it were nothing at all. No other loss can occur so quietly; any other loss – an arm, a leg, five dollars, a wife, etc. – is sure to be noticed.
> (Kierkegaard 1980: 32–3; all references to 1980 will be to Kierkegaard's book)

Penetrating? Insightful? How so? What's the big idea in this short paragraph?

The toughness of the passage, I trust, is obvious. Suppose we assume, as I have said we should, that talk of selves just is talk of ourselves. Speaking of your self just is a way of referring to you. Speaking of my self just is a manner of speaking of me. If so, how is it that you are 'the most dangerous thing' for *you*, the person, to 'show signs of having'? You don't *have* you. You are you. Or how is it that losing oneself can 'occur so quietly', more so than losing, say, 'an arm, a leg, five dollars'? An arm? A leg? Some money? You surely can lose those things without disappearing from the face of existence. You cannot lose yourself, however, without utterly ceasing to exist. Nothing quiet in that. Self-loss is personal-existence loss, assuming that talk of your self just is talk of yourself. Is it so, for Kierkegaard?

Kierkegaard writes:

> A person cannot rid himself of the relation to himself any more than he can rid himself of his self, which, after all, is one and the same thing, since the self is the relation to oneself.
>
> (1980: 17)

Such a remark seems premised on the proposition that a person's self and the person themselves are one and the same thing. If so, then Kierkegaard's view is my view, namely that my self is none other than me. So, then, what is the meaning of Kierkegaard's puzzling remark about a self being the most dangerous thing to possess? Is Kierkegaard utterly incapable of lucidity?

Indeed no. He is eminently capable of lucidity: of brilliantly lit views of the ground, to use the phase of David Lodge's fictional character of Passmore. Here is another one of my favorites in *Sickness*:

> When someone faints, we call for water, eau de Cologne, smelling salts; but when someone wants to despair, then the word is: Get possibility; get possibility, possibility is the only salvation. A possibility – then the person in despair breathes again, he revives again, for without possibility a person seems unable to breathe.
>
> (1980: 38–9)

To be in despair is to lose hope: to lose one's sense of positive possibility. To be hopeful about something (in a manner that is incompatible with despairing) is to believe that something truly and deeply positive is possible. Not in the anemic sense of being merely or logically possible. But in the robust sense of empirically or actually possible. Good things may really come to pass – things may work out well and matters may improve. Things may look bleak, but may well have a positive issue. 'Get possibility.'

So, Kierkegaard certainly can be lucid, engagingly so. But how, then, interpret the meaning of the difficult passage?

Here is another one of his passages about self. In this he does try to define it, but note the swirling gray mist.

> But what is the self? The self is a relation that relates itself to itself or is the relation's relating to itself in the relation; the self is not the relation but is the relation's relating itself to itself. A human being is a synthesis of the infinite and the finite, of the temporal and the eternal, of freedom and necessity, in short a synthesis. A synthesis is a relation between two. Considered in this way, a human being is still not a self.
>
> (1980: 13)

We seem to have moved from a hard-to-understand paragraph (our very first above) to an immensely difficult-to-understand paragraph (the one just offered). This, it may seem, makes our interpretational chores worse.

Actually it does not. The passage makes things better. It makes one fact perfectly clear. This is that Kierkegaard is *not* using the word 'self' as I recommend we should. He is not using it for us as such. He is using it for something about us. What this something is and what it has to do with 'sickness' or our existential malaise is my next topic.

One popular view in the literature on selfhood is that the 'self' of a self-responsible or self-reflective and self-controlled agent is not the whole person, is not me per se, but somehow is a privileged aspect or dimension of me, namely those of my values, desires or aspirations that I endorse through reflective deliberation or perhaps, objectively speaking, *ought* to endorse if I am to understand my best interests or true good (see Wolf 1990). It is me kept intact and motivationally uncorrupted by bringing my behavior in line with my best interests or true good. Is this the reference of 'self' being deployed by Kierkegaard? In relating myself, to use his language, to my self am I relating to (reflecting on, endorsing) my best interests? My true good?

Quite clearly for him the answer is no. For consider this next special paragraph:

> Just as a physician might say that there very likely is not one single living human being who is completely healthy, so anyone who really knows mankind might say that there is not one single living human being who does not despair a little, who does not secretly harbor an unrest, an inner strife, a disharmony, an anxiety about an unknown something or a something he does not even dare to try to know, an anxiety about some possibility in existence or an anxiety about himself, so that, just as a physician speaks of going around with an illness in his body, he walks around with a sickness, carries around a sickness of the spirit that signals its presence at rare intervals in and through an anxiety he cannot explain.
>
> (1980: 22)

Kierkegaard above certainly is not speaking of an ideal self or core-values self. He is not speaking of a better judgment about our selves or of desires or preferences with which we ought to identify. He is speaking of acknowledging a discord, strife or instability within us, within ourselves as whole human beings navigating through the world. To cut to the chase, here is my hypothesis for the best interpretation of Kierkegaard's loss-of-self talk.

In speaking of self as the last thing to care about, the 'most dangerous' thing of all to possess, and whose loss may go quietly, Kierkegaard is identifying something about us that, he believes, we must recognize (although we may try to forget about it or to keep it quiet) if we are adequately to understand ourselves and responsibly to manage our lives. This is that as human beings we are sick or afflicted in spirit, sick with the "most dangerous kind of illness" (1980: 26). This is an illness in our person or psychological composition or make-up. It is in response to recognition of this unique affliction or malaise, which I plan to describe in a moment, that Kierkegaard is urging us to redirect our health-and-illness-centered attention. Rather than strive to perfect our mental and physical health, our minds and bodies, so that we aim to be free of disease and illness (which for him is quite impossible), and perhaps deceive ourselves into believing that we are not afflicted or existentially ill, we should invest more of our intellectual and emotional energies in attending to our sickness in 'self'. Our existential discord as persons. And what is that discord? Our sickness unto death?

Well, for one, its full nature and total significance or purport is "hidden ... so hidden in a man that he himself is not aware of it" (1980: 27). (This is part of why it can be lost without being consciously noticed.) For another, it stems from the fact that we are all, as persons, composed of divisive or discordant elements ('an inner strife') in our psychological make-up. In *Sickness* Kierkegaard refers to these discordant elements as a disharmony or tension between the finite and infinite, the temporal and eternal, and the necessary and free. As earlier mentioned, he has a religious motive to promote. Talk of infinitude, eternality and so on suits his religious assumptions. There is, for him, a touch of God in all of us. ("The self," he writes, "is healthy and free only when ... it rests transparently in God" [Kierkegaard 1980: 30].) But here I am interested in his more general and not specifically religious contention that our psychological make-up as persons is discordant, unstable or disharmonious. So, I prefer to speak of our being mixtures not of the infinite and finite, and so on, but of psychological stability and instability, the ordered and disordered – notions from the present book's very first chapter. "The coloring" of each element contains "the reflection of the ... opposite" (1980: 30). Our stability is what it is because of our instability and vice versa. The forces of the one penetrate the powers of the other. If, for example, I am generous in one circumstance but stingy in another, my generosity is what it is because, at times, it runs up against my stinginess. If I am courageous in the public positions that I take on matters political, but cowardly about publicly confronting people about their bizarre religious claims, my courage is not an all-encompassing character trait. It is situated within specific limits.

What is the upshot of the discord in us? Kierkegaard offers the following hypothesis. We are afflicted with an inescapable and complex existential malaise (a sickness unto death, a disorder of spirit): affordances squandered, trusts sabotaged, responsibilities unrecognized, relationships with other people undermined; propensities to guilt, shame and regret; cowardice and stinginess displayed; proclivities to anxiety, hopelessness, and selfishness and egoism; absences of compassion, forgiveness and love. We are 'sick'. We are 'unreasonable'. Being 'sick' (being unreasonable) our lives frequently come apart, sometimes utterly apart. We are unable to hold ourselves together in a rational or reason-responsive way and to recognize and pursue our best interests or true good.

Let us briefly consider a concrete example of the malaise, the sickness unto death, as it were, of which Kierkegaard writes. Sometimes we are trapped by limited abilities to imagine ways out of deeply unwelcome or undesired situations. We may be in an unhappy job or marriage. We may be beleaguered by a chronic bodily infirmity or disease. We may believe that we have hit on a way to escape through, say, flight to a new job, divorce or alternative drug therapy. But flight to a new job possesses holes in its wings and no engine. The prospect of divorce or experimental therapy fares no better. We may get temporarily lost in contemplating an imagined possibility only to realize that the mere thought of escape contributes to our forlornness and misery. I can't get a new job. I can't abandon my spouse. Drugs have never worked for my condition.

Now what? Seek distraction. Become resigned. End it all. Stuff one's belly with mash potatoes and ice cream. Have an affair. Pave the road of aspiration with new but still unrealistic imagined intentions. These alternatives, too, taste sour. Then, it may finally seem as if no alternative will do for a person. An individual may feel stuck, hopelessly stuck. A person may literally collapse in despair. Such is Kierkegaard's diagnosis and lament: the virtual inescapability of despair, of hopelessness about one's situation.

It's a bleak picture. But if I understand his view correctly, Kierkegaard does offer a response. What does a person need in such circumstances – really need? What one really needs, on Kierkegaard's account, is hope: hope in being able, as it were, to breathe again, psychologically. Not hope in the presence of a successful flight plan (new job, divorce, etc.). But hope in the positive possibility of something perhaps as yet unseen or unpredictable, something as yet not fully describable or concretely imaginable. That is the very attitude we need. Hope that *something* good (we know not precisely what) will happen. A hope or attitudinal optimism that is sufficient for a person to function again and that helps to give them the courage to withstand profoundly disappointing situations.

Kierkegaard notes: "Legends and fairy tales tell of the knight who ... finds himself separated from his companions and lost in the woods" (1980: 37). His hope and also courage, were he to possess it, may be all that he has left under such forbidding circumstances. The world otherwise is lost to him and he in it.

Something like a hope of last resort or breath of unarticulated but optimistic possibility is reported in John Stuart Mill's *Autobiography* (1969). Mill, as noted earlier, describes a form of personal unhappiness, a depression that he experienced as a young man, during which he seemed to have "nothing left to live for" (Mill 1969: 94). As a matter of biographical fact, Mill experienced several periods of "morbid despondency" throughout his life (as Stillinger notes in his editorial introduction to Mill 1969: xiii). Mill claimed in a letter that to such periods of despondency, "I have been indebted for ... the most valuable [insights] as I have into the most important matters" (quoted in Mill 1969: xiv).

Mill reports that, at first, while a young man he wished that his depression would lift, but it did not. "Advice," he said, "if I had known where to seek it, would have been most precious" (Mill 1969: 81–2). (Psychotherapy in any formal sense was as yet an undiscovered country in the early nineteenth century.) His depression persisted without outside assistance. Then, he tried to do something that one may not expect would work: to delve into his condition on his own, to notice whatever it might reveal to him about his self or situation. This took courage, no doubt, but the results, he says, astonished him. He discovered things that he had "previously disbelieved or disregarded." The discoveries became "cardinal points" in his "philosophical creed" (118, 101). Part of his depressed state, for instance, had consisted in believing that a person is a "helpless slave of ... circumstances" (119). Given, however, that he pulled himself out of his despondency, as it turned out by reading poetry, by enjoying nature, he believed that he had discovered a power to breathe again. He had discovered a capacity, albeit limited or contextualized, to rebuild himself in a hopeful manner. So, ironically, the depression served the unintended outcome of revealing a power or capacity whose assumed absence appeared to induce it. Arguably, Mill thereupon gained a deeper appreciation of his feelings and their sources "than palliation though medication can provide" (Horwitz and Wakefield 2007: 190).

One astute interpreter of Kierkegaard makes the following point:

> It is not important to be healthy and sound at all costs, because sickliness contains the possibility of knowledge ... a possibility from which the healthy and conflict-free person is cut off.
>
> (Nordentoft 1978: 300)

A similar observation is made by William James: "Few of us are not in some way infirm ... and our very infirmities [may] help us unexpectedly" (James 2002: 28). A person can owe a debt to an illness. This is a debt for insight or the felt necessity of personal self-transformation. Suffering a condition or infirmity or mental illness can lead to a person's "having kinds of understanding and knowledge that one would not otherwise have" (Wilkinson 2000: 295).

This does not mean that a case of mental illness actually is a good thing or desirable. It should not lead us to abandon the view that mental disorder is a disorder. It is harmful. It's just that an illness may induce or enhance one's recognition or appreciation of valuable things.

Also to be noted: Different persons and different cases demand different responses. It would be simplistic and dangerous to expect depressions more severe or disabling than Mill's to respond to his salamander-like self-reclamation. Depression can be anything from a serious impediment to a young philosopher's enthusiasm to a cause of tragic suicidal death. Wordsworth's poetry or walks in the woods are no substitute in extreme (prototypical) cases for seeking professional medical help. The aspiration for self-reclamation is commendable only when a person is sufficiently reason-responsive to learn from experience how to self-improve.

Clinical psychologist Kay Redfield Jamison was a senior in high school when she had her first attack of manic-depressive illness. It was not until she was on the faculty of the University of California, Los Angeles, that she recognized that she needed medical help. She writes:

> The debt I owe my psychiatrist is beyond description. I remember sitting in his office a hundred times during those grim months and each time thinking, What on earth can he say that will make me feel better or keep me alive? Well, there never was anything he could say, that's the funny thing. It was all the stupid, desperately optimistic, condescending things he *didn't* say that kept me alive; all the compassion and warmth I felt from him that could not have been said; all the intelligence, competence, and time he put into it; and his granite belief that mine was a life worth living.
>
> (Jamison, in Sattler et al. 1998: 79)

Indeed, the experience of regeneration and reclamation, autonomous (as in the case of Mill) or assisted (as in the situation of Jamison) has produced an abundance of personal narratives about descent into and release out of, or recovery from, mental disorder. Some of the best-selling books have been on depression, such as William Styron's *Darkness Visible* (1990), Elizabeth Wurtzel's *Prozac Nation* (1994), Jamison's *An Unquiet Mind* (1995) (just quoted), and Andrew Sullivan's *The Noonday Demon* (2001). No disorder, whether prototypical or non-prototypical, seems to be without its autobiographical records. MPD has "Quiet Storm." Alcohol addiction has Caroline Knapp. Schizophrenia is represented by Carol North. The literature is vast (for short representative samples see Sattler et al. 1998).

To my knowledge no one has truly surveyed or systematically canvassed the memoir or narrative recollection or reconstruction literature to learn how subjects of a disorder tend to understand or explain what has happened to them, how they managed (or didn't), and what may have helped them to recover (when they did). But one fact is clear on the basis of representatives of the literature with which I am familiar. Narrative rehearsal often is an effective and powerful way of integrating the episodes of a disorder into patterns of a newly reclaimed life, drawing lessons from the experience of disorder, and showing how the experience may contribute not just to an understanding of one's past but, most importantly, to leading a purposeful life and achieving a new-found measure of fulfillment or satisfaction. Hope for the future, the memoirs reveal, has transformative effects. As Jamison says: "Most difficult to put into words ... that I could make it" (Jamison 1998: 79). One can make it even if, at times, one cannot imagine exactly how or even just what making it may mean.

Onsets or episodes of a disorder often appear like storms or waves that rise up out of the sea and dissemble a life. Post-episode a tempest may reverberate in the sorrow one feels that a disorder struck or in emotional ambivalence about how best to put oneself back together again. If, as a victim, a person is sensitive to the actual and potential ambiguities of disorder, she may be less than firm or decisive in her interpretation of how to regain her life. A person may be drawn to contrary renderings and appraisals. Imagine: You did not know that you may seriously value religion until you became a victim of religious delusions. You are a person (you thought) who had ably managed stress and disappointment without believing in a personal God to whom to pray. Should you now believe (post-delusionally) in such a God? With a little imagination you can appreciate that you may have been suppressing religious impulses. Yield to them more wisely now? Or suppose: Your spouse had been urging you not to drink; in self-deception you overestimated your capacity to safely consume alcohol. You slid down a slippery slope. Your heavy drinking dissolved your marriage and desiccated your economic circumstances. You don't have the foggiest idea how now to put things back together again. But you do know that guilt should be avoided and that shame would foster a self-pity that will deform your efforts to reconnect with your spouse and children. You have a tough road ahead but with steely resolve you hope to make it. Hope.

What sort of road should it be? A road wherein you seek or perhaps continue to seek medical assistance? Or a path along which salamander-like you try to grow back your own mental limbs? Seeking help is not a weakness and it may be utterly necessary. But there are borderline or non-prototypical cases. You don't want your tolerance for painful or negative emotions to decline. You wish to be faithful to yourself: to be authentic, to be self-responsible. To be reasonable. But you also need to acknowledge your distress and it may be too much to leave its management totally and completely in your own hands.

A person may wish for a simple way to tame a decision about seeking help, to make it algorithmic in its basis. "No need for a therapist in Case Type A." "No role for medication in Case Type B." "This is a situation of an A/B kind, and so it's the sort that I should address all by myself." But if Kierkegaard is right the human condition just is not like that. Little is firm and decisive. Lives are riskily led. There is no unambiguous divide separating or demar-cating when we need others from when we don't, when we underestimate ourselves from when we overestimate, when we are autonomously able to achieve a goal from when we are not. Instability is inseparable from stability. Discord is in our concord.

Just as there is no hard-and-fast rule for when a disturbance is a disorder, so there is no precise criterion for when a person is ill enough to seek medical help. There are borderline cases. Zones of contestability. Prototypes blend or bleed into foils. It is here, too, at clini-cally fuzzy and imprecise borders, that in order to lead or direct a life various aspects of personhood that we cherish or towards which we aspire may perhaps wisely prevent an individual from relying on Zoloft, Valium, Prozac or Paxil. A person may reasonably refrain from 'medicalizing' themselves (from seeking medical help) in such borderline circum-stances even if no criterion of mental disorder precludes taking a medically assisted route. But a person may also reasonably choose a path of medicalization. Medication may work. The reason-responsiveness of mind and the enabling mechanisms of brain may be directed into a less deleterious or distressing state with a right prescription.

I use the expression 'final affliction' to help to title this epilogue. Kierkegaard's sickness unto death is not a mental disorder *per se*, perhaps some ultimately resistant one. It's a different and more general type of disturbance. It is a malaise or affliction, as noted, of human nature, the human condition or the human spirit. It is also Copenhagen without a pharmacist. Human decision-making without a medical authority or ready cure. A story with indeterminate dimensions whose character depends on the editorial decisions one makes. Certain ways of composing the story may result in an unhappy outcome; certain others may not. For each of us also the details of the affliction vary. The mix of stability and instability, of the reasonable and unreasonable, is uniquely personal. For some the malaise contains an imprudent proclivity to depression, for others anxiety, for still others being obsessive, and so on. It's the Personal Place where we as persons have to decide whether to seek assistance or not. No one else can make that decision for us. Reason may line up on either side.

Weighing the benefits of possible self-reconstruction against the risks or costs may depend, in part, on a matter mentioned in the chapter on addiction. Distant future mental health may be discounted just because it is temporally distant and we may pick a path towards it that appears, mistakenly perhaps, to require the least personal effort. We may be impatient to secure a present benefit through, we think, drugs or a quick dose of therapy, and this may overwhelm whatever benefit we may otherwise anticipate for ourselves if we make the Millian effort to help our selves autonomously. Impatience may often need to be checked, as difficult as this may be in a case of, say, acute anxiety or profound grief. The benefit of being mentally healthy may not have the same value, reliability or resilience for a person no matter how it is achieved. To secure the benefit as a result of an effort at self-reconstruction may make two improvements in a person's life. One is in personal health itself. The other is in the sense of personal achievement at having secured well-being on one's own and therein exercising the basic psychological capacities of self-responsibility, self-comprehension, enduring commitment and so on. To determine the wisdom of seeking help, therefore, a person must answer or decide on personal values questions about themselves. In the elimination of a disturbance or distress should a person risk a process that perhaps strips them of, or at least diminishes, the sense of personal achievement – Paxil or Zoloft? Or should they assume unalloyed responsibility for themselves? Or somehow mix forms of reliance on others with forms of self-reliance and autonomy. The future is one thing; how we try to get there is another.

The zones of vagueness or imprecision in the theory of mental disorder that is offered in this book are in fact, such is my claim now, ultimately tied to the 'sickness' or affliction of which Kierkegaard speaks. No theory of mental disorder that is sound and sensible can eliminate personal decisions that need to be made if we are to manage borderline cases of disorder (or even, on occasion, some questions about exemplary disorder). This result may not be what some critics of our psychiatric culture seek, but it is a useful and, I believe, inescapable result nonetheless. There are ways in which our mental lives are indeterminate between health and illness, reasonableness and truncated reason, the brain serving mental health or undermining it, wise treatment and unwise clinical attention.

The quotes I offered at the top of this section are taken from David Lodge's *Therapy: A Novel* (1995). Lodge's is a satirical book about a person, Laurence 'Tubby' Passmore, who follows the very route that Kierkegaard says that self-responsible individuals should not follow. Tubby seeks counselors or therapeutic help for just about every dilemma or distress he faces. Passmore is also caught up in a rapt and ironic infatuation. He is an unadulterated admirer of Kierkegaard. He commits to reading the Copenhagen philosopher for personal advice and direction, as he tries to navigate his way through life. This is not Kierkegaard's way, of course. For Kierkegaard searching for an authority about how to lead a life represents a form of self-responsibility avoidance or denial. It constitutes a failure to come to terms with responsibility for self. Passmore's self-comprehension, however, is so utterly caught up in a Kierkegaardian fantasy that he hopes that just by visiting Copenhagen he may become a better, happier or healthier person.

So he visits. On arrival a traveling companion mentions early evidence of Passmore's likely disappointment in the pilgrimage: nothing ultimately worth journeying for.

> Have you ever been to Copenhagen? Neither had I till this weekend. It's very nice, but just a little dull. ... Tubby had never been there before either. He wanted to get the feel of the place.
>
> (Lodge 1995: 183–4)

The feel of the place? If I am right, there is no place in which a person should feel truly safe from internal discord or instability. We carry a mixed and discordant bag of attributes. Proneness to mental disorder may be the most troubling mark of this mixture. But it is a proneness whose power may be blunted and after whose harmful decrements of mental integrity we persons, in one way or another, may acquire fresh mental limbs. In some cases with or only with the help and compassion of other people, whereas in other cases by ourselves alone. The task either way is not even close to being 'dull'. Nothing about it may be 'nice'. But the fruits of reconstruction may richly reward the labor.

Bibliography

Abramson, L. Y., Metalsky, G. I. and Alloy, L. B. (1989). Hopelessness depression: a theory-based subtype of depression. *Psychological Review* 96, 358–72.

Abramson, L. Y., Seligman, M. E. P. and Teasdale, J. D. (1978). Learned helplessness in humans: critique and reformulation. *Journal of Abnormal Psychology* 78, 40–74.

Adams, R. M. (1999). *Finite and Infinite Goods: A Framework for Ethics*. Oxford: Oxford University Press.

Adler, J. (2007). Faith and fanaticism. In L. Antony (ed.), *Philosophers without Gods: Meditations on Atheism and the Secular Life*. Oxford: Oxford University Press.

Ainslie, G. (2001). *Breakdown of Will*. Cambridge: Cambridge University Press.

Alloy, L. and Abramson, L. (1979). Judgment of contingency in depressed and nondepressed students: sadder but wiser? *Journal of Experimental Psychology: General* 108: 441–85.

Alloy, L. and Abramson, L. (1988). Depressive realism: four theoretical perspectives. In L. Alloy (ed.), *Cognitive Processes in Depression*. New York: Guilford Press.

Andreasen, N. C. (1984). *The Broken Brain: The Biological Revolution in Psychiatry*. New York: Harper & Row.

Andreasen, N. C. (2001). *Brave New Brain: Conquering Mental Illness in the Era of the Genome*. Oxford: Oxford University Press.

APA (American Psychiatric Association) (1952). *Diagnostic and Statistical Manual of Mental Disorders*, 1st edn. Washington, DC: APA.

APA (American Psychiatric Association) (1968). *Diagnostic and Statistical Manual of Mental Disorders*, 2nd edn. Washington, DC: APA.

APA (American Psychiatric Association) (1980). *Diagnostic and Statistical Manual of Mental Disorders*, 3rd edn. Washington, DC: APA.

APA (American Psychiatric Association) (1987). *Diagnostic and Statistical Manual of Mental Disorders*, 3rd edn rev. Washington, DC: APA.

APA (American Psychiatric Association) (1994). *Diagnostic and Statistical Manual of Mental Disorders*, 4th edn. Washington, DC: APA.

APA (American Psychiatric Association) (2000). *Diagnostic and Statistical Manual of Mental Disorders*, 4th edn, text rev. Washington, DC: APA.

Applebaum, P. (2004). Foreword to J. Radden (ed.), *The Philosophy of Psychiatry: A Companion*. Oxford: Oxford University Press.

Arpaly, N. (2005). How it is not "just like diabetes": mental disorders and the moral psychologist. *Philosophical Issues* 15, 282–98.

Augustine (1992). *Confessions*, trans. H. Chadwick. Oxford: Oxford University Press.

Baier, A. (1989). Trusting ex-intimates. In G. Graham and H. LaFollette (eds), *Person to Person*. Philadelphia: Temple University Press.

Baker, L. R. (1997). Persons in metaphysical perspective. In L. Hahn (ed.), *The Philosophy of Roderick Chisholm*. Chicago, IL: Open Court.

Baker, L. R. (2000). *Persons and Bodies: A Constitution View*. Cambridge: Cambridge University Press.

Barber, C. (2008). *Comfortably Numb: How Psychiatry is Medicating a Nation*. New York: Pantheon.

Barlow, D. H. (1988). *Anxiety and Its Disorders*. New York: Guilford.

Barlow, D. H., Chorpita, B. and Turovsky, J. (1996). Fear, panic, anxiety and disorders of emotion. In D. Hope (ed.), *Perspectives on Anxiety, Panic and Fear*, vol. 43. Nebraska Symposium on Motivation. Lincoln, NE: University of Nebraska Press.

Battin, M. (1982). *Ethical Issues in Suicide*. Englewood Cliffs, NJ: Prentice-Hall.

Bauer, R. (1984). Automatic recognition of names and faces: a neuropsychological application of the Guilty Knowledge Test. *Neuropsychologica* 22, 457–69.

Bayne, T. and Levy, N. (2005). Amputees by choice: body integrity identity disorder and the ethics of amputation. *Journal of Applied Philosophy* 22, 75–86.

Bayne, T. and Levy, N. (2006). The feeling of doing: deconstructing the phenomenology of agency. In N. Sebanz and W. Prinz (eds), *Disorders of Volition*. Cambridge, MA: MIT Press.

Bayne, R. and Pacherie, E. (2004). Bottom-up or top-down? Campbell's rationalist account of monothematic delusions. *Philosophy, Psychiatry, and Psychology* 11, 1–11.

Beam, A. (2001). *Gracefully Insane: The Rise and Fall of America's Premier Mental Hospital*. New York: PublicAffairs.

Bear, M., Connors, B. and Paradiso, M. (2007). *Neuroscience: Exploring the Brain*, 3rd edn. Philadelphia: Lippincott Williams & Wilkins.

Bechtel, W. (2008). *Mental Mechanisms: Philosophical Perspectives on Cognitive Science*. New York: Routledge.

Bechtel, W. and Graham, G. (eds) (1998). *A Companion to Cognitive Science*. Malden, MA: Blackwell.

Becker, G. and Murphy, K. (1988). A theory of rational addiction. *Journal of Political Economy* 96, 675–700.

Bell, A., Halligan, P. and Ellis, H. (2006). Explaining delusions: a cognitive perspective. *Trends in Cognitive Sciences* 10, 219–26.

Bentall, R. (2004). *Madness Explained: Psychosis and Human Nature*. London: Penguin.

Bentall, R. (2007). Clinical pathologies and unusual experiences. In M. Velmans and S. Schneider (eds), *The Blackwell Companion to Consciousness*. Malden, MA: Blackwell.

Berridge, K. (2004). Motivation concepts in behavioral neuroscience. *Physiology and Behaviour* 81, 179–209.

Berridge, K. and Robinson, T. (1995). The mind of the addicted brain: neural sensitization of wanting versus liking. *Current Directions in Psychological Science* 4, 71–6.

Berrios, G. E. and Luque, R. (1995). Cotard's syndrome: analysis of 100 cases. *Acta Psychiatrica Scandinavica* 91, 185–8.

Blasfield, R. (1996). Predicting DSM-V. *Journal of Nervous and Mental Disease* 184, 4–7.

Bolton, D. (2001). Problems in the definition of "mental disorder." *Philosophical Quarterly* 51, 182–99.

Boorse, C. (1975). On the distinction between health and illness. *Philosophy & Public Affairs* 5, 49–68.

Bortolotti, L. (2004). Can we interpret irrational behavior? *Behavior and Philosophy* 32, 359–75.

Bovet, P. and Parnas, J. (1993). Schizophrenic delusions: a phenomenological approach. *Schizophrenia Bulletin* 19, 579–97.

Bracken, P. and Thomas, P. (2005). *Postpsychiatry: Mental Health in a Postmodern World*. Oxford: Oxford University Press.

Braude, S. (1991). *First Person Plural: Multiple Personality and the Philosophy of Mind*. London: Routledge.

Brentano, F. (1995 [1874]). *Psychology from an Empirical Standpoint*, trans. A. Rancurello, D. Terrell and L. McAlister. London: Routledge.

Breuer, J. and Freud, S. (2000). *Studies in Hysteria*, trans. and ed. J. Strachey. New York: Basic Books.

Brooks, V. (1986). *The Neural Basis of Motor Control*. New York: Oxford University Press.

Broome, M., Woolley, J., Tabraham, P., Johns, L., Bramon, E., Murray, G., Pariante, C., McGuire, P. and Murray, R. (2005). What causes the onset of psychosis? *Schizophrenia Research* 79, 23–34.

Brülde, B. and Radovic, C. (2006). What is mental about mental disorder? *Philosophy, Psychiatry, and Psychology* 13, 99–116.

Brumberg, J. J. (1988). *Fasting Girls: The History of Anorexia Nervosa*. Cambridge, MA: Harvard University Press.

Cahill, C. and Frith, C. (1996). False perceptions or false beliefs: hallucinations and delusions in schizophrenia. In P. Halligan and J. Marshall (eds), *Method in Madness: Case Studies in Cognitive Neuropsychiatry*. Hove, East Sussex, UK: Psychology Press.

Campbell, J. (1999). Schizophrenia, the space of reasons and thinking as a motor process. *Monist* 82, 609–25.

Campbell, P. (1996). Challenging loss of power. In J. Read and J. Reynolds (eds), *Speaking Our Minds: An Anthology*. London: Macmillan.

Caplan, P. (1995). *They Say You're Crazy: How the World's Most Powerful Psychiatrists Decide Who's Normal*. New York: Addison-Wesley.

Charney, D. S., Nestler, E. J. and Bunney, B. S. (eds) (1999). *Neurobiology of Mental Illness*. New York: Oxford University Press.

Chung, M., Fulford, K.W.M. and Graham, G. (eds) (2007). *Reconceiving Schizophrenia*. Oxford: Oxford University Press.

Church, J. (2003). Depression, depth, and the imagination. In J. Phillips and J. Morley (eds), *Imagination and Its Pathologies*. Cambridge, MA: MIT Press.

Colombo, A. (2008). Models of mental disorder: how philosophy and the social sciences can illuminate psychiatric ethics. In G. Widdershoven, J. McMillan, T. Hope and L. van der Scheer (eds), *Empirical Ethics in Psychiatry*. Oxford: Oxford University Press.

Confer, W. N. and Ables, B. S. (1983). *Multiple Personality: Etiology, Diagnosis, and Treatment*. New York: Human Sciences Press.

Cooper, J. and Oates, M. (2000). Principles of clinical assessment in general psychiatry. In M. Gelder, J. J. Lopez-Ibor and N. Andreasen (eds), *New Oxford Textbook of Psychiatry*, vol. 1. Oxford: Oxford University Press.

Costin, C. (1998). Your dieting daughter. In D. Sattler, V. Shabatay and G. Kramer (eds), *Abnormal Psychology in Context: Voices and Perspectives*. Boston: Houghton Mifflin.

Cotard, J. (1882). Du délire des negations. *Archives de Neurologie* 4, 152–70.

Crowley, C. and Lodge, H. (2004). *Younger Next Year*. New York: Workman.

Currie, G. (2000). Imagination, delusion, and hallucinations. In M. Coltheart and M. Davies (eds), *Pathologies of Belief*. Oxford: Basil Blackwell.

Davidson, D. (2004). Representation and interpretation. In D. Davidson (ed.), *Problems of Rationality*. Oxford: Oxford University Press.

Davis, S. (2002). Was Jesus mad, bad, or God? In S. Davis, D. Kendall and G. O'Collins (eds), *The Incarnation*. New York: Oxford University Press.

DeBaggio, T. (2003). *Losing My Mind: An Intimate Look at Life with Alzheimer's*. New York: Free Press.

Dennett, D. C. (1969). *Content and Consciousness*. London, Routledge & Kegan Paul.

Dennett, D. C. (1978). Intentional systems. In *Brainstorms: Philosophical Essays on Mind and Mentality*. Cambridge, MA: MIT Press.

Dennett, D. C. (1984). *Elbow Room: The Varieties of Free Will Worth Wanting*. Cambridge, MA: MIT Press.

Dennett, D. C. (1987). *The Intentional Stance*. Cambridge, MA: MIT Press.

Dennett, D. C. (1991). *Consciousness Explained*. Boston: Little, Brown & Co.

Dennett, D. C. (2009). Intentional systems theory. In B. McLaughlin, A. Beckermann and S. Walter (eds), *The Oxford Handbook of Philosophy of Mind*. Oxford: Oxford University Press.

Dennett, D. C. and Humphrey, N. (1989). Speaking for ourselves: an assessment of multiple personality disorder. *Raritan* 9, 68–9.

Descartes, R. (1984). *The Philosophical Writings of Descartes*, vol. 1, trans. J. Cottingham, R. Stoothoff and D. Murdock. Cambridge: Cambridge University Press.

Dretske, F. (1988). *Explaining Behavior: Reasons in a World of Causes*. Cambridge, MA: MIT Press.

Edwards, D. and Kravitz, E. (1997). Serotonin, social status and aggression. *Current Opinion in Neurobiology* 7, 811–19.

Ehrman, B. (1999). *Jesus: Apocalyptic Prophet of the New Millennium*. Oxford: Oxford University Press.

Eisenberg, L. (2000). Psychiatry as a worldwide public health problem. In M. Gelder, J. J. Lopez-Ibor and N. Andraesen (eds), *New Oxford Textbook of Psychiatry*, vol. 1. Oxford: Oxford University Press.

Elliott, C. (2002). Who holds the leash? *American Journal of Bioethics* 2, 48.

Elliott, C. (2003). *Better Than Well: American Medicine Meets the American Dream*. New York: Norton.

Elliott, C. (2004). Mental health and its limits. In J. Radden (ed.), *The Philosophy of Psychiatry: A Companion*. New York: Oxford University Press.

Ellis, H. D. and Young, A. W. (1990). Accounting for delusional misidentifications. *British Journal of Psychiatry* 157, 239–48.

Emmons, R. A. (1999). *The Psychology of Ultimate Concerns: Motivation and Spirituality in Personality*. New York: Guilford Press.

Enoch, M. D. and Trethowan, W. H. (1991). *Uncommon Psychiatric Syndromes*, 3rd edn. Oxford: Butterworth-Heinemann.

Erikson, E. (1968). *Identity, Youth, and Crisis*. New York: Norton.

ESEMeD/MHEDEA 2000 Investigators (European Study of the Epidemiology of Mental Disorders) (2004). Prevalence of mental disorders in Europe: results from the European study of the epidemiology of mental disorders. *Acta Psychiatrica Scandinavica* (suppl.) 420, 21–7.

Esiri, M. and Nagy, Z. (2002). Neuropathology. In R. Jacoby and C. Oppenheimer (eds), *Psychiatry in the Elderly*, 3rd edn. Oxford: Oxford University Press.

Farah, M. (2008). Neuroethics and the problem of other minds: implications of neuroscience for the moral status of brain-damaged patients and nonhuman animals. *Neuroethics* 1, 9–18.

Feinberg, J. (1970). What is so special about mental illness?. In *Doing and Deserving: Essays in the Theory of Responsibility* (pp. 272–92). Princeton, NJ: Princeton University Press.

Feinberg, J. (1989). *Harm to Self*. New York: Oxford University Press.

Fingarette, H. (1988). *Heavy Drinking: The Myth of Alcoholism as a Disease*. Berkeley: University of California Press.

First, M. B. (2005). Desire for amputation of a limb: paraphilia, psychosis, or a new type of identity disorder. *Psychological Medicine* 35, 919–28.

Flanagan, O. (2007). *The Really Hard Problem: Meaning in a Material World*. Cambridge, MA: MIT Press.

Flynn, J. (1998). Cocaine: Helen's story. In D. Sattler, V. Shabatay and G. Kramer (eds), *Abnormal Psychology in Context: Voices and Perspectives*. Boston: Houghton Mifflin.

Foucault, M. (1977). *Discipline and Punish*, trans. A. Sheridan. London: Allen Lane.

Frances, A. and First, M. (1998). *Your Mental Health: A Layman's Guide to the Psychiatrist's Bible*. New York: Scribner.

Frankfurt, H. (1988). *The Importance of What We Care About: Philosophical Essays*. Cambridge: Cambridge University Press.

Frankfurt, H. (2004). *The Reasons of Love*. Princeton: Princeton University Press.

Freud, S. (1958 [1900]). *The Interpretation of Dreams*. In *Standard Edition of the Complete Works of Sigmund Freud*, ed. James Strachey, vols. 4 and 5. London: Hogarth Press.

Freud, S. (1963 [1905]). *Dora: An Analysis of a Case of Hysteria*. New York: Collier.

Freud, S. (1986 [1924]). Neurosis and psychosis. Trans. J. Strachey. In A. Freud (ed.), *The Essentials of Psychoanalysis: The Definitive Collection of Sigmund Freud's Writing*. London: Penguin.

Freud, S. (1989 [1930]). *Civilization and Its Discontents*, trans. and ed. J. Strachey, intro. Peter Gay. New York: Basic Books.

Freud, S. (2000 [1917]). Mourning and melancholy. In J. Radden (ed.), *The Nature of Melancholy: From Aristotle to Kristeva*. Oxford: Oxford University Press.

Frith, C. D. (1992). *The Cognitive Neuropsychology of Schizophrenia*. Hillsdale, NJ: Erlbaum.

Frith, C. D. (1998). Deficits and pathologies. In W. Bechtel and G. Graham (eds), *A Companion to Cognitive Science*. Malden, MA: Blackwell.

Frith, C. D. and Johnstone, E. (2003). *Schizophrenia: A Very Short Introduction*. Oxford: Oxford University Press.

Frith, C. D. and Rees, G. (2007). A brief history of the scientific approach to the study of consciousness. In M. Velmans and S. Schneider (eds), *The Blackwell Companion to Consciousness*. Malden, MA: Blackwell.

Fulford, K. W. M. (1989). *Moral Theory and Medical Practice*. Cambridge: Cambridge University Press.

Fulford, K. W. M. (1993). Thought insertion and insight: disease and illness paradigms of psychotic disorder. In M. Spitzer, F. Uehlin, M. Schwartz and C. Mundt (eds), *Phenomenology, Language, and Schizophrenia*. New York: Springer-Verlag.

Fulford, K. W. M. (1994). Value, illness, and failure of action: framework for a philosophical psychopathology of delusions. In G. Graham and G. L. Stephens (eds), *Philosophical Psychopathology*. Cambridge, MA: MIT Press.

Fulford, K. W. M., Thornton, T. and Graham, G. (2006). *Oxford Textbook of Philosophy and Psychiatry*. Oxford: Oxford University Press.

Gallagher, S. (2000). Self-reference and schizophrenia: a cognitive model of immunity to error through misidentification. In D. Zahavi (ed.), *Exploring the Self*. Amsterdam: John Benjamins.

Gallagher, S. (2009). Delusional realities. In M. Broome and L. Bortolotti (eds), *Psychiatry as Cognitive Neuroscience: Philosophical Perspectives*. Oxford: Oxford University Press.

Garner, A. and Hardcastle, V. (2004). Neurobiological models: an unnecessary divide – neural models in psychiatry. In J. Radden (ed.), *The Philosophy of Psychiatry: A Companion*. Oxford: Oxford University Press.

Garrett, R. (1989). Love's way. In G. Graham and H. LaFollette (eds), *Person to Person*. Philadelphia: Temple University Press.

Garrett, R. (1994). The problem of despair. In G. Graham and G. L. Stephens (eds), *Philosophical Psychopathology*. Cambridge, MA: MIT Press.

Gerrans, P. (2000). Refining the explanation of the Cotard delusion. In M. Coltheart and M. Davies (eds), *Pathologies of Belief*. Oxford: Blackwell.

Gerrans, P. (2002). A one-stage explanation of the Cotard delusion. *Philosophy, Psychiatry, and Psychology* 9, 47–53.

Gert, B. and Culver, C. (2004). Defining mental disorder. In J. Radden (ed.), *The Philosophy of Psychiatry: A Companion*. New York: Oxford University Press.

Gillett, G. (1991). Multiple personality and irrationality. *Philosophical Psychology* 4, 103–18.

Gillett, G. (2008). *Subjectivity and Being Somebody: Human Identity and Neuroethics*. Exeter, UK: Imprint Academic.

Glannon, W. (2007). *Bioethics and the Brain*. Oxford: Oxford University Press.

Glass, A. and Holyoak, K. (1986). *Cognition*. New York: Random House.

Glasser, W. (2003). *Warning: Psychiatry Can Be Hazardous to Your Health*. New York: HarperCollins.

Glover, J. (2003). Towards humanism in psychiatry. Tanner Lectures on Human Values, Princeton University, 12–14 February.

Goffman, E. (1961). *Asylums: Essays on the Social Situation of Mental Patients and Other Inmates*. New York: Doubleday.

Goffman, E. (1963). *Stigma: Notes on the Management of Spoiled Identity*. New York: Simon & Schuster.

Gold, P. and Charney, D. (2002). Diseases of the mind and brain: depression, a disease of the mind, brain, and body. *American Journal of Psychiatry* 159, 1826.

Goldman, A. (1970). *A Theory of Action*. Princeton, NJ: Princeton University Press.

Goldman, A. (2006). *Simulating Minds: The Philosophy, Psychology, and Neuroscience of Mindreading*. Oxford: Oxford University Press.

Goodman, N. (1968). *The Languages of Art: An Approach to a Theory of Symbols*. Indianapolis, IN: Hackett.

Goodwin, D. and Guze, S. (1996). *Psychiatric Diagnosis*, 5th edn. New York: Oxford University Press.

Gorenstein, E. (1992). *The Science of Mental Illness*. San Diego: Academic Press.

Graham, G. (1986). Russell's deceptive desires. In L. Stevenson, R. Squires and J. Haldane (eds), *Mind, Causation, and Action*. Oxford: Blackwell.

Graham, G. (1990). Melancholic epistemology. *Synthese* 82, 309–28.

Graham, G. (1996). Review of Hacking *Rewriting the Soul*. *Ethics* 106, 845–8.

Graham, G. (1998). *Philosophy of Mind: An Introduction*, 2nd edn. Malden, MA: Blackwell.

Graham, G. (1999). Fuzzy fault lines: selves in multiple personality disorder. *Philosophical Explorations* 3, 159–74.

Graham, G. (2002). Recent work in philosophical psychopathology. *American Philosophical Quarterly* 39, 109–34.

Graham, G. (2004). Self-ascription: thought insertion. In J. Radden (ed.), *The Philosophy of Psychiatry: A Companion*. Oxford: Oxford University Press.

Graham, G. and Horgan, T. (2002). Sensations and grain processes. In J. Fetzer (ed.), *Evolving Consciousness*. Amsterdam: John Benjamins.

Graham, G. and Horgan, T. (2008). Qualia realism: its phenomenal contents and discontents. In E. Wright (ed.), *The Case for Qualia*. Cambridge, MA: MIT Press.

Graham, G. and Stephens, G. L. (1994). Mind and mine. In G. Graham and G. L. Stephens (eds), *Philosophical Psychopathology*. Cambridge, MA: MIT Press.

Graham, G. and Stephens, G. L. (2007). Psychopathology: minding mental illness. In P. Thagard (ed.), *Philosophy of Psychology and Cognitive Science*. Amsterdam: Elsevier.

Graham, G., Horgan, T. and Tienson, J. (2007). Consciousness and intentionality. In M. Velmans and S. Schneider (eds), *The Blackwell Companion to Consciousness*. Malden, MA: Blackwell.

Graham, G., Horgan, T. and Tienson, J. (2009). Phenomenology, intentionality, and the unity of mind. In B. McLaughlin, A. Beckermann and S. Walter (eds), *The Oxford Handbook of the Philosophy of Mind*. Oxford: Oxford University Press.

Gross, G. and Rubin, I. (2002). Clinical theory. In E. Erwin (ed.), *The Freud Encyclopedia: Theory, Therapy and Culture*. New York: Routledge.

Grunbaum, A. (1984). *The Foundations of Psychoanalysis*. Berkeley, CA: University of California Press.

Guze, S. B. (1992). *Why Psychiatry is a Branch of Medicine*. New York: Oxford University Press.

Hacking, I. (1995). *Rewriting the Soul: Multiple Personality and the Science of Memory*. Cambridge, MA: Harvard University Press.

Hacking, I. (1998). *Mad Travelers*. Charlottesville, VA: University of Virginia Press.

Hacking, I. (1999). *The Social Construction of What?* Cambridge, MA: Harvard University Press.

Halligan, P. W. and Marshall, J. C. (eds) (1996). *Method in Madness: Case Studies in Cognitive Neuropsychiatry*. Hove, East Sussex, UK: Psychology Press.

Harman, G. (1998). Intentionality. In W. Bechtel and G. Graham (eds), *A Companion to Cognitive Science*. Malden, MA: Blackwell.

Harrison, B. (1998). I am not afraid. In D. Sattler, V. Shabatay and G. Kramer (eds), *Abnormal Psychology in Context: Voices and Perspectives*. Boston: Houghton Mifflin.

Haynes, S. (1992). *Models of Causality in Psychopathology: Toward Dynamic, Synthetic and Nonlinear Models of Behavior Disorders*. New York: Macmillan.

Heineman, M. (1998). Losing your shirt. In D. Sattler, V. Shabatay and G. Kramer (eds), *Abnormal Psychology in Context: Voices and Perspectives*. Boston: Houghton Mifflin.

Hempel, C. (1965a). Fundamentals of taxonomy. In *Aspects of Scientific Explanation and Other Essays in the Philosophy of Science*. New York: Free Press.

Hempel, C. (1965b). Science and human values. In *Aspects of Scientific Explanation and Other Essays in the Philosophy of Science*. New York: Free Press.

Hempel, C. (1966). *Philosophy of the Natural Sciences*. Englewood Cliffs, NJ: Prentice-Hall.

Heninger, G. (1999). Special challenges in the investigation of the neurobiology of mental illness. In C. Charney, E. Nestler and B. Runney (eds), *Neurobiology of Mental Illness*. New York: Oxford University Press.

Hobson, J. A. and Leonard, J. (2001). *Out of Its Mind: Psychiatry in Crisis – A Call for Reform*. Cambridge, MA: Perseus.

Hocutt, M. (2000). *Grounded Ethics: The Empirical Basis of Normative Judgments*. New Brunswick, NJ: Transactions Press.

Horgan, T. and Graham, G. (2008). Phenomenal intentionality and content determinacy. In R. Schantz (ed.), *Prospects for Meaning*. Berlin: De Gruyter.

Horgan, T., Tienson, J. and Graham, G. (2003). The phenomenology of first-person agency. In S. Walter and H.-D. Heckmann (eds), *Physicalism and Mental Causation: The Metaphysics of Mind in Action*. Exeter, UK: Imprint Academic.

Horwitz, A. (2002). *Creating Mental Illness*. Chicago: University of Chicago Press.

Horwitz, A. and Wakefield, J. (2007). *The Loss of Sadness: How Psychiatry Transformed Normal Sorrow into Depressive Disorder*. Oxford: Oxford University Press.

Howard-Snyder, D. (2004). Was Jesus mad, bad, or god? ... or merely mistaken? *Faith and Philosophy* 21, 456–79.

Hyder, O. Q. (1977). On the mental health of Jesus Christ. *Journal of Psychology and Theology* 5, 3–12.

Institute of Medicine (1996). *Pathways to Addiction: Opportunities in Drug Abuse Research*. Washington, DC: National Academy Press.

Jackson, M. (2007). The clinician's illusion and benign psychosis. In M. Chung, K. Fulford and G. Graham (eds), *Reconceiving Schizophrenia*. Oxford: Oxford University Press.

James, W. (1890). *The Principles of Psychology*, vol. 2. New York: Henry Holt.

James, W. (1961 [1892]). *Psychology: The Briefer Course*. New York: Harper.

James, W. (1997 [1910]). *Psychology*. New York: Henry Holt; reprinted as "The stream of consciousness," in N. Block, O. Flanagan and G. Gulzedere (eds), *The Nature of Consciousness: Philosophical Debates*. Cambridge, MA: MIT Press.

James, W. (2002 [1901–2]). *The Varieties of Religious Experience: A Study of Human Nature*. New York: Modern Library.

Jamison, K. (1995). *An Unquiet Mind*. New York: Knopf; excerpted as An unquiet mind. In D. Sattler, V. Shabatay and G. Kramer (eds), *Abnormal Psychology in Context: Voices and Perspectives*. Boston: Houghton Mifflin, 1998.

Jarvik, L. F. and Chadwick, S. B. (1972). Schizophrenia and survival. In S. B. Hammer, K. Salzinger and S. Sutton (eds), *Psychopathology*. New York: Wiley.

Jaspers, K. (1963). *General Psychopathology*, trans. J. Hoenig and M. Hamilton. Chicago, IL: University of Chicago Press.

Kagan, J. (1994). *Galen's Prophecy: Temperament in Human Nature*. New York: Basic Books.

Kandel, E. R. (1998). A new intellectual framework for psychiatry. *American Journal of Psychiatry* 155, 457–69.

Kane, R. (2005). *A Contemporary Introduction to Free Will*. New York: Oxford University Press.

Kant, I. (2000 [1793]). On the cognitive faculties. In J. Radden (ed.), *The Nature of Melancholy: From Aristotle to Kristeva*. Oxford: Oxford University Press.

Kapur, S. (2003). Psychosis as a state of aberrant salience: a framework linking biology, phenomenology, and pharmacology in schizophrenia. *American Journal of Psychiatry* 160, 13–23.

Karmiloff-Smith, A. (1998). Development itself is the key to understanding developmental disorders. *Trends in Cognitive Sciences* 2, 389–98.

Keeley, B. (1999). Of conspiracy theories. *Journal of Philosophy* 96, 109–26.

Kendall, R. E. (1975). The concept of disease. *British Journal of Psychiatry* 127, 305–15.

Kendall, R. E. (1985). What are mental disorders. In A. Freedman, R. Brotman, I. Silverman and D. Hutson (eds), *Science, Practice, and Social Policy*. New York: Human Sciences Press.

Kendall, R. E. (2001). The distinction between mental and physical illness. *British Journal of Psychiatry* 178, 490–3.

Kennedy, R. and Graham, G. (2007). Extreme self-denial. In M. Marraffa, M. De Caro and F. Ferretti (eds), *Cartographies of the Mind: Philosophy and Psychology in Intersection*. Netherlands: Springer.

Kenny, A. (1988). *The Self*. Marquette, WI: Marquette University Press.

Kessler, R. C. (2005). Prevalence and treatment of mental disorders, 1990 to 2003. *New England Journal of Medicine* 352, 2515–23.

Kessler, R. C., Bergland, P., Demler, O., Jin, R., Merikangas, K. R. and Walters, E. E. (2005). Lifetime prevalence and age-of-onset distributions of DSM-IV disorders in national comorbidity survey replication. *Archives of General Psychiatry* 62, 593–602.

Kessler, R. C., Chiu, W. T., Demler, O., Merikangas, K. R. and Walters, E. E. (2005). Prevalence, severity, and comorbidity of 12-month DSM-IV disorders in the national comorbidity survey replication. *Archives of General Psychiatry* 62, 617–27.

Kessler, R. C., McGonagle, K. A., Zhao, S., Nelson, C. B., Hughes, M., Eshleman, S., Wittchen, H. and Kendler, K. S. (1994). Lifetime and 12-month prevalence of DSM-III-R psychiatric disorders in the United States from the national comorbidity survey. *Archives of General Psychiatry* 51, 8–19.

Kierkegaard, S. (1980 [1849]). *The Sickness unto Death: A Christian Psychological Exposition for Upbuilding and Awakening*, trans. H. Hong and E. Hong. Princeton: Princeton University Press.

Kim, J. (1998). *Mind in a Physical World: An Essay on the Mind–Body Problem and Mental Causation*. Cambridge, MA: MIT Press.

Kim, J. (2003). Lonely souls: causality and substance dualism. In T. O'Conner and D. Robb (eds), *Philosophy of Mind: Contemporary Readings*. London: Routledge.

Kinderman, P. and Bentall, R. (2007). The functions of delusional beliefs. In M. Chung, K. Fulford and G. Graham (eds), *Reconceiving Schizophrenia*. Oxford: Oxford University Press.

King, C. (2007). They diagnosed me a schizophrenic when I was just a Gemini: "the other side of madness." In M. Chung, K. Fulford and G. Graham (eds), *Reconceiving Schizophrenia*. Oxford: Oxford University Press.

Kitcher, P. (1992). *Freud's Dream: A Complete Interdisciplinary Science of Mind*. Cambridge, MA: MIT Press.

Kleinman, A. (1988). *Rethinking Psychiatry*. New York: Free Press.

Kleinman, A. (2000). Social and cultural anthropology: salience for psychiatry. In M. Gelder, J. J. Lopez-Ibor and N. Andreasen (eds), *New Oxford Textbook of Psychiatry*, vol. 1. Oxford: Oxford University Press.

Kleinman, A. and Good, B. (1988). *Culture and Depression: Studies in the Anthropology and Cross-Cultural Psychiatry of Affect and Disorder*. Berkeley: University of California Press.

Klinger, E. (1977). *Meaning and Void: Inner Experiences and Incentives in People's Lives*. Minneapolis: University of Minnesota Press.

Kluft, R. P. (1986). Personality unification and multiple personality disorder. In B. Braun (ed.), *The Treatment of Multiple Personality Disorder*. Washington, DC: American Psychiatric Press.

Klume, S. (2007). Best selling drugs. On-line at http://psychcentral.com/blog/archives/2006/02/28/best-selling drugs.

Knapp, C. (1998). My descent into alcoholism. In D. Sattler, V. Shabatay and K. Kramer (eds), *Abnormal Psychology in Context: Voices and Perspectives*. Boston: Houghton Mifflin.

Kraepelin, E. (1919). *Dementia Praecox and Paraphrenia*, trans. R. Barclay, ed. G. Robertson. Edinburgh: E. & S. Livingstone.

Kraepelin, E. (1968). *Lectures in Clinical Psychiatry*, trans. Thomas P. Johnstone. New York: Hafner.

Kraepelin, E. (1990 [1899]). *Psychiatry: A Textbook for Students and Physicians*, 6th edn, trans. H. Metoui and S. Ayed, ed. J. Quen. Canton, MA: Science History Publications.

Kutchins, H. and Kirk, S. (1999). *Making Us Crazy: DSM, the Psychiatric Bible and the Creation of Mental Disorders*. London: Constable.

Lahav, R. (1993). What neuropsychology tells us about consciousness. *Philosophy of Science* 60, 67–85.

Langdon, R. and Coltheart, M. (2000). The cognitive neuropsychology of delusions. In M. Coltheart and M. Davies (eds), *Pathologies of Belief*. Oxford: Blackwell.

Laureys, S. (2007). Eyes open, brain shut. *Scientific American* 296 (May), 84–9.

Lear, J. (1998). *Open Minded: Working Out the Logic of the Soul*. Cambridge, MA: Harvard University Press.

Leff, J. (2000). Transcultural psychology. In M. Gelder, J. J. Lopez-Ibor and N. Andreasen (eds), *New Oxford Textbook of Psychiatry*, vol. 1. Oxford: Oxford University Press.

Leshner, A. (1997). Addiction is a brain disease. *Science* 278, 45–7.

Levin, M. (1979). *Metaphysics and the Mind–Body Problem*. Oxford: Oxford University Press.

Levine, J. (2009). The explanatory gap. In B. McLaughlin, A. Beckermann and S. Walter (eds), *The Oxford Handbook of Philosophy of Mind*. Oxford: Oxford University Press.

Levy, N. (2006). Autonomy and addiction. *Canadian Journal of Philosophy* 36, 427–47.

Levy, N. (2007). *Neuroethics: Challenges for the 21st Century*. Cambridge: Cambridge University Press.

Lewis, C. S. (1952). *Mere Christianity*. New York: Macmillan.

Litvan, I. (1999). Parkinson's disease. In J. G. Beaumont, P. Kennedy and M. Rogers (eds), *The Blackwell Dictionary of Neuropsychology*. Malden, MA: Blackwell.

Locke, J. (1975 [1690]). *An Essay Concerning Human Understanding*, ed. with intro. P. H. Nidditch. Oxford: Clarendon Press.

Lodge, D. (1995). *Therapy: A Novel*. New York: Viking.

London, J. (1982). John Barleycorn. In D. Pizer (ed.), *Jack London: Novels and Social Writings*. New York: Macmillan.

Lovestone, A. (2000). Dementia: Alzheimer's disease. In M. Gelder, J. J. Lopez-Ibor and N. Andreasen (eds), *New Oxford Textbook of Psychiatry*, vol. 1. Oxford: Oxford University Press.

Luhrmann, T. (2000). *Of Two Minds: The Growing Disorder in American Psychiatry*. New York: Alfred A. Knopf.

Lycan, W. (2003). The mind–body problem. In S. Stich and T. Warfield (eds), *The Blackwell Guide to the Philosophy of Mind*. Malden, MA: Blackwell.

Maher, B. (1974). Delusional thinking and perceptual disorder. *Journal of Individual Psychology* 30, 98–113.

Maher, B. (1988). Anomalous experience and delusional thinking. In T. F. Oltmanns and B. Maher (eds), *Delusional Beliefs*. Chichester, UK: John Wiley & Sons.

Maher, B. (1999). Anomalous experience in everyday life: its significance for psychopathology. *Monist* 82, 547–70.

Malenka, R. C. (2004). The addicted brain. *Scientific American* 290, 78–85.

Margolis, E. and Laurence, S. (2003). Concepts. In S. Stich and T. Warfield (eds), *The Blackwell Guide to the Philosophy of Mind*. Malden, MA: Blackwell.

Marks, I. and Nesse, R. (1994). Fear and fitness: an evolutionary analysis of anxiety disorders. *Ethology and Sociobiology* 15, 247–61.

Matthews, E. (2007). Suspicions of schizophrenia. In M. Chung, K. Fulford and G. Graham (eds), *Reconceiving Schizophrenia*. Oxford: Oxford University Press.

Maudsley, H. (1867). *The Physiology and Pathology of Mind*. London: Macmillan.

May, R. (2004). Making sense of psychotic experience and working towards recovery. In J. Gleeson and P. McGorry (eds), *Interventions in Early Psychosis: A Treatment Handbook*. Chichester, UK: Wiley.

McGinn, C. (1993). *Problems in Philosophy: The Limits of Enquiry*. Oxford: Blackwell.

McGinn, C. (1999). *The Mysterious Flame: Conscious Minds in a Material World*. New York: Basic Books.

McKay, A., McKenna, P. and Laws, K. (1996). Severe schizophrenia: What is it like? In P. Halligan and J. Marshall (eds), *Method in Madness: Case Studies in Cognitive Neuropsychiatry*. Hove, East Sussex, UK: Psychology Press.

Mellor, C. S. (1970). First rank symptoms of schizophrenia. *British Journal of Psychiatry* 117, 15–23.

Metzinger, T. (2004). *Being No One: The Self-Model Theory of Subjectivity*. Cambridge, MA: MIT Press.

Mill, J. S. (1969). *Autobiography*, ed. J. Stillinger. Boston: Houghton Mifflin.

Moore, M. S. (1980). Legal conceptions of mental illness. In B. Brody and T. Englehardt (eds), *Mental Illness: Law and Public Policy*. Dordretcht: Reidel.

Morrison, A. P. (1998). Cognitive behavior therapy for psychotic symptoms of schizophrenia. In N. Tarrier, A. Wells and G. Haddock (eds), *Cognitive Therapy for Psychosis: A Formulation-Based Approach*. London: Brunner-Routledge.

Muneoka, K., Han, M. and Gardiner, D. (2008). Regrowing human limbs. *Scientific American* 298, 56–63.

Munro, A. (2006). *Delusional Disorder: Paranoia and Related Illnesses*. Cambridge: Cambridge University Press.

Murphy, D. (2006). *Psychiatry in the Scientific Image*. Cambridge, MA: MIT Press.

Nagel, T. (1974). What is it like to be a bat? *Philosophical Review* 83, 435–50.

Nesse, R. M. (1990). Evolutionary explanations of emotions. *Human Nature* 1, 261–89.

Nesse, R. M. (2000). Is depression an adaptation? *Archives of General Psychiatry* 57, 14–20.

Nesse, R. M. (2001). Motivation and melancholy: a Darwinian perspective. In J. French, A. Kamil and D. Leger (eds), *Evolutionary Psychology and Motivation*, vol. 47 of the Nebraska Symposium on Motivation. Lincoln, NE: University of Nebraska Press.

Nesse, R. M. and Williams, G. (1996). *Why We Get Sick: The New Science of Darwinian Medicine*. New York: Times Books.

Nordentoft, K. (1978). *Kierkegaard's Psychology*, trans. B. Kirmmse. Pittsburgh, PA: Duquesne University Press.

Nozick, R. (1974). *Anarchy, State, and Utopia*. New York: Basic Books.

Nussbaum, M. (2006). *Frontiers of Justice: Disability, Nationality, Species Membership*. Cambridge, MA: Harvard University Press.

Odean, T. (1998). Volume, volatility, price, and profit: when all traders are above average. *Journal of Finance* 53, 1887–1934.

Olson, E. (1997). *The Human Animal: Personal Identity without Psychology*. New York: Oxford University Press.

Olson, E. (2007a). There is no problem of the self. In B. Gertler and L. Shapiro (eds), *Arguing about the Mind*. Oxford: Routledge.

Olson, E. (2007b). *What Are We? A Study in Personal Ontology*. Oxford: Oxford University Press.

Oppenheimer, C. (2006). I am, thou art: personal identity in dementia. In J. Hughes, S. Louw and S. Sabat (eds), *Dementia: Mind, Meaning, and the Person*. Oxford: Oxford University Press.

Ostwald, P. (1985). *Schumann: The Inner Voices of a Musical Genius*. Boston: Northeastern University Press.

Perry, J. (1979). The problem of the essential indexical. *Noûs* 13, 3–21.

Pickard, H. (2009). Mental illness is indeed a myth. In M. Broome and L. Bortolotti (eds), *Psychiatry as Cognitive Neuroscience: Philosophical Perspectives*. Oxford: Oxford University Press.

Pinker, S. (1997). *How the Mind Works*. New York: Norton.

Place, U. T. (1999). Ryle's behaviorism. In W. O'Donohue and R. Kitchener (eds), *Handbook of Behaviorism*. San Diego: Academic Press.

Poland, J. (2001). Review of *DSM-IV Sourcebook*, vol. 1. On-line at *Metapsychology*: http://mentalhelp.net/books.php&type = de&id = 557.

Poland, J. (2007). How to move beyond the concept of schizophrenia. In M. Cheung, K. Fulford and G. Graham (eds), *Reconceiving Schizophrenia*. Oxford: Oxford University Press.

Poland, J., von Eckardt, B. and Spaulding, W. (1994). Problems with the DSM approach to classifying psychopathology. In G. Graham and G. L. Stephens (eds), *Philosophical Psychopathology*. Cambridge, MA: MIT Press.

Powell, G. (2000). Cognitive assessment. In M. Gelder, J. J. Lopez-Ibor and M. Andreasen (eds), *New Oxford Textbook of Psychiatry*, vol. 1. Oxford: Oxford University Press.

Proust, J. (2006). Agency in schizophrenia from a control theory viewpoint. In N. Sebanz and W. Prinz (eds), *Disorders of Volition*. Cambridge, MA: MIT Press.

Putnam, F. W. (1989). *Diagnosis and Treatment of Multiple Personality Disorder*. New York: Guilford Press.

Rachels, J. (1986). *The End of Life: Euthanasia and Morality*. Oxford: Oxford University Press.

Radden, J. (2007). Defining persecutory paranoia. In M. Chung, K. Fulford and G. Graham (eds), *Reconceiving Schizophrenia*. Oxford: Oxford University Press.

Radden, J. (2009). *Moody Minds Distempered: Essays on Melancholy and Depression*. Oxford: Oxford University Press.

Ramachandran, V. S. (2003). *Reith Lectures: The Emerging Mind*, lecture 5. BBC Radio 4, 30 April 2003. Available at the website of the BBC: www.bbc.co.uk/radio4/reith2003/lecture5/transcript/html.

Ratey, J. and Johnson, C. (1998). *Shadow Syndromes*. New York: Random House.

Rawls, J. (1971). *A Theory of Justice*. Cambridge, MA: Harvard University Press.

Reed, E. (1996). *Encountering the World: Toward an Ecological Psychology*. Oxford: Oxford University Press.

Rescher, N. (1987). *Ethical Idealism: An Inquiry into the Nature and Function of Ideals*. Berkeley: University of California Press.

Reznek, L. (1987). *The Nature of Disease*. London: Routledge & Kegan Paul.

Richardson, R. (2007). The adaptive programme of evolutionary psychology. In P. Thagard (ed.), *Philosophy of Psychology and Cognitive Science*. Handbook of the Philosophy of Science Series. Amsterdam: Elsevier.

Robinson, T. (2004). Addicted rates. *Science* 305, 951–3.

Robinson, T. and Berridge, K. (2003). Addiction. *Annual Review of Psychology* 54, 25–53.

Rogers, M. (1999). Apraxia. In J. Beaumont, P. Keneally and M. Rogers (eds), *The Blackwell Dictionary of Neuropsychology*. Malden, MA: Blackwell.

Rosch, E. (1978). Family resemblances: studies in the internal structure of categories. In R. Rosch and B. Lloyd (eds), *Cognition and Categorization*. Hillsdale, NJ: Lawrence Erlbaum Associates.

Ross, D. (trans.) (1971). *The Nicomachean Ethics of Aristotle*. Oxford: Oxford University Press.

Ross, D., Sharp, C., Vuchinich, R. and Spurrett, D. (2008). *Midbrain Mutiny: The Picoeconomics and Neuroeconomics of Disordered Gambling*. Cambridge, MA: MIT Press.

Russell, B. (1921). *The Analysis of Mind*. London: Allen & Unwin

Russell, B. (1989 [1917]). A free man's worship. In T. Penelhum (ed.), *Faith*. New York: Macmillan.

Russell, B. (1993 [1919]). *Introduction to Mathematical Philosophy*. London: Routledge.

Sadler, J. (2004a). A madness for the philosophy of psychiatry. *Philosophy, Psychiatry, and Psychology* 4, 357–9

Sadler, J. (2004b). Diagnosis/antidiagnosis. In J. Radden (ed.), *The Philosophy of Psychiatry: A Companion*. Oxford: Oxford University Press.

Samuels, R. (2009). Delusions as a natural kind. In M. Broome and L. Bortolotti (eds), *Psychiatry as Cognitive Neuroscience: Philosophical Perspectives*. Oxford: Oxford University Press.

Sass, L. (1992). *Madness and Modernism: Insanity in the Light of Modern Art, Literature, and Thought*. Cambridge, MA: Harvard University Press.

Sass, L. (1994). *The Paradoxes of Delusion: Wittgenstein, Schreber, and the Schizophrenia Mind*. Ithaca, NY: Cornell University Press.

Sass, L. (1999). Schizophrenia, self-consciousness and the modern mind. In S. Gallagher and J. Shear (eds), *Models of the Self*. Thorverton, UK: Imprint Academic.

Sass, L. and Parnas, J. (2007). Explaining schizophrenia: the relevance of phenomenology. In M. Chung, K. Fulford and G. Graham (eds), *Reconceiving Schizophrenia*. Oxford: Oxford University Press.

Satel, S. (2008). Science and sorrow. A review of A. Horwitz and J. Wakefield, *Loss of Sadness*. *New Republic*, 27 February, 37–43.

Sattler, D., Shabatay, V. and Kramer, G. (1998). *Abnormal Psychology in Context: Voices and Perspectives*. Boston: Houghton Mifflin.

Schaff, P. (1918). *The Person of Christ*. New York: American Tract Society.

Schoeman, F. (1994). Alcohol addiction and responsibility attributions. In G. Graham and G. L. Stephens (eds), *Philosophical Psychopathology*. Cambridge, MA: MIT Press.

Schopenhauer, A. (1965 [1841]). *On the Basis of Morality*, trans. E. Payne. Indianapolis, IN: Bobbs-Merrill.

Schopenhauer, A. (2004). On the sufferings of the world. In D. Benatar (ed.), *Life, Death, and Meaning*. Lanham, MD: Rowman & Littlefield.

Schweitzer, A. (1948 [1913]). *The Psychiatric Study of Jesus*, trans. C. Joy. Boston: Beacon Press.

Searle, J. (1983). *Intentionality*. Cambridge: Cambridge University Press.

Searle, J. (2001). *Rationality in Action*. Cambridge, MA: MIT Press.

Searle, J. (2007). *Freedom and Neurobiology: Reflections on Free Will, Language, and Political Power*. New York: Columbia University Press.

Sellars, W. (1997). *Empiricism and the Philosophy of Mind*. Cambridge, MA: MIT Press.

Shorter, E. (1997). *A Brief History of Psychiatry*. New York: Wiley.

Silverman, H. (1995). Review of Kluft and Fine, *Clinical Perspective on MPD*. *Contemporary Psychology* 40, 589.

Simonton, D. K. (1994). *Greatness: Who Makes History and Why*. New York: Guilford.

Slavney, P. and McHugh, P. (1987). *Psychiatric Polarities: Methodology and Practice*. Baltimore: Johns Hopkins University Press.

Smith, A. (1976 [1759]). *The Theory of the Moral Sentiments*, ed. D. Raphael and A. Mackie. Indianapolis: Liberty Fund.

Soble, A. (2004). Desire: paraphilia and distress in DSM-IV. In J. Radden (ed.), *The Philosophy of Psychiatry: A Companion*. New York: Oxford University Press.

Spanos, N. (1996). *Multiple Identities and False Memories: A Sociocognitive Perspective*. Washington, DC: American Psychological Association.

Stephens, G. L. and Graham, G. (2000). *When Self-Consciousness Breaks: Alien Voices and Inserted Thoughts*. Cambridge, MA: MIT Press.

Stephens, G. L. and Graham, G. (2004). Reconceiving delusion. *International Review of Psychiatry* 16, 236–41.

Stephens, G. L. and Graham, G. (2007). The delusional stance. In M. Chung, K. Fulford and G. Graham (eds), *Reconceiving Schizophrenia*. Oxford: Oxford University Press.

Stephens, G. L. and Graham, G. (2009a). Mental illness and the consciousness thesis. In S. Wood, N. Allen and C. Pantelis (eds), *The Neuropsychology of Mental Illness*. Cambridge: Cambridge University Press.

Stephens, G. L. and Graham, G. (2009b). An addictive lesson: a case study in psychiatry as cognitive neuroscience. In M. Broome and L. Bortolotti (eds), *Psychiatry as Cognitive Neuroscience*. Oxford: Oxford University Press.

Stich, S. (1983). *From Folk Psychology to Cognitive Science*. Cambridge, MA: MIT Press.

Stone, T. and Young, A. W. (1997). Delusions and brain injury: the philosophy and psychology of belief. *Mind & Language* 12, 327–64.

Strawson, G. (1997). The self. *Journal of Consciousness Studies* 4, 405–28.

Strawson, P. F. (1959). *Individuals: An Essay in Descriptive Metaphysics*. London: Methuen.

Strawson, P. F. (1966). *The Bounds of Sense: An Essay on Kant's "Critique of Pure Reason."* London: Methuen.

Styron, W. (1990). *Darkness Visible: A Memoir of Madness*. New York: Vintage Books.

Sullivan, A. (2001). *The Noonday Demon: An Atlas of Depression*. New York: Scribner.

Swoyer, C. (2008). Abstract entities. In T. Sider, J. Hawthorne and D. Zimmerman (eds), *Contemporary Debates in Metaphysics*. Malden, MA: Blackwell.

Szasz, T. (1960). The myth of mental illness. *American Psychologist* 15, 113–18.

Szasz, T. (1972). Bad habits are not diseases. *Lancet* 128, 83–4.

Szasz, T. (1974). *The Myth of Mental Illness*. New York: Harper & Row.

Szasz, T. (1982). The psychiatric will: a new mechanism for protecting persons against "psychosis" and "psychiatry." *American Psychologist* 37, 762–70.

Szasz, T. (2001). Mental illness: psychiatry's phlogiston. *Journal of Medical Ethics* 27, 297–301.

Taylor, C. (1976). Responsibility for Self. In A. Rorty (ed.), *The Identities of Persons*. Berkeley: University of California Press.

Taylor, M. A. (1999). *The Fundamentals of Clinical Neurology*. New York: Oxford University Press.

Taylor, R. (1992). *Metaphysics*, 4th edn. Englewood Cliffs, NJ: Prentice-Hall.

Taylor, S. E. (1991). *Positive Illusions: Creative Self-Deception and the Healthy Mind*. New York: Basic Books.

Taylor, S. E. and Brown, J. (1988). Illusion and well-being: a social psychological perspective on mental health. *Psychological Bulletin* 103, 193–210.

Thagard, P. (1999). *How Scientists Explain Disease*. Princeton, NJ, Princeton University Press.

Torrey, E. Fuller (1995). *Surviving Schizophrenia: A Manual for Families, Consumers, and Providers*, 3rd edn. New York: HarperCollins (2001, 4th edn).

Velleman, D. (1991). Well-being and time. *Pacific Philosophical Quarterly* 72: 48–77.

von Wright, G. E. (1963). *Varieties of Goodness*. London: Routledge.

Wakefield, J. C. (1992). Disorder as harmful dysfunction: A conceptual critique of DSM-III-R's definition of mental disorder. *Psychological Review* 99, 232–47.

Wakefield, J. C. (1997). Diagnosing DSM-IV – part I: DSM-IV and the concept of disorder. *Behavioral Research in Therapy* 35, 633–49.

Wakefield, J. C. (1999). The measurement of mental disorder. In A. V. Horwitz and T. L. Scheid (eds), *A Handbook for the Study of Mental Health: Social Contexts, Theories, and Systems*. New York: Cambridge University Press.

Wakefield, J. C. (2006). What makes a disorder mental? *Philosophy, Psychiatry, and Psychology* 7, 123–31.

Watson, P. and Andrews, P. (2002). Toward a revised evolutionary adaptationist analysis of depression: the social navigation hypothesis. *Journal of Affective Disorders* 72, 1–14.

Weiskrantz, L. (1986). *Blindsight: A Case Study and Implications*. Oxford: Clarendon.

West, R. (2006). *Theory of Addiction*. Oxford: Blackwell.

WHO (World Health Organization) (1992). *International Statistical Classification of Diseases and Related Health Problems*, 10th rev. edn. Geneva: WHO.

WHO (World Health Organization) (2002). *Mental Health Global Plan: Close the Gap, Dare to Care*. Geneva: WHO.

Wilkes, K. (1988). *Real People: Personal Identity without Thought Experiments*. Oxford: Oxford University Press.

Wilkes, K. (1991). How many selves make me? In D. Cockburn (ed.), *Human Beings*. Cambridge: Cambridge University Press.

Wilkinson, S. (2000). Is "normal grief" a mental disorder? *The Philosophical Quarterly* 50, 289–304.

Wittgenstein, L. (1951). *Tractatus Logico-Philosophicus*. New York: Humanities Press.

WMHSC (World Mental Health Survey Consortium) (2004). Prevalence, severity, and unmet need for treatment of mental disorders in the World Health Organization World Mental Health Surveys. *Journal of the American Mental Health Association* 291, 2581–90.

Wolf, S. (1990). *Freedom within Reason*. New York: Oxford University Press.

Wood, J. and Grafman, J. (2003). Human prefrontal cortex. *Nature Reviews Neuroscience* 4, 139–47.

Woodward, J. (2003). *Making Things Happen: A Theory of Causal Explanation*. New York: Oxford University Press.

Wurtzel, E. (1994). *Prozac Nation: Young and Depressed in America*. New York: Riverhead Books.

Young, A. W. (2000). Wondrous strange: the neuropsychology of abnormal beliefs. In M. Davies and M. Coltheart (eds), *Pathologies of Belief*. Oxford: Blackwell.

Young, A. W. and Leafhead, K. (1996). Betwixt life and death: case studies in the Cotard delusion. In P. Halligan and J. Marshall (eds), *Method in Madness: Case Studies in Cognitive Neuropsychiatry*. Hove, East Sussex, UK: Psychology Press.

Index